101 PROJECTS FOR YOUR Corvette
1984 - 1996

RICHARD NEWTON

MOTORBOOKS
INTERNATIONAL

This edition first published in 2003 by Motorbooks International, an imprint of MBI Publishing Company, Galtier Plaza, Suite 200, 380 Jackson Street, St. Paul, MN55101-3885 USA.

Motorbooks International titles are also available at discounts in bulk quantity for industrial or sales-promotional use. For details write to the Special Sales Manager at Motorbooks International Wholesalers & Distributors, Galtier Plaza, Suite 200, 380 Jackson Street, St. Paul, MN 55101-3885 USA.

ISBN 0-7603-1461-6

Portions of materials contained herein have been reprinted with permission of General Motors Coporation, Service Operations. Licensee Agreement #0310806

Editor: Peter Bodensteiner
Layout: LeAnn Kuhlmann
Section Openers: Lee Klancher

On the front cover: *(primary photo)* This red C4 looks like a standard Corvette, but is in fact a prototype version of the "King of the Hill" ZR1 model. *Randy Leffingwell*

On the title Page: The convertible is a favorite among the Corvette crowd.

On the frontispiece: These rectangular lights appeared with the Corvette's 1991 redesign.

On the back cover: A removable top was a standard feature of the Corvette during the entire 1984-1996 production run. *Randy Leffingwell*

About the author: Richard Newton has been writing about Corvettes since the early eighties. This is his third Corvette book, and the first dealing with the 1984 to 1996 Corvette. All of his books are designed for the home mechanic and the person who enjoys working on their Corvette. While he was trained as an historian, he ended up becoming an ASE Master Technician and spent fifteen years in the service industry. "One of the reasons people enjoy my books is that I'm one of the few people in the field that was actually trained as a technician. I can help them separate fact from fiction."

Newton edited *Corvette Fever* magazine and brought that magazine into prominence with astounding circulation numbers. "I guess my big mistake at *Corvette Fever* was making it look too easy. Now everyone is trying to replicate our success."

"I don't think I ever intended to devote so much time in my life to the Corvette but it's been a great deal of fun. If I've helped a few people along the way that's even better." Most would agree that he's helped more than just a few people with their Corvette experience, and this book should continue in that tradition.

Printed in China

CONTENTS

This book almost didn't get written. After several false starts and a number of intervening years, I finally got around to completing it. The C4 Corvette was a milestone in Corvette history. How could a Corvette that lasted for thirteen years be anything but legendary? And how do you put all this history into a book that gives the reader some new information?

During the thirteen years the C4 was produced, I spent a lot of time with the cars. I wrote hundreds of different articles about the C4 Corvette. For several years I edited *Corvette Fever* magazine. I also managed to take a perfectly good 1985 Corvette and make it one hell of a weekend track car. And, in doing so, I created a car that was almost impossible to drive on the street for more than an hour or two. Yes, I know about the C4. And when it came to this generation of Corvette, I came to appreciate the good, the bad, and even the ugly.

I've driven every type of C4 that was ever produced and have purchased half the faulty parts that the aftermarket ever manufactured. Over the years I came to appreciate just how good a car the 1984 to 1996 Corvette really was. I discovered the weak spots and figured out how to accentuate its strong points.

I hope that you can use this book as a starting point in your Corvette repair journey. You can take your old C4 and do some very basic things with the car. As you gain confidence and experience, you'll find yourself doing more than you ever imagined you could. After you finish reading this book, you'll need to get the appropriate factory manual for your particular car. The best way is to contact Helm, which publishes the GM factory manuals. Helm can be reached at 1-800-782-4356 or on line at www.helminc.com. A manual costs around one hundred dollars, and it's worth every cent. Skip all of the other manuals and go right to the original source.

One of the reasons I decided to finish this book is that I felt the Corvette community needed an honest approach to repair and performance when it came to the 1984 to 1996 Corvette. Over the past few years, the economics of the magazine industry have made advertising revenue more critical than ever. This means that the Corvette magazines have become more of an infomercial than an honest source of information. Some of the writers and editors have never taken a car apart, and many can't even grasp the concept of how a car actually works. Far too many of the articles in today's Corvette magazines are actually written by the people who produced the parts being highlighted in the article. This is how all of those magic "Add 20 More Horsepower" stories get into circulation.

Of course, I'm not trying to criticize all writers and editors. Instead, I'm trying to point out the economics of the industry. Today, good repair technicians can easily make six-figure incomes. Technical editors for the various Corvette magazines make slightly more than minimum wage. Magazines have reached the point where they can no longer afford to hire truly skilled professionals.

The Corvette became more complex from 1984 to 1996, and the people writing about the car have very little training and knowledge about the complex systems found in the C4 Corvette. As hard as the writers may try, they simply can't keep up with the current technology. And I believe the situation is only going to get worse. This is why I recommend that you get the factory manuals and find a good Corvette shop if you're going to own a C4 Corvette.

Finding a good Corvette shop is a major effort. You should search for a shop that specializes in Corvette repair and one that, if at all possible, works solely on Corvettes. You don't need employees practicing their skills on your Corvette.

The problem with the C4 Corvette is that although it's an old car, it's not old enough for a restoration shop. On the other hand it's old enough that the average Chevrolet dealer has no interest in the car. The technicians have long since moved on to the C5 and the C6 Corvette. Most dealerships don't even have technicians who remember the L98 engine.

This disinterest among dealership technicians is greatest with the ZR-1. The optional LT5 engine was a technological wonder for its time, but so few were produced that most shops never worked on one. Today the number of people who can work on the LT5 engine can be counted on the fingers of your two hands.

ZR-1 prices are very low right now. However, should you have a problem with these Corvettes, you're in for a major shock. The ZR-1 is one of those unique cars that can evoke tremendous bouts of frustration and its repair bills can nearly push you to the brink of bankruptcy.

Before you purchase a ZR-1, find out if anyone in your area has experience working on these cars. If there's no one within a two-hundred-mile radius of your home, you need to reevaluate how badly you want a ZR-1 Corvette.

You also need to seriously consider whether you should modify your Corvette. The 1984 to 1996 Corvettes are really good cars just the way Chevrolet designed them. The factory drivetrain and the suspension are about as good as they get. These cars are faster than anything you can drive on the street, and any engine modifications will detract from the general drivability of the car. The same is true of most suspension modifications.

Yes, there were 1983 Corvettes. A number of 1983 Corvettes were built and even given serial numbers. When the C4 was introduced to the media in California, the cars were actually 1983, not 1984, Corvettes. Today the only 1983 Corvette remaining is at the National Corvette Museum in Bowling Green Kentucky.

After purchasing one of these Corvettes, your first plan of action should be to make sure that all of the stock systems are working as effectively as they can and are functioning in the way they were originally designed. You should change the coolant, have the ignition system checked, and have the computer downloaded to check for any possible problems. Only when you have everything in first-class condition should you even think about making changes in the stock configuration.

The same holds true with the braking and suspension systems. Even the earliest cars, the ones with the single-piston sliding calipers in the front, are fine for normal driving. The priority here is to flush all the old brake fluid and check to see that the brake pads are wearing evenly on both the inboard and outboard sides of the rotor.

The only problem with the suspension is that once you go over 100,000 miles the rubber bushings tend to wear out. At that point, the shock absorbers are also in need of replacement. If you have a burning desire to work on your Corvette, the suspension might be the best place to start. I've found that simply replacing all of the rubber bushings with the polyurethane bushings is a nice improvement. Polyurethane bushings won't cause any deterioration of ride quality, and the new ones don't squeak if you use the correct lubricant.

My suggestion is that you shouldn't attempt any real changes during the first year you own a used Corvette. You'll be busy enough just catching up on all the normal maintenance items that the last owner neglected. Get to know and love your Corvette before you start making changes.

My second bit of advice is to avoid most of the parts sold by aftermarket companies. In my opinion, they will actually detract from your Corvette's performance. Over the years, I've dyno tested a variety of aftermarket chips and most of them caused a decrease in horsepower. The

same can be said of most aftermarket exhaust systems as well as of many other aftermarket parts.

Of course, I have to admit that I don't always heed my own warnings. I personally drive a highly modified 1985 L98 with the 4+3 standard transmission. I've gone through a huge number of parts to simply find the correct combination. Once you start down the modified road, you're in for a lot of aggravation and expense. Sure, if you stay with it, you'll have a pretty fast Corvette. But you'll also end up with a Corvette that is less useful for the daily commute or the weekend trip. Trust me on this.

The 1984 to 1996 Corvette may well be one of the best performance bargains on the market. If you manage to find a good one, you're going to love the car. If you happen to get a bad one, you're in for a series of problems. However, if you know what to look for, you can turn a problem-ridden car into a praise-worthy vehicle.

When examining a Corvette, it's important to check for any indication the previous owner has attempted an electrical repair. Any signs of electrical system modifications should be a sign of impending doom. If you notice non-GM electrical connections under the hood, start deducting money from the asking price. A good rule of thumb is to lower your offer $500 for every non-factory electrical connection you find.

Also keep in mind that the reason you own a Corvette is to have fun. Enjoy the car and think about what a bargain you got. Don't worry about investment value and silly stuff like appreciation. Remember that cars don't stop depreciating until they're at least twenty years old. That gives you a lot of time to just enjoy the car.

As you begin to delve into the Corvette projects detailed in this book, it's best to begin with the easiest ones. Don't start your Corvette experience by removing the motor. The C4 is best enjoyed by blasting down the last few open roads left in America, not resting in a garage.

Most of us are tool junkies. It seems that almost anyone who likes cars also has an equally serious addiction to tools. That's why when the family goes shopping at the local mall, most of us find a way to sneak off to the Sears tool department. The way I see it, you can never own enough tools. In fact, when it comes to tools, I'm like the alcoholic who can never drink enough.

The other day I was looking for my carbide cutting tool and found a spring compressor that I had used on my old '68 Corvette. I seriously doubt if I'll ever own another '68 Corvette in my life, but I just felt better knowing that I had the tool in my tool chest.

By the time you get around to owning a Corvette, you have probably already amassed a huge number of tools. It's likely that you purchased some of these while you were in high school. Others were probably presented to you at Christmas by your wife. But regardless of how you acquired them, I'll bet you've never thrown out a tool since the tenth grade. Sure, you may have lost any number of tools, but you've never willingly disposed of a single wrench or screwdriver. And because you have this wide range of useful, and not so useful, tools, you have no need for one of those 1,000-piece tool sets found in the Sears catalog. Rather, you're looking to add to what you already own or maybe even upgrade your Chinese box-end set to the Snap-On level.

Everyone makes a big deal about tool warranties today. The truth is that every hand tool sold today comes with a lifetime warranty. The only question is how easy it is to make good on that warranty. When I was in the professional end of the automotive service business, I hated the Sears warranty and loved the Snap-On warranty. If I broke a tool in my shop, the Snap-On dealer would replace the tool on his next weekly visit. Breaking a Craftsman tool meant getting in my car and driving more than twenty miles to get the replacement item.

I'm no longer in the service business, and the Snap-On truck no longer arrives on a weekly basis. Now it's easier to replace the Craftsman tool than the Snap-On item. Still, I need to state that nothing is as good as a Snap-On tool. Of course, there is nothing as expensive as a Snap-On tool. Snap-On prices are beyond belief. To be honest, no weekend warrior needs Snap-On tools. However, being able to use them to work on a car can make you feel really good. I call this phenomenon the lust for professional-grade quality. It makes no sense but neither do a lot of other things in this world.

Screwdrivers: I have to admit that I have more than fifty screwdrivers. I even have a complete set of Snap-On Posidriv screwdrivers. They can best be described as an English version of the Phillips-head tip. For those of you who missed out on the joy of taking English sports cars apart, you will never know the joy of Posidriv screwdrivers.

The only screwdrivers I use on a regular basis are the Snap-On or Matco models. Screwdrivers are not a place to save money. Get the ones with the hardened tips, and you'll get a lifetime of use out of them. The big advantage of using these is that it's virtually impossible to strip a Phillips-head screw with a quality screwdriver.

The one screwdriver you really need is the electric version. I have the ten-dollar Home Depot model. You shouldn't use electric screwdrivers to break screws loose, but they certainly can make fast work of the interior screws. Take a look at all the screws on the C4 Corvette door panels, and you'll understand just how valuable a ten-dollar, battery-operated screwdriver can be.

Adjustable Wrench: No one admits to owning an adjustable wrench. Yet you'll always find a couple of them in every professional toolbox. However, I can't remember ever using one on a Corvette. If you do buy an adjustable wrench, make sure that it's something you can use around the house since you really won't need to use it on your Corvette.

Pliers: I put pliers in the same category as screwdrivers. You can never really have too many. The big difference between the two tools is that good pliers are a lot more expensive than screwdrivers.

Everyone has the ubiquitous Vise-Grip, or locking pliers. These are nice to use around the house, but they really don't belong near a Corvette. The most useful types of pliers for working on your vehicle are the long needle-nose pliers. I have the needle-nose pliers in three different sizes and find them to be the most useful of all the pliers in my collection.

Sockets and Drivers: Here's where you get to spend some serious money. You can probably spend more money on sockets and drivers than some of us paid for our Corvettes. The three basic sizes for drivers are 1/4-inch, 3/8-inch, and 1/2-inch. Sockets are described as shallow, deep, and a new size that can best be described as "in between." And every single socket comes in a 12-point version and a 6-point version. The good news is that you don't need to purchase them all at one time. The bad news is that you need all three sizes of sockets to work on the C4 Corvette.

I'm a huge fan of 1/4-inch sockets, but you can really get by with three-eighth sockets for most of your work. The other good news is that Craftsman makes some very nice sockets. I suggest that you start with the basic set and then add a few sockets on either end of the range. That should give you complete coverage.

A deep socket will always work where you could use a short socket, but if you need a deep socket then that's the only thing that will suffice. A good collection of deep 12-point sockets is more useful than you can imagine.

Hammers: In addition to being crucial, hammer collections are fun. The two most important hammers are the soft face and the ten-pound mini sledgehammer. I love my rawhide mallet and that's probably the most-used hammer I have in my collection. I prefer a rawhide mallet to a plastic one because it leaves even fewer marks on the items you are hitting.

The ten-pound, mini sledgehammer is wonderful. You can get the basic steel version or the plastic-covered version. When all else fails, you need a BMFH. The BMFH is great for taking apart the rear suspension on the C4. I also love to use a ten-pound hammer as a rotor removal tool. I would rather hit the parts twice with a big hammer than beat them to death with a smaller hammer.

I'm not a big fan of ball peen hammers, but a lot of people seem to find them attractive. I'm not even sure what a ball peen hammer is good for, but I own three of them. Go figure.

Timing Light: I can't remember the last time I used timing light on my 1985 Corvette. I may be crazy for not checking my timing more often, but I would certainly put this at the bottom of any list of necessary tools. Besides, the only place you can really use timing light is on the L98 engines. Skip this item and buy some additional 1/4-inch metric sockets.

Torque Wrenches: Buy a really good torque wrench and then get it calibrated every couple of years. You should be careful with it and don't let it bang around in your toolbox. This is a precision instrument and should be treated as such. The most common use for a torque wrench is for checking your lug nuts when you remove and replace your tires.

Most warped brake rotors come from not tightening the wheels evenly and with the proper torque setting. The price of a good 1/2-inch drive torque wrench is about the same as a new Corvette rotor.

When working on your Corvette, a 1/2-inch drive torque wrench will be the most useful of all of the sizes. Unlike the 1/2-inch version, the 1/4-inch torque wrench is basically useless. I know this because I actually own one. In the five years I've owned it, I still haven't figured out where I can use it. The way I see it, confessing that I own this torque wrench is a way of admitting my addiction. I can feel like proclaiming, "Yes I have a problem with purchasing tools, and I hope to do something about it." Of course, it's a hard addiction to

overcome, and I'd really like a 1/2-inch digital-readout torque wrench.

Wrenches: If you don't have any wrenches at all, the best thing to do is to purchase a set of metric combination wrenches. These are the kind with the box on one end and the open end opposite it. In case you don't remember, the box end is the part you should use for breaking nuts loose, or for tightening them. The open end is best for getting a nut all the way off the bolt once you've gotten it loose.

There's a whole world open to you once you have the basic combination set of wrenches. I like the ones with a swivel socket on one end and an ordinary open-end wrench on the other end.

Line Wrenches: Line wrenches are special open-end wrenches used to loosen and tighten hydraulic lines. They resemble a box end, but with a smaller opening. Line wrenches are sometimes called flare nut wrenches. You'll need three of them in the metric size if you plan on replacing the master brake cylinder or the brake caliper lines. They're certainly vital when working on tight hydraulic or fuel lines, but they'll certainly wipe out at least one month's tool budget.

Having tried every type of line wrench on the market, I would recommend that you purchase a Snap-On set. I suggest Snap-On because the jaws of these wrenches won't spread apart, causing the corners of the fitting to round off. The jaws of the less expensive wrenches actually spread, defeating the whole purpose of a line wrench. As ridiculous as the prices of these Snap-On wrenches might seem, they're a whole lot cheaper than having to replace a brake line because you rounded the corners of the fitting off.

Lighting: You really only need a couple of kinds of lights. The most important is a small flashlight. The C4 Corvette has more nooks and crannies than any car I've ever owned. A really good flashlight lets you shine a finely focused light on the areas under examination. I've seen professionals actually take a dash apart while holding a flashlight in their mouth. The flashlight is a great tool.

You'll also need the ubiquitous extension cord light. Everyone today is using the fluorescent type. These are great to use when you want to light a large area. I prefer the shorter versions to the long ones. The long ones get hung up too often and never seem to fit into the place where you really need the light.

The latest thing is the portable halogen light. These throw out a tremendous amount of light. They're not only portable, but sold at very low prices at places like Home Depot and Lowes. The downside is they get very hot, so much so that it's actually uncomfortable working around them. I've got a couple of these and rarely use them. However, they're so cheap that even if you only use them a couple of times a year, they're still worth having in the shop.

Electrical Repair: It's hard to say how much electrical equipment you'll really need when working on the C4. The electronics on the C4 are complicated, and you really need a lot of skill before you charge into the electrical system. Life with the C4 Corvette is a series of relays and special weather pack fittings. The factory manual has an outstanding section about electrical repairs. You should read it at least twice before you mess around with any of the wires on your Corvette.

Should you decide to work on the electrical system, the most important tool you'll need is the multimeter. It measures voltage, resistance, and amps. You can purchase a good multimeter for under fifty dollars. Once you learn how to use it, you'll be surprised how many problems you can solve.

It seems we always want a reason to buy more tools. The projects in this book will give you plenty of reasons to seek out the tool vendors at all the car shows. My only suggestion is that you stick to quality tools. Here's a selection of some tools that I frequently use.

1 – You need a quality tire gauge more than any other tool in your box. I like this type of gauge because it has a handy bleed-down button. That means I can put a bunch of air in the tire and then bleed it down to the correct pressure. I also like the huge dial since it's so easy to see.

2 – This type of combination wrench is really nice. It has the standard open end plus a swivel socket. I use this type of wrench a lot.

3 – I'm an absolute nut about open-end, flare nut wrenches. You need to spend serious money here since the cheap ones tend to spread open when you apply extra torque. Don't attack brake lines or fuel lines without a selection of these.

4 – You can never have too many pliers, and it's easy to just keep collecting them over the years. Every type of pliers has a special use. This one is great for cutting cotter pins on the tie rod ends and the ball joints.

5 – Flex-head sockets are extremely useful. They may not be your first purchase, but you'll eventually need them.

6 – Screwdrivers are just like pliers – you can never own too many. Make sure you get the ones with hardened tips. In my opinion, the screwdrivers with the largest handles are the easiest to use. I hate wimpy handles on screwdrivers.

7 – Sockets can kill your budget, but you really need them. You may find yourself purchasing quite a few as you work through the various Corvette projects.

8 – You'll need two torque wrenches. The 1/2-inch size and the 3/8-inch are both useful. If you can only budget for one torque wrench, make it the larger 1/2-inch version.

9 – When it comes to breaker bars, bigger is always better. The only reason you'll ever need a breaker bar is to loosen a very stubborn nut and to do that, you want the extra leverage of the large bar.

10 – A long-handled, 3/8-inch ratchet wrench with a swivel head is a must for these projects. It allows you to reach places that are otherwise inaccessible. You'll find a lot of those types of places on the C4 Corvette

The other tool that's nice to have is a wire stripper. Getting the insulation off a wire is a real trick without this tool. The price of a top-quality wire stripper is so low that it's foolish not to have one in your toolbox. Since this is a tool you're going to have for the remainder of your life, spend an extra couple of dollars and get a good one.

Air Compressor: I can't imagine working in a garage without an air compressor. You don't need a gigantic unit, just one that lets you fill tires and run a few air tools. However, if you have a bead-blasting cabinet in your garage, you'll need a fairly large air compressor to produce the required volume of air. When you purchase an air compressor, make sure you think of ways you might use the compressor in the future and buy one that can accommodate your potential needs.

I recommend that you get a compressor that can be plugged into the normal 120-volt home electrical supply. You should also give some serious thought to the vertical models since they'll take up a lot less space on the floor of your garage. If you live in the South, you can actually place the compressor outside your garage and run some plumbing into the garage. This cuts down on the noise inside your garage considerably. To complete the system, you'll also need 25 feet of air hose, a good quality blow gun nozzle, and an air chuck for filling your tires.

THE ADVANCED COLLECTION

When you purchase these tools, you'll usually end up spending some serious money – on tools that you'll seldom use. However, in times of need, these expensive items can make all he difference.

Dial Indicators: Dial indicators are most useful for brake work. You really can't check for rotor runout, or warpage, without a good-quality dial indicator. When you shop around, remember that the mounting system is more important than the actual dial gauge. Keep in mind that when you check your brake rotors, you want the dial positioned at ninety degrees to the face of the rotor. Make sure you purchase a mounting system that will allow you to do this.

The big question is whether you should purchase a dial indicator that reads out in metrics or one that reads out in the English system. The C4 Corvette is a totally metric car. However, the factory manual gives specifications in both millimeters and inches. You should base your decision on the other cars you have in your garage. If your other toy is an old, straight-axle Corvette, then you should get a dial indicator that reads out in inches. If there's a Porsche in your garage, then I suggest you get the metric version.

Micrometers: I have countless micrometers left over from the days when I used to build engines. Most haven't been

out of the box in five years. The only reason to have a micrometer around is to measure brake rotor thickness. You can find a special micrometer just for this task, but it's really not essential to have. A normal micrometer will do the job just fine.

The biggest problem with micrometers is that they usually only have a range of one inch. That means you'll need several of them. And you'll need to know how to properly calibrate them. The most useful micrometer is the one that measures distances between zero and one inch. If you aren't doing precision work, you can save some money by purchasing a Chinese product. If you need really accurate readings, you need to spend some serious money.

Dial Caliper: The dial caliper is my favorite tool for measuring things. It's the easiest to use, and it can measure things ranging from a few thousandths of an inch to six inches. Dial indicators can be used to measure everything from the size of a piece of sheet metal to the diameter of an exhaust pipe. I even have a cheap one that I use for measuring things such as exhaust pipes. I keep the high-quality dial caliper in its case for the few times when I need precision measurements.

Engine Tools: The days of rebuilding your own engine are long gone. You can now purchase a crate motor for far less than it costs to rebuild your own motor. As a result, you can skip buying all of the traditional engine-building tools like ring compressors and valve spring compressors.

Air Tools: We're not trying to make a living working on our Corvettes. We're just having fun and pretending that we're technicians. There's really no need for speed or air tools. But, if you have your heart set on buying air tools, the best purchase is a 3/8-inch air ratchet. It's great for running nuts down on bolts. Plus, it's fairly small and won't get in the way like an impact gun does.

There's really no need for 1/2–inch impact guns in the home shop. They're expensive and can do a lot of damage if you aren't careful with them. If a bolt is really tight, you can usually remove it with a 24-inch breaker bar placed on your 1/2-inch socket. I suggest that you save your money and skip the impact guns.

Digital Camera: You should strongly consider getting a cheap digital camera before you start taking things apart. There's a very good chance that your project will drag out several days – or weeks – beyond your original time schedule.

The new programs will allow you to store a lot of images on your computer. When the time comes to put things back together, you can simply look at the computer screen or print out the images to use as references. Just remember that too many pictures are better than too few.

At the beginning of each project listed in this book, you'll find a list of topics and little picture icons. These guides will help you figure out if you really want to tackle the project or if you'd rather leave it for another time – or even another person. The purpose of these guides is to give you a good idea of what's involved with the project and tell you what you'll need in the way of tools, knowledge, and money. The list should be self-explanatory. But, to give you a little insight about what went into creating these guides, here is some background on my thought process.

TIME: Time is a rough estimate of how long it would take a person with reasonable skills and knowledge to complete the project. It's not easy to come up with concrete time estimates. GM has a flat-rate manual that lists how long it should take to complete every possible task you can perform on a Corvette and even GM experts can't always make these time goals. A good service technician can beat the flat-rate book all day long. Another technician, working in the same dealership, will have trouble making a decent living because every job takes him two to three times longer than the time listed in the GM flat-rate manual. I generally estimate a Corvette project will take twice as long as I originally thought that it would.

TOOLS: This should give you a rough idea as to which tools you're going to need for each project. For the simple projects, I've listed the wrenches and even the sizes you might need. If I detailed all the tools you may need for the advanced projects, the lists would be longer than the project description. Therefore, I've only listed the specialty tools. Remember that no matter what you have in the way of tools, you'll probably be making more trips to the Sears tool department than you could ever imagine. With this in mind, you might even want to add the cost of new tools into the cost of a given project.

TALENT: Determining the talent level needed for a project is even more difficult than trying to decide what tools you might need. Over the years I hired a bunch of professional technicians and their range of abilities was tremendous. And, while that range may have been wide, the range of abilities is even wider when it comes to the talent levels of weekend warriors. I've seen amateur mechanics who were every bit as skilled as the top techni-

cians in a dealership. They may not have had the speed of a highly skilled professional, but they made up for that shortcoming with pure ability and a proper attitude.

In this book, the suggested skill level for a project is revealed by the number of little mechanic icons listed next to the project. If a project has one icon anyone can give it a shot. Two of the little guys mean that you should be slightly proficient with wrenches. To do a project with three mechanic icons, you need to have done enough work so that you are comfortable working on cars with very little guidance. To tackle a level-four project, you better know what you're doing and have a lot of tools in your toolbox. These are not projects for the great masses. Generally, level-four projects are jobs best left to the professional – or the very brave.

APPLICABLE YEARS: There aren't a lot of variations in the 1984 to 1996 Corvette. There were really only four engines used over these years, and if you take the low-quantity LT5 and 1984 engines out of the equation, you're left with only two engines. The chassis is almost the same for all the years the C4 was in production. When the suspension was modified in 1988, it was basically a matter of only changing the locating points because the parts all come apart the same way.

TAB: This is a ballpark idea of how much money you're going to spend. Over the years I've developed a formula that can be used for any project. First, you should look up all the prices for a project in the various catalogs. Then make a detailed list of the parts and prices. Now take that total and double it. This should give you a number that is fairly close to what you'll end up spending. Every project will take on a life of its own and will undoubtedly exceed your preliminary budget at least twofold. Oftentimes it's best not to keep detailed records because they're too embarrassing.

Most of the hard-core restoration guys are now spending over $100,000 on a National Corvette Restorers Society restoration. The only reason they won't admit to this is because they haven't kept decent records of the actual costs. Sometimes it's better not to know.

TORQUE: When your Corvette was assembled in Bowling Green, Kentucky, every single nut and bolt was set to a very specific torque setting. I'm not advocating that you be as precise as the factory, but you can't disregard all the torque settings on your Corvette either. There are a few areas that truly deserve accurate settings – the specifications for the brake system, the chassis, and obviously any engine work you might perform. I've only listed the most critical torque settings in this book. The factory manual gives every single specification, which is another reason you should purchase a factory manual.

TIP: Here I try to point out some of the little tips that will help you through a particular job. In most cases, the tip is something that a technician discovered years ago but failed to pass on to others. In some cases, it may well be something that most of you already know. I hope that you'll find some of the tips to be useful.

PERFORMANCE GAIN: As I pointed out in the introduction, there's very little you can do to improve the performance of the C4 Corvette in one area without detracting from another area. I try to explain here what gains you can expect from a modification and how these are going to affect another area of your Corvette.

COMPLEMENTARY MODIFICATION: Once you replace one part on your Corvette, you'll probably notice two other areas that might also need some help. Sometimes when you're doing some work on one item, you should consider working on an adjacent part. Other times it's best to just concentrate on a specific area. When we talk about combining some jobs, the real trick is knowing when to stop. Getting started is usually the easy part.

There are some-stand alone jobs on your Corvette. You need to enjoy these jobs for what they are. Don't try and stretch every task into a series of tasks. There are some things best enjoyed alone.

And don't forget the "work/drive" ratio. The longer you work on your Corvette without driving it, the quicker you will lose interest in the car. Remember that you originally bought your Corvette to *drive*. When the fixing-up time exceeds the driving time, your interest will wane. If this happens, you'll probably end up selling your Corvette to a person who still has the passion that you once possessed.

BASICS

Parts courtesy Corvette Central

PROJECT 1

Jacking Up the C4

Time: 10 minutes

Tools: Hydraulic floor jack, jack stands

Talent:

Applicable Years: 1984 to 1996

Tab: $75

Tip: AutoZone and Wal-Mart usually have the best prices and the largest selection for jacks and jack stands.

PERFORMANCE GAIN: Starting point for all work underneath the car.

COMPLEMENTARY MODIFICATION:
Check front suspension bushings.

Getting your Corvette up in the air is rather easy, especially if you use a hydraulic floor jack. You simply have to treat the car as if it's coming in for a pit stop in a NASCAR race. You just raise the whole side of the car up in the air with your floor jack.

Attempting to raise the back, or front, of the car only leads to frustration. There just isn't a decent way to do it. More important – why even bother? The only decent place to put a jack under the rear is the differential housing. Once you finally get your jack under the car, you'll find you really can't move the handle. In addition, using a jack on the center of the differential housing means the car is really unstable. I think the differential is really the last place you want to use a jack. You really don't need to drop your prized Corvette on the ground.

The best jack to use on your Corvette is what's known as a trolley jack. Just leave the jack that came with your Corvette right where the factory placed it and remind yourself it's just for roadside emergencies. The discount parts houses like Pep Boys and AutoZone constantly advertise these small hydraulic trolley jacks. Simply place the jack at the center of the side frame rail and raise the entire

side of the car at once. Remember, if you think of a NASCAR pit stop, you've got the idea.

Now let's get back to jack stands. If you do any serious work, you might want to purchase two sets. Low sets are really great for changing tires and greasing the car. They give you the safety you need and aren't as big and heavy as the taller ones. Four of these short jack stands will support 8,000 pounds, which is more than enough for your Corvette. If you have an 8,000-pound Corvette, send me a picture of it. The best part is that these little jack stands are usually the ones that are placed on sale since most people are looking for a set of jack stands that will support a pickup truck, not a smaller vehicle like a Corvette.

If you feel the need to take a transmission out or replace an exhaust system, you'll need to get the car a little higher than the bargain jack stands allow. This means the larger jack stands are going to be needed.

One trick that I picked up from the race teams is that an 8-inch by 8-inch block of wood makes a great jack stand. And if you put a handle on the block, everything will be wonderful. The only problem is the wood actually costs more than a set of decent jack stands at the local discount parts house, and if you don't use them properly, they can be less stable then jackstands.

If you place the jack in the middle of the car, you can easily raise the entire side. Be careful that the jack pad is centered on the rail that runs directly behind the fiberglass rocker panel. Sometimes the panel rests slightly lower than the rail.

Lower jack stands are much more useful than the larger models. You really don't need to get the Corvette all that high off the ground for most of your work. The big jack stands provide more support than you'll ever need. This one here has a 4,000-pound capacity.

During the past few years, it seems everyone has been trying to fit a lift into their home garage. But, having worked with lifts for several decades, I have to say that I don't think a lift is a great idea. Most of the time a lift is just in the way. There are a few jobs that can be made easier by using a lift, but those things are so rarely done that having a lift is really not worth the trouble. Every single job that needs to be done on your Corvette can be done in your home garage with a good floor jack and jack stands.

When it comes to lifts, the best choice is the twin-post model with the adjustable arms. The only problem is that to use it you need a very solid concrete floor for mounting. The average home garage simply doesn't have enough concrete to support this type of lift.

Before installing any lifts in my shops, we always did a test boring into the concrete and then had it analyzed to see if it was of sufficient strength. You only need to have a lift collapse once before you get real nervous. Anyone who's been in the trade more than ten years has seen a car fall off a lift. It's not pretty.

For home garages, the basic four-post lift is about as useful as the two-post model. It's great for changing the oil on your Corvette but doesn't facilitate much else. The provision for getting all four wheels off the deck of the ramp is primitive at best. This means that you have a lift that really isn't much good for brake jobs. In addition, you have a lot of steel posts taking up room in your garage.

Just in case you think I'm overstating the problems associated with lifts, look around any race car shop. If you examine pictures of any NASCAR race team shop, you'll notice that there are no lifts. The owners of these shops dislike them for the same reasons I do. The aggravation of having a lift hanging out in your garage is far greater than the ease it provides every few months.

PROJECT 2

Changing the Oil

Time: 30 minutes

Tools: Metric sockets (3/8-inch drive) and metric combination wrenches

Talent:

Applicable Years: 1984 to 1996

Tab: $30 if you use synthetic oil

Torque: Oil drain plug – 20 foot-pounds

Tip: Place newspaper under the drain plug and the oil filter since some oil will always run down on your garage floor.

Changing the oil is very easy with the 1984 to 1996 Corvette. Your local discount parts houses have everything you need to do the job. The oil filter you will use is the very common Chevrolet oil filter. Only the ZR-1 uses a different filter, and I'll get to that in the ZR-1 section.

The best advice for choosing oil brands was volunteered by a friend of mine who observed one day, "I've never seen an engine explode because of the brand of oil. I've seen a lot of them, though, that had serious problems because the oil was low or never changed."

Everyone has an opinion on which oil is best, and it's usually an uninformed opinion. Very few people have the qualifications to actually judge the quality of an oil. A petroleum engineer once told me that there really are significant differences between the various brands of oil. But, he explained, "The only problem is that by the time I get the research completed everyone has changed their formulations."

Commercial oil sales prove that advertising works. People are extremely brand-loyal. They'll give you a bunch of reasons why the oil they use is the best oil on the market. The interesting thing is that all this information usually comes from the ads.

There's a myth that says you need to use a heavy oil in an older or high-mileage car. But truth be told, old cars

If you haven't used one of these filter wrenches, you're doing way too much work. When working on a Corvette, these seem to work a lot better than the strap wrenches. Even though it's a huge temptation, don't use this wrench to tighten the oil filter. If you get the filter too tight, you'll run the risk of pinching the gasket and setting up a leak. I won't even mention the trouble you'll have removing the filter at the next oil change.

When you remove the old oil filter, take a second to make sure the old gasket came off with the old filter. If you don't see the old gasket, go back and remove it from the filter housing before you install the new oil filter. If you make a mistake here and leave the old gasket in place and install the new filter, you'll soon have an instant oil leak. Every year professional shops end up having to replace motors because the technician failed to check for the old filter gasket. It's really just a matter of developing good habits. As stupid as this mistake may sound, it's amazingly common.

really don't need heavier oil. All the 20W-50 oil does is get hotter than a thinner oil. If your Corvette is running over 200 degrees all the time, then you really need to be using 5W-30 or 10W-30. There is no benefit in running heavy oil in a Corvette. The heavy oil myth is left from the days when oils were much less sophisticated.

Another myth is that of the 3,000-mile oil change. It, too, is false. You can actually stick to the factory-recommended oil change interval. In the case of the C4 Corvette that means changing the oil every 7,500 miles. Later models only need their oil changed when the oil change light goes on. The 3,000-mile oil change is an idea that has been promulgated by the oil companies. If they can convince you to change your oil twice as often as necessary, they get to sell twice as much oil.

Before I close the book on automobile mythology, I need to address the oil filter question. Very few people are qualified to judge the quality of an oil filter. Just ask someone the size of particles that the filter is designed to trap, and you'll realize how little the person knows about the oil filter.

I saw an excellent oil filter study done over a decade ago. It showcased scientific research done under highly controlled conditions. Interestingly, the study showed that a couple of the filters actually filtered too much. The filters were catching every little microscopic element. This meant that the filter material was totally plugged after just 1,000 miles of vehicle use. After 1,000 miles, the oil was being sent through the bypass circuit and not getting any filtration.

Today the average filter is designed to catch particles in the range of 25 to 30 microns. The average human hair is usually 67 microns in diameter. That should give you an idea as to how well your oil is being filtered.

The single most important part of an oil filter is the gasket. If this gasket fails, you'll lose the oil, and that's the end of one very nice Corvette engine. The cheap oil filter companies use a lower quality material in the construction

The Oil Change Light

The 1990 to 1996 Corvette is equipped with an Engine Oil Life Monitor. This system uses the Central Control Module, or CCM, to calculate the lifespan of the engine oil. It does this by measuring engine rpm and oil temperatures over the time you drive the car. It makes these calculations based on certain things that happen to the car. It's not like some of the European systems that actually look at the condition of the oil.

You should reset the Engine Oil Life Monitor after every oil change. To do that, follow these directions:

• Turn the key to the ON position, but don't start the engine.

• Press the ENG MET button on the Trip Monitor and release it. Then, within five seconds, press and release the ENG MET button again.

• Within five seconds of completing the above step, press and hold the RANGE (1990-1991) button or the GAUGES (1992-1996) button on the Trip Monitor. The CHANGE OIL light will flash.

• Hold the RANGE or GAUGES button until the CHANGE OIL light stops flashing and goes out. When the light goes out, the Engine Oil Life Monitor is reset. This should take about ten seconds. If it doesn't reset, turn the ignition to OFF and repeat the procedure.

of this base gasket. That's just one reason to stick with a quality brand filter.

In 1992, Chevrolet did away with the optional Corvette oil cooler and switched to Mobil 1 as the factory oil. The cooler was eliminated to reduce manufacturing costs, and the synthetic oil could function very well in the high heat. If you have a 1992 to 1996 Corvette, you should continue to use synthetic oil.

If you own a 1984 to 1991 Corvette, there isn't much to be gained from the more expensive oil. On the other hand, it won't cause any problems. You have to decide if the little extra protection in high-heat situations is worth the cost. Havoline once told me that conventional oil was just fine in conditions up to 250 degrees.

Heat causes the oil to break down. The nice thing about a Corvette is that it has an oil temperature gauge. If, for any reason, your oil gets into an abnormally high range, you should change it at the earliest possible opportunity. I've had times at track events where I've seen a reading of 270 degrees on my gauge. The next day that oil was changed.

Typically, engines overheat because of a burst hose or low coolant levels. If you've overheated from these problems, change your oil at the same time you make the other repairs. Don't take a chance by using cooked oil in your Corvette.

Don't forget that you need to dispose of your used oil and filter in an appropriate fashion. The EPA calculates that about 75 percent of oil filters, a hidden source of used oil as well as recyclable steel, are still ending up in landfills. Most of the major parts stores have programs in place now to help you dispose of used oil.

It's not a bad idea to replace the drain plug gasket every time you change the oil. The only gaskets that seem worth buying are the ones from the Chevrolet dealer. They use a rubber sealing ring surrounded by metal. You would have to be a gorilla to squeeze the gasket too tight on these.

Serpentine Belt Replacement

 Time: 30 to 60 minutes

 Tools: 1/2-inch breaker bar

 Talent:

 Applicable Years: 1984 to 1996

 Tab: Under $50

 Torque: Belt tensioner to engine block – 30 foot-pounds

 Tip: Consider purchasing the tool designed to release the belt tensioner. This works very nicely and is cheap. Otherwise use a 1/2-inch breaker bar.

 PERFORMANCE GAIN: There's a performance gain only if the pulleys are changed, and that's usually not a good idea.

COMPLEMENTARY MODIFICATION: Replace the serpentine belt tensioner if you've been hearing a noise coming from the belt area.

There's just one belt on a Corvette. If this belt breaks on the highway, call the tow truck – you aren't driving anywhere. This means you should probably replace this serpentine belt a bit earlier than you think is necessary rather than wait for bad things to happen.

It would be a good idea to replace this belt around 30,000 miles. Heat and mileage are the main causes of wear. Every time this belt passes around a pulley, it bends and flexes. This produces heat, which hardens the rubber over time. After millions of journeys around the pulleys, even the best drive belt begins to suffer the effects of age. The rubber begins to crack and fray, and the internal cords become weak and brittle.

The best check is to examine the belt for cracks and frayed edges. Some small cracks are going to be normal. If you have more than eight or ten cracks per inch, it's time to replace the belt. If there are chunks of rubber missing from your belt, you're living on borrowed time, and you should replace the belt as soon as possible.

Frayed edges are another sign that you should start thinking about replacing the belt. You should also look around and see if all the pulleys are in alignment. Frayed edges are not a normal wear pattern.

After having several bad experiences with parts catalogues, I generally take the old belt to the parts store with me when I purchase a new belt. This way I know I'm getting the correct length.

The actual belt change couldn't be simpler. You just need to be sure you still have the label that diagrams how the belt should positioned. If your Corvette has been hit at any time, the body shop probably didn't replace the label. In fact,

a missing label is usually a good indicator that a Corvette has been in an accident at some time during its life. If you don't have the label, get one before you change the belt.

The only thing you have to do to replace the belt is release the tensioner. I've used a 1/2-inch breaker bar for years, but there is an actual tool designed to perform the task. The tool costs less than thirty dollars, and it definitely makes the job go a little quicker.

If you don't get enough movement with the tensioner tool, you can't move the air intake hose. To do this, simply

Before you get started, make sure that this diagram is still on your car. You need to make sure that you have a drawing of how the belt is installed. This is one case in which you really shouldn't trust your memory.

release the two clamps and loosen the hose clamp that's on the throttle body. You'll only need to move it a few inches so you can leave the MAF sensor plugged in to the harness.

Noise Problems

Sometimes you'll hear a chirping sound coming from the area of the belt. This could indicate a problem with the alignment of your pulleys. Using a spray bottle filled with water, mist the belt lightly. If the noise level recedes for several seconds, then returns at a louder volume, a misalignment problem is most likely the problem.

If the noise immediately increases after the belt is sprayed, slipping is the likely culprit. If the water spray test is inconclusive or not successful at diagnosing the problem, remove the belt and re-install it so that the belt runs in the opposite direction. Because misalignment noise is influenced by the direction of misalignment in the drive, flip-

These cracks will eventually lead to belt failure. A few cracks are nothing to be concerned about, but when you find more than eight cracks for every inch of belt, you should really consider changing the belt. Considering that a new belt is going to cost a whole lot less than a tow truck, just replace it a little sooner than you think is necessary.

Here are the belt-tensioner wear indicators. Not only does the belt stretch slightly during its lifespan, the spring in the tensioner also suffers from fatigue. You can tell how much the spring has weakened or how much the belt has stretched by looking at this indicator.

ping the belt around in this manner will temporarily eliminate or diminish any noise caused by drive misalignment. If the noise remains unchanged, the problem is not likely related to drive alignment.

Serpentine Belt Tensioner

There are a variety of things that can cause your Corvette to make a chirping sound. Oftentimes this noise isn't coming from the belt, but rather from the tensioner. The tensioner is designed to keep constant tension on the serpentine belt.

To address this problem, turn off the motor and take a look at the tensioner. This drive belt tensioner is a spring-loaded device that sets and maintains the drive-belt tension. The drive-belt should not require tension adjustment during the life of the drive belt. Automatic drive-belt tensioners have drive-belt wear indicator marks. If the indicator mark is not between the MIN and MAX marks, the drive belt is worn and both the tensioner and belt should be replaced.

Changing Pulley Size

Several companies sell different-size pulleys that are supposed to give you more horsepower. What they usually give you are more problems. All of the drive pulleys on the C4 Corvette are carefully calibrated. The water pump and the alternator are designed to run at specific speeds. GM engineering looks at how most people drive their cars and then calculates how fast these items should revolve.

If you start changing the drive pulleys, be prepared to have coolant temperature problems and a dead battery every now and then. True, you'll get a couple more horsepower at 5,000rpm, but you'll pay a price for this. Changing pulley size is like messing with nature. It can be done, but the results aren't always very pleasant and the performance gain is truly minimal.

You can either purchase the special tool that's designed for this job or use a 1/2-inch breaker bar for releasing the tension on the belt. Here is a breaker bar that was heated and bent, which will make the job just a little easier. For the average home mechanic, it's easier to simply remove the air intake hose along with the MAF sensor.

Changing the Air Filter

 Time: 15 minutes

 Tools: None

 Talent:

 Tab: $15 to $45

 Tip: Make sure that the air filter lid is square on the housing before you tighten everything down.

PERFORMANCE GAIN: There's very little performance gain in the various air filter brands.

COMPLEMENTARY MODIFICATION:
Clean the throttle body-intake passage with air intake cleaner.

Corvette air filters are very easy to change. It's simply a matter of loosening the large thumbscrews and removing the lid on the intake housing. You don't even need tools to do this, although pliers sometimes help.

The big thing you have to be careful of is the soft urethane sealing gasket molded in place on the filter element. Make sure that you get the gasket sealed carefully in the housing before you tighten everything down. If the filter isn't properly seated, you're going to have a place where unfiltered air can enter the engine.

The C4 Corvettes all use what's called a linear flow air filter. This means the air passes directly through the air filter, and doesn't have to turn any corner. This path facilitates low airflow restriction. The stock AC-Delco air filter is a pretty good air filter, and a change to a different brand will result in only minimal, if any, power gains.

One of most common aftermarket items sold is an open lid for the housing. Every Corvette vendor sells one of these "performance enhancing" covers. These covers are nothing more than a stock lid with the front of the factory housing cut off. There's very little performance gain with these covers.

The only gains would come at very high rpm, and there are other more serious air restriction points in the intake system. On the other hand, they're not very expensive and can't cause any damage.

Interestingly, the only time the factory ever saw water ingestion problems was with the factory air filter housing. A friend of mine who worked at the Bowling Green plant said the factory never encountered a problem with the aftermarket air filters, but saw several with the factory unit.

There's little to be gained from switching to an Accel or K&N air filter. I've tested air filters on the dyno, and there's not enough of a power gain to justify their cost when being used in a street car. When we totally removed the air filter, we lost several horsepower. That's not a good thing.

The biggest advantage of Accel and K&N filters is that they last for as long as you own your car. However, they cost more than twice as much as stock filters. You'll have to decide how long you're going to keep your Corvette to see if buying one is a worthwhile expenditure.

If you're running your Corvette at the drag strip or a road racetrack, you'll pick up a few horsepower (maybe two or three) with the modified air filter lid and a K&N air filter. This will only happen at the highest rpms, though. The only sure way to lose horsepower is to run with a dirty air filter – or without any air filter at all.

Above left: This is an air filter housing that's been modified. Virtually every aftermarket manufacturer sells this type of filter housing. Here the front section has been cut off the standard GM housing. There's a slight gain in horsepower but not enough to justify the price.

Above right: The best part of the K&N filter is that you can clean it and keep it forever. If you intend to keep your C4 Corvette for a number of years, this filter might be a benefit. If you only keep your car a few years, the standard AC-Delco filter will be just fine.

Be very careful spraying oil on the K&N filter. You only want a very light misting. If you apply too much oil, it will go right through the air filter and contaminate the mass airflow sensor. This is especially critical when dealing with the cars from 1994 to 1996 since they don't have a burn-off cycle for the MAF. Some people have had this problem, and it took them a while to diagnose the situation. The solution is to clean the inside of the MAF sensor with air intake cleaner. Just remember, you don't need to soak the air filter with the oil. More oil is not better.

Changing the Fuel Filter

 Time: 30 minutes

 Tools: Flare nut metric wrenches, safety glasses

 Talent: ♟♟

 Applicable Years: 1984 to 1996

 Tab: $25

 Tip: Make sure you use flare nut, or line wrenches, to remove the filter. Standard open-end wrenches can create problems.

COMPLEMENTARY WORK: While this can easily be a stand-alone job, it's often combined with an air filter and oil change.

This is the part where you need to pay attention. Look for the little arrow on the filter and make sure you have the filter pointing in the correct direction. By the way, the gasoline goes from the back of your car to the front. The arrow should point toward the front of the car.

Corvette fuel filters are extremely easy to change. The only problem you may encounter is actually finding the filter. Remember, you should change this filter in a well-ventilated area since you're going to spill gas on the floor – there's just no way to avoid it. If possible, you should change the filter outside on your driveway.

Fuel filters became critical once the change to fuel injection was complete. The fuel passages in a fuel injector make a carburetor look like an expressway. Given the price of a Corvette fuel filter, you should be changing it every year – maybe more often if the spirit moves you.

You'll need a couple of flare nut, or line wrenches, to perform this job. These flare nut wrenches are great for any type of fuel or brake line. They make it almost impossible to round the corners of the fittings. The last thing you want to do is round the edges off a fuel line. Fuel lines in the C4 Corvette are long and complicated. Round the edges off a fitting, and you'll see just how long and complicated they really are.

The first trick is to simply locate the fuel filter. Most people over a certain age think that fuel filters have to be in the engine compartment. That's not the case with these Corvettes. Their filters are located on the inside of the right frame rail. This means you're going to have to place the right side of the car up on jack stands for this job. You should make sure that everything is secure before you crawl under the car and start removing the old filter.

Many people choose to release the pressure in the fuel system before they exchange the old filter for a new one. You'll find a Schrader valve located on the fuel rail up in the engine compartment. This is a valve that looks just like a tire valve. If you push down on this valve the same way you would let air out of your tire, you can release the pressure in the fuel system. Don't do this on a hot engine since you could end up burning down the car right in your driveway. Just try explaining that one to your wife.

With the pressure in the fuel system released, jack the car up on the right side and place two jack stands under the frame. The front jack stand position may require some thought since you don't want it to get in the way of your effort to remove the fuel filter.

This isn't the easiest filter to locate. If the car is on a lift, it's easy to change. If your Corvette is on jack stands in your driveway, it's not nearly as much fun.

If you haven't released the fuel pressure in the system, be prepared for a shot of gasoline when you loosen the filter nuts. Sometimes I cover the whole area around the nuts with a shop rag just so I won't get gasoline in my face. Safety glasses are a good thought at this point.

The only other thing you need to be concerned about is getting the new filter pointing in the correct direction. Luckily, there is usually an arrow on the filter to help you do this properly. Take a few seconds and double-check this before you install the filter.

While you're under the car, you may notice there's a bracket that holds the fuel line against the frame rail. I find that things go a little easier if you remove the bracket while you're changing the filter. It's not necessary when you're removing the old filter, but when you install the new one it helps you line up the threads properly.

Once the new filter is in place you can remove the jack stands and start the engine. Let it run for a couple of minutes and then turn it off. Now poke your head under the car and check for any fuel leaks. Anytime you replace a fuel filter you need to make absolutely certain that all the connections are tight. A leaking fuel filter is a major cause of car fires.

It's not a bad idea to push down on the Schrader valve on the engine's fuel rail to relieve any fuel pressure. You could have as much as forty pounds of residual pressure in the fuel line when you remove the old fuel filter. Gasoline shooting out with forty pounds of pressure just isn't my idea of fun.

Radiator Cleaning

BASICS

Time: 2 to 3 hours

Tools: Metric sockets (3/8-inch drive and 1/4-inch drive) and metric combination wrenches

Talent:

Applicable Years: 1984 to 1996

Tab: Minimal

Torque: Fan shroud to upper housing — 15 foot-pounds

Tip: This should be done every few years.

PERFORMANCE GAIN: Greatly improved cooling will keep the engine from detonating.

COMPLEMENTARY MODIFICATION: Replace the upper radiator hose if it hasn't been changed in the last two years.

The first step is to drain the cooling system. The radiator drain is on the passenger side and is plastic. Simply screw it out turning it to the left just like a normal bolt, not in the opposite direction as with some drain plugs. Be careful with this plug since it's plastic, and you really don't want to break it. You don't have to drain the entire cooling system unless it's been over a year since you last changed the coolant.

The digital temperature gauge in the 1984 to 1996 Corvette is truly a curse. Fortunately, in 1990 a gauge was added in the instrument cluster redesign. As a result, you can turn off the electronic readout and just pretend it's not there. The Corvettes made between 1984 and 1989 only have the digital readout. This has probably caused more anxious moments than any other gauge in the history of the Corvette. Nothing is worse than being stuck in traffic and watching the numbers slowly climb. With a basic analog gauge you wouldn't even notice a two-degree temperature change. Not so with a digital gauge. You can anxiously watch the water temperature increase degree by degree.

As if the digital gauge weren't disconcerting enough, Corvettes were also designed to run hot. Temperatures between 200 degrees and 225 degrees are nothing to be alarmed about. Actually in some of the C4s the fans don't turn on until the coolant is at 226 degrees. This means that your cooling system needs to be operating at peak efficiency to keep things under control. This is a case of where normal can become borderline very quickly.

The Big Culprit

The major cause for unusually high coolant temperatures in your C4 is that it's a bottom-breather. The C4 Corvette sucks air from the bottom of the car. Look at the front of the car, and you'll see that the air for the radiator is actually pulled from the bottom. The problem is that this system also sucks up a tremendous amount of road trash. The C4 cooling system is so efficient that it literally acts like a giant vacuum cleaner as it goes down the road.

All of this road trash gets sucked up into the space

We have several items here that need to be unplugged. With this car the manifold air temperature sensor, or MAT, has been moved to the air intake passage. This typical GM plug has locking tabs holding the two parts together. Use a very small screwdriver to move the locking tab and then pull the two parts apart. Don't break the tabs off when you do this. In this case it was easy enough to simply remove the sensor from the rubber grommet.

The whole air intake assembly can be removed. You can do this with the MAF sensor still connected. But since it's so easy to disconnect, just take it off and set the entire assembly aside.

between the radiator and the air conditioning condenser. You literally have your own trash dump between the two components. This is the single biggest cause of high temperatures in your cooling system. It's also an easy thing to fix. And luckily, you won't need any special tools or any highly developed professional skills to fix it.

Plan on spending the good part of the day on this project. The job isn't all that difficult – it's just that there are a lot of bolts that have to be removed. This means you should be very careful not to break these bolts. One idea is to spray all the bolts down with WD-40 a few days before you start the project. Every little thing can help in a situation like this.

Also make sure that you stack everything in nice little piles so you can put it all back together properly and efficiently. When I'm doing this job I usually replace the upper radiator hose at the same time. The upper radiator hose is the most susceptible to bursting, and it's not a bad idea to

The two thumb screws, or knobs, hold the entire air filter assembly to the radiator housing. Sometimes you'll need pliers – especially if the last guy who owned the car feared the air filter was going to fall off or enjoyed using the knobs as a test of strength. This is also a good time to replace the air filter.

Now remove the upper radiator hose. If this hose is more than two years old, go ahead and replace it. The upper radiator hose is the most vulnerable to bursting for a variety of reasons —none of which we're going to get into right now. Regardless of the reason, just remember it's going to be a lot easier to replace the hose now than it will be when you're stranded on the side of the road six months from now.

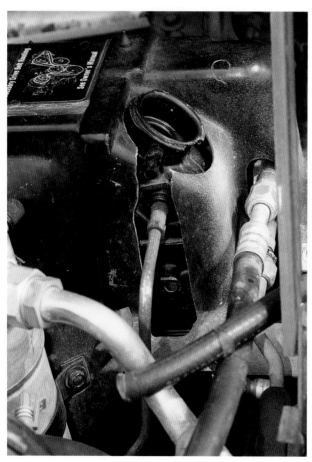

You might find a hard steel line that threads into the plastic end cap on the radiator. This is an oil cooler line and will have to be removed. Fortunately this line is flexible enough that you can simply hold it back as you pull the top of the radiator housing off. Be very careful when you replace this line since the steel nut is screwed into the plastic radiator housing.

Now you can start removing the bolts around the perimeter of the housing. Be careful since these may have rusted into place if they haven't been removed lately. In addition to the bolts you can readily see, the fan shroud hides several more.

When you have the housing off, you can remove all the trash you'll find lodged there. A vacuum cleaner with a very small nozzle is very effective in removing this rubbish. You can also use compressed air to blow the debris out. Just make sure you do it outside and wear safety glasses.

PROJECT 7

Detailing Your Corvette

Time: Several hours

Talent: 👤👤

Applicable Years: 1984 to 1996

Tab: Under $20

Tip: Always use the least aggressive product that will restore the finish. Never start with the industrial-strength product. Regular maintenance will ensure that these milder products get the job done.

❗ PERFORMANCE GAIN: Your Corvette just looks better, which means it feels faster.

More time is spent on detailing the Corvette than on any other job. We can talk about new computer chips and exhaust systems at great length, but wax is the one thing that is vital to every Corvette owner.

I'm going to assume that you already know how to wash your car. Just make sure you don't use dish soap since it removes all the wax from the car. I usually buy the cheapest car wash I can find at the local discount parts store.

Once you've gotten all the dirt off the car you can now use detailing clay. To avoid floating dust particles, I would do this inside the garage. Detailing clay is one of the best inventions of the last several decades. It was originally

designed as a product to help body shop employees remove overspray from repaired cars. It acts as a very fine abrasive and removes any surface blemishes from the paint. It actually doesn't remove any paint, just debris.

Use a lot of lubricant, such as Meguiars No. 34 Final Inspection, and then simply hydroplane the clay across the surface to abrade any little bumps from the existing paint. You can "float" this clay back and forth across the paint until the resistance ceases. This indicates that the unwanted droplets have been ground off.

When you're doing this in your home garage, you're usually removing tree sap and insect remnants, not overspray. The clay never really abrades the clear coat, but rather just removes anything that is on the surface. Clay smoothes the surface of the paint by grinding off the microscopic high spots of your paint, much like sandpaper smoothes a piece of wood. You'll feel the difference when all the surface imperfections are gone. Using these detailing clays is the best way to remove paint overspray, tree sap, insects, and other hard-to-remove surface blemishes.

If you're not careful, detailing clay can create scratches. It should only be used on a well-lubricated area, and you should constantly check your clay for contaminants. If you rub it on areas of the paint that have not been well lubricated, or if a piece of grit lodges in the clay, you've just

All of the C4 Corvettes use a clear coat paint system. You need to be very careful that you don't wear through this clear coat with a product that's too abrasive. If the bottle says "polish" on the label, the product inside probably has an abrasive in it. Always test out a new product on some painted surface that isn't important to you. You don't want to use your Corvette as a test case. The best way to test for abrasives is to put some of the product on a white rag and then polish something that isn't clear coated. If this white rag picks up the color from what you're polishing, it's a pretty abrasive product. Don't let it near your Corvette.

created sandpaper. You should constantly refold the clay to expose a fresh, clean surface. If contaminants lodge in the clay, simply tear off the contaminated section and throw it out. As soon as you're done using the clay you should place it in a sealed plastic bag.

Wax

It seems everyone is still praising the virtues of carnauba wax. You need to get off the carnauba kick and start using the synthetics. Many people argue that carnauba is better for your Corvette because it's a natural product. The only problem with this argument is that there's nothing natural about the paint on your Corvette.

The paint on your Corvette is a miracle of chemistry. From a chemist's point of view, synthetic waxes are much closer in substance to your Corvette's paint than a wax taken from trees.

Generally Zaino Brothers and Liqui-Tech's Finish-First, both synthetic products, will hold up better than a carnauba-based wax. The range of durability will depend on a lot of factors, but the broad statement is still true.

Where you live will have more of an effect on the staying power of your wax than the specific product you use. Most of the chemists in the detailing industry choose a polymer wax over a carnauba wax. Basically, if you want to protect the paint on your Corvette, you need to use synthetic wax products.

Interior

Even though your car may have leather seats, there's a tremendous amount of vinyl in the C4 Corvette. You might want to think of vinyl as a raw semi-liquid that is held in place by a solid skin. Ultraviolet rays constantly bombard the dash and other vinyl parts. These UV rays break down the molecules in the skin, allowing the raw vinyl to escape. This is referred to as "off-gassing." This escaped vinyl deposits itself on the glass, forming a haze.

Most products don't contain UV protectants, and the silicone oils in some products may actually act as a magnifying glass, intensifying the UV degradation. Silicone oil may also dissolve the oils in the vinyl skin, hastening the premature formation of cracks.

A quality vinyl cleaner/dressing product will contain a UV protectant. After a few moments of allowing it to work into the surface, buff off the excess. The top of the dash should be treated more often than any other area since it's subject to the most severe attack by UV rays and heat

My favorite vinyl treatment is from a company called Just Dashes. Their main business is the reproduction of dash panels. Since they spend so much time making some of the best dashes in the industry, it's only natural that they would help owners keep their dashes looking good.

Leather

When it comes to leather seats, I have real reservations about most of the products on the market here. Lexol is

The 1984 to 1996 Corvette used great leather on the seats. All you have to do is clean it and use a leather conditioner on a regular basis. I've tried almost every product I can purchase at my local parts discounter, and I keep going back to Lexol. I don't think it's an amazing product — it's just not as bad as the rest of the stuff on the market.

still the number one product on the market, followed closely by Duragloss. I'm not in love with any of this stuff. I just find that Lexol and Duragloss are the better choices in the large bunch of bad choices. People are always asking how often they should treat the seats and steering wheels in the C4 Corvette. The answer is really simple – the product will let you know.

Remember, what you're doing is replacing the oils in the leather. If you do this a little too often, the Lexol will simply build up on the seat. This means that the leather has more than enough oil. If you wait too long, the Lexol will soak quickly into the leather. Just let your Corvette seats talk to you, and you'll understand how often they need to be treated.

The steering wheel on the 1984 to 1996 Corvette is one huge issue. The leather is usually bad on the older cars. Dirt and perspiration from your hands get on the leather every day you're behind the wheel. One solution is to wear gloves every time you drive. But, as we all know, that's not a very feasible plan.

A more sensible solution is to use a good leather cleaner on the wheel on a regular basis. The other thing is to make sure that you keep the steering wheel treated with a good leather treatment. You're also fighting the sun on this one. It seems that between the sun and your hands these wheels have a lifespan of less than ten years. Considering the price of a new wheel, ten years of leather treatment is very cheap.

The leather seats in the 1984 to 1996 Corvette are really tough. The interesting thing is that the stitching will usually give out before the leather goes bad. I've had my seats re-stitched several times now. I think a lot of the leather conditioners actually weaken the stitching so don't get too carried away with treatments. This is a case where more may be worse than just enough.

Wheels

When it comes to wheel cleaner, choose the least aggressive product you can locate. If you keep up with the accumulation of brake dust, a simple car wash solution is enough.

The biggest problem with wheels is brake dust. The metallic dust given off during braking is red hot and will actually burn tiny holes in the finish of your wheels. The small droplets that look like road tar on your wheels may not be road tar at all. They may, in fact, be re-polymerized brake pad adhesive.

This brake pad adhesive is the root of most of our problems. These polymer adhesives form droplets that wind up on the wheels where they adhere with a vengeance. When the adhesive residue becomes wet, it turns acidic and will actually etch your wheels. Again, the only solution is to clean your wheels often.

All of the stock wheels for the 1984 to 1996 Corvette have either a painted surface or a clear coat. This actually makes life easy. You can treat these wheels the same way you handle any painted surface. If you clean your car regularly, you can just use the normal soap and simply clean the wheels with a separate rag. And, as you've probably been told numerous times, it's best to clean them when they're cool.

The only wheel cleaner I use on a wheel is P21S, a product made in Germany. Most of the popular brands are highly acidic and can do more harm than good. In fact, GM advises that acidic cleaners will attack and ruin the rear suspension spring! That's a very high price to pay for clean wheels. The active ingredient in a lot of wheel cleaners is hydrofluoric acid. This is the same stuff normally used to etch glass. P21S may not be as aggressive as other brands, but it won't strip the finish off your wheel either.

Most wheel cleaners work best on a dry wheel. Spray the cleaner on the wheel and work evenly into all areas of the wheel with a soft cloth or a small sponge. Allow the wheel cleaner three to five minutes to work and then gently scrub the wheel with your cloth or sponge.

If you have stock Corvette wheels, you might consider waxing them. This wax acts as a sacrificial protectant. The damaging effects of red-hot brake dust, brake dust acids, pollution, and ozone will be unleashed on the wax and not on your wheel. Liqui-Tech makes a very nice synthetic wax that's good for this purpose.

If the wheels are slightly faded or dull looking, 3M Imperial Hand Glaze may help. Apply the glaze to a soft cloth and gently rub out the clouding and buff out. If this doesn't do the trick, put a generous amount of 3M on your cloth and add a small amount (about the size of the nail on your pinkie finger) of P21S Metal Finish Restorer Metal

Polish. Polish out the clouding with this combination. The P21S/3M combination will usually get the job done. Then follow up with a coat of wax. Treat your wheels just like you would any other painted surface on your Corvette.

If you're crazy enough to have polished aluminum wheels, it'll take longer to detail the wheels than it will to detail the whole rest of the car. I've gone back to Simichrome polish after experimenting with several other products. It never ceases to amaze me how the old standby products have yet to be eclipsed.

Tires

When it comes to tire dressing, I'm back to an old product after messing around with every other product on the market. I gave up on One Touch tire dressing several years ago because the look was too glossy, and the results always looked streaked. Eventually I decided to give One Touch another try with one of the new applicators on the market. It worked so well I use One Touch all the time now.

Brake dust is the biggest enemy of your wheels. This stuff will actually eat through the paint if you don't clean your wheels on a regular basis. All the Corvette wheels were painted during this era. If you decide to have this clear coat removed and want to polish the wheels, you've just added several hours to your weekly maintenance program.

Detailing spray is great. It's mostly glycerin, and it gets rid of a lot of water spots. I love using it on glass for a special effect. I'm not sure if it protects anything, but your car will sure look better when you're done.

My other choice for tire care is a product by Stoner. This company got started making release agents for the tire molds at Goodyear. Stoner knows about tires. The company's product is easy to apply since it comes in an aerosol can, and all you have to do is spray it on. The One Touch holds up a little better, but Stoner gives you a little less gloss. I currently only use these two tire detailers.

You need to be very careful about tire dressing since some of the products use raw silicone. This may actually lead to sidewall cracking over time. In addition, a lot of the tire treatments contain formaldehyde. I would like to tell you which ones do, but they are not required to disclose this information – and they don't.

Carpet

Carpet is carpet. Anything you use on the carpet in your house is good for the carpet in your Corvette. The best carpet cleaner is the stuff you buy at the grocery store – the exact same stuff you use on your home carpets. If you vacuum the inside of your Corvette on a regular basis, you can probably avoid the use of any carpet cleaners.

SECTION TWO

ENGINE

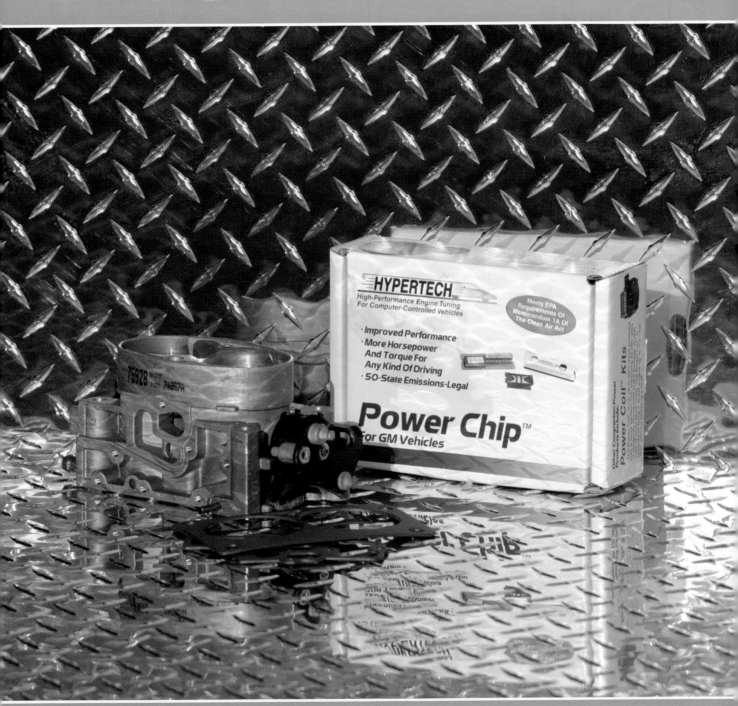

Parts courtesy Corvette Central

Removing the Engine

ENGINE

 Time: Hours to days

 Tools: Just about everything you can fit into a toolbox. Remember, everything is going to be Torx head or metric.

 Talent:

 Applicable Years: 1984 to 1996

 Tab: $750 to $5,000

 Tip: This is a major task. Don't try to do this on your own the first time unless you've got some really experienced help nearby. The problems won't be in removing the engine. All of the really serious problems will occur when you start to put the engine back in the car — and try to get it running.

⚠ PERFORMANCE GAIN: Even a simple rebuild will give you a performance gain compared to the previously worn-out motor.

COMPLEMENTARY MODIFICATION:
The list of possible changes is endless. As you put the engine back together, the problem is trying to decide what not to change. You might want a new 383 cid short block. Or maybe you'd prefer an induction system change. Just make sure you make these choices from an educated perspective. Talk to someone who's completed this task before. Also disregard most of the stuff you read in the magazines since they're trying to sell parts.

 Removing the engine from a C4 Corvette is a big deal. Anytime you have to pull the motor out of a Corvette, you're in for a lot of work. But with a C4, you also have a lot of computer controls to keep track of. The first thing you have to decide is whether the engine really has to be removed at all. There aren't too many reasons to take the engine out of a C4.

The engines in the C4 Corvettes seem to be lasting forever. There's minimal piston ring wear, and bearing wear is almost nonexistent. A lot of the older cars are getting well over 150,00 miles before they have any serious sort of problem.

The major reasons for removing the engine won't occur until the car has well over 150,000 miles on the engine. Even then you may not need to remove the whole engine.

The clutch and transmission can easily be removed with the engine left in place. There's just no reason to take a motor out of a C4 Corvette to perform any of these tasks. If a shop tells you that the engine has to come out of the car to work on the transmission, you should find another shop.

One occasion to remove the engine is when you decide to replace the camshaft. This may sound a little strange since once you remove the radiator there's more than enough room to install a new camshaft. The problem is the seal at the bottom of the timing cover. It's almost impossible to get this seal to seat correctly unless you have the engine out of the car. A lot of people have tried to work on the front of the engine and the timing chain cover with the engine in place, but it usually results in an oil leak at the bottom of the timing cover. This is a case where it's best to do things correctly the first time rather than have to do them over again.

Should you finally make the decision to remove the engine, you should start with the battery. This needs to be disconnected before you start removing anything from the car. You're going to be moving a lot of stuff around so you certainly don't need any electrical shocks. An electrical short can damage a lot of equipment in a C4 Corvette. Be very careful.

After you have the battery disconnected you can drain the radiator. Then remove the radiator and all of the attached shrouds. Try to label everything you remove. You'll think you can remember everything you've done to the car, but the reality is that it may be months, or even years, before you start to put things back together again.

If you're taking the engine out of the car, you should really consider buying a digital camera so you can see how everything looked before you began working on it. The age of digital photography is a tremendous help for all of us working on cars. You don't need a fancy camera that costs hundreds of dollars. Just remember to burn the pictures on a CD for permanent storage.

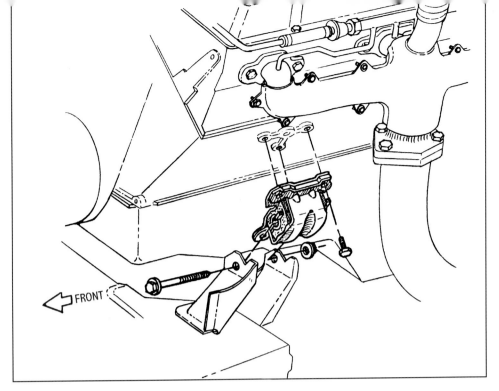

This is a good example of how crowded the engine compartment on the C4 really is. These engine mounts are really easy to remove once you find them. If you're considering removing your own engine, go out in the garage and look under the hood. Now try to find the engine mounts. Next, try to envision getting to them and removing the bolts. This may answer any questions you might have about doing this project in your home garage.

FRONT

You should also get a bunch of Ziplock bags and hundreds of labels. Put every part you remove into a bag and identify it on the label. No matter how good you think you are, you'll never remember where everything goes. Don't lie to yourself about how good your memory is. The more bags and labels you use, the better off you're going to be.

Now that you've gotten the radiator out of the way, you need to remove the exhaust system. Look at the chapter on the exhaust system to remind you how to take the system apart. When you remove the engine, you should plan on dropping the entire exhaust system. It takes very little effort, so why bother with anything other than removing the entire system and just sliding it out from under the car?

Now that you have the exhaust and cooling systems removed you can start unplugging electrical connections. You definitely must develop a labeling system for everything you disconnect. There are so many relays and connections you'll never remember where they all go when this Corvette finally goes back together.

Most people seem to remove these engines with the transmission left in place. While you could pull the transmission and engine as a total unit, you may find this to be a disadvantage. The transmission will need some sort of support while the engine is out of the car so plan on devising a system that works for you. Keep in mind that it may be some time before the engine is returned to its normal home.

Another issue you have to deal with is the hood. The engine will easily come out of the car sideways if you use the cherry picker type of engine hoist. The good thing is that these can be rented by the day. The last thing your garage needs is a C4 hood leaning against the wall for an undetermined amount of time.

One critical thing is that you should never attempt to remove the engine from the chassis by yourself. When you

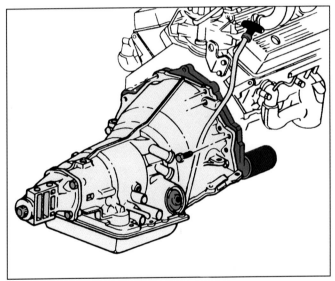

The transmission can generally stay in place when you remove the motor. The bolts that run around the top half of the transmission case are all fairly easy to access. You will, however, need to make arrangements to support the front of the transmission while the engine is out of the car.

finally have everything disconnected, make sure you have a couple of friends around to help you with the next step in the process. An engine swinging around on a hoist is a sure way to cause a lot of damage to both yourself and your car.

Putting the engine back in the chassis will be the easy part. Just get some friends to help you carefully lower the engine into place. Then you can begin digging out all those digital pictures and labeled baggies. This is also the point during which you need a friend who's been through this process before. Engine removal is not for the inexperienced, nor the faint of heart.

PROJECT 9

Opti-Spark Solutions

 Time: 2 hours

 Tools: A credit card with a large credit line.

Talent:

 Applicable Years: 1992 to 1996

 Tab: $500 to $1,000

 Tip: Don't ever let any water get in the area of the Opti-Spark when you detail your engine compartment.

COMPLEMENTARY MODIFICATION: This would be a very good time to install new spark plug wires. Spark plug wires on the LT1 are a major effort. It usually takes around four hours to install them. I would install the new Opti-Spark, and once I'm sure the engine runs properly, I would get started on the spark plugs and the spark plug wires.

This new Opti-Spark distributor was supposed to be the greatest thing since GM did away with ignition points. Instead they had an internal mistake, and the Opti-Spark caused Corvette owners a tremendous amount of aggravation.

One of the goals of the distributor was to control spark scatter during transient maneuvers, such as acceleration. GM also wanted to eliminate the large timing errors that occur during starting. This was a well-known problem with magnetic reluctance timing sensors.

The Opti-Spark is a distributor with a two-track optical position sensor, a keyed drive shaft, an ECM, a single ignition coil and driver, and conventional secondary wires and spark plugs. Contrary to what many people believe, most spark errors actually occur at low speeds, especially starting, rather than at high rpm. Spark errors also occur during transient movements such as acceleration, deceleration, and transmission shifts.

A key element in this Opti-Spark system was the increased overall diameter of the distributor. This allowed

for greater separation between the secondary terminals within the cap. This reduced cap and rotor wear by reducing the ozone formed when the spark is jumping large rotor-to-cap gaps.

The Problem
Despite all of the Opti-Spark's innovations, one major problem occurred in the transition to actual production. The casing of the Opti-Spark, which was mounted to the front of the engine, just behind the water pump, was designed with a small hole at the base. This would allow any condensation formed within the distributor to drain out. The design engineering team was very precise about the size of this hole.

After the design was completed, the unit was passed on to a group called validation engineering. This group changed the size of the hole without communicating this change to anyone else. The validation team felt the hole was simply too large and would allow water to enter into the distributor. Unfortunately, this new drain hole was simply too small to allow condensation to flow out of the distributor.

To make matters just a little worse, the validation team changed the composition of the internal components, making them less corrosion resistant. That was all that was needed to make this one of the most failure-prone components in Corvette history. Eventually a recall campaign led to all (or most) of the units being replaced.

Today there are several units on the market that incorporate some design changes that make the very reliable. This is important since there are no alternatives on the market for the Opti-Spark. It's not as if you can simply install a different type of distributor.

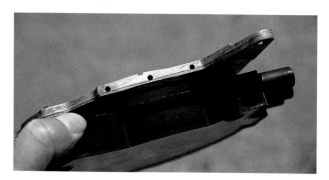

These dreaded holes create the infamous Opti-Spark problem. If you kill the unit, you must be prepared to spend some very serious money to fix your mistake. I would search out one of the upgraded units — don't even consider another original equipment part.

This is the Opti-Spark distributor cap. You can easily see how far the terminals are from each other. This greatly improved the low speed performance of the new LT1 engine – at least until the whole distributor failed.

This assembly hides directly behind your water pump and almost directly under the thermostat housing. It's a shame that the various groups within GM didn't have a chance to talk to each other and resolve the whole Opti-Spark issue. The LT1 is a great engine with one huge problem – a problem that could cost you more than a thousand dollars.

One Type of Retrofit

At one time, Borg Warner offered an Opti-Spark repair kit called C400. It was listed for the 1992 to 1996 Corvettes. This kit worked fine on 1995s or 1996s, but it needed a little help to fit the earlier units. You might want to look around and see if it's still available.

At $153, the kit isn't cheap so be careful with the installation. The kit gives you a vented cap and rotor, and the inside cover is different than the stock unit. The ECM plug is on the new part, but the old unit had the plug already molded and attached to the base. It goes in a notch in the old cover.

It is tempting to use the old inside cover, but, keep in mind, it may have carbon tracks due to its close proximity to the rotor and may not work when you are done. Using a Dremel tool or a small hobby saw, carefully cut the plug snout off of the new cover flush with the outside diameter.

Saw a notch in the new cover working a little at a time until you are satisfied with the fit. Leave a little room for some epoxy or JB weld.

You'll notice the flange in the center will not clear the photo receptor on the base. Remove a small section of the flange until it just barely clears. Now clean everything as well as possible and put the unit together. Put a very small amount of Vaseline on just the portion of the cap seal directly above the ECM plug so the epoxy won't stick to it. Leave the screws a little loose until the epoxy sets and then tighten them to compress the seal.

Corvette Clinic in Sanford, Florida, is the only firm that sells the Opti-Spark with all the upgrades. They actually use a flow-through ventilation system that circulates air through the distributor cap. I've never heard of anyone having a problem with one of their units.

Before you do any detailing, you should take a towel or shop rag and cover the hole in the Opti-Spark casing. I use a shop rag and then duct tape it so no moisture can possibly destroy the unit. You simply can't take chances. You have to be very careful when you do any engine detailing with the LT1. A lot of folks have gotten a little carried away cleaning their engine compartments and killed the Opti-Spark in the process. That's a very expensive mistake.

This cutaway LT1 picture from GM shows exactly what is going on with the infamous distributor. When you look at the distributor, also look at the spark plug wire routing for the LT1. If you have to replace your spark plug wires, you can expect to pay for about four hours of labor. That sort of bill makes me happy that I have an L98 engine.

PROJECT 10
Replacing Rocker Arm Cover Gaskets

 Time: 2 to 3 hours

 Tools: Metric socket set, Brake Clean, Torx drivers

 Talent:

 Applicable Years: 1984 to 1996

 Tab: $10 to $20

 Torque: 90 inch-pounds for center-bolt style

 Tip: Use Brake Clean to clean the valve covers.

 PERFORMANCE GAIN: None

COMPLEMENTARY MODIFICATION: After you've completed installing the new gaskets, you should warm up the car and change the oil. No matter how careful you are, some particles will fall into the rocker arm area and will circulate with the oil in the engine.

There are two types of stock Corvette rocker arm covers—actually three if you count the LT5 engine. From 1984 to 1986, the Corvette used the cast-iron cylinder heads that had been first designed in 1955. These early rocker arm covers all leak and will continue to leak despite your best efforts. You can slow the leaks down, but don't expect that you can eliminate the leaks.

When the small block was designed in 1955, the idea was that only one side would be machined. Obviously this saved money. The only problem was that the mounting surface for the gasket was left as a rough cast surface. The gasket could never totally seal this area.

From 1984 to 1986, the Corvette used a magnesium rocker arm cover. This fixed most, but not all, leakage problems. The issue really wasn't solved until the aluminum cylinder head was introduced.

In 1987 Chevrolet released the new aluminum cylinder heads which incorporated a new gasket and mounting system. This system uses a center-bolt mounting system and a U-shaped gasket where the cover joins the cylinder head. These aluminum heads seldom leak.

The first round of valve covers for the aluminum heads used a magnesium casting. These are almost indestructible, and you should have very few problems with them. In 1993 the construction was switched to a polyester resin. This switch was done in the interest of noise dampening, since no weight was saved. All you really need to know is that the magnesium covers and the polyester rocker arm covers are interchangeable.

When you install a new gasket, whether it's for the steel heads or the aluminum heads, make sure that everything is as clean as you can possibly get it. Any little particles left on either the cylinder head or the rocker arm cover will be potential starting points for leaks.

Be careful when you're removing the old gasket material. You're dealing with soft materials here. If you get a little too aggressive with your cleaning, you're going to remove material. This is really a case where it's important to take your time and do it properly.

The holes for the oil filler cap and the PCV hoses on this aftermarket cover just aren't right for the Corvette. You have to use a push-in oil filler cap, and then you have to rig a new system for the emissions plumbing. As beautiful as these are, they make you wonder why companies just can't make things correctly.

When it comes to replacing the gaskets, the most important part of the process is removing everything that gets in the way of getting to the gaskets. Clearing the right side is usually a walk in the park. Removing everything from the left side will test your drive for perfection. There's just a whole lot of stuff you have to remove in order to get at the actual valve cover.

The best procedure is to take several pictures so you can have a visual record of where everything goes. Then take a couple of additional pictures of the process as you go along.

Several companies make aftermarket rocker arm covers for the engines with the aluminum heads. While most Corvette owners prefer to keep the stock appearance, there's a growing trend toward the use of high quality aftermarket parts.

There's one giant issue with these aftermarket parts, however. Most of them will not meet emission standards. If you look at your standard rocker arm covers, you'll notice that there are usually two lines attached to the cover, and the oil fill cap seals solid to the rocker arm cover. This means that your rocker arm covers are really a part of the total emissions system. I haven't found one yet that really meets emissions standards. If you live in a tough place for emissions tests, they'll fail you in a second. If you don't have emissions tests in your area, you can install these aftermarket covers.

Make sure you get this ridge very clean. Any old gasket material here could be the source of a future oil leak.

You should use a torque wrench on the rocker arm cover bolts. Remember, it's 90 inch-pounds of torque — not 90 foot-pounds. This is a case where tighter is not necessarily better. If you get the bolts too tight, you're squeezing the gasket and just asking for a leak. This is much more critical on the old four-bolt steel cylinder heads than it is on the aluminum heads. Of course, you should use caution regardless of which type of rocker arm cover is on your Corvette.

PROJECT 11

Installing a Throttle Body Air Foil

 Time: 30 minutes

 Tools: Screwdrivers

 Talent:

 Applicable Years: 1985 to 1996

 Tab: $40

 Torque: Thermostat housing to intake manifold— 25 foot-pounds

 Tip: A new 52mm throttle body is an option if you've made any other improvements to the intake system. If you have a stock intake system, though, it's best to stay with a stock throttle body.

PERFORMANCE GAIN: You should notice an improvement in the idle quality.

COMPLEMENTARY MODIFICATION: Before you install an air foil, it isn't a bad idea to clean the throttle body intake with air intake cleaner from Wynn's or 3M.

People love to make fun of throttle body air foils. People see them as gimmicks. Don't expect to see any great change in your Corvette after you install the air foil. If you're lucky, you might get a couple of extra horsepower at very high rpm. You'll probably never be able to actually feel any difference but then again when did you get much power for 1/2 hour's worth of work and less than fifty dollars?

Installing air foils is quite easy. You'll need to remove the air intake hose to get into the throat of the throttle body. Most of the throttle body air foils for the C4 are aluminum, although I have seen some in a high-tech resin configuration. The material makes very little difference since the only thing that will have contact with the air foil is air.

A lot of us grew up with carburetors and still have trouble understanding exactly what fuel injection is all about. To clarify, with fuel injection the fuel isn't added to the intake system until the last possible moment. Look at your engine and note where the fuel injector is.

The injector on Corvettes is right at the edge of the intake runner, just before the cylinder head. That means the intake system is dealing with dry air until it hits the injector. All the things you know about fuel atomization really don't apply here. The distance the fuel has to travel in a Corvette intake system is really very short.

From the very front of the air filter until the fuel injector, the air is totally dry. This dry air is also the reason these air foils work. Any improvement you can make to airflow will help improve the power. The bigger the changes in airflow, the more power you should get. This air foil is only going to produce a little change so you won't actually feel much difference. Remember, however, you aren't spending a lot of money and time. That's why this is a good deal even if you might not be able to notice much of a difference.

Above left: This is one version of the air foil. There are a lot of vendors for this item, and it's found in almost every catalog. The idea is that it smooths the airflow into the plenum — it actually works and does help fill the plenum with air. Keep in mind, though, that your engine is really drawing air from the plenum. The plenum is more than large enough to store air for normal use, so the real utility of the air foil is limited. Only when you're running at maximum rpm is there a real need to get more air into the plenum.

Left: A very common modification is to remove the screens from the Mass Airflow sensor. The idea is that the screens block the air from reaching the plenum. The only problem is that any extra air you might allow into the engine will only be used at higher revolutions. Think about how often you drive your Corvette at 5,000 rpm and ask yourself if you truly need this modification. These screens were designed to keep dirt out of the MAF sensor. You have to make a decision about which is more of a problem for your Corvette. Are you most concerned that any dirt might somehow find its way past the air filter? Or are you most concerned about extra airflow at high rpms? Just because all the racers remove the screens from the MAF sensor doesn't make it a good idea for your street-driven Corvette.

PROJECT 12

Throttle Body Cleaning

 Time: 30 minutes to several hours

 Tools: Screwdrivers, metric sockets, and metric open-end wrenches

 Talent:

 Applicable Years: 1985 to 1996

 Tab: $40

 Torque: Throttle body to plenum — 18 foot-pounds

 Tip: A new 52mm throttle body is an option if you've made any other improvements to the intake system. If you have a stock intake system, it's best to stay with a stock throttle body.

 PERFORMANCE GAIN: You should notice an improvement in the idle quality.

COMPLEMENTARY MODIFICATION: Replace the air filter when you're done with the cleaning.

We never really think about the throttle body much. We can't even see a problem about to happen unless we start taking things off the car. We just assume all the air gets to the combustion chamber. We know it has to get through the air filter, but we never think too much about the throttle body. Still, this throttle body gets just as dirty as the old carbs used to get. The throttle body on your Corvette can really benefit from a good annual cleaning.

One thing you need to remember about the throttle body is that it's a system for controlling dry air. Keep in mind where your fuel injectors are located. Until the air reaches the fuel injectors you simply have a dry air passage. Those of us raised with carburetors have a tendency to forget that very simple fact.

The other thing to keep in mind is that these throttle bodies have been around since the 1985 Corvette. That means some of them are simply worn out. It also means that some of them are incredibly dirty. This filth can cause a variety of problems, the most common being a fairly high or erratic idle speed. This happens because the vacuum can't completely close the throttle plates. The throttle plates are normally drawn shut with engine vacuum. If the plates remain slightly open, you'll have a higher idle speed.

We're going to deal with several types of cleaning here. The best way is to simply keep everything clean on a regular basis. The process is so easy you could probably do it on a bi-monthly basis. It's just a matter of removing the air intake assembly and spraying some air intake cleaner on the throttle plates.

A lot of us bought our cars on the used market. The only thing we could afford was a high-mileage Corvette with an unknown maintenance history. These Corvettes are usually candidates for a major throttle body service. This means taking the throttle body completely off the car. It also means cleaning the Idle Air Control, or IAC.

The first step is to remove the intake hose that runs between the Mass Airflow sensor, or MAF, and the throttle body. Now you can get a good look at the amount of dirt in your throttle body. If there's very little dirt, a simple cleaning with an air intake cleaner will get the job done. Remember, though, that most of the buildup will be behind the throttle plates. You have to open the throttle plates to see what the back side looks like to make a true determination on the condition of your throttle body.

41

If your throttle body hasn't been cleaned in the last decade, it's a good idea to remove the entire assembly from the car. When you do this, you can get the rear half of the intake areas really clean. The first step is to remove the throttle linkage from the throttle body. This linkage is held together by a couple of small clips. You don't have to worry about anything special at this point.

Don't expect the throttle body to simply fall off easily. You might have to tap it with a small rubber mallet. Resist any temptation you might have to pry it off with a screwdriver. Any gouges in the surface will cause a major air leak when you put things back together. Remember, aluminum is a very soft material.

Removing the throttle body from the car will also require that you drain some coolant from the radiator since you're going to have to remove the coolant hoses at the lower part of the throttle body. If you live in Florida or California, you might just plug them or buy the little kit that was designed for this purpose. If you live in Minnesota or Michigan, you better hook them back up when you place the throttle body back on the plenum. This heated water really is important in a cold climate.

If you own a late model C4 Corvette, you can probably skip the removal step. If you aren't experiencing any problems, just clean the throttle plates from the outside with some air intake cleaner. Don't get too carried away with the cleaner since most of it will puddle on the floor of your plenum. It won't harm anything, but it won't do any good either. If a simple spray doesn't clean the throttle plates, try using a toothbrush on the plates.

Here we can see how black the rear part of the throttle body has become. There are times when the buildup is so bad that the entire unit has to be submerged in solvent for a day or so. These cases are unusual, but possible — especially if your old Corvette has not been properly maintained.

The best way to clean the unit is to spray it down with the Wynn's Air Intake Cleaner and then use a toothbrush to scrub the area. Don't use anything stiffer than a toothbrush for this job because you don't want to scratch any of the aluminum. A couple of scratches here, and you could find yourself looking at a new throttle body. If the residue won't come off with solvent and a toothbrush, let it sit overnight.

PROJECT 13

Thermostat Replacement—L98

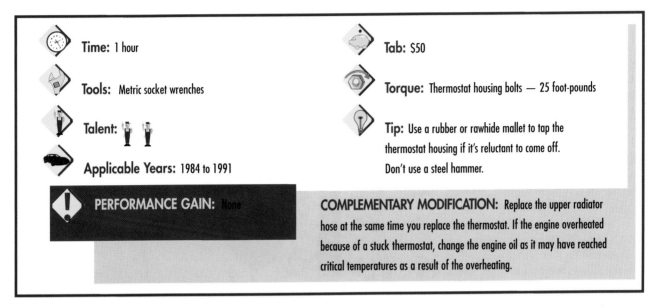

Time: 1 hour

Tools: Metric socket wrenches

Talent: ★ ★

Applicable Years: 1984 to 1991

PERFORMANCE GAIN: None

Tab: $50

Torque: Thermostat housing bolts — 25 foot-pounds

Tip: Use a rubber or rawhide mallet to tap the thermostat housing if it's reluctant to come off. Don't use a steel hammer.

COMPLEMENTARY MODIFICATION: Replace the upper radiator hose at the same time you replace the thermostat. If the engine overheated because of a stuck thermostat, change the engine oil as it may have reached critical temperatures as a result of the overheating.

More confusing things have been said about thermostats than any other part of the C4 Corvette. People claim all sorts of incredible gains from simply installing a new thermostat in their car, yet most don't have the first clue about what a thermostat really does.

Let's take a minute and get rid of one major myth. The thermostat in your Corvette does not set the coolant temperature. Think about basic physics for a minute. Your Corvette produces heat energy every time combustion takes place. If we left all that heat in place, the entire engine would melt down in a very short time.

In an effort to save the engine from melting down, combustion chamber heat is transferred to the coolant that circulates around the engine. Eventually all that coolant would itself become too hot. After all, the coolant can only absorb so much heat. That's why we have radiators in our Corvettes. All of the hot coolant from the engine is passed through a series of radiator tubes that have little fins on them. The heat from the coolant is transferred to the little fins and then dispersed into the atmosphere.

Your Corvette's cooling system is really nothing more than a study in the transfer of heat energy. It makes sure all the heat from the combustion chamber gets out into the atmosphere before the engine melts down. That's what the radiator and all those hoses in your Corvette really do.

The thermostat is nothing more than a gate in this system. When you start your car every morning, the coolant that's resting in the engine block is the same temperature as the air in your garage. The thermostat is designed to hold all the water in the engine block until it reaches a certain temperature. Once the coolant reaches that temperature, the thermostat, or gate, is opened, and coolant is allowed to flow around the entire system, including the radiator.

This means the thermostat has absolutely no influence on the temperature of your engine's coolant after things are at operating temperature. Yet every year, thousands of people swap thermostats around thinking they're going to get a performance gain.

The only way to lower the temperature of your Corvette's cooling system is to get more air to the fins on the radiator, or increase the amount of surface on the radiator. Changing the thermostat will have absolutely no effect on the temperature of the coolant once it's in a fully open position.

Remember, the operating temperature of your engine is determined by the size of your radiator and by whether or not you have an oil cooler. It's also a function of how much airflow is passing through the radiator. The idea is to disperse all the heat energy into the atmosphere. Moving air over that radiator will result in cooler temperatures.

If you install a 180-degree, or even worse, a 160-degree thermostat, all you're doing is opening the gate a little sooner. In the winter, this means your coolant may never get warm enough to allow the oil to function at optimum temperature. It also means that your heater won't be operating at peak efficiency.

There is an optimum temperature for your engine. Running the coolant as cold as you can get it makes no more sense than it does to run it extremely hot all the time. Temperature is especially critical to the engine oil. It has to be hot enough to get rid of any accumulation of moisture.

The myth about the thermostat got started with drag racers. A Corvette will run slightly faster if it's a little on the cool side. I've run dyno tests to compare a cold engine with a hot engine. The tests showed there were a few more horsepower when the engine was cold. As the engine temperature rose, we lost a couple of horsepower. The thing to keep in mind is that the thermostat had absolutely no effect on this change in temperature. We got this outcome by letting the car sit on the dyno with ice bags packed all over the plenum.

Now that we've decided you really don't need to change the thermostat unless it's stuck in either a closed or open position, we can move on. This is a really easy part to change. It's slightly different on the L98 and the LT1 engine, but, in both cases, it's on top of the engine. It's a little awkward to reach but not impossible.

When you install a new thermostat, make sure that you have really spotless surfaces on both the thermostat and the housing. Use a paper gasket with no RTV sealer. If you insist on using sealer, stick to the Permatex aviation cement or something like the old Indian Head gasket shellac. Also, be sure the thermostat sensor is oriented downward.

Changing the PROM

 Time: 30 minutes

 Tools: Screwdriver and battery terminal wrench

 Talent:

 Applicable Years: 1984 to 1995

 Tab: $250

 Tip: Be very careful not to bend the prongs when installing a new chip into your ECM.

 PERFORMANCE GAIN: Simply changing the chip, or PROM, will not give you any noticeable increase in power. It may even decrease the power you currently have. The only real reason for changing the PROM is if a series of other modifications have been carried out.

COMPLEMENTARY MODIFICATION: This modification literally demands that other things be modified — things like the camshaft or intake system.

ENGINE

Let's take a minute and look at what a PROM really does. Its basic purpose is to store computer control strategy and look-up tables. These look-up tables indicate how an engine should perform. For instance, if the MAP sensor sends the message that the engine has 20 inches Hg of absolute manifold pressure, this information is combined with information from the engine speed sensor and compared to a table for spark advance. The PROM tells the computer what the spark advance should be under these conditions. The computer then modifies this spark advance value by consulting other tables.

The computer makes decisions based on three basic sources of information: the look-up tables, the system strategy, and the input from the sensor. By comparing information from these sources, the computer can make informed decisions.

The major goal of the whole computer system is to keep the air/fuel ratio as close to 14.7 to 1 as possible. This ratio allows maximum catalytic converter efficiency. You can fool the computer a little bit, or for a short time, but eventually it's going to get everything back on track with the 14.7 to 1 air/fuel ratio.

Open loop refers to the engine when it's still cold and the computer is not operating in a complete cycle. Closed loop is when the system is in a full feedback cycle. This means that a constant series of decisions and changes are being made based on sensor output.

Every car magazine in the world has talked about how to change the chip in your Corvette. Changing the Programmable Read Only Memory, or PROM, usually doesn't work really well. Because they are commercial enterprises, these magazines have a hard time discussing how some parts their advertisers sell are really just a waste of money. Advertising pays the bills at the magazine offices. As a result, whole generations of Corvette owners have been led to believe that by simply changing the chip in the Corvettes' computer, they're going to gain a whole bunch of horsepower that General Motors never knew existed. This is a about as logical as saying Santa Claus arrives at your house every twelve months.

Over the years I've seen more people lose horsepower from installing a new chip than gain power. This doesn't mean that the chips are bad. It just means they won't get close to offering the miracles the advertising promises.

This is a custom chip that I had created for my 1985 Corvette after we ported the plenum and installed larger intake runners on the L98 engine. It gave us about three more horsepower over the stock chip. Considering all the dyno time we used testing the new chip and all the effort we went through to change the chip, I have to admit that GM did a pretty good job with the stock chip.

The main reason that aftermarket PROM changes don't provide much horsepower is that, no matter what you do, the system will try to get back to that ideal 14.7 to 1 air/fuel mixture. You can change the spark advance curve and the length of time the injectors are on, but ultimately the closed loop system is self-correcting.

Some of the aftermarket chips simply throw the system into an open loop status. This gives you a rich fuel mixture that feels like more power. Rich motors generally feel powerful, but lean-running engines actually produce more power.

Unless you make a great number of changes to the mechanical systems of your Corvette engine, an aftermarket chip isn't going to do too much for your car. Keep in mind that you're constantly battling the 14.7 to 1 air/fuel ratio. Since your stock Corvette is already optimized, a simple chip change isn't going to change anything. The computer will adjust everything back to where you get the correct air/fuel mixture.

However, if you change the camshaft or the compression ratio, you're going to have to make some changes in the engine management system. That's why you're going to need a custom chip to optimize the mechanical changes you just made. A simple over-the-counter chip just won't get the job done.

You really can't get enough horsepower out of a standard mail-order chip to justify the expense. I once tested a half dozen chips on the dyno. It took the good part of the day, and when we were all done the stock GM chip provided the best power.

This is the whole ECM for the 1985 Corvette. Very few people have a clue about what goes on inside this box. When it comes to ECMs and the Programmable Read Only Memory, you really need to ask a lot of questions and find someone with a dyno and lots of experience. This is one case where the mail-order solution may not be the best idea.

The later model C4s moved the computer out from under the dash and directly over the master cylinder for the clutch. This makes it a lot easier to open the box and swap chips. In fact, it was probably too easy because in 1996 the government ruled that the PROMs had to be potted in plastic so that they couldn't be removed.

Replacing the Oxygen Sensor

 Time: 30 minutes

 Tools: Special oxygen sensor socket, 3/8-inch ratchet and extensions

 Talent: ▮▮

 Applicable Years: 1984 to 1996

 Tab: $40 to $200

 Torque: 40 to 44 foot-pounds

 Tip: It's often easier to remove the sensor if the exhaust is still hot rather than after the entire system has cooled down. You may need several different socket extensions and a universal joint for your ratchet wrench. Also, make sure you use a proper O2 socket for the sensor and use anti-seize compound on the threads when you install the new sensor.

 PERFORMANCE GAIN: The biggest difference will be in improved idle performance. You could see a performance gain across the board depending on how badly the old O2 sensor was deteriorated.

You probably won't have to replace the O^2 sensor on your Corvette. On the other hand, an oxygen sensor is cheap enough that you might want to simply replace the sensor every 50,000 miles as part of a routine maintenance program. Even if you own a C4 with the LT1 engine and two sensors, the price is still low. You might even treat it like a spark plug and replace it before it causes a problem.

The oxygen sensor is a key element in the engine computer system when the car is operating in closed loop system. The data that's derived from this sensor is used to maintain a balanced air/fuel mixture. If the sensor is sending out false or even sluggish readings, your engine is not going to be at peak performance.

A problematic oxygen sensor may not fail completely. Often times, on older cars they simply start to act sluggish. The usual signs of this are a slight loss of power, a rougher idle, or a slight drop in fuel mileage coupled with increased emissions.

Almost any shop can hook a scan tool up to your Corvette and read the number of oxygen sensor counts, or the number of times it's actually measuring your exhaust gases. This is a foolproof diagnosis and might eliminate an unnecessary replacement, although the diagnosis may cost more than a new oxygen sensor.

Depending on which engine is in your Corvette, you may have to look for the oxygen sensor in two different places. On the L98 engine, there's only one sensor. It's located down on the exhaust pipe, on the driver's side just forward of the catalytic converter.

The ZR-1 uses two oxygen sensors. They're located forward of the catalytic converters. These are both heated, which means the price is about double that of the older style sensors. The procedure for removing them is no different than the process for replacing the single sensor in the L98.

Before you start to remove an oxygen sensor, it's a good idea to remove the negative battery cable. Anytime you do electrical work on your Corvette, it's not a bad idea to disconnect the battery. This is especially true when you start to mess around with any of the sensors. Although it's not critical when removing the O^2 sensor, you might feel safer with the battery disconnected.

Most oxygen sensors come with the threads already coated with a special anti-seize compound. GM uses a special compound composed of graphite and glass beads. The graphite will quickly burn away, but the glass beads will remain. If you have to remove and reinstall the old oxygen sensor(s), make sure that you coat the threads with an anti-seize compound.

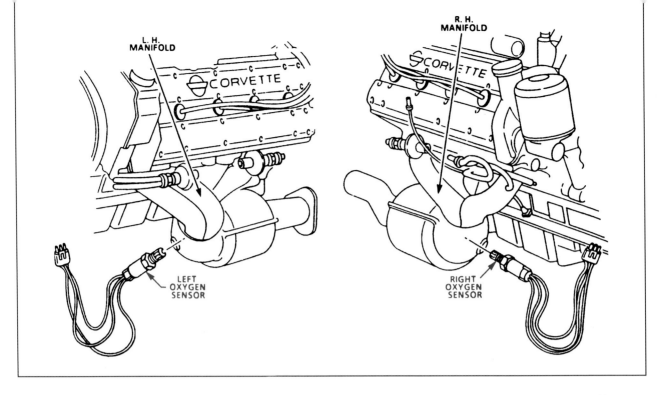

The LT5 engine has two oxygen sensors, and both are fairly easy to reach with a wrench. The bad part is they're very expensive. A single sensor costs roughly twice as much as an LT1 sensor. That's because they use a heated tip to keep the emissions clean at start-up.

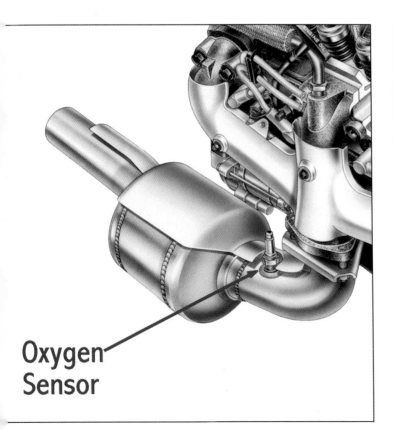

Oxygen Sensor

When the LT1 engine was introduced, the Corvette returned to a true dual exhaust system. This meant that the system now had to have two O_2 sensors — one for the right side and one for the left side. The good part is that they're fairly easy to get to.

This special socket is used to remove the O_2 sensor from the exhaust system. The slit down the side is a provision for the wiring. I would disconnect the harness first. Then you might as well start out with a 1/2-inch breaker bar on the end of this socket since these sensors don't like to be removed. In some cases you can use a box-end wrench and just thread the wires through the box end. And remember, it's best to try this project when the exhaust is hot.

PROJECT 16

LT1 Coolant Change

 Time: 1 hour

 Tools: Screwdrivers for hose clamps, and pliers

 Talent:

 Applicable Years: 1992 to 1996

 Tab: $25

 Tip: You should change the coolant on an annual basis with any C4 Corvette.

 PERFORMANCE GAIN: None

COMPLEMENTARY MODIFICATION: This is also a good time to consider replacing your upper radiator hose. The hose is cheap enough that you can and should replace it every two or three years. It's also the first hose that will go bad on your vehicle. Usually the lower hose lasts twice as long.

The introduction of the LT1 in 1992, with the new reverse cooling system, complicated the changing of the engine coolant a little bit. This reverse flow cooling was the key to the enhanced performance of the LT1, but it requires a little more care when flushing the cooling system.

Reverse flow cooling is superior to the cooling systems used in the L98 since it cools the cylinder heads first, preventing detonation. This in turn allows for a higher compression ratio and more spark advance on a given grade of gasoline. A fringe benefit is that cylinder bore temperatures are higher and more uniform, thus reducing piston ring friction. Because of the new cooling system, the LT1 could meet the ever-increasing emissions standards with significant gains in power, durability, and reliability.

The incoming coolant first encounters the thermostat, which now acts both on the inlet and outlet sides of the system. Depending on the engine coolant temperature, cold coolant from the radiator is carefully metered into the engine. This allows a more controlled amount of cold coolant

to enter the engine. The cold coolant immediately mixes with the bypass coolant already flowing. This virtually eliminates the thermal shock that existed in the old system.

After entering through one side of the two-way thermostat, the cold coolant is routed directly to the cylinder heads where the combustion chambers, spark plugs, and exhaust ports are cooled. Then the heated coolant returns to the engine block and circulates around the cylinder barrels. The hot coolant from the block re-enters the water pump and hits the other side of the two-way thermostat. Depending on the temperature, it is either re-circulated back through the engine or directed to the radiator.

The main concept behind reverse flow cooling is to cool the heads first. This greatly reduces the tendency for detonation and is the primary reason that the LT1 can run 10.5 to 1 compression and fairly significant ignition advance on modern lead-free gasoline. Reverse flow cooling is the key to the Generation II LT1s increased power, durability, and reliability over the earlier small block engines.

This is the LT1 water pump. One of the reasons it seems twice as large as the traditional Chevy water pump is that the distributor is mounted directly behind the water pump. The other reason is that this water pump is gear driven. If you have to replace the Opti-Spark, you might want to consider a new water pump. You can't just remove the distributor. The water pump has to be removed in an effort to get to the distributor. Luckily, this water pump isn't much more expensive than the traditional Chevy water pump. Unfortunately, when it starts to leak, it often destroys the Opti-Spark, and fixing this will add more than $600 to your bill.

Corvette LT1 applications use a pressurized coolant recovery reservoir instead of the nonpressurized overflow tank that was used with conventional cooling systems. All of the coolant flows continuously through the pressurized reservoir, which is an integral part of the cooling system. The pressurized reservoir in the LT1 is connected to the cooling system in three places. One inlet hose connects to the top of the right-hand radiator tank, a second inlet hose is attached through a "tee" connection on the heater inlet hose, and a third outlet hose is connected to a "tee" connection in the throttle body heater outlet.

The pressurized reservoir is mounted at the highest point in the system, and it provides a place where all air can be continuously scavenged from the coolant. Any steam and bubbles are allowed to rise to the surface, eliminating foam and providing pure liquid coolant back to the engine. Pure liquid coolant is returned to the system via the heater outlet hose connection. The pressure relief/vent cap in these systems is rated at 15psi and is located on the reservoir rather than the radiator.

Unless you know the little tricks, flushing the coolant can aggravate you. The problem is getting all the air out of the system so that it's completely full. Often you'll think you have the radiator full, but after driving down the road, you'll start overheating and see a Low Coolant message appear on the dash.

The first problem to address is just getting all the old coolant out of the system. You need to take special care with the LT1 to keep any coolant off your Opti-Spark distributor, which is located in the front lower portion of the engine. This is especially important on 1993 and 1994 models, as they're not properly vented. Water will destroy your Opti-Spark.

You'll need to open this bleed screw to release the air out of your cooling system. This bleed screw is mounted on the top of the thermostat housing, placing it at the highest point in the system. When you bleed the cooling system, remember to protect the Opti-Spark from any water.

This will also be an issue when filling your cooling system. Make sure that you bleed the cooling system by opening the air bleed valve on top of your engine. This will allow any air to escape. Once again, though, be careful as this valve is located directly above the Opti-Spark. It's a lot easier to get to this valve if you remove the air intake duct that connects the air filter to the throttle body.

If you remove the cap on the fill reservoir that's up on the passenger side and then open the air bleed valve, the water will come out faster. Also, don't completely remove the petcock from the right lower part of the radiator—it's designed to stay there.

In order to completely flush the cooling system, you'll have to remove both knock sensors out of the block. You'll find one on each side, just above the oil pan. Remember, the engine block holds almost 60 percent of the coolant in the system. Removing these knock sensors will require a 23mm socket and ratchet or a 23mm offset box-end wrench. The knock sensors will come off fairly easy if they were tightened to the correct specification in the first place. Avoid rounding off the bolt on the sensor. Resort to the vice grips only as a last resort, grasping the round base of the sensor. If you damage a sensor, you can get a new one for about thirty-five dollars from your local Chevy dealer. Always stick with the genuine AC/Delco stuff and don't use the cheapies from places like Auto Zone or Pep Boys since they may be calibrated to different specs and can cause Trouble Code 43. When reinstalling the knock sensors, set your torque wrench to 11 to 15 foot-pounds.

Once you have the system completely flushed, you can close the petcock in the bottom of the radiator, replace the knock sensors, and start to slowly fill the radiator with new DEX-COOL mixed in a 50/50 ratio with distilled water. Use a funnel and pour very slowly so as not to slosh stuff on your engine or your car's paint job. If you crack open the pressure side-bleed screw on the thermostat housing while slowly refilling, you can displace most of the trapped air. Fill the system, retighten the bleed screw, and replace the radiator cap.

I've actually heard of people who jack the front of the car up so that the air bleed valve is above the level of the recovery tank in an effort to get all of the air out of the system. I've never found that necessary, but it's a thought worth considering. But, as far as I'm concerned, just getting everything up to temperature and then letting it cool down so that you can fill the recovery tank a second time seems to work very well.

After you think the cooling system is full, take the car for a five-mile ride and watch your coolant gauge very carefully. Get the car up to its normal operating temperature before you return home to the garage. If everything goes smoothly, park the car in your driveway and check the coolant level in the reservoir. Just remember that it's a lot easier to do all this now than to have a surprise problem on the road later.

Relocating the Intake Air Temperature Sensor

ENGINE

 Time: 60 minutes

 Tools: Drill and wiring tools

 Talent:

 Applicable Years: 1985 to 1996

 Tab: $45 to $50

 Tip: A really easy modification.

 PERFORMANCE GAIN: Very slight increase in power. However, it's a very inexpensive and easy modification.

COMPLEMENTARY MODIFICATION: This is a good time to install an aftermarket air foil in the throttle body.

This is a really easy project that will give you a slight gain in performance. It may be so slight that you won't even feel anything. On the other hand, you won't be spending a lot of money either. The basic idea is to get an accurate reading of the air entering the intake plenum.

The Manifold Air Temperature sensor, or MAT, is really a thermistor, or a resistor, which changes its value based on temperature. This sensor is normally mounted in the throttle body extension. The kits that are offered for this task relocate the sensor to the area just behind the air filter.

The MAT sensor is responsible for sending air temperature information to the ECM. It is located underneath the plenum and, because of this location, the sensor picks up engine heat. As a result, the air temp readings are incorrect

This is a case where the aftermarket has the correct solution. When you place the intake air temperature sensor in the intake tube behind the air filter, you'll get a much more accurate reading of the temperature. Chevrolet couldn't do it this way because of manufacturing problems, and the company thought the horsepower gain, or lower tailpipe emissions, were not significant enough to merit any changes in the manufacturing process. It's a really easy project to do on a Saturday morning, and it costs less than fifty bucks.

This is the thermistor that actually measures the temperature. Before you plug it into its new home, it wouldn't be a bad idea to spray it down with your air intake cleaner. Just don't try to scrub it or polish it.

or, to say the least, "not optimal." A sensor relocation kit moves the MAT to a cold air duct where the air temp is correct, and drivability is improved.

High air inlet temperature can lead to a change in the detonation characteristics of a given mixture. This is because the computer monitors the air inlet temp and modifies the recommended ignition advance accordingly. Thus, when the inlet air temperature is measured at a given level, the computer retards the ignition timing.

GM placed the MAT sensor in the plenum. This wasn't an ideal plan given that the surrounding heat soaks into the sensor and gives a false reading, thereby causing a false ignition retard condition. GM engineers put the sensor in the plenum because they believed that an engine should be a complete assembly by the time it left the production facility. There are many sound reasons that support this approach – checking system integrity and reducing instal-lation time at the vehicle assembly plant to name but two. The location they chose made perfect sense at the time most Corvettes were built.

Today you can pick a better location for the sensor so that it picks up the actual intake air temperature. You want

a location that's insulated from the heat of the engine, yet is still in the inlet airflow. This is why the relocation of the MAT sensor to the filter housing makes a lot of sense. Here the sensor can measure inlet air before it becomes heated. This means that the ignition won't be retarded quite so often.

To begin the process, all you need to do is drill a 7/8-inch hole in the area around the air filter. Then install the rubber grommet in the housing. Next attach the new wiring harness and push the sensor through the rubber grommet. It's that simple.

After making this change, you'll get slightly more power and better throttle response out of your Corvette. Because the air in the filter housing is 50 to 50 degrees cooler than in the intake, the engine will think it's running cold all the time and won't be so eager to retard the timing. Most modern engine management systems are now calibrated very close to the detonation limit of the fuel. However, most of the C4 Corvettes were cali-brated very conservatively, and they can tolerate ignition advance under most circumstances, especially if you run premium gasoline.

PROJECT 18

Mass Airflow & Speed Density

The C4 Corvette used two different methods of measuring the airflow into the Corvette engine. From 1985 to 1989, it used what is called a mass airflow approach. In 1990 a switch was made to a speed density system. While this speed density system was a noble idea created to save money, it simply didn't work out in practice. When the 1994 model was introduced, the Mass Airflow sensor was back in place, although this time AC/Delco, not Bosch, produced the unit.

The MAF based systems are far more accurate since they measure airflow directly, whereas the speed density system infers airflow indirectly. A multitude of things can throw the calculation of a speed density system off calibration. This is why Corvette returned to the MAF system beginning with the 1994 C4. The speed density system algorithms were kept intact, but this approach was used as a backup to the MAF system.

The MAF sensor works on the "hot wire" principle. A constant voltage is applied to a heated wire. This wire is positioned in the air stream and is heated by electrical current. As airflows across it, the wire cools down. This heated wire is really a positive temperature coefficient, or ptc, resistor.

The resistance of the wire drops as its temperature drops. This drop in resistance allows more current to flow through it in order to maintain the programmed temperature of the wire. This current is changed to a frequency or a voltage which is then sent to the computer and interpreted as airflow. Adjustments for air temperature and humidity are taken into consideration since they also affect the temperature of the heated wire.

It's really easy to tell if you have a speed density system since there's nothing between the air filter and the throttle body except the air intake tube.

Humidity always affects the density of air since humid air is denser than dry air. Air temperature also affects density since colder air is denser than warmer air. The Corvette uses an air temperature sensor to compensate for this factor. You'll find this intake air temperature sensor in the manifold or the intake piping.

The 1985 through 1989 C4 engines used a Bosch MAF sensor that heated the wire to 100 degrees Celsius. The 1994 and later C4 models used an AC/Delco MAF that heated the wire to 200 degrees Celsius. The amount of current required to reach the temperature is measured in each case. (Note: the LT5 engine used in the ZR-1 used a speed density system and continued to use that system in 1994 and 1995 since the engines had already been made prior to the last two years of production. Therefore, even after Corvette went back to the MAF based system, the ZR-1 had no MAF.)

Theory of Operation

As the air travels past the heated wire on its way to the intake manifold, it will cool the wire. Additional current is added to heat the wire to the design temperature. Since the amount of air moving past the sensor is directly related to the amount of cooling experienced by the heated wire, a feedback condition is established whereby the exact amount of moving air is directly related to the amount of current passing through the wire. Thus, the intake air is precisely measured.

Once the amount of air is known, the computer controlling the engine can add or subtract fuel as required to maintain the magic 14.7 to 1 air/fuel mixture. This ratio results in the cleanest burn possible. It does this by varying the "on time" of the fuel injectors. The injectors are pulsed on and off, and the width of the pulse is lengthened or shortened as required.

When you first start a typical engine, the pulse width is around 4 milliseconds. But as soon as the engine "catches," the pulse width is shortened to about 2.2 milliseconds for idle. During operation, the measured airflow through the MAF will cause the computer to increase or decrease the pulse width as explained above.

MAF Operating Conditions

The earlier Bosch MAF is more complex than the AC/Delco version used in the later Corvettes. While both measure airflow, the Bosch MAF has a circuit called the "burn-off circuit." It cycles on for about two seconds when you shut the engine down. This circuit heats the wire to a high enough temperature to burn off any residue that may have collected on the wire during operation. If you're in a

This is a Bosch MAF sensor with the screens intact. You can remove the screens if you wish, but the power gain is minimal. On the other hand, if you're building a motor with mega-power, you'll want to remove the screens since you'll need all the air you can get. There's really no downside to removing the screens. Other companies that use Bosch sensors have never installed them. The screens are just something that GM thought could act as a little additional protection against MAF sensor damage. Be careful cutting the screen out, however, because if you have a lifetime warranty, cutting the screen out will most likely void that warranty.

quiet area, you can actually hear the relays click on and then off as the burn-off cycle occurs.

There are two relays involved with the Bosch MAF: a power relay that passes current to the MAF wire during normal operation and the burn-off relay that provides the current for the cleaning cycle. Both are located on the fire-wall in the engine compartment, just behind the battery on the driver's side of the car. Bad MAF power and burn-off relays can cause hard starting problems and should be changed as a preventative measure.

The AC/Delco MAF, used in the 1994 to 1996 Corvette, has a power relay but no burn-off relay. For this reason, you need to pay close attention to the condition of your air filter on these cars. A contaminated wire in an AC/Delco MAF is going to stay contaminated and cause false signals to be passed to the computer.

MAF Modifications

Removing the two screens found in the front and rear of the Bosch MAF cylinder is fairly common. This procedure increases the airflow through them, and this results in more horsepower. Removing the screens is an old trick from the Corvette Challenge days in 1988 and 1989. It works, but it's illegal in many states so be advised. Most of the time, this modification will go totally unnoticed. But if you get a sharp emissions inspector, he may discover your secret.

You have to keep in mind that the speed density system does NOT work well on modified engines that lose manifold vacuum upon throttle opening. These systems won't tolerate internal engine modifications because the airflow will no longer be accurate based off of the manifold pressure. MAF systems, on the other hand, actually measure mass airflow directly, eliminating the need for more complicated calculations. This is the major reason that the MAF systems are the most tolerant of internal engine modifications, especially performance camshafts.

If you're going to purchase a C4 Corvette and intend to modify it with a camshaft and ported heads, you should probably avoid the 1990 to 1993. The modification on this generation of car can be made to work, but it's just a little more hassle.

Bosch made these early Mass Airflow Sensors. These are great units, but when they fail, you should be prepared for a sizable bill. I try to make sure I purchase the replacement from someplace like AutoZone or Pep Boys, which offers a lifetime replacement. This little guy is expensive, and I only want to pay for it once.

Engineering gave up on the speed density system at the end of 1993. This MAF sensor was manufactured by GM. It wasn't quite as good as the earlier Bosch unit, but it was a heck of a lot cheaper. It still is, if that's important to your budget.

PROJECT 19
Cooling System Problems

 Time: 4 to 6 hours

 Tools: Screwdrivers and pliers for the hose clamps

 Talent:

 Applicable Years: 1984 to 1996

 Tab: $200 to $400

 PERFORMANCE GAIN: The car will run cooler and be less likely to overheat. You will also get less spark knock in a cooler engine. This means the knock sensor won't retard the engine timing quite as often.

COMPLEMENTARY MODIFICATION:
This is a good time to think about installing new air and fuel filters.

ENGINE

As the C4 Corvette ages, we're finding out the single biggest problem is the cooling system. Almost all of the cars are starting to lose coolant. The bad news is that it's not always leaking in the same place. There are no major weaknesses in the cooling system. Rather, it seems that the entire cooling system is one giant weakness.

A large number of early C4s are rusting out freeze plugs. This isn't something that normally happens in a car. The same goes for the heater cores. An unusually high number of C4 Corvettes have had heater core problems. You have to understand that in any car the heater core is really the weakest link in the cooling system.

The heater core is really nothing more than a miniature radiator. The coolant that flows through your engine block and radiator is the very same coolant that flows through your heater core. If your coolant is bad enough to cause a corrosion problem with the heater core, the rest of the cooling system cannot be far behind. Think of your heater core as an early warning system. But, like most early warning systems, the warning is usually a little too late.

The only way to prevent cooling system problems is to exceed the normal recommended maintenance procedures. It wouldn't be overzealous to change the coolant on an annual basis. The expense of new anti-freeze every year is a minor figure compared to what it'll cost to have the heater core replaced.

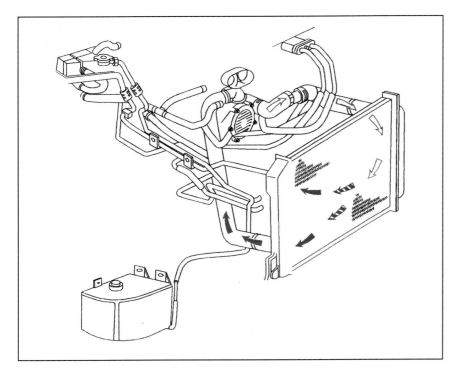

This is the LT1 cooling system. With all of these hoses and connections, is it any wonder that the cooling system becomes problematic after a decade or two? If you purchased a ten-year-old C4 Corvette with over a hundred thousand miles on it, the hoses for the cooling system might make a good winter project. You'll have to order most of the hoses from the dealer. If you're involved in a restoration project, make sure you retain the original clamps.

In the LT1, the recovery reservoir is located at the highest point in the system — on the passenger side of the car. If you're going to truly cleanse your cooling system, you should remove this and clean it thoroughly. There's no point to flushing the entire system and then letting all the dirt stay in the reservoir.

You might think about simply replacing the coolant reservoir tank on the L98 engine. This plastic reservoir is in the right front corner of the engine compartment, just beside the radiator. These tanks are so easy to replace, and the price is so reasonable, it's foolish not to replace them every five years or so. You'll never be able to clean one completely, so it's just easier to install a new one.

I feel the same way about the radiator cap. While you can have the one in your car tested, why bother? The price of the cap is less than what a shop will charge you to pressure test your system. Just stay with the stock 17psi radiator cap. There's nothing to be gained by changing to a different pressure rating.

One little trick I learned from Cadillac a few years back is to use a small container of Barr's Stop Leak when you refill the cooling system. Cadillac had a tremendous problem with cylinder head gaskets leaking into the cooling system. They recommended that a can of Barr's be used every time the coolant was changed.

Barr's eventually dissolves into the coolant so there's no problem with it clogging your system. This was actually a recommended warranty repair with the Cadillacs. I figure the same procedure can't hurt on a Corvette. Just don't dump the whole can into your cooling system at one time.

Remove the radiator cap and let the coolant come up to temperature. As the water is circulating through the radiator slowly, let the Barr's mix with the hot coolant. Then replace the radiator cap and go for a twenty-mile drive to make sure everything is evenly distributed through the cooling system.

Hose Replacement

The upper radiator hose is the one that will cause you problems. That's a good thing since it's also the easiest one to reach. The lower hose will last twice as long as the upper hose. There's a complex chemical reason for this but I won't get into it here. Should you be interested, the Gates website explains all this in detail at www.gates.com .

When it comes to replacement hoses, you're best sticking with the items from GM. The original hose design was changed so often that the aftermarket suppliers simply can't stock all the varieties. Take your VIN number to the dealer and have him look up the correct hose for your car.

The other thing you should consider is using some gasket sealant on the inside of the hoses before you install them. Take something like aviation sealant and coat the inside of the hose. This will create a perfect seal. It may be a belt-and-suspenders type of solution, but it involves so little effort, why not take every possible precaution?

PROJECT 20

Replacing Knock Sensors

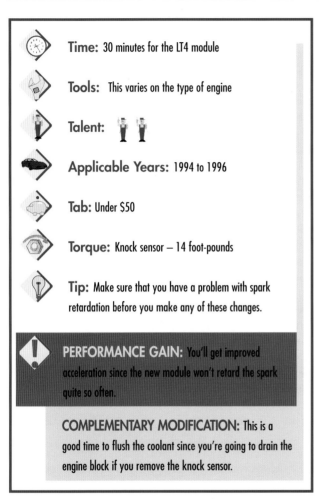

Time: 30 minutes for the LT4 module

Tools: This varies on the type of engine

Talent: 👤👤

Applicable Years: 1994 to 1996

Tab: Under $50

Torque: Knock sensor – 14 foot-pounds

Tip: Make sure that you have a problem with spark retardation before you make any of these changes.

PERFORMANCE GAIN: You'll get improved acceleration since the new module won't retard the spark quite so often.

COMPLEMENTARY MODIFICATION: This is a good time to flush the coolant since you're going to drain the engine block if you remove the knock sensor.

The C4 Corvette uses a knock sensor to detect spark detonation. The purpose is to keep you from burning holes in your pistons. The only problem is that sometimes the knock sensor is a little too sensitive. As soon as the knock sensor hears a noise that resembles detonation, it retards the ignition spark in an effort to save your pistons. This means your Corvette gets slower.

The LT1 Knock Module (not the sensor, but the module) found in the ECM of the 1992 to 1996 LT1s is a little too sensitive. This means it's subject to picking up false knock. The computer thinks it's picking up knock, or detonation, and it begins to retard the timing. The knock module can cause the timing to be retarded up to 22 degrees. This results in a serious loss of performance.

The knock sensor itself is on the side of the engine block and is nothing more than a microphone. Once it picks up a noise, it transmits a message to the Electronic Spark Control Module, or ESC. The ESC module then

transmits a message to the ECM, or main computer, that the ignition timing should be retarded. In layman's terms, this means the engine produces less power.

Keep in mind that the exact time to fire the plug is controlled by the distributor or, in the case of the LT1, the Opti-Spark. Remember, though, that the degree of spark advance is not a static point in time, like the old 1963 Sting Rays, but rather is a dynamic point depending on engine load and rpm. In the C4 Corvette, the ECM/PCM (Engine Control Module/Powertrain Control Module) monitors

The knock sensor is hidden near the depths of the engine block. It's a gold anodized device, about 1-1/2 inches in diameter that you'll find almost midway on the engine block near the oil pan gasket. You'll also know it by the wiring harness that goes to the sensor. Normally you'll have no reason to seek out this sensor. The only reason to seek it out would be to drain the coolant for the engine block. The LT1 has two sensors, while the L98 gets by with one.

several sensors to determine exactly when is the best time to fire the spark plugs.

The real problem is that the spark control system, and more specifically the knock sensor, isn't very sophisticated. It simply picks up noise, any noise, and transmits the signal to the ESC module. An exhaust leak, a set of headers, or different rocker arms can set off a noise that is interpreted as ignition knock.

This false knock has been reported by a lot of people at higher rpms, which is usually indicated by your car "searching" and "surging" under WOT (wide-open throttle).

The general consensus seems to be that if you run 93-octane gas and are normally aspirated, you should have no knock whatsoever. The knock module interprets the signal from the knock sensor in the side of your engine block. The LT4 engine is a normally "noisier" engine due in part to roller rockers in the valve train. Engineers did a much better job on the LT4 when it came to listening for true knock and weeding out the normal engine noises. The reactions to installing an LT4 Knock Module in the ECM on a 1992 to 1996 LT1 engine have been anywhere from, " I really didn't notice much of a difference," to, "WOW!" The results will vary from Corvette to Corvette. They will also vary depending on how high you normally wind the engine. The typical result is smoother acceleration and no "searching" at high rpms. Plus, it is still able to sense true knock. Remember, the more you modify your car, the more susceptible it is to false knock and reduced performance.

The L98 Knock Sensor

There's another way to deal with the spark retardation problem in the L98 engines. If you simply disconnect the harness right at the sensor, you won't have an engine code set until the coolant goes over 194 degrees. The engine code is based on the coolant temp sensor. The ECM will automatically retard timing a tremendous amount during wide-open throttle applications if there's no signal from the knock sensor. This means you have to keep your temperature under 194 degrees – not a real practical solution.

However, you can hook up a 1/4-watt 4.5k-ohm resistor in place of the sensor and fool the ECM into thinking everything is great with detonation. This will cure the unnecessary ignition retardation problem.

Before you disconnect your knock sensor, check to make sure you don't have any detonation. Your knock sensor can become a very valuable tool in reducing a lot of strain on your pistons. You can typically see what is happening with a scanner or Diacom software.

Remember, this knock sensor was installed for a reason. It's there to protect your engine. If you're willing to take a major risk, it's fine to run without this insurance policy. The LT4 ESC module installation keeps your policy in effect – it just changes the terms of the policy. Taking the knock sensor out of the system is like canceling your insurance. This means the folks with the LT1 engines should feel free to change the module. It means the L98 owners can modify the wiring at their own risk.

One way to locate this sensor is to follow the wiring harness until you find some wires going to the side of the block. It's the only thing down there that's round and attached to wires.

FUEL SYSTEM

Fuel Pump Replacement

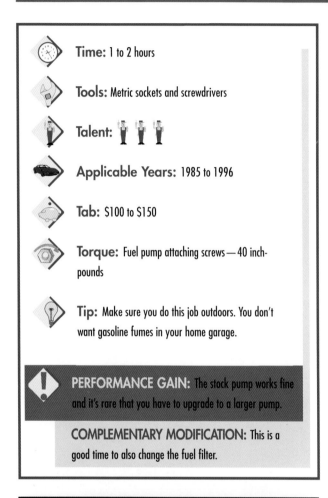

Time: 1 to 2 hours

Tools: Metric sockets and screwdrivers

Talent: ▮▮▮

Applicable Years: 1985 to 1996

Tab: $100 to $150

Torque: Fuel pump attaching screws—40 inch-pounds

Tip: Make sure you do this job outdoors. You don't want gasoline fumes in your home garage.

PERFORMANCE GAIN: The stock pump works fine and it's rare that you have to upgrade to a larger pump.

COMPLEMENTARY MODIFICATION: This is a good time to also change the fuel filter.

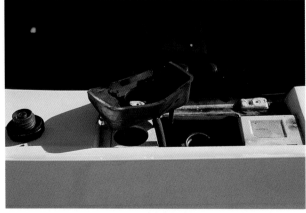

The gas cap door is easily removed by simply removing the four No. 10 Torx screws. Then remove the gas cap and start to wiggle the rubber housing off the filler neck. Don't be surprised if you tear it during removal. You did order a new one, didn't you? Now you can reach the various hoses and bolts that attach to the fuel pump/gauge unit.

The one thing you can be almost certain of is that your fuel pump won't go bad while the car is on your property. That would make things too easy. It's more likely the fuel pump will go bad as you're on the way to work some morning—at least that's when it usually fails in my car.

The best replacement solution is to stay with the stock GM fuel pump. While you can use some of the aftermarket pumps, you'll find that installing them is quite aggravating. Unless you have some sort of monster horsepower motor, there's no reason to install anything other than the stock pump.

This fuel pump is a combination of both a fuel pump and a sending gauge. The gasoline is pumped at very high

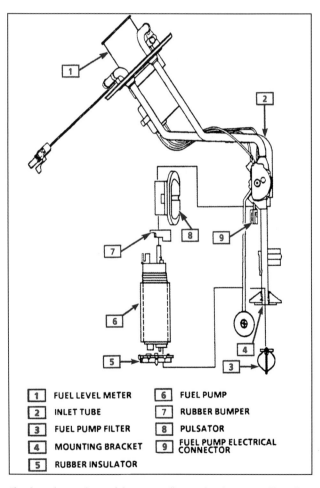

1	FUEL LEVEL METER	**6**	FUEL PUMP
2	INLET TUBE	**7**	RUBBER BUMPER
3	FUEL PUMP FILTER	**8**	PULSATOR
4	MOUNTING BRACKET	**9**	FUEL PUMP ELECTRICAL CONNECTOR
5	RUBBER INSULATOR		

This shows the complexity of the unit. You'll notice that the pump itself is only #6 in the diagram. The problem is that almost everyone sells this as part of a complete unit rather than offering the individual part. It's common for the filter sock (#3) to deteriorate. At one time, you could purchase that part separately, but it's no longer available for individual sale. The only good part about this unit is that it's very reliable.

Don't forget to check the gas cap for tears or rips in the rubber O-ring seal. This is your last defense against rainwater running into your gas tank should the filler-neck drain hole become plugged.

surface on your fuel filler cap. On the older cars, these are starting to deteriorate and no longer seal properly.

The worst scenario is to have the drain hole in the rubber filler housing get plugged and then have a bad gas cap seal. During a heavy rain, your gas tank will fill up with the rainwater. Make sure you check both the drain and the gas cap seal fairly often.

This whole job basically consists of disconnecting a lot of things and then trying to remember how to reconnect them. You really should finish this job at one sitting. It's easy enough to do and, if you take a break, you might forget where you left off.

pressure to the engine, and then the excess gasoline is returned to the gas tank. A lot of the gasoline is actually making a round trip journey from the pump to the fuel rails—and then back to the gas tank. The idea is to provide a constant amount of fuel pressure at all times.

A plastic sock is used as a strainer and is attached to the lower end of the fuel pump. On some of the older cars, we're starting to see deterioration of this plastic sock. The bad news is that the sock is no longer available as a separate unit.

The first thing you should do when you replace the fuel pump is put the car in the driveway. Fuel vapors are highly explosive. I've seen several shops burn to the ground because of fuel vapors, and these shops were full of professionals doing the work. Your family will not be very happy if you set your home on fire changing a fuel pump in your Corvette.

Once you get the car in the driveway, you should disconnect the battery and make sure you won't get a spark from the loose terminal. The best way to do this is to wrap the battery terminal with some electrical tape. If you think I sound a little paranoid about working around gasoline, you're very perceptive. It scares the hell out of me. Hopefully you have a little fear of it, too.

Once you've gotten the battery connection out of the way, you need to release the fuel pressure from the system. Here you do the same thing you did when you replaced the fuel filter. Simply push down on the Schrader valve and let the gas run out. Just make sure you have a rag in the area. And you might want to put some glasses on since the gas may spurt out in your face.

Now go around to the rear of the car and remove the fuel filler door. Take the entire panel off by removing the four Torxhead screws. Leave the door attached to the panel and take everything out at one time.

Now you have to wiggle the rubber fuel filler housing off the filler neck. Over the years, the rubber gets very hard and brittle, and it will probably rip when it comes off. I would suggest that you simply order a new one at the same time you order the new fuel pump. While we're on the topic of ordering parts, take a second and check the gasket

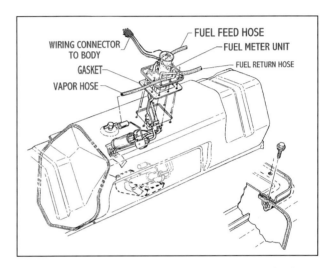

There are a lot of hoses at the top of the gas tank. The good part is that they're all different sizes and coming from different directions, so it shouldn't be too hard to reinstall them correctly.

This cutaway does little to explain why you should always have at least a half tank of gas when you're at the track. Under normal driving, fuel pickup is never a problem. At the track, the pump just can't pick up enough gas in a corner. Most of us have gotten in the habit of arriving at the track with a full tank of gas, and then filling it up again at the lunch break. It's easy to purchase some Sunoco 100-octane unleaded gas at the track. The hard part is trying to explain to your family why five gallons of gas cost almost fifty dollars.

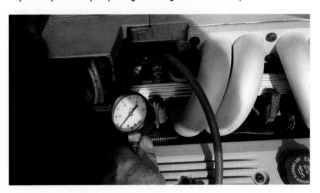

Checking your fuel pressure is quite simple. Simply attach your fuel pressure gauge to the Schrader valve and see how things are doing. You should have at least 42 pounds of pressure. If you only have about 35 pounds, then you should start checking around for the best price on a new fuel pump.

Installing an Adjustable Fuel Pressure Regulator

FUEL SYSTEM

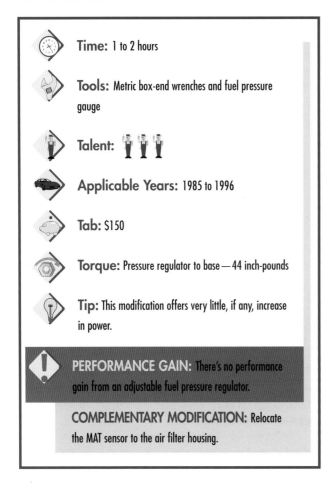

Time: 1 to 2 hours

Tools: Metric box-end wrenches and fuel pressure gauge

Talent: ▮▮▮

Applicable Years: 1985 to 1996

Tab: $150

Torque: Pressure regulator to base — 44 inch-pounds

Tip: This modification offers very little, if any, increase in power.

PERFORMANCE GAIN: There's no performance gain from an adjustable fuel pressure regulator.

COMPLEMENTARY MODIFICATION: Relocate the MAT sensor to the air filter housing.

Every Corvette parts supplier in the world sells an adjustable fuel pressure regulator. All of these regulators are fairly cheap and extremely easy to adjust. The problem is that they don't do much good. These were sort of a fad for a few years, but as people began to understand what little impact they had, they fell out of favor.

I've heard of many people gaining 20 horsepower just by increasing the fuel pressure. However, regardless of where I have it set, I seem to run the same times. Currently I have mine set at 44 psi (with the vacuum hose disconnected).

The idea is that by increasing the pressure you can force a little more gas into the fuel mixture. This theory is true—at least for a few minutes. Once the oxygen sensor begins to sense that the car is running rich, it will decrease the amount of time that the injector is open. Now you're right back to where you started.

You should consider using a wide band oxygen sensor in conjunction with this modification so that you can get a more accurate reading of what your air/fuel mixture is. Optimum is, in theory, supposed to be 12.5 to 1 at wide-open throttle. That's somewhere in the neighborhood of a 900mv signal from the oxygen sensor. The problem is that a wide band sensor will cost you a great deal more than the adjustable fuel pressure regulator. That's just one more reason to leave the fuel pressure regulator alone.

If you're running lean or too rich, I can see why some setups could manage respectable gains with the adjustable fuel pressure regulator. However, most Corvettes seem to work just fine as long as the fuel pressure is set between 42 and 50psi.

The biggest problem with changing the fuel pressure regulator occurs on the L98 engines. The regulator is underneath the intake plenum. This means the intake runners have to be loosened (not removed) and the plenum removed. You can cheat a little bit by simply raising the rear of the plenum enough to gain access to the regulator.

You'll find a vacuum hose leading off the regulator, and the entire assembly is held in place by two 5/32-inch hex bolts. Remove the vacuum line and unbolt the regulator. Fuel is going to spill on the manifold so be careful. There's not much you can do about it, really, except to clean it up with a rag and keep your garage door open. Actually, it's a good idea to do this whole job outside.

You need to be careful when you remove the regulator. There are two fuel ports on the bottom of the regulator, and one of them has an O-ring that is critical. The new regulators usually don't come with a replacement. Pull the regulator off gently and keep an eye out for the O-ring. Save this ring and put it back in its seat during reassembly. The new one will go into the same location as the stock regulator. The only difference is that you'll have a pressure regulating screw that was installed by the aftermarket company.

After you go to all this trouble, you'll realize that your computer is actually pretty smart. When you lower fuel pressure to achieve a better air/fuel ratio, the computer sees this as part throttle and adds injector pulse width to compensate. If you raise the fuel pressure, the computer will eventually subtract band width for the same reason.

This means that the horsepower will always fall back to where it started. Logic seems to indicate that because oxygen values are not measured during wide-open throttle, changing the fuel pressure should have a long-lasting effect – at least when you have the throttle wide open. But in actual practice, it doesn't work that way.

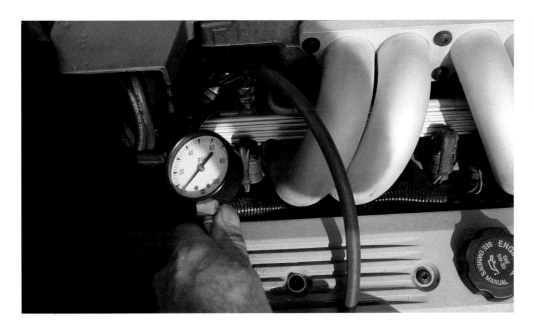

You can check the fuel pressure by attaching a pressure gauge to the Schrader valve on the fuel rail. Stock fuel pressure should be between 41 and 47psi.

An adjustable fuel pump is helpful for getting the block learns as close to zero percent as possible. This gives the computer the widest range of adjustment, but not more horsepower. For more horsepower, you need a computer program with a different target air/fuel ratio. Unless you make that change, an adjustable fuel pressure regulator is just a waste of time and money.

If you're going to play with the fuel pressure, I recommend that you do it at a shop where the car can be analyzed on a chassis dyno. If you decide to install an adjustable fuel pressure regulator because you've made a lot of other changes, make sure you budget enough money for a day of dyno time. When you're finished, the price of the adjustable fuel pressure regulator will look comparatively cheap.

If you look underneath the intake plenum, you can see the adjustable fuel pressure regulator. Take a look at your L98 engine and decide if you really want to start taking the whole intake system apart for no real gain in power. Of course, once you go through all the effort of assembling and reassembling all this, you'll find yourself telling people how much better your car runs—even if it's not true. After all, when you put that much effort into changing the stock system, you have to say something. Just don't let anyone see your dyno sheets.

Replacing the Fuel Injectors: The Options

FUEL SYSTEM

 Time: 1 to 8 hours depending on whether you have an LT1 or L98.

 Tools: The L98s take a large number of tools to remove the intake runners, while the LT1 requires very few tools. The LT1 intake manifold can stay in place for injector replacement.

 Talent:

 Applicable Years: 1985 to 1996

 Tab: $75 to $500

 Tip: Make sure you take your time to diagnose the problem correctly.

 PERFORMANCE GAIN: The biggest change will be that the car will idle without a miss.

COMPLEMENTARY MODIFICATION: You can switch to larger injectors, but there's very little performance gain unless you've performed a host of other modifications.

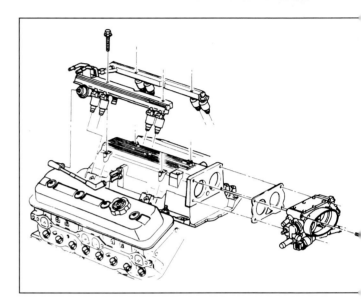

Always install the injectors in the fuel rail first. Then carefully place the assembly into the intake manifold. Make sure all the O-rings have lubricant applied. This is going to involve a little jiggling and pushing, but you shouldn't need to apply force. This also shows why it's so much easier to replace the injectors on the LT1 engines. One of the goals in designing the LT1 engine was to reduce the number of warranty hours billed back to General Motors. I strongly suspect that the LT1 project paid for itself in a just a couple of years due to the reduction of warranty claims.

You'll know when you have a fuel injector go bad. If you're lucky, you'll be able to find a shop that can figure it out as well. A bad fuel injector will give you a tremendous miss. The trick is that it'll feel almost like an electrical miss—which is probably why the first shop I took my car to tried to solve the problem by replacing all the spark plugs and the ignition wiring. The local Chevrolet dealer finally got it right and replaced one injector for several hundred dollars. At that point I didn't even care what type of injectors the dealer installed. I was just happy the car worked.

There are a number of different fuel injectors on the market. Even GM shops around for injectors. The company has used Lucas, Bosch, Rochester, and Multec. The prices vary considerably and performance differences are hard to detect.

Fuel injectors are sized for application. For instance, the 5.0-liter Ford injector is sized to deliver approximately 4.05 milligrams of fuel with a 2.5-millisecond pulse, or 18.13 pounds per hour at approximately 36psi. The 5.7-liter injector is sized to deliver approximately 4.83 milligrams of fuel with a 2.5-millisecond pulse, or 23.92 pounds per hour at approximately 43.5psi. This information is typical for all manufacturers even though flow rates will vary slightly even between identical injectors.

Lucas has been pushing its High Output Disc Injector, which is referred to as a high-performance injector. This product was introduced about ten years ago and is usually priced at about $60. A wide variety of flow rates are available to include 18 24, 28, and 37 pounds per hour. These are all 16.2 ohms and will work well with all GM TPI ECMs. Rochester injectors are presently furnished for the 1990 to 1994 GM 5.7L engine. This Rochester injector has an all-metal nozzle and performs well. It has a price in the neighborhood of $75. Bosch injectors are also an excellent choice and cost approximately $87 each.

While there are significant differences between the TPI and LT1 induction systems and computers, the injectors are essentially the same. The first use of ball injectors was on General Motors' throttle body injector, or TBI, systems. Some TBI and MFI injectors are bottom-feed ball injectors. Many other vehicle manufacturers also use ball-type injectors, and their design is basically the same. A ball-type injector uses an armature that performs the fuel metering.

Armatures may be two- or one-piece designs. Both types consist of a shaft section and a ball tip that looks like part of a hollow ball bearing. In a two-piece design, the shaft section has one end machined to allow the ball tip to slip over it. The ball is then swaged slightly. This holds it in place but still allows it to move slightly. The slight movement helps the ball seal more consistently. One-piece design ball armatures have the ball attached to a disc of metal that moves in a bore in the injector. When the injector is pulsed, the ball is lifted, and fuel sprays out from the nozzle.

Some ball injectors have a singular orifice similar to a pintle-type injector. Other ball injectors spray the fuel through a series of very small holes. Typically there are six or more holes in a circular pattern on the injector nozzle. This provides a conical spray pattern. Some multi-valve engines even have injectors with two circular spray patterns. These engines use one injector for two intake valves. The nozzles are designed to aim the fuel spray patterns at both valves. On two-piece design injectors, the ball can separate from the shaft. The injector will click as the ECM pulses the injector, but the fuel pressure keeps the ball tip on its seat, and no fuel is delivered. When this happens, the injector must be replaced.

Disc-Type Injectors

The disc injector can be very similar to a pintle-type injector. Internally they are also similar. The main difference is on the discharge end of the injector. The nozzle can have one or more orifices or tubes through which the fuel is discharged. The disc is spring-loaded against its seat. The disc is large enough to cover all of the orifices or tubes to provide a seal for the fuel. When the injector is energized, the disc is lifted, and fuel sprays from the injector. The main advantage of both ball- and disc-type injectors is that they are less likely to have deposits that will restrict fuel flow. The pintle-type injectors have the most problems with deposits.

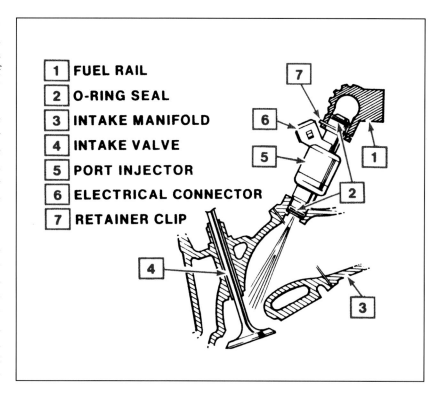

1 FUEL RAIL
2 O-RING SEAL
3 INTAKE MANIFOLD
4 INTAKE VALVE
5 PORT INJECTOR
6 ELECTRICAL CONNECTOR
7 RETAINER CLIP

Even though fuel injection has been around for several decades, there's still a lot of misunderstanding concerning it. Here you can see that the Corvette injectors spray the fuel almost directly on the valve head. Always keep in mind that fuel is added only at the last instant. All of the passages from the air filter to the cylinder head intake port are for the flow of dry air.

Injector O-rings

The O-rings are critical for the proper operation of the fuel system and the life of the injector. The O-ring provides a seal to prevent fuel leaks on one end. It also prevents false air from entering the engine on the wrong end. The O-ring also acts as a shock absorber to keep engine vibrations and harmonics from damaging the injector.

The O-ring also insulates the injector from heat transferred from the throttle body or intake manifold. Aging can cause the O-rings to harden and this can result in drivability problems. Some applications have top and bottom O-rings that are different colors. This color-coding can indicate different heat properties of the O-rings or indicate slight differences in diameter or size of the O-ring. Because of the possibility of false air or fuel leaks, it's important to always install the correct O-rings for the location and the vehicle application.

Cleaning Injectors

There are two ways to clean your injectors. The first way is to clean them on your car. This involves purchasing a kit from a company like Matco or Snap-On. The kit is a major expense, and it's actually cheaper to have a shop perform the work than for you to purchase the necessary equipment. The injector cleaners that can be found at your local parts discounter aren't worth your money.

The next step up is to remove all your injectors and send them out to be tested and cleaned. Obviously this is a project to be done during those months when you don't drive your car. Several companies will accurately measure the flow of your injectors for a set amount of time and then calculate fuel flow. They also check the injector spray patterns using strobe lights.

The injectors are then transferred to an ultrasonic cleaning machine and connected to injector drivers where they're submerged in a cleaning solution. At this point, they're pulsed while being subjected to ultrasonic waves. The combination of the solution and the ultrasound aggressively cleans the internal and external parts of the injectors.

Injector Installation

The L98 and LT1 engines require similar procedures for injector replacement. The big difference is that on the L98 a lot of items have to be removed so you can get to the injectors. When working on the L98, it will take at least an hour before you even get to the injectors.

Regardless of the style, always install the injector onto the fuel rail first, making sure the O-ring is properly seated. You want to lube the O-rings with oil and then slide the

injector into the fuel rail. The electrical connector should face the harness connector.

When the injector feels snug in the manifold, align the clip groove on the fuel rail with the clip groove on the injector that gives you the best alignment. If you're installing a disc style in place of a pintle or ball style, the second clip groove is often the best fit.

When you replace a disc style with a pintle style or even a ball style, the first clip groove usually produces the best fit. You might want to remember that some pintle-style injectors have disc-style grooves.

Use a lubricant like WD-40 to help the O-rings slide into position. Insert the injectors into the fuel rails (electrical connection facing out) and snap the retaining clips into place. Now press each rail assembly into position, making sure all of the injectors are completely seated.

Take a minute and make sure the fuel transfer tube is properly seated between the two rails. Now loosely install the hard fuel lines to the fuel rails. Select the proper fittings from the fuel rail kit to connect the fuel lines to your car. Once this is done, tighten the hard lines at the fuel rails.

Now reconnect the battery and turn your ignition key to the run position to energize the fuel pump. If you have an adjustable fuel pump, you can adjust the pressure to 47psi as a starting point.

Before you start putting everything away, take a minute and carefully check for leaks. You can never be too careful when you're working with gasoline. Take a look around a Corvette salvage yard and notice how many cars landed in the yard because of an engine fire. That will give you new respect for gasoline.

1	SOLENOID ASSEMBLY
2	SPACER & GUIDE ASSEMBLY
3	CORE SEAT
4	BALL VALVE
5	SPRAY TIP
6	DIRECTOR PLATE
7	SPRAY HOUSING
8	CORE SPRING
9	SOLENOID HOUSING
10	SOLENOID
11	FUEL INLET FILTER

Very few people have ever seen the inside of a fuel injector. It's amazing how many little parts have to cooperate in the effort to get fuel into your cylinder head. These little guys are a testament to quality engineering and manufacturing.

After several hours of dismantling the entire induction system, you'll eventually reach the goal. If you take your car to a shop, be prepared for a labor charge of at least three or four hours. The real question is do you just replace the one injector that failed or do you replace all eight of them? That's a personal decision. I had the shop replace the one bad injector, and 20,000 miles later there has yet to be a hint of a problem.

TRANSMISSION

Parts courtesy Corvette Central

Servicing the Overdrive on the 4+3

TRANSMISSION

Time: 1 hour

Tools: Drain pain, sockets, and 3/8-inch torque wrench

Talent:

Applicable Years: 1984 to 1988

Tab: $45

Tip: Treat this job the same way you would treat changing the fluid and filter with an automatic transmission. You'll probably end up making just as big a mess on your garage floor.

COMPLEMENTARY MODIFICATION: As long as you're going to have a mess on your garage floor, you might as well change the gear oil inside the four-speed part of the transmission.

The overdrive unit was simply hung off the back of the four-speed transmission. In a great many ways, the overdrive was very similar to the old two-speed Powerglide. This particular overdrive unit was originally designed for the Jeep CJ-7 and CJ-5. Chevrolet was working on such a tight deadline for the fourth generation Corvette that there was no time to develop a new unit specifically for the Corvette.

Delco Electronics solved the computer problems and made sure that the manual section and the overdrive were truly integrated units. All of this was really done to meet the EPA fuel mileage regulations. The added bonus was that the overdrive fourth gear provided a high-speed cruising capability that easily exceeded all the earlier Corvettes. Thanks to the EPA, the Corvette became a 150-mile-per-hour car.

The electronics necessary to create this dual transmission weren't all that complicated, but they did make for some interesting driving. There are actually three unique algorithms programmed into the overdrive ECM—one

each for second, third, and fourth gears. The overdrive ECM logic is incorporated into the main ECM, or the chip.

This program monitors miles per hour, engine temperature, and throttle position in an effort to properly engage the overdrive. The program will normally not engage under 184 degrees, although my 1985 always liked 176 degrees. I guess all computers are not created equal. The real trick is to get rid of all the complicated electronics and turn this transmission into an eight-speed.

A Quick and Easy Modification

Chris Petris, who used to build transmissions for the Corvette Challenge racing series, helped me with this modification. There's a switch on the side of the transmission that tells the computer which gear is engaged. On the 4+3, the second-gear switch is engaged every single time you shift the transmission, whether the overdrive is engaged or not. It's no wonder that this is usually the first item to wear out.

When my second-gear switch went bad, the car simply wouldn't engage overdrive properly. I could hit the switch on the console to turn on the overdrive, and it might not actually engage until I drove some twenty miles down the road. You can imagine how aggravating this was. When Chris and I couldn't locate a replacement switch

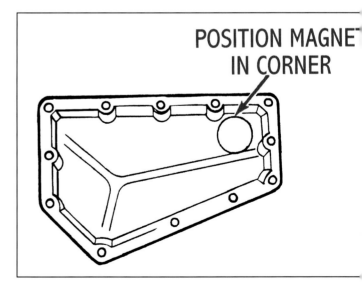

GM placed a magnet in the oil pan to capture any metallic particles. Don't be shocked if your magnet is covered with steel shavings. This simply means the magnet is doing what it is designed to do. You can remove the magnet for cleaning and then place it back in the correct location.

right away, we simply grounded the switch by running a very short shunt from one terminal to the other. This effectively made the overdrive a completely mechanical unit, operated only by the interior switch, which, in this case, was on the console.

Eliminating this switch made all the difference in the world. While Chevrolet designed all the electronics to pass the EPA fuel mileage cycle, I simply wanted a useful transmission. The 4+3 actually works better if you take some of the sophistication out of the system.

What we did was fool the computer into thinking that I'm always in second gear or higher. The second-gear switch is on the left side of the transmission, and can be seen easily if you have the car on a lift. This switch was assigned many different locations throughout the years, but it was always located toward the rear. Remove the wiring harness from the switch and hook it out of the way with a cable tie. You won't be using this harness. Now make a little jumper wire that will fit into the two terminals. You can remove the switch from the transmission and make the jumper wire on your workbench if you prefer. If it takes more than fifteen minutes to create this, you're goofing off.

The Filter

Since the overdrive unit in the 4+3 transmission is really a version of the old Powerglide automatic transmission, it shouldn't be a surprise that it has a transmission filter. You

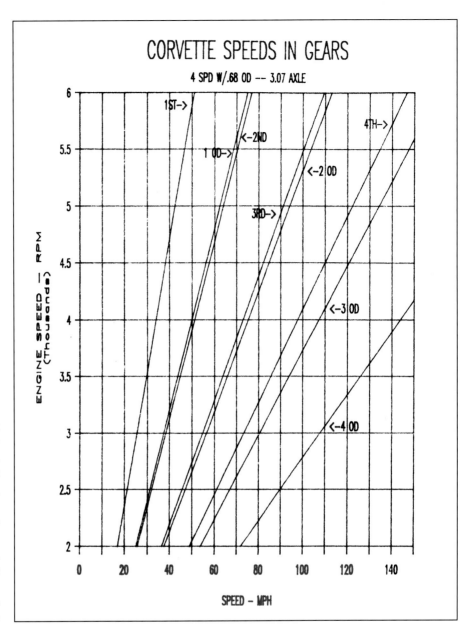

The overdrive gave the C4 an incredible top speed for a vehicle built in the mid-eighties. You'll notice that the difference between fourth gear and fourth gear overdrive is almost forty miles per hour at 4,000 rpm. Since most of us don't drive much over 80 miles per hour on the highway, this simply means the C4 will give us pretty incredible gas mileage. I'm still wondering where you can actually use all that gear ratio. Even at Sebring, which is a very fast course, I only get into third overdrive. Maybe I need to drive the banking at Daytona—that ought to get me into fourth overdrive.

should approach this task just as you would the job of removing any automatic transmission. You'll even create the same type of mess on your garage floor.

The technique is to simply drop the oil pan on the bottom of the overdrive unit and hope that most of the fluid goes into the large drain pan you've placed under the pan. Be careful not to lose any of the bolts.

When working in your home garage, the best way to clean the pan is to use spray cans of Brake Clean and a roll

of paper towels. Pay particular attention to the sealing edges of the pan. At one time, GM used RTV sealant on this surface. That wasn't such a great idea but now you can get the filter kits with gaskets. If you don't find a gasket in your car, you can assume that the fluid hasn't been changed in a few years.

Make sure that you also clean the transmission surface. These overdrive units are notorious leakers. Using a gasket on the surface will solve most of the sealing prob-

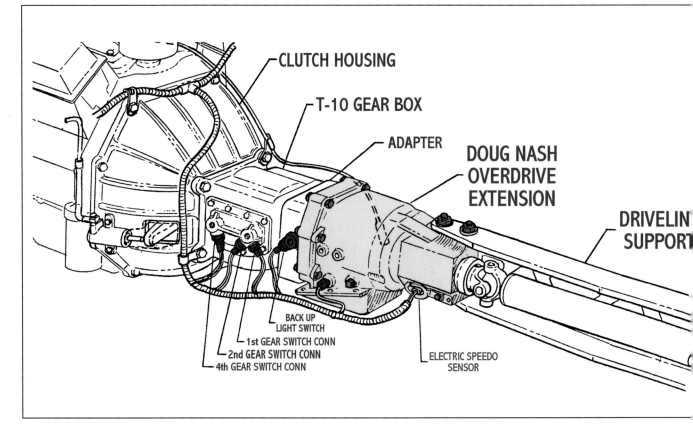

CLUTCH HOUSING

T-10 GEAR BOX

ADAPTER

DOUG NASH
OVERDRIVE
EXTENSION

DRIVELIN
SUPPORT

BACK UP
LIGHT SWITCH

1st GEAR SWITCH CONN
2nd GEAR SWITCH CONN
4th GEAR SWITCH CONN

ELECTRIC SPEEDO
SENSOR

This is an interesting combination of parts. The traditional small block Chevrolet engine is bolted to the very traditional T-10 transmission. Then that's hooked to yet another transmission, one that looks strangely similar to the old Powerglide from the 1950s. The second transmission, or overdrive, is bolted to a huge length of aluminum U-channel, or the Driveline Support. This is, in turn, bolted to a differential carrier in the rear of the car. With all of this, it's amazing that it works so well.

lems. Once everything is clean, you can install a couple of bolts to hold the oil pan back in place. Carefully tighten the bolts using a cross pattern to get it nice and even.

I would use Dexron III in the unit. It seems everyone has a different preference when it comes to choosing a synthetic type of fluid. Just ask some other owners what they are using.

Once they got past the 1984 model year, these units have proven pretty reliable. There were some internal changes made, and the clutch material is different on the later cars. When it comes to this overdrive, the best thing you can do is change the fluid and filter once a year or at least every 15,000 miles.

This little jumper switch did wonders for my driving enjoyment. Placing the jumper wire in this switch turned my overdrive into a manual overdrive. All of the stuff that was designed to meet fuel mileage requirements is now gone. I even have overdrive in first gear now—not that I really need it. The switch is easy to modify, but if you have any questions, just call the Corvette Clinic in Sanford, Florida.

Improved Shifting for the 4+3

 Time: 1 hour

 Tools: Pliers and a variety of screwdrivers

 Talent:

 Applicable Years: 1984 to 1988

 Tab: $50

 Tip: Replace the reverse lockout rod as soon as possible if your C4 has over 75,000 miles. You'll love the difference.

 PERFORMANCE GAIN: If you can shift the car faster, you'll not only go faster, but you'll also like the car a whole lot more.

COMPLEMENTARY MODIFICATION: Since all this work is going to be done inside the car, and you're going to be looking at the console and dash while you work, you might decide to detail the console and dash panels as well. There's no point in crawling under the car and getting dirty. There are so few opportunities to work on clean Corvette jobs, you might as well just enjoy things for as long as you can.

In 1984, you could order your new Corvette with a four-speed manual transmission that had overdrive on the top three gears. This meant that you suddenly had a seven-speed transmission in your Corvette. This 4+3 transmission was really nothing more than two separate transmissions mated together to form one unit. By combining these two transmissions, Chevrolet was able to give us seven forward gears.

Although the idea was exciting, people complained about the 4+3 transmission from day one. They complained about the way it shifted and about the way the overdrive worked. Most of the complaints weren't justified. In reality, a lot of the people who complained about the 4+3 had simply never driven one that was properly adjusted. The fact that the average Chevrolet dealership didn't know enough, or didn't care enough, to properly adjust the transmission didn't help the reputation of the transmission one

single bit. This unit also suffered because the German six-speed that replaced it in 1988 was really much better. Nevertheless, if you have a 4+3 in your Corvette, don't get all worked up. It really is a good transmission.

Upshift Indicator Light
The Corvettes made between 1986 and 1988 have a light in the upper left corner of the tachometer. You can simply ignore this light unless you're trying to set a fuel mileage record. This light is designed to let you know how to get the best fuel mileage. The idea is that you'll accelerate slowly and then shift into the next higher gear when the light comes on. Under normal operation, this light goes off if you simply lift off the accelerator. It's a lot of effort to get rid of this light so just ignore it.

Reverse Lockout Lever
The reverse lockout lever should be one of the very first things to replace in your 4+3 Corvette. Corvette Clinic in Sanford, Florida, produces a heavy-duty lockout rod for the 4+3 transmission. Installation only takes less than an hour, and you won't believe the difference it makes.

Three different people tried to adjust my shifting linkage, and three different shops pretended that they made a difference. The truth is that the only thing that made a difference was replacing the rod known as the reverse lockout rod.

Left: This is the reverse lockout rod. It's hard to believe that this item could result in so many ragged shifts. These are caused when the rod wears on the end. After a few thousand shifts, the shift lever and the assorted linkage prevent you from shifting properly.

Below: The first step is to remove the plastic cover from the shift lever. Then you just keep removing things until you get to the reverse lockout rod. Make sure that you remember how things came apart. Some of the parts can fit in backwards, but if you put them in that way, you won't be able to shift the transmission. This whole job should take you less than a half-hour. Although this job takes so little time, you'll be amazed at the difference it makes.

PROJECT 26

Installing a Short Throw Shifter in the 4+3

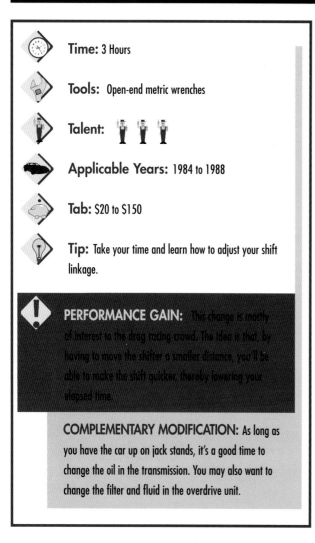

Time: 3 Hours

Tools: Open-end metric wrenches

Talent: 🔧 🔧 🔧

Applicable Years: 1984 to 1988

Tab: $20 to $150

Tip: Take your time and learn how to adjust your shift linkage.

PERFORMANCE GAIN: This change is mostly of interest to the drag racing crowd. The idea is that, by having to move the shifter a smaller distance, you'll be able to make the shift quicker, thereby lowering your elapsed time.

COMPLEMENTARY MODIFICATION: As long as you have the car up on jack stands, it's a good time to change the oil in the transmission. You may also want to change the filter and fluid in the overdrive unit.

Kits for short throw shifters have been around for the last thirty years. Very few folks install them on the 4+3, but most companies still offer them. The idea is that by moving the holes in the shifter arms, or levers, you won't need to move the lever quite so far during each shift. In other words, the distance the shifter knob moves from second to third will be shorter. The same would be true for the third to fourth shift, although this isn't that important for drag racing since you normally never get the Corvette into fourth gear at the drag strip. The idea is that you'll be able to shift faster with these shorter arms in place. The theory is true, but there are secondary implications.

Basically, the goal of these shift kits is to bring the holes for the shift linkage closer together. That means you have to move the lever a shorter distance. These shorter levers mean that you'll have to use more force. Remember,

a shorter lever will require more force to move the same mass. You may not have to move the lever as far, but you'll have to push the lever harder to engage the next gear.

There's one more reason to keep the stock shifter arms. When you're driving on the track, it's very easy to tell which gear is engaged by simply touching the shift lever. A simple touch on the lever will remind you that you're in third gear, and not fourth. When you shorten the lever arms, all the gears seem to be too close. If you're going fast enough, you probably only have time to rely on your sense of touch. And, with the gears closer together, you'll have a harder time figuring out which gear you're in. If you're going slow, telling which gear you're in won't be a problem. If your racing, it's a lot like reading a tachometer. If you have time to look at the tachometer, you're going too slow.

The biggest problem with this task is that you're working under the car and in very cramped quarters. Make sure you get some really decent lighting for this task. This is one job where the portable halogen lights are wonderful – as long as you don't let the intense heat of the lights get to you.

To begin, place the lever in neutral and disconnect the spring clips that hold the shift arms in place. Place these clips where you can locate them again since you're going to reinstall them.

Now remove the nuts that fasten the shift arms to the side of the transmission case. The shift arms should come right off. Then it's simply a matter of putting the new arms in place and adjusting the shift levers.

Adjustment

The factory manual lists a shift-lever adjustment procedure that calls for the use of gage pins. Jim Ingle, a former Corvette engineer, developed a way to adjust the transmission without using gage pins. He suggested that once you have the retaining nuts tightened, you should rock the lever back and forth in the neutral gate just to be sure the shifter forks are in neutral position.

The adjustment is keyed to the block plate. The order of adjustment is:

    Reverse
    1-2 lever
    3-4 lever

The procedure is to compare the position of each lever (except the 3-4) to the block plate shown in the drawing. You simply adjust the shift rod to equalize the step, or distance, at the front and rear to the block plate.

For example, if the reverse lever is aligned to the block plate as shown in Figure 2, the shift rod will have to be length-

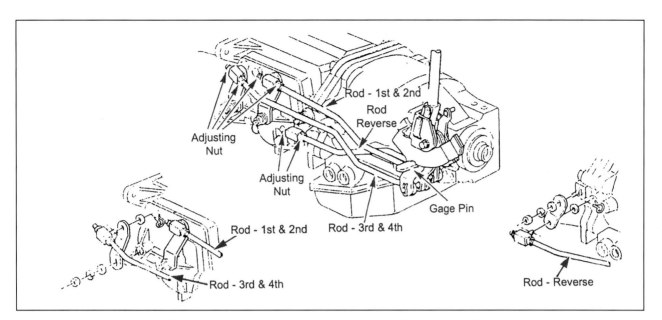

Adjusting Nut

Adjusting Nut

Rod - 1st & 2nd

Rod Reverse

Gage Pin

Rod - 1st & 2nd

Rod - 3rd & 4th

Rod - 3rd & 4th

Rod - Reverse

You're going to be dealing with three shifter rods under the car. Before you start, make sure you can identify the three rods when you're lying on your back with the car up on jack stands. It's often easiest to unbolt the 3-4 shifter rod first to get it out of the way. Then you'll have a direct approach to the 1-2 shift rod. Once you get the 1-2 lever bolted up, you can turn to the 3-4 shift lever.

ened by turning the arm nuts until the step is equalized. Don't forget that the motion of the shifter knob is the opposite of the motion of the lower levers. You may have to repeat this process several times until everything is equalized.

The other trick with this system is to tighten the front and rear jamb nuts in an alternating fashion. This will minimize any movement when you tighten them to the final torque.

Now that you have the reverse lever set in position, you can go to the 1-2 lever. The best way to do this is to simply disconnect the 3-4 shift rod and let it hang out of the way. With the 3-4 lever out of the way, you can get a wrench on the 1-2 lever.

The procedure for the 1-2 adjustment is the same as the procedure for the reverse gear lever. Have your helper pull up on the reverse trigger while you compare the front and rear steps between the 1-2 lever and the block plate. Now just adjust the shift rod as necessary to equalize the distances.

With the 1-2 rod adjusted, you can reconnect the 3-4 shift rod. The adjustment procedure is the same as before except here you're going to use the steps that exist between this lever and the 1-2 lever. These steps are usually very

small so take your time.

Most of the time you'll only have to adjust one of the shift levers. Usually two out of the three will be within specifications. Once you complete this procedure a few times, the process shouldn't take you more than ten minutes.

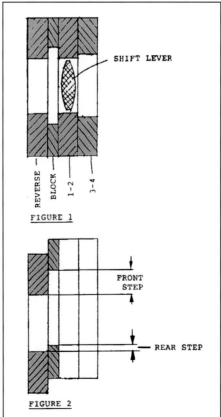

SHIFT LEVER

REVERSE

BLOCK

1 - 2

3 - 4

FIGURE 1

FRONT STEP

REAR STEP

FIGURE 2

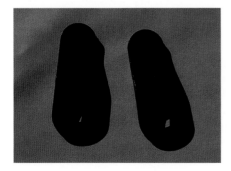

This is what you get for your twenty bucks. If you have a shop install these two shifter arms, the labor charge will be at least $150.

This drawing helps to explain the Jim Ingle approach to shift lever adjustment. It may take you a few times to master it, but once you catch on, the task should take no time at all. Jim can adjust the shift linkage in about five minutes, – although I haven't seen anyone else do it quite that quickly.

ZF Six-Speed Transmission Maintenance

TRANSMISSION

 Time: 1 hour

 Tools: 1/2-inch drive metric sockets

 Talent:

 Applicable Years: 1989 to 1996

 Tab: $50

 Tip: Use the Castrol gear oil that's available from your local BMW dealer.

COMPLEMENTARY MODIFICATION: As long as you have your Corvette up on jack stands and oil drain pans out, this might be a good time to change the oil in the differential.

The ZF six-speed has a unique look since everything is contained inside the case. There are no shifter rods hanging off the side just waiting to collect the snow and salt found on northern roads. This may well be the best standard shift transmission ever found in a Corvette.

I still remember the first time I drove a C4 with the ZF transmission. I was at Lime Rock and decided to take the people at Chevrolet up on their offer to try this new six-speed transmission. I came back into the pits after about ten laps, exclaiming that it shifted like a Toyota. I had no idea that, at the time, the Toyota MR2 had actually been the engineering benchmark for shifting ease. It was absolutely incredible. Even though I never even got into the top three gears, I loved it.

The old 4+3 Corvette transmission was developed to help the Corvette meet fuel mileage standards. The combination of a four-speed transmission and an overdrive hooked on the back simply didn't send a high-tech message to the public. Remember, this was the era when Corvette engineers wanted customers to think of the Corvette as a technological statement.

The old transmission was actually the Borg Warner Super T-10 that had been used in the Corvettes made between 1974 and 1981. However, you can actually trace its lineage back to the original T-10 that arrived in 1963.

Dave McLellan, then a Corvette chief engineer, went to his superiors and got approval for a brand-new transmission that would be good until the new C5 Corvette arrived in the early nineties—at least that was the planned time period for its arrival. This was no small achievement since management looked at the sales figures and really questioned the need for any standard shift transmission in the Corvette. And management certainly wasn't interested in creating a budget for a brand-new one.

In 1985 the case for a new transmission was strong enough that GM Powertrain went to Zahnradfabrik Friedrichshafen A. G. in Germany for help designing and building the new six-speed. This contract arrangement was common for the Corvette since GM hadn't manufactured a manual Corvette transmission since 1973. Besides, ZF had done a lot of earlier work with GM, and the partnership usually worked very well.

The gear ratios are very close in both the 4+3 and the ZF six-speed. This wasn't surprising since the whole idea was to use the engine's torque curve for the maximum amount of acceleration. Once you get past the basic 1 to 1 ratio of fourth gear, you can think of the fifth gear as being a high-speed cruising gear and sixth as the fuel economy gear. In reality, most of us use the sixth gear on the expressways, which gives us up to 25 miles per gallon.

The best thing about this transmission was that everything was placed inside the transmission case. For decades the Corvette shifter mechanism had resided outside the

If you crawl under your six-speed, you'll find a nice metal tag that lists all the relevant information on your six-speed. If your transmission needs any seals or other items, make sure you locate this tag and give the parts supplier all the necessary information.

actual transmission. Road dirt, mud, and salt all took their toll on the shifter mechanism.

The CAGS Deal

The best thing you can do with this Computer Aided Gear Selection system is get rid of it as fast as possible. See project 31 for information on how to do this. The CAGS system exists only because the federal government wanted it there. It was used only to meet the federal fuel-economy regulations. There was no way for a six-speed transmission to meet federal fuel-economy standards without forcing early upshifts during normal driving.

The Powertrain engineers called it a "skip shift." It used an electric solenoid controlled by the car's ECM to lock out second and third gears under certain conditions. Looking at it from a pessimistic point of view, the goal of the CAGS system seems to be to annoy you all the time. But in reality, the system kept the original owner from paying a gas-guzzler tax. Long ago, GM decided that no GM car would ever be subject to a gas-guzzler tax. And the CAGS system was the tool that helped the engineering team meet this goal.

The EPA mileage cycle allowed upshifting from first to second gear at fifteen miles per hour. The CAGS system then forces you into fourth gear. As long as you get into the throttle with a certain amount of aggressiveness, the system won't engage.

The system actually works with five parameters:
• Transmission in first gear
• Engine speed less than 1200 rpm
• Coolant temperature greater than 158 degrees

At the right is the dreaded dual mass flywheel. If you have a problem with this unit, you'll get a dreaded bill for replacement. Fortunately it can be replaced with a single flywheel. Don't expect that to be cheap, but it will cost a lot less than the factory original. Some people opt for an aluminum flywheel, but that creates some problems in street driving. Aluminum flywheels are great for rpm, but lousy for leaving stop signs.

- Vehicle speed between 12 and 19 miles per hour
- A full stop for at least two-second duration after a previous skip shift operation

The Flywheel

This is where you'll learn the term "dual mass" flywheel. The dual mass flywheel was really all about noise and customer satisfaction. When the engine is at idle, the torque sets off a rattling noise as the teeth of the mainshaft gears bounce back and forth in the teeth of the countershaft gears. The sound is most apparent in neutral. It's not something found only in the ZF transmission—it happens in any manual transmission where there's a significant distance between the centers of the shafts.

This fix has been around for a while and consists of using what amounts to two flywheels to dampen the vibration. There's the primary flywheel and a secondary flywheel. The secondary flywheel is mounted on this primary unit. It rides on ball bearings and has a set of dampening springs that link the two. This system dampens the torque fluctuations and quiets the gear rattle.

The initial system used in the 1988 version was pretty good, but there were still customer complaints. As a result, it was redesigned in 1991. Today the real issue is cost. A dual mass flywheel is expensive. The good news is that it can be replaced with a single mass example.

The only downside to this swap is that you'll end up with the rattle that GM worked so hard to get rid of. Just keep telling yourself that the rattle is just fine. If you pride yourself on having a quiet car, you probably aren't the best candidate for switching to a single mass flywheel.

Most owners go to the single mass flywheel as a way to save money. The OEM type of unit will cost you more than $1,000 by the time you purchase all the parts. You can save at least $300 by switching to the single mass. Just remember, you'll save money, but you'll get more noise in return.

Clutch Issues

You need to pay attention to your clutch hydraulics. Rebuilders say that 85 percent of the ZF six-speeds that come across their bench failed because the hydraulic clutch systems were operating in a degraded condition. If you own a Corvette with a ZF six-speed, pay particular attention to the chapter on clutch hydraulics.

Maintenance

There's some confusion about normal service on this transmission. The Corvette owner's manual clearly states that this transmission does not need service. Chevrolet says that you only need to check the fluid level. The people who made the transmission don't agree with GM's recommendation. Instead, ZF recommends that the transmission oil be changed every 30,000 miles. People who repair these transmissions in the field suggest changing the fluid every 15,000 miles.

ZF recommends using either the GM factory fill (GM Part No. 1052931) or Castrol Formula RS Synthetic. The RS has been superceded by TWS10W-60. The Castrol oil is not available in the usual discount parts stores but is available from your local BMW dealer.

The advantage of using synthetic oil is the lack of carbon buildup in the transmission. The factory oil seems to leave a film on everything. Many Corvette owners have switched to a 5W-50 synthetic oil, and that seems to work very nicely as well.

Most of the wear on this transmission seems to occur on the phosphor-bronze-lined synchronizers. If you change the lubricant every 15,000 miles, this bronze material won't end up floating around the internals of the transmission. You should change the lubricant in your six-speed ZF at least once a year, or every 15,000 miles if you drive a great deal.

ZF S6-40 Quick Data

Gear ratios

Gear	Ratio
1st	2.68
2nd	1.80
3rd	1.29
4th	1.0
5th	0.75
6th	0.50
Reverse	2.50

Weight (w/shifter) 145 pounds

Lube Capacity - 2.2 quarts

Automatic Transmission Service

Time: 1 hour

Tools: 1/2-inch drive metric sockets

Talent: ♛ ♛ ♛ ♛ ♛

Applicable Years: 1984 to 1996

Tab: $50

Tip: Make sure you ask plenty of questions before you let a shop tear into your transmission. The expense of automatic transmission service is great, and a lot of things can happen to your car while it's in the shop. Make sure you find a top-quality shop. The quality of the work is going to be a lot more important than final price.

COMPLEMENTARY WORK: If you're considering the installation of a shift kit in your automatic, keep in mind that you'll also be changing the fluid and filter at that time.

If you own a 1984 to 1996 Corvette, you probably have an automatic transmission. Most Corvette owners prefer the automatic transmissions to the manual transmission.

The good part is that few things ever go wrong with these automatics. These are very solid transmissions, and they seldom need repair. The most common reason for repair is simple abuse, and the most damaging abuse comes from neglect.

Since most of you purchased your C4 Corvette on the used-car market, there's a need to check out the transmission. You can make two very simple checks. First, you should check the fluid level. Make sure you do this when the car is completely warmed up. Also, make sure you always check the fluid when the engine is running.

Checking the Fluid Level

You'd think that the job of checking the fluid level would be so obvious that I shouldn't even have to write about it. However, after twenty years in the service business and a few years with a major transmission chain, I have to admit that very few people know how to properly check the level of the automatic transmission fluid. Low fluid levels are a major reason that automatic transmissions have to be repaired.

You should never check the fluid immediately after coming off the interstate. High-speed driving will give you a false reading on the dip stick, or, as GM calls it, the fluid level indicator blade. Wait at least three minutes with the car in park before you check the fluid level.

You not only need to see if the transmission is properly filled, but you also want to get an indication about the condition of the fluid. After you remove the dip stick, place it on a white paper towel. The fluid should soak into the towel fairly easily. If the fluid doesn't readily soak into the paper towel and/or is black in color, it's probably compacted with fiber material. This is the first sign of clutch wear.

If you can actually see clutch material on the paper towel, you can be almost certain that the clutches need to be replaced. Just for comparison, drop some new Dexron III ATF fluid next to the spot being checked. This will give you a good side-by-side comparison of how drastically your fluid may have changed since it was last serviced.

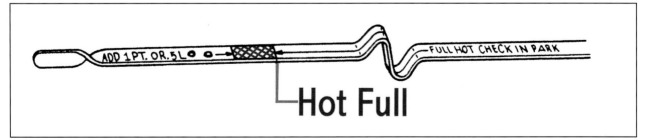

It's important to keep track of the fluid level in your transmission. This sounds obvious, but neglect is the single largest cause of transmission failure. Make sure you read the dip stick correctly and check the condition of the fluid at the same time.

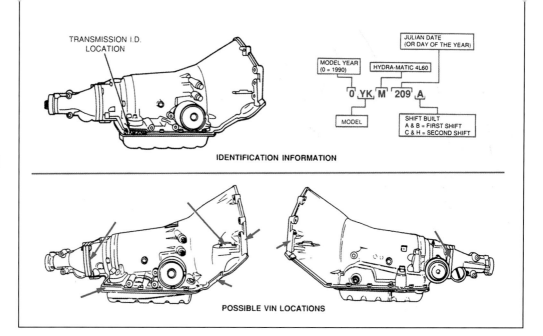

TRANSMISSION I.D. LOCATION

IDENTIFICATION INFORMATION

JULIAN DATE (OR DAY OF THE YEAR)

MODEL YEAR (0 = 1990)   HYDRA-MATIC 4L60

0 YK M 209 A

MODEL

SHIFT BUILT
A & B = FIRST SHIFT
C & H = SECOND SHIFT

POSSIBLE VIN LOCATIONS

Check the VIN number before you take the car to a transmission shop. The vehicle identification number could be in any one of six different locations. Just keep looking until you find it. While you're under the car, you can also find and copy down the car's identification code.

Maintenance

To practice good maintenance, you should change the fluid and filter on a regular basis. I'm a fanatic about regular fluid and filter changes on cars with automatic transmissions. I recommend that you change them on an annual basis even though that may be a little excessive.

I will offer one suggestion. If you have over 75,000 miles on your car, and you're pretty certain it still contains the original factory installed fluid, don't change anything. There's a good chance that the dirt and crud inside your transmission are actually holding it together. At this point, any possible damage has already been done and changing the fluid and filter might only make things worse. You should, instead, start putting money aside for a rebuilt transmission.

Corvettes haven't had a factory-equipped drain plug since the old Powerglide days. Changing the automatic

transmission fluid in a Corvette requires dropping, or removing, the oil pan. Some shops use transmission service equipment that can replace the fluid without dropping the transmission pan. This equipment either taps into the ATF oil cooler lines or connects to the dipstick filler tube. The problem with this approach is that the service doesn't include a filter change. The only way to change the filter is to drop the oil pan. You should be more concerned about changing the filter than you should be about changing the fluid.

If you decide to change your own transmission filter, make sure you get the car as high up in the air as possible. The higher the car is off the ground, the easier this job will be. Next put some large plastic sheeting on the garage floor. Make sure that you spread it the width of the entire car and possibly three feet in front of and behind the transmission. You should just assume you're going to make a mess. It wouldn't hurt to have a bag of kitty litter handy to soak up spilled fluids.

Pan gasket and filter sets are available at your local discount parts house. They may be either boxed or in flat shrink-wrap packages. Flat shrink-wraps are typically used with cork pan gaskets to protect the gaskets from bending. Rubber, or neoprene, pan gaskets, on the other hand, are flexible and can be folded to fit in a box. Different technicians have different preferences as to which is the best gasket material to use.

There is one type of gasket material that you don't need—silicone gasket material that comes in a tube. Silicone gasket material can cause you more problems than you can imagine. When you use silicone gasket material, it's squeezed between the transmission body and the pan. You'll notice how it squeezes out of the sealing faces. Just as much material has been squeezed into the oil pan area. If this material gets loose inside the pan, there's a very good chance it will find its way into internals of the transmission and clog a very important passage.

In addition to the pan and gasket set, you'll also need four or more quarts of Dexron III ATF to refill the transmission.

The automatic transmission in the C4 Corvette began life as the 700 R4 and ended up being called the 4L60-E. Basically it was the same transmission as the 700 R4 except that, in the later years, a lot of the hydraulic functions were handled by electronics. It was still a four-speed transmission, and it still had fluid and a filter that needed changing. All of the changes were part of the quest for improved fuel mileage and smoother shifting.

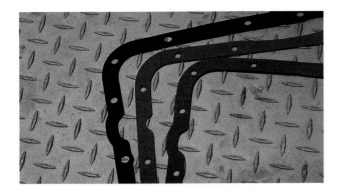

Transmission builders will probably argue the merits of different gaskets for the next several decades. The real secret to keeping your transmission oil pan from leaking is to make sure that both surfaces are very clean. You should employ a torque wrench to tighten the oil pan bolts evenly, using a variation of the star pattern you utilize when tightening lug nuts.

The transmission's fluid capacity is important because automatics must be run very close to the full level. In addition, they must never be run over that level. Overfilling your automatic transmission can aerate the fluid, causing shifting problems. Underfilling can cause slow engagement and slipping. The amount of ATF required is usually listed in the vehicle owner's manual.

Don't forget proper lighting. It's dark under your Corvette, and you want to make sure that you can see everything that's going on. This is one case in which those inexpensive halogen lights sold by Home Depot come in very handy. They focus the light directly into the correct areas.

When you have the oil pan down, check for metal shavings and other debris. These things are indicators of impending transmission problems. Some shavings in the oil pan are normal and shouldn't alarm you. If you do find a lot of material, the best thing you can do is just continue on the task. But once the job is done, you need to start setting some money aside for a rebuilt transmission.

Additives

A lot of additives are sold for transmissions. None of them are good for your transmission. The only time I would

When your transmission is rebuilt, everything comes out of the case. The parts are checked, replaced, and everything goes back in as a stack.

When you take your transmission to a shop to be rebuilt, make sure you specify that you want a total rebuild. Some shops only repair the first broken item they find and then stop. Stay away from that sort of shop. Ask questions and shop around.

use an additive would be if I were desperate. For example, if the seals have started to leak, I would postpone any real repair and try using an additive. The additives that are designed to stop leaks contain chemicals that swell the seals and gaskets to reduce fluid leakage. These chemicals might hold you over until you can reduce the balance on your credit card so your transmission can be properly repaired. Just don't think of it as a real repair.

Getting Your Transmission Back

When your Corvette comes back from the shop, always make sure that it was returned with its own transmission. The large transmission shops always keep a variety of units on the shelf. This allows them to offer same-day service on a transmission repair. Since the transmission used in the Corvette is popular across the GM product line, shops may have a couple on the shelf. And, shop employees may be tempted to just switch out your transmission and replace it with one of the many transmissions on the shelf.

You need to carefully explain to the shop employees that you want your transmission rebuilt. Make sure they know that you don't simply want a rebuilt transmission. Just to be on the safe side, crawl under the car with a light and locate the VIN number on your transmission. This VIN number can be in more than a half-dozen locations so be diligent when trying to find it. Write down the number and, when you get your car back home, check to make sure the number has remained the same.

Having your original transmission might not seem important to you right now, but at some point it will be a big deal. Just ask the people who own 1968 and 1972 Corvettes how much they would be willing to pay to get the original transmission back in their Corvettes.

MAJOR COMPONENTS

CONVERTER CLUTCH
CONVERTER
VANE TYPE PUMP ASSEMBLY
INPUT CLUTCH HOUSING
INPUT ROLLER CLUTCH ASSEMBLY
INPUT PLANETARY GEAR SET
REVERSE INPUT CLUTCH
OVERRUN CLUTCH
FORWARD CLUTCH
3-4 CLUTCH
LO AND REVERSE CLUTCH SUPPORT
LO AND REVERSE CLUTCH
LO ROLLER CLUTCH ASSEMBLY
REACTION PLANETARY GEAR SET
SPEEDOMETER DRIVEN GEAR ASSEMBLY
GOVERNOR DRIVEN GEAR
CONTROL VALVE ASSEMBLY
2-4 BAND
OIL FILTER ASSEMBLY
REACTION SUN SHELL

Clutch Master and Slave Cylinder Replacement

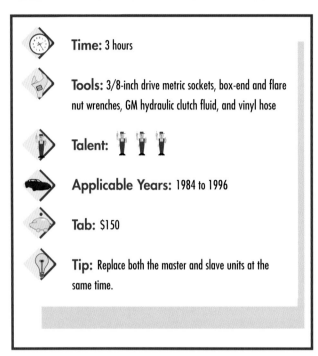

Time: 3 hours

Tools: 3/8-inch drive metric sockets, box-end and flare nut wrenches, GM hydraulic clutch fluid, and vinyl hose

Talent: ¶ ¶ ¶

Applicable Years: 1984 to 1996

Tab: $150

Tip: Replace both the master and slave units at the same time.

TRANSMISSION

When the 1984 Corvette was introduced, it used a totally different system for working the clutch. Previously the Corvette had used a series of rods and pivots to connect the clutch to the clutch pedal. Suddenly the Corvette had a hydraulic system.

The Corvette engineering team felt that the engagement of the clutch was much smoother with a hydraulic system. This system uses two major components. The clutch pedal is attached to the clutch master cylinder, and the fluid is transmitted to the slave cylinder.

The C4 clutch hydraulic system is both self-bleeding and nonadjustable. Cycling the clutch pedal multiple times while on a level grade before driving will displace any trapped air pockets formed within either cylinder. If the threaded fittings of the hydraulic line between the clutch master and slave cylinder are tight, there are only three places where air can enter into the slave cylinder assembly—the slave cylinder seal, the master cylinder seal, and the fluid reservoir inlet.

Both the master and slave cylinder assemblies are horizontally mounted. The master cylinder assembly faces forward, and the slave cylinder assembly faces rearward. When the vehicle is parked facing uphill, the clutch hydraulic master cylinder is more likely to develop an air pocket. When the vehicle is parked facing downhill, the clutch actuator cylinder is more likely to develop an air pocket.

A Simple Test

There's a fairly simple test to check out your clutch hydraulic system. The first step is to make sure that you've bled the hydraulic system. When doing this, use GM hydraulic clutch fluid (P/M 12345347). When you're convinced that you've done a good job and all the air is out of the system, you need to do the following things to check the master and slave cylinder for leakdown, or internal leaks:

Simulate that the vehicle is parked on an incline for 12 to 24 hours. You can do this by placing jack stands under the front of the car, making it at least one foot higher than the rear.

Lower the car, being careful not to depress the clutch.

With the clutch pedal to the floor, start the vehicle.

Try to put it into reverse when it first gets started.

If you have difficulty getting it into reverse, there's a very good chance that the clutch master cylinder is not at 100 percent.

The following day, you need to perform the same procedure with the rear of your Corvette raised. This is the leakdown test for the slave cylinder.

The first thing you need to realize is that you can't rebuild these units. Even though there are rebuild kits available for both cylinders, they simply aren't worth the effort.

A master or slave cylinder goes bad as a result of wear in the bore. The anodizing wears out and leaves a rough spot in the bore. That spot accelerates the wear on the rubber O-ring. You can hone the cylinder out—when you do that you'll enlarge the size of the bore. The O-ring seals only come in standard sizes. This means that, after rebuilding, the unit will fail again in a very short time because the seal will not be up to standard specs.

The other thing to remember is that you've got two units, and both are used every time you push down on the clutch pedal. If one of the units fails, the other one is also going fail eventually. The best idea is to replace both units at the same time. This means you only have to do the job once. This is an especially good idea since bleeding the system can be aggravating.

Don't hesitate to replace the slave cylinder if it doesn't bleed properly. Some people have found that they need to replace the clutch master hydraulic cylinder once for every two slave cylinder replacements. The hydraulic clutch system should always operate in at least the 97 percent efficiency range to provide for normal transmission life expectancy—typically 75,000 to 150,000 miles.

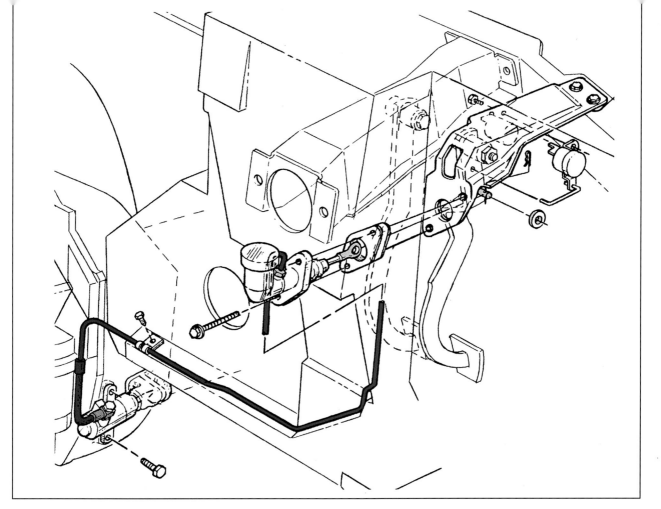

The most difficult part of working on the clutch system is getting under the dash to release the small clevis pin that holds the clutch master cylinder actuating rod to the clutch pedal. This job goes a lot quicker if you have the car up on four jack stands. You don't have to twist around quite so much to access the pin. Since the car will have to be on jack stands anyway for the bleeding process, start this project off right by getting it up in the air.

The first thing you want to do is get the car as high up on four jack stands as you can. Is this beginning to sound familiar? You're going to be under the car to replace the master and slave units, and then you'll be under it again to bleed the system.

On the later cars, you'll have to move the computer unit out of the way in order to access the clutch master cylinder. Luckily, everything will come apart easily. Start at the top and use your flare nut wrench to break the hydraulic lines loose. Don't remove them yet, just make sure they can be loosened. It's easier to do this before you start to unbolt the actual cylinders.

Now comes the hard part. You have to unhook the clutch hydraulic master cylinder linkage. This has to be done from the inside of the car, from under the dash. If you have the car up on jack stands and have the hush panel removed, the clip can be accessed from directly below. You can see this clip by looking through the hood release handle with a flashlight.

Accessing the clip isn't a hard job as long as you have a long screwdriver and extra-long needle-nose pliers. The trick is to have the vehicle up on jack stands. That way you can sit on the floor and have your eye level be at the lower door jam level.

Bleeding the Clutch Hydraulic System

The best method for bleeding this system is to run fluid through the system until the fluid coming out is clean. Once the fluid runs clear, climb in the car and press down on the clutch pedal about fifty times. Then go back under the car and bleed the system one last time.

Some people simply open the bleeder screw and let gravity draw fluid through the system. The problem is that a lot of dirt and residue never leaves the system during that process. Instead, the fluid will run around the dirt and out the bleeder screw.

The best bleeding process is still the conventional method where one person actuates the clutch pedal while another opens and closes the bleeder after the pedal is depressed to the floor and before the pedal is let back up.

After the bleeding process is complete, fill the reservoir to 1/16 of an inch below the "low" mark so that when the "clean and dry" moisture barrier is re-inserted and lid screwed on, the fluid level remains between the low and high mark. This method provides the best level of atmospheric pressure isolation within the hydraulic system.

Shift Kits for the Automatic

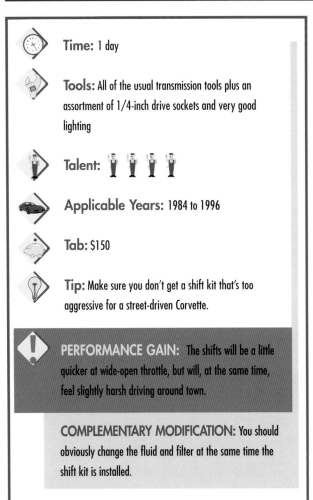

TRANSMISSION

Time: 1 day

Tools: All of the usual transmission tools plus an assortment of 1/4-inch drive sockets and very good lighting

Talent: ★★★

Applicable Years: 1984 to 1996

Tab: $150

Tip: Make sure you don't get a shift kit that's too aggressive for a street-driven Corvette.

PERFORMANCE GAIN: The shifts will be a little quicker at wide-open throttle, but will, at the same time, feel slightly harsh driving around town.

COMPLEMENTARY MODIFICATION: You should obviously change the fluid and filter at the same time the shift kit is installed.

Shift kits work by altering the control pressure and oil flow within the transmission. They usually include a redesigned control plate and different gaskets that mount between the valve body and transmission housing. This new plate may have different orifice sizes; relocated, new, or blocked ports; and/or come with recalibrated control springs.

A shift kit generally makes changes to the valve body in order to produce firm shifts. Not all shift kits improve shift firmness a great deal. Some are made specifically to correct and prevent problems that can wreak havoc on the transmission later on down the road—at least that's what the folks who sell these kits tell you.

Even though the Corvette transmission is the same as that found in the Camaro, it works differently. Any number of internal parts are Corvette specific and are not used for the rest of the GM product line. One of the things that the Camaro guys love to do is put the Corvette servos into their Camaros. GM has already given the Corvette crisper shifts than the other cars in the company. You need to decide how much more you want—or need.

Some of the high-performance aftermarket shift kits can actually change the operation of the transmission. They can alter the valve body significantly enough to change how the transmission behaves. For example, several high-performance kits can convert an automatic transmission into having full manual shifts. This converts the transmission into a clutchless standard transmission.

The kits have a number of downsides. For starters, there's a coupling in the 700R4 transmission that is prone to breaking. Some of the shift kits on the market can cause an enormous amount of strain on that coupling, wearing it out and eventually breaking it.

One solution to the 700R4 coupling problem is to do what the GM does. The company replaces the servo with a larger one and raises the line pressure. This takes a lot of the strain off the coupling and puts the additional strain on the plates. The best part is that the parts you need are all standard GM parts:

8634940	valve
8647351	seal
8639164	spring
8673039	housing
8642079	piston

The 8634940 line pressure valve is a .470; now you can get a .490 or .500. You'll find that the higher the number, the higher the line pressure and the harder the shifts. The other thing you might consider adding is a larger servo. This will help bring out the most of any shift kit.

The crux of all this is that improving your Corvette's transmission is not as easy as going down to the local Pep Boys store and purchasing a shift kit. Shift kits simply don't come in a standard size. The difficult part is that very few people even have the knowledge necessary to advise you on your choices.

Skilled transmission technicians are extremely rare, and the good ones all have six-figure incomes. They are the only people you should listen to if you're considering the installation of a shift kit. They cannot only install the kit for you, but they can get you pointed in the right direction.

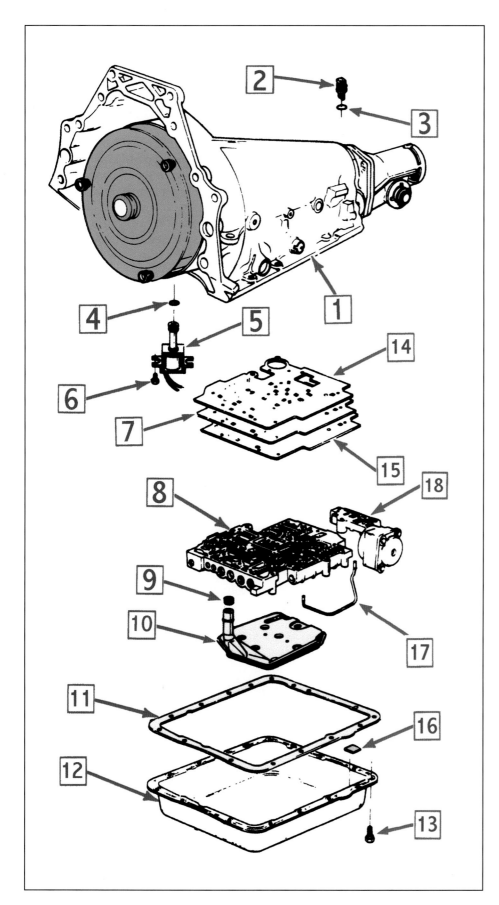

1 - Transmission Case
2 - Electrical Connector
3 - O-Ring Seal (electrical connection)
4 - O-Ring Seal (solenoid)
5 - Solenoid
6 - Washer for Bolt (solenoid)
7 - Valve Body Spacer Plate
8 - Control Body Valve Assembly
9 - Filter Seal
10 - Transmission Oil Filter Assembly
11 - Transmission Oil Pan Gasket
12 - Transmission Oil Pan
13 - Screw (pan)
14 - Spacer Gasket (plate to case)
15 - Spacer Gasket (spacer plate to
        valve body)
16 - Magnetic Chip Collector
17 - Auxiliary Accumulator Valve Tube
18 - Auxiliary Accumulator Valve Body
        Assembly

CAGS Eliminator Installation

TRANSMISSION

 Time: 30 minutes

 Tools: Screwdriver

 Talent: 👤👤

 Applicable Years: 1989 to 1996

 Tab: $15

 Tip: If you haven't already eliminated the skip shift on your Corvette, do it as soon as possible.

 COMPLEMENTARY WORK: This is such an easy job, you really needn't bother looking around for other things to do. You should just enjoy the fact it's an easy job.

The ZF six-speed used in the Corvette from 1988 to 1996 utilizes a Computer-Aided Gear Selection, or CAGS, system. This CAGS system was designed to improve fuel economy during normal driving situations by forcing the driver from first gear to fourth gear under light acceleration from a dead stop.

The GM Powertrain engineers coined the term "skip shift." They used an electric solenoid that's controlled by the car's ECM to lock out second and third gears under certain conditions. It seems that it's there to totally annoy you all the time. In reality, the annoyance is just a side benefit. The system really kept the original owner from paying a gas-guzzler tax.

The EPA mileage cycle allowed upshifting from first to second at fifteen miles per hour. The CAGS system then forces you into fourth gear. As long as you get into the throttle with a certain amount of aggressiveness, it won't engage. The system actually works with five parameters:

Transmission in first gear

Engine speed less than 1200 rpm

Coolant temperature greater than 158 degrees

Vehicle speed between 12 and 19 miles per hour

A full stop for at least a two-second duration after a previous skip shift operation

The good news is that it's easy to defeat the skip shift. All of the major Corvette suppliers sell a little plastic cap that fits over the terminals when you disconnect the skip-shift system. This is used to protect the open ends of the harness. Dirt and corrosion can enter the open ends and cause problems. These plugs are custom made for the harness and allow you to reconnect it, if necessary, with no modifications or problems. The best part is they're less than twenty dollars and do a much better job than black tape.

Prior to 1996, when OBD-II went into effect, you could simply unplug the CAGS solenoid connector. However, OBD-II is required to detect failures that impact emissions so disconnecting the CAGS solenoid on a 1996 Corvette will cause a service emissions system, or SES, warning light.

If you simply unplug the system in the 1996 Corvette, the ECM will see an open circuit, or infinite resistance, and set a trouble code to warn of CAGS solenoid failure. To prevent this, a 2.2K-ohm 1/2-watt resistor is placed in the end of the wiring harness after it is unplugged from the solenoid. Now the ECM will see the same coil resistance as it did when the wiring harness was connected to the CAGS solenoid. No codes will be set, and the CAGS lockout solenoid will cease to function. Now, you will no longer be prevented from shifting into second gear from first during conservative driving. Just remember that this plug will not prevent the skip shift light from illuminating on the console. But after you install the new plug, the light will be meaningless so you can ignore it.

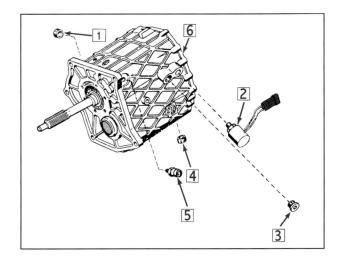

1 – Fill Plug, 2 – Transmission Computer Aided Gear Selection Solenoid (CAGS)
3 – Detent Plus, 4 – Drain Plug, 5 – Backup Light Switch, 6 – Front Transmission Case

Transmission Removal

 Time: Several hours—or even several days

 Tools: Wrench and sockets for each size: 21, 19, 17, 16, 15, 14, 13, 10, and 8 millimeter; a 12-inch pry bar; full-size rolling floor jack, 4 jack stands

 Talent:

 Applicable Years: 1984 to 1996

 Tab: $300 to $2,500

Tip: A lift is a real help on this job since the bolts are often difficult to remove.

COMPLEMENTARY WORK: Almost everything is possible when you take on a task of this magnitude. It isn't really a question of what else you could do—it's a question of when to stop doing things.

Taking the transmission out of your Corvette is a big deal. If it's the first time you've ever tried something like this, it's *really* a big deal. It's actually not terribly difficult if you have a lift, a transmission jack, and a bunch of very long socket extensions. Most good dealer technicians can have a Corvette transmission out of the car in thirty minutes. They do it all time—you don't.

Transmission removal is primarily a matter of taking everything apart in a logical sequence—then remembering what that sequence was when it's time to put things back together.

As with most tasks, it's the process of putting everything back together that will give you fits of frustration. The big stuff will always go well. It's the details like getting all the bolts lined up that usually cause problems. When doing this, the trick is to use your floor jack as a movable pry bar. Jack the transmission up and down until the holes line up. Whatever you do, don't force things into place. If something doesn't fall readily into place, just keep moving things around until it does.

The big difference between the 4+3 and the six-speed is that with the six-speed everything is contained inside the transmission. With the 4+3, all the shift linkage is external. The 4+3 linkage actually runs inside your car. If you remove the inner panel on the driver's side of the transmission tunnel, you'll be able to see all of the linkage. This makes the 4+3 removal a little more difficult.

One of the other big issues is deciding how many parts you really want to replace. Let's assume that you take the transmission out to have an internal problem fixed. You need to make a decision about replacing the clutch now as well. Let's assume you have the dual mass flywheel. Do you feel the need to replace it at this time? Remember, all of these decisions will add additional cost to the project.

If you feel brave enough to take on this task, you need to have a copy of the factory manual. It takes you step-by-step through all the procedures. You should follow these procedures exactly. In addition to the manual, you'll need a good friend who's done this job before. If you can't find an experienced friend, try to recruit any friend who doesn't mind hanging out in your garage for a couple of days. You shouldn't even think about doing this job on your own.

I'm going to walk you through the process of a ZF six-speed removal. Most of the steps can be applied to any manual transmission and will need only slight variations. The important point of this section is to show you how involved this process truly is.

Transmission Removal (1989 to 1996 six-speed):
- Free up the shifter from the interior. Remove cap, wedge, knob, lockout mechanism if equipped, leather-boot shift-lever eyelet and four nuts.
- Remove the entire exhaust system as one piece.
- Remove all the electrical connections and mark them carefully.
- Support the transmission with the floor jack centered at the drain plug.
- Remove the drive shaft and support beam bolts.
- If you vary the support height of the transmission with the floor jack, you will be better able to remove the driveline support beam bolts.
- Slide the support beam forward from the differential mount.
- Carefully watch the firewall clearance while you tilt the engine and transmission slightly backwards allowing the drive beam to clear the emergency brake cable.
- Slide the support beam out from the transmission.
- Remove the transmission to bell housing bolts.
- Select third gear with the shifter (removal clearance).

Carefully watch the firewall clearance while slowly and very carefully tilting the engine and transmission back (lowering jack) until the transmission can be pulled away from the bell housing. This will be the relaxed position of the engine and bell housing (minus trans) balanced at rest on the engine mounts.

Slowly remove transmission from under the car.

Remove the bell housing by aligning the fork on the two flats of the release (throw out) bearing. Pull the fork back from the bearing while rotating the bell housing in a clockwise direction. Note: If the clutch has extreme wear, you may have to loosen the ball stud to disengage the fork and bell housing.

The 6-millimeter Allen socket ball stud locking screw has a counter-clockwise turn-to-loosen thread and is tightened to 20 foot-pounds.

The 12-millimeter Allen socket fork ball stud is a clockwise turn-to-loosen thread and is tightened to 33 foot-pounds. Caution: Don't let the bell housing hang by the hose. Be sure to secure it off to the side in a horizontal position. This might save the seals inside the slave cylinder from debris-lodging damage if the system is dirty.

Do not, under any circumstance, use any type of pry bar between the transmission and bell housing. It's best to move things around by varying the height of the floor jack to get the holes aligned.

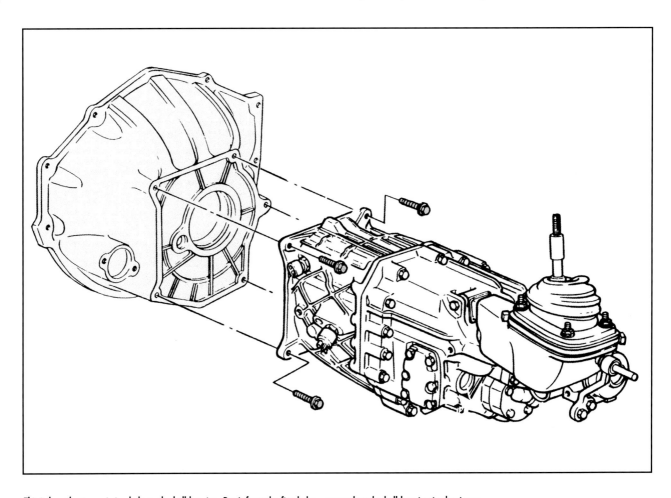

This is how the transmission bolts to the bell housing. Don't force the five bolts—remember, the bell housing is aluminum.

EXHAUST

CAR SOUND
Catalytic Converter
h-Flow Catalytic Converter. EPA and CARB Approved.

www.car-sound.com

Parts courtesy Corvette Central

Replacing the Catalytic Converter

 Time: Several hours

 Tools: Metric sockets and a 1/2-inch breaker bar

 Talent:

 Applicable Years: 1984 to 1996

 Tab: $150 to $300

 Tip: A lift is a real help on this job since the bolts may be rusted in place. The alternative is to simply remove the entire exhaust system from the car as a complete unit.

 PERFORMANCE GAIN: The L98 engines can really benefit from a low restriction catalytic converter. The gain is less with the LT1, and you have to purchase two catalytic converters.

COMPLEMENTARY MODIFICATION: Think about why your catalytic converter became clogged. It may be something as simple as a dirty air filter that caused the car to run very rich, or it could be a sensor failure in the computer system.

The catalytic converter is a sensitive topic. First, it's illegal to remove the catalytic converter. Secondly, there is very little power to be gained from removing the converter or, in the case of the LT1 and LT5, the multiple converters. Why, then, are you considering a replacement? Make sure you can answer this question before you get started.

It's going to be real difficult to get a shop to replace a perfectly good converter. It's illegal for a professional shop to remove a converter, and it's also illegal for them to *replace* a *good* converter. The EPA is monitoring for this type of violation continually, and the fines are substantial. This means you'll either replace the catalytic converter at home, or you'll have to live with what you have—neither of which is a bad thing.

There were two systems used on the C4 Corvette. The 1984 to 1991 Corvettes all used a single converter. This means that these early cars do not have a dual exhaust system. So even though you have a couple of tailpipes sticking out the rear, you really have a single exhaust system.

The Corvette didn't get a true dual exhaust system until the advent of the LT1 engine in 1992. When that engine was introduced, the exhaust system went back to cast manifolds and dual converters were added. The most common problem with converters occurs when you have an engine problem that builds excessive heat in the exhaust system. This can melt the insides of a converter. The converters can actually get so hot that they will glow bright red.

When the converter gets that hot, the molten mass plugs the exhaust system. When this happens, the car may start and idle fine, but it simply won't run. One really simple way to check for this problem is to look under the car at night to see if the converter is glowing red. If it is, shut the car down and get it to a shop. You've got a defective converter, and it's likely been caused by your engine running way too rich. I've seen a case where this happened simply because the air filter hadn't been changed for about ten years.

A defective converter isn't the easiest thing to catch. There's a tendency to assume that you have an engine performance problem and start replacing plugs and playing with the fuel injection system. A real easy test for a bad converter is to simply drop the converter out of the system and drive the car with the exhaust coming directly out of the down pipe. If the engine revs freely when you do this, you've got a bad cat. In the case of the C4, you can do this test by just dropping the whole system out and driving around the block.

The other way to check on the status of your catalytic converter is to run a pressure test. Drill two holes in the exhaust system, one directly in front of the catalytic converter and another behind it. Now hook up a pressure gauge and see what the pressures are at the two openings. If the rear pressure reading is significantly lower than the front one, you have a bad catalytic converter.

By the time the converter goes bad, the bolts are very rusted. The trick is to get them loose without breaking them. I find that the oxy-acetylene torch does a wonderful job of heating the nuts up. When the nuts are cherry red, you can loosen them easily. This isn't something that can be done in the typical home shop, however.

The best way to replace a catalytic converter on the C4 Corvette is to simply drop the whole exhaust system and then remove the converter on the floor of your garage. Try soaking the bolts with WD-40 for a day or so ahead of time.

Under no circumstances should you try to save money by getting a "universal fit" converter. This kind of converter should really be called a "no-fit" converter. The C4 Corvette used a variety of different converter mounting systems over the years. Make sure you get the one designed for your car.

When it comes to the C4 Corvette, it's easy to drop the entire exhaust system as a total unit. Get the car up on jack stands and have your neighbor come over to help you slide the whole system out from under the car. Now you can dismantle the system in your driveway. This approach is a lot better than fighting nuts and bolts while lying on your back under the car.

When it comes to replacing the converter, don't try to save money and purchase one of the white-box specials. Most of those don't fit properly. These cheap converters are designed to fit a half-dozen cars—in other words, they really don't fit anything.

Very few C4 Corvette converters actually go bad. They'll never rust out since they are made of high-quality steel. If there's a problem, it's usually because the material inside the converter starts to break up. In fact, one of the easiest ways to test the status of your converter is to simply remove the converter and see how much stuff falls out of the converter when you stand it on end.

On high mileage cars, the converter(s) may very well need replacing. I'm talking about Corvettes that have more than 150,000 miles on them. But even when a car has that many miles on it, it's unusual to see a defective catalytic converter. The other thing to keep in mind is that with the LT1 and LT5 engines it wouldn't hurt to replace the oxygen sensors at the same time you replace the converters. If things got bad enough to destroy your converter, there's a good chance your oxygen sensor was killed as well. Of course, you can simply wait until you have everything back together and then have the oxygen sensors tested.

To summarize, replacing a catalytic converter is against the law unless you can prove that the original equipment unit was defective. There's also very little horsepower gain in installing a new converter. The only gains of any significance will be with the L98 engines with the single exhaust system. The LT1, LT4, and LT5 engines will show almost no performance gain by replacing a good converter with a brand-new one.

Installing an Aftermarket Exhaust System

 Time: 3 to 6 hours

 Tools: Metric sockets and a 1/2-inch breaker bar

 Talent:

 Applicable Years:

 Tab: $150 to $1,500

 Tip: A lift can be a big help on this job since the bolts may be rusted in place. If you're using jack stands, get the car as high up as possible because the exhaust system will come off in one giant piece.

COMPLEMENTARY WORK: If your car has over 100,000 miles, you might consider replacing the converter(s) at this point.

You need to consider several things before you purchase an exhaust system. First, can you really live with the added noise? A lot of Corvettes sound really cool when they drive by you, but the driver suffers on a long trip. Hearing a great-sounding Corvette drive past you and living with one every day are really two different propositions.

The noise issue is really a huge one with the C4 Corvette since it's very susceptible to a resonance problem. A resonance is a mild or, in some cases, a loud booming noise that occurs at certain rpms. The strange part is that it's more apparent with certain models than others. The early cars, as well as convertibles, are particularly prone to this resonance. You can't truly tell how bad the resonance is going to be until you actually have the system in place.

My own personal experience provides an interesting take on the exhaust system problem. I had installed a

There's a large range of exhaust system choices in the marketplace. Most of the options are expensive. I've used the Power Effects system shown here and have been very happy with the system. The mufflers are actually cast aluminum and should last longer than the rest of the car.

Power Effects system on my 1985. I did this after trying several systems. Power Effects was a wonderful system. The key word here is "was."

When I replaced the stock cylinder heads, I bumped the compression ratio up about a point. That one change created a whole new sound, and what had once been a wonderful car became the home of tremendous resonance. Although nothing on the exhaust system was altered, the changes in the engine made a dramatic difference in the noise level of the car. It's just very hard to predict what a system is going to sound like on your car.

It's also important to realize that there are very few horsepower to be gained with the installation of an aftermarket exhaust system. The earlier L98 cars all have what is really a single exhaust. Remember, even though there are two down pipes and two tailpipes, everything is routed through the single catalytic converter. That makes it a single exhaust system. A true dual exhaust system didn't arrive until the LT1.

All of the L98 aftermarket systems are really single exhaust systems as well since they begin behind the catalytic converter. On the other hand, all of the LT1, LT4, and LT5 aftermarket systems are true dual systems. This is only natural since the factory system is a dual system.

Another option is to use what is called a muffler eliminator. This is simply a straight pipe that replaces the muffler. It's very cost effective and produces just about as much power as a complete system. The noise level isn't very high since the catalytic converter acts as a muffler.

The best part of the muffler eliminators is that they're much easier to install than a complete system. A couple of

EXHAUST

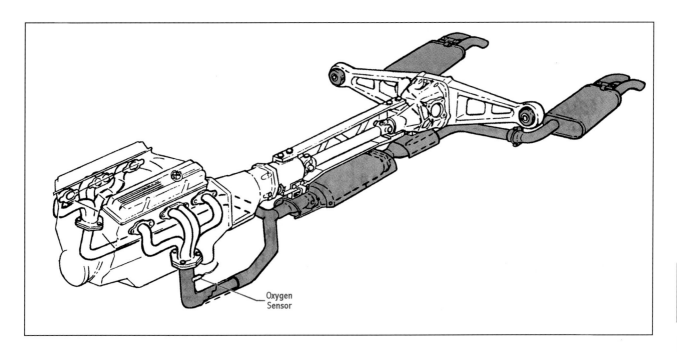

Oxygen Sensor

The C4 Corvette exhaust system is one of the easiest I've ever seen to remove. The trick is to simply drop the whole thing out from under the car. You start by unplugging the oxygen sensor(s) from the wiring harness and then proceed to remove any connections that might be found on the catalytic converter. Once you're certain that everything is free from the rest of the car, put some blocks under the system and unbolt the exhaust manifolds from the system.

The final step is to unbolt the hangers from the chassis and carefully drop the entire system on the floor. This is a two-person job so plan ahead. If you can get a couple of helpers, that's even better than having just one friend assist you. The original system isn't the lightest thing in the world, but it's not unmanageable.

You want the car on a very tall set of jack stands for this little trick. Once the system is on the garage floor, you can simply slide the whole thing out into the driveway and begin the final disassembly. You might want to reuse everything from the catalytic converter forward since most aftermarket systems only go from the catalytic converter to the rear of the car. The good part is you can clean up the forward portion of the original system, and you're in business. It's actually fairly easy to assemble the new system on the car. Just remember not to tighten anything down until you have all the parts lined up.

cuts with a reciprocating saw, and you're in business. Then it's simply a matter of putting a couple of clamps in place and driving on down the road.

The most difficult part of the entire exhaust system replacement process is having to deal with where the catalytic converter meets the rear part of the system. On the earlier cars, this joint is a flange with bolts. These nuts and bolts get rusted and can be very difficult to remove. The hardest part of the whole job will be getting these bolts loose.

I still like using heat for these bolts, but that's usually not an option available in the home shop. Don't even try drilling these bolts out. The only thing you'll do is destroy a lot of drill bits. One technique is to let the bolts soak in penetrating oil in your driveway for a couple of days and then try loosening them again. The one thing you don't want to do is break off a bolt.

A unique feature of the Power Effects system is that you can change the flow of the exhaust by simply turning a knob on the muffler. This knob changes the position of the baffles inside the muffler and routes the exhaust differently at the various positions. There are several positions, but I tend to use only wide open and fully closed. This makes a great setup for a track car that is occasionally driven on the street.

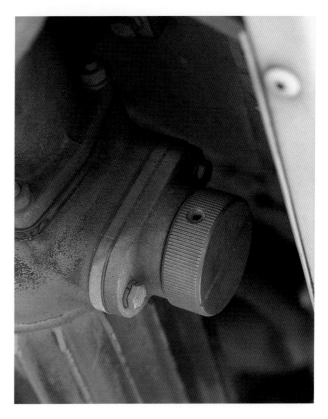

Installing Headers

 Time: Several hours to a day

 Tools: Metric sockets and a 1/2 -inch breaker bar

 Talent:

 Applicable Years: All

 Tab: $750 to $1,500

 Tip: A lift really helps with this job since you have to navigate the headers in place, and the more clearance you can get between the car and the ground, the better. If you only have jack stands, make sure that you get the car up as high as possible.

 PERFORMANCE GAIN: There's no question you'll gain some horsepower from installing headers. Unfortunately, it probably won't be as much as you hope. Considering the cost and effort it takes to install headers, you need to seriously think about this installation. You need to have a very good reason to install headers in your Corvette.

COMPLEMENTARY MODIFICATION: The only real gain from headers will come when you modify the induction system. Corvette engines are really all about air in and air out. It doesn't do much good to have an impressive exhaust system unless you increase the volume of air coming in through the induction system.

EXHAUST

Installing headers isn't a bad job. But you should plan on spending at least a day to do it.

You won't see a lot of significant horsepower gain from just installing headers. The earlier cars will experience the greatest horsepower gain. The exhaust manifolds on those cars is the most restrictive of all the cars. There will be even less of a horsepower gain with the LT1 engines and almost none with the LT4 cars. The later exhaust manifolds are really very efficient.

Don't be fooled by the stock exhaust manifolds on the LT1. The cast manifolds that the factory used are very effective. The tubular shorty headers that are sold by the aftermarket companies are less effective than the stock manifolds. GM tested both types of exhaust manifolds when it was developing the LT1. The company found that cast headers offered improved flow over a welded manifold because of the smoother interior surfaces at the transition points. The fact that the cast manifolds offer reduced noise is simply a bonus. This is a case where the aftermarket is selling a part that GM rejected. Don't get seduced by the advertising.

You should consider doing the whole exhaust system from the cylinder heads on back at the same time you install headers. This will cost a lot more money, but it's the only way to see a real gain in power. As long as you're going to spend time taking everything apart, it makes sense to do the whole system. Most of the time you spend installing the headers will involve simply removing a whole lot of parts and then putting most of them back on. Take some photos and make lots of notes as you take things off the car. This will make the installation go smoothly.

When it comes to installing the headers, the best approach is to simply take the complete exhaust system off the car. Put the whole exhaust system in your driveway and start reassembling things starting at the front with your new headers. This assumes, of course, that you're putting what is called the long tube header system in the car.

These long tube headers go in from the top of the engine compartment. This means the higher you have the car on jack stands, the easier things will go. You're going to literally have to turn a corner with these long tube headers as you feed them down into the depths of the car. This is another occasion when it really helps to have a second person underneath the car.

There are a lot of things that have to come together when you install a set of headers. It takes some time to get all of the various pieces aligned properly. Get it all loosely together first and then go around tightening things down in stages.

I've worked with two different brands of headers for the C4 Corvette, and neither is perfect. Hooker makes a nice set of long tube headers for the Corvette. The nice thing about this company's headers is that they tuck up in the car nicely. The bad part is that the oxygen sensor is in the wrong place. This means that you'll need to drill a hole and weld a flange on the pipe after the four pipes meet.

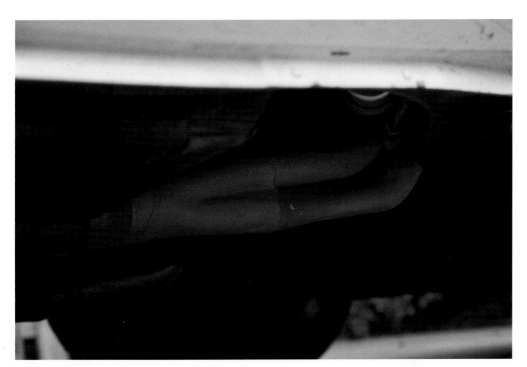

Here's the problem with some of the headers — they're really pretty low. Ask around at the Corvette shows to learn how people feel about the system they have on their car. You're going to end up spending around a thousand dollars, or more, for the headers when everything is all done. Please be an informed consumer.

If you're keeping the air injection system intact, and you should, make sure you inquire about this before you order the system. Not all the aftermarket headers have provisions for this.

The other header I've worked with is from TPIS. Its oxygen sensor is in the correct location, but the downside is that the headers hang pretty low in the chassis. This isn't a problem if you mainly use your car for drag racing and track events. If you lower your Corvette and drive it on the street, though, it's a major problem.

My recommendation is that you hold off on doing the header installation until you've made some other engine modifications. Only after you've increased the airflow *into* the engine should you start to worry about getting all that air out of the engine.

BRAKES

Parts courtesy Corvette Central

Bleeding and Flushing the Brake System

 Time: 1 hour

 Tools: Pressure bleeder, brake fluid, and vinyl tubing

 Talent:

 Applicable Years: 1985 to 1996

 Tab: $10 to $100

 Tip: This is a necessary task and should be done once a year.

PERFORMANCE GAIN: You'll improve the braking force and have far less of a chance of experiencing brake pedal fade.

COMPLEMENTARY MODIFICATION: Check your brake pads for wear. You should consider replacing the brake pads anytime they're below half of their original thickness.

Although very few people do this, you should be bleeding and flushing the brake system once a year. If you run track events with your Corvette, you should do it before every event.

Your brake fluid actually sucks the moisture out of the air. After a year or two, there's bound to be a pretty high moisture content in your brake fluid. This happens even if you never take the caps off the master cylinder.

Once your fluid gets contaminated with a lot of moisture, you have two problems. First, the water can set up rust problems in your brake system. This is minimized by all the aluminum components in the C4 Corvette brake system, but the problem still exists in the steel brake lines.

The other problem is that water boils at 212 degrees Fahrenheit. That's a pretty common temperature for your brake system. Knowing that my calipers run around 550 degrees at the track, you'll realize that 212 degrees is no big deal. All that moisture in the brake system will turn to steam. As a result, you'll have water vapor, or steam, in your brake lines, which is compressible, unlike the brake fluid.

Bleeding is NOT Flushing

Flushing your hydraulic system is a little different than simply bleeding the brake system. When you bleed the brake system, you're simply trying to get all the air bubbles out of the system. When you flush the brake system, you're

These pressure bleeders are available for around fifty dollars. One real advantage is that they use a hand pump to build pressure. This means you don't need to have a compressed air source in your home garage. Secondly, they'll never build enough pressure to damage your hydraulic system. You only need about four to five pounds of compressed air to effectively flush or bleed your brake system. The thing to remember is that you never want to let the tank run dry of brake fluid. Also, when you're done, throw all the unused brake fluid out. Every time you flush the brake system you should start with new cans of fluid. Open cans of brake fluid around the garage do nothing but collect moisture. That's exactly what you're trying to avoid by flushing the brake system.

getting rid of all the fluid that's been in the system since the last flush. More accurately, you're replacing the current brake fluid with brand-new, fresh brake fluid. You might think of a brake system flush as being more complete than a simple bleeding of the system.

If you kept on bleeding the hydraulic system even after you had expelled all the air in the system, you would be doing a complete flush of the braking system.

Four Ways to Flush the Brake System

There are four methods of bleeding the brake system. It really doesn't make much difference which one you use since they all accomplish the same thing. It's mostly a matter of which tools you have available and how much time you have.

Pressure Bleeding: With this system, you have a reservoir of brake fluid in a pressurized tank. You then place a positive air pressure force on the opposite side of the fluid, forcing it into the brake system, pushing all the old brake fluid out of the system.

Vacuum Bleeding: This is where you fill the reservoir and then apply a vacuum at the caliper bleeder nipple. The vacuum pump pulls the fluid through the system.

Family & Friends Bleeding: This is a system where you recruit a family member or friend who owes you a favor and have them push on the pedal repeatedly until the entire system is bled.

Gravity Bleeding: This is a unique procedure where you simply open all the bleeder screws and let the fluid run out. The key point here is that you never let the master cylinder run dry. A lot of race teams use gravity bleeding when they have completely rebuilt the brake system.

I prefer bleeding the system with the pressure tank because most folks don't really know how to push the brake pedal during the bleeding process.

From the Bleeder to the Bottle

It's really not a good idea to simply let the fluid run all over the shop floor. The best way to deal with these fluids is to take a couple of feet of vinyl tubing and push one end onto the bleeder screw and place the other end in a bottle. This minimizes the mess on the floor and on the car. Brake fluid is the best paint remover on the market. You don't want it on any painted surfaces unless you intend to strip the paint. There is no such thing as being too careful with brake fluid.

Pushing the Pedal

During normal use, the piston in a master cylinder only goes into the cylinder about one-third of the its possible travel. New master cylinders have clean and smooth pistons, but pistons on older master cylinders are dirty and corroded.

As the piston is depressed into the bore of the master cylinder, the seals and fluid help to keep that smaller portion of the piston bore clean, smooth, and well lubricated. The remaining two-thirds of the bore is exposed to dirty brake fluid and doesn't get the benefit of regular cleaning. When your friend or family member depresses the piston during the bleeding process, the cylinder is pushed into this dirty, corroded area and drags across the seals. This is a perfect situation for tearing and nicking the little O-ring seals.

The more dirt or corrosion on the interior of the master cylinder, or the more frequently and vigorously the person pumps the pedal, the worse the damage will be. The net effect is a leaky master cylinder. The best way to prevent this is to place a block of wood under the brake pedal so the person in the seat can never push the brake pedal all the way to the floor.

The person pumping the pedal should do so with slow, even strokes. There is no need to go crazy on the pedal. Over the years, I've seen unskilled people do more damage to master cylinders than to any other item. With this in mind, I prefer a pressure bleeder to any of the other systems.

Vinyl tubing is great for bleeding and flushing brakes. When you insert the other end of the tubing into a bottle, it keeps all the brake fluid off both the car and the garage floor. This also allows you to see any air bubbles that might have been trapped in the brake system. I suggest that you keep flushing fluid through the system until you see new, clean brake fluid coming out of the caliper.

Replacing Front Brake Pads

 Time: 1 hour

 Tools: 1/2-inch metric sockets

 Talent:

 Applicable Years: 1984 to 1996

 Tab: $75 to $150

 Torque: Caliper mounting bolts – 165 foot-pounds

 Tip: This is an easy task that just requires time and attention to detail. The most important step is preparing the brake rotors for new pads.

 PERFORMANCE GAIN: Your car will stop faster, and, more importantly, it should stop smoother.

COMPLEMENTARY MODIFICATION: Flush all the old brake fluid from the system after the new pads have been installed.

BRAKES

You can always pay someone to do this job. But, since it's so easy, you may as well do it yourself. Plus, you can usually do a better job than most shops. Most shops make very little money if they simply replace brake pads. The only way to improve the profit margin on brake work is to complete the job as quickly as possible, or sell you a bunch of extra parts.

Doing a brake job at home is simply a matter of checking everything carefully and taking your time. One thing to remember is that you should only take one side apart at a time. That way, if you get confused, you'll still have a good sample to examine.

The C4 Corvette used two different front brake calipers. If you look at the early cars, those made between 1984 and 1987, you'll find a sliding brake caliper with a single piston. This brake system is just fine for the street-driven Corvette. There's very little need for improvement. Just remember to use a top-quality brake pad designed for street driving.

The ZR-1, along with the cars that were equipped with a heavy-duty brake package, utilized a two-piston sliding caliper. This design is the same as the earlier caliper except that, instead of a single piston, it has two pistons on the inboard side of the caliper.

The brake rotors on these later cars are also larger. Actually, the increased

The first thing is to check the condition of the rotors. Don't just replace them. Take a minute and measure them. Notice how I've used the lug nuts to hold the rotor firmly to the hub to measure for rotor warping. The dial gauge should be at a right angle to the hub and near the outer edge. If the dial moves more than 0.006 inches, you should pick up the phone and order new rotors.

97

Left: Now that you've checked for runout, or warping, you should check for thickness. The brake rotor is really one giant heat sink. If it's too thin, it's not going to pull enough heat away from the pads, and you risk boiling the brake fluid under hard braking. In addition, your caliper pistons will have to extend too far when the brake pads wear. Pay attention to the manufacturer's specifications. The minimum thickness is usually stamped inside the rotor. If you can't find this information, just call your local machine shop, and they will tell you the specification. Take a measurement in several places and compare the numbers you find. If the numbers vary by more than 0.013 inches, buy some new rotors.

brake rotor diameter may be more effective in improving brake performance than the larger caliper. If you think back to your high school physics class and try to remember the principles of leverage, you'll understand that a brake caliper located farther from the hub is going to exert more leverage. That's why big rotors are important.

Before you start taking your Corvette apart, you should decide what brand of brake pad you want to purchase. In order to do this, you'll have to decide what's important to you in a brake pad.

If you only drive your Corvette on the street, your biggest concerns are going to be about brake dust and noise. Almost every brake pad on the market will stop your street-driven Corvette, and most of the major brands come with a lifetime warranty.

When it comes to brake pads, the important thing isn't the composition of the pad, but rather the preparation of the rotor. People seem to forget that stopping involves the brake pad rubbing against the rotor. The rotor and the brake pad are equally vital.

You should make sure you break in your new pads very carefully. Take the car for a drive and get it up to about 40 miles per hour. Then bring the car to a complete stop. Now drive a mile or so and repeat the process. Once you've done this about fifteen times, you've started the bedding process. Now just be careful for the next hundred miles, and you'll have a great set of brakes.

Above: You should put a proper finish on both new and used brake rotors with an orbital sander and 100-grit paper. This gives the rotor a non-directional finish. You should sand it until you've removed the usual high spots, especially the areas at the outer edge. There should be a series of little scratches and swirls in the surface of the rotor when you're done.

Another reason for doing this is to ensure you remove all the remnants of the old brake pad material. Your brake rotor is coated with the material from that earlier brake pad. By sanding the rotor, you're ensuring that the new pads make contact with the rotor, not with a surface layer of the old brake pad. A lot of the squealing problems come from the new pad material being exposed to the old pad material.

Now scrub the rotor with soap and water. This should be done with new brake rotors as well as used ones. You'll need a stiff brush and lots of soapsuds. Finish the cleaning process by spraying down the brake rotor with brake clean. After all this effort, you should be able to rub a white paper towel on the rotor surface and not get it dirty.

No one ever talks about brake caliper hardware. When you remove your calipers, take time to examine these pins very carefully. If you see any wear, replace them. If you can't remember the last time you replaced these pins, just order a new set when you order your brake pads. I found that the most expensive place to purchase these pins was the local Chevrolet dealer. I actually walked out without my parts because the price was so outrageous. I ended up getting a better deal from Baer Racing. Even with the shipping cost, it was only a fourth of what my local dealer wanted to charge me. When I ordered the pins, I also ordered about a dozen of the little circlips that hold the pins in place. You should use new clips every time you replace the brake pads.

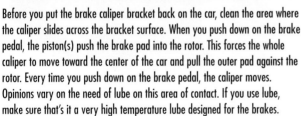

Before you put the brake caliper bracket back on the car, clean the area where the caliper slides across the bracket surface. When you push down on the brake pedal, the piston(s) push the brake pad into the rotor. This forces the whole caliper to move toward the center of the car and pull the outer pad against the rotor. Every time you push down on the brake pedal, the caliper moves. Opinions vary on the need of lube on this area of contact. If you use lube, make sure that's it a very high temperature lube designed for the brakes.

Replacing Rear Brake Pads

 Time: 1 hour

 Tools: Metric box wrenches, 1/2-inch Metric sockets, and brake piston tool

 Talent:

 Applicable Years: 1984 to 1996

 Tab: $75

 Torque: Upper Guide Pin Bolt — 26 foot-pounds; Lower Guide Pin Bolt — 16 foot-pounds

 Tip: Purchase the special tool that pushes the caliper piston back into the caliper. Using the tool is much better than using a pair of pliers.

 PERFORMANCE GAIN: Improved braking is always a good thing. New pads will allow for greater braking power.

COMPLEMENTARY WORK: You might want to consider the installation of new hydraulic brake hoses at this time.

BRAKES

Two types of rear brake calipers were used on the C4 Corvette. From 1984 to 1987, the Corvette parking brake was essentially a miniature brake drum complete with brake shoes and springs. Then, in 1988, the Corvette began using a rear brake caliper that incorporated the parking brake into the caliper.

In terms of preparation, you should treat the rear brakes the same way you treated the front brakes. The rotors should be taken off and sanded with 100-grit paper. Then you need to carefully scrub them to clean off all the metal particles. Take another look at the chapter on front brake pad installation to remind yourself how to install brake pads that won't squeal at the first stop sign you come to. Don't skimp on rear brake rotor preparation.

Above: This is the best tool to use for pushing the caliper piston back into the caliper housing. It's a lot easier to use than the traditional C-clamp or even a pair of slip-joint pliers. The tool is so inexpensive that you would be foolish not to purchase one. Always push the pistons back into the caliper with the bleeder screw open. Opening the bleeder screw gets rid of all the nasty old brake fluid that's been living in the caliper for the last few years. You don't want to push all this nasty fluid back into your brake system. Unless you open the bleeder screw as you push the piston into the caliper, all you're doing is pushing dirty nasty brake fluid backwards through the system. That's not a good thing.

Left: This parking brake was used from 1984 to 1987. If your parking brake is working fine, you don't need to do much to it at this point except adjust it once you get the brake rotor back into place. It's easier to adjust the parking brake prior to replacing the brake caliper. Doing any major service on this style of parking brake is a major source of aggravation. Anyone who has previously worked on the 1967 to 1982 Corvette parking brake can attest to that. The best time to do a complete service on these parking brakes is when you replace the rear wheel bearings.

Brake Rotor Prep and Replacement

Time: 1 hour

Tools: Orbital sander with 100-grit paper, soap, hot water, and brake clean.

Talent:

Applicable Years: 1984 to 1996

Tab: $5 to $400 for a set of brake rotors

Tip: Avoid the drilled rotors if you expect to do any heavy braking or attend any track events with your Corvette.

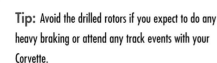
PERFORMANCE GAIN: Proper brake rotor preparation will result in smoother stopping with less brake noise.

COMPLEMENTARY MODIFICATION: This job is usually coupled with the installation of new brake pads.

Squealing brakes are the single biggest complaint that repair shops have. Luckily, brake squeal is generally not an indication of a safety hazard. It's just one gigantic and very embarrassing annoyance. There's really no reason for most of the brake squeal you hear coming from Corvettes. Brake squeal is a problem that you can avoid if you spend an extra half-hour installing your new brake pads.

It helps if you understand that brake squeal is really a vibration. When the pad touches the brake rotor, it sets up a vibration, or oscillation. The noise you hear when you pull up to the red light is really a vibrating rotor or caliper. Try to think of your brake rotors and calipers as a tuning fork. The noise you hear when you strike a tuning fork is nothing more than a vibrating piece of steel. Your brake rotor is steel, and your caliper is aluminum—at least on the C4 Corvette.

Brake rotor warpage is not as common as people think. Often the brake pedal will feel like it's pushing back at your foot, but warpage is not always the reason. Sometimes when people install new brake pads, they leave the old rotors on the car. These rotors are coated with the friction material from the previous pads. When you apply your new brake pads, they never even touch the rotor—they simply interact with the old friction material. As a result, the brakes will grab, and the whole braking application will feel like your rotors are warped.

When you install new pads, you not only need to measure them for thickness and runout, you also need to prepare the surface properly. This means taking an orbital sander with 100-grit paper and sanding both the inside and outside surfaces. You want a series of small circular sanding marks on the rotor.

The very first thing you need to do is check the condition of the rotors. Don't just replace them. First, take a minute to measure them. Notice how I've used the lug nuts to hold the rotor firmly to the hub to measure for rotor warpage. The dial gauge should be at a right angle to the hub and near the outer edge. If the dial moves more than 0.006 inches, you should pick up the phone and order new rotors. Rotors can be machined, but it's really not the best idea. In a perfect world, a brake lathe can deliver a precision cut. It's just too bad that we don't live in a perfect world. In fact, we live in a world where the average brake lathe is a worn-out piece of junk. GM actually used to forbid dealerships from machining any rotors when the brake work was being done under warranty. Corvette rotors are not so expensive that you need to take a chance with questionable machining.

BRAKES

101

Left: Now that you've checked for runout, or warpage, you need to check for thickness. The brake rotor is really one giant heat sink. If it's too thin, it's not going to pull enough heat away from the pads, and you risk boiling the brake fluid under hard braking. In addition, your caliper pistons will have to extend too far when the brake pads wear. Pay attention to the manufacturer's specifications. The minimum thickness is usually stamped inside the rotor hat. If you can't find the number, just call your local machine shop and they can tell you the specification. Take a measurement in several places and compare the numbers you find. If the numbers vary by more than 0.013 inches, buy some new rotors.

Once you have the surfaces sanded, scrub your rotors with soap and hot water. The idea is to remove all the little metallic particles. Once you've done a good job of scrubbing the rotors, dry them off and spray them with Brake Clean.

The good news is that brake squeal is preventable. The bad news is that, once you have a squeal, it's very hard to get rid of it. It's best to make sure the brake pads are installed with a lot of care so you can prevent a noise before it starts. I've installed several hundred brake pads and only a few ever developed a squeal. I always took just a little bit longer to do the job than most people, but I never had to deal with the comebacks.

This is the best type of rotor for your Corvette. The grooves allow any hot brake pad gases to dissipate, and you don't have those nasty little holes that set up cracks in your rotor. These aren't cheap, but they really work.

It seems everyone wants drilled rotors on their Corvette. The only problem is drilled rotors don't work very well if you drive your car at the track. Under severe braking, cracks begin to emanate from all the holes. Drilled brake rotors on the C4 Corvette are really a cosmetic item that will actually detract from braking performance.

BRAKES

Preparing Brakes for a Track Car

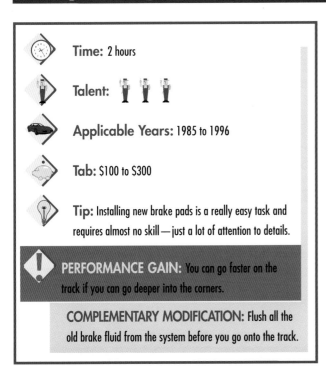

Time: 2 hours

Talent: ⫩ ⫩ ⫩

Applicable Years: 1985 to 1996

Tab: $100 to $300

Tip: Installing new brake pads is a really easy task and requires almost no skill—just a lot of attention to details.

PERFORMANCE GAIN: You can go faster on the track if you can go deeper into the corners.

COMPLEMENTARY MODIFICATION: Flush all the old brake fluid from the system before you go onto the track.

People spend too much time worrying about the power their motors put out and not enough time thinking about how they're going to get their beasts stopped.

Brakes can generate a lot of heat. The reason your Corvette stops at all is because the brake system converts kinetic energy into heat energy.

Because your brakes give off so much heat, all the braking system components have to be in really good shape to withstand the tremendous temperatures. It's important to figure out some new ways to get rid of the heat that's going to be coming off your rotors and calipers.

Brake Fluid

You should always change your brake fluid before you go to a track event. Brake fluid is like oil in that the act of changing it is far more important than choosing which brand to use. In the chapter on your brake's hydraulic system, I talked about the moisture content of your brake fluid. This moisture is an even greater concern at the track where your rotors may reach 1,000 degrees Fahrenheit.

Ford heavy-duty brake fluid has been extremely popular for years and years. It's still the most economical choice. Lately, I've been using Wilwood and have never had a problem. If you have trouble making a choice, ask around at the track for recommendations. Regardless of which fluid you pick, make sure it's brand new and has no moisture.

Rotors

Rotors are very basic items. When you head out to the track, you want them as thick as possible. You don't want the kind with holes drilled in them. Take some time and check your rotors for thickness and warpage.

Pad Material

If you only do a couple of track events a year, a top quality street pad will be just fine. Many people spend way too much money on brake pads they don't really need. Regardless of the pad material you use, never go to a track event with less than half of the brake pad thickness left on your pads.

Brake pads have torque curves just like engines. If you put the coefficient of friction on one axis and temperature on the other axis, you can plot the torque curve of a brake pad. The interesting thing is that you want the same sort of torque in a brake pad that you want in an engine. The last thing you want is a spike on the torque curve. To avoid very grabby brakes, you want a high, flat torque curve.

To make a heavy car stop you're going to need huge amounts of torque. The other thing you have to realize is that, most of the time, your brake pad material really isn't making direct contact with the steel of your brake rotor. Remember, there's friction material left on the rotor from the previous brake application. This is especially true when using race pads. It's just one more reason to pay tremendous attention to rotor preparation and proper break-in procedure.

Before you install a set of race pads in your Corvette, you need to ask yourself how you really feel about brake dust and noise. Although these things may be of little concern to racers, they are the two biggest issues for people who drive their Corvettes on the street.

Front to Rear Balance

The Corvette is biased to use a lot of front braking force. The rear brakes are more or less just there to help out. The front brakes are responsible for roughly eighty-five percent of your braking. This isn't necessarily a bad thing, because locking up your rear brakes can get very exciting very fast. As soon as they lock up, the rear of the car comes around to the front, and you're staring back at the road you just drove down.

It's possible to give your Corvette improved rear braking. First, you can play with the front to rear balance by changing the brake bias spring. Doug Rippie Motorsports has been doing this for a long time. It's a relatively easy task to replace the spring, and the process results in giving you a decent amount of rear brake.

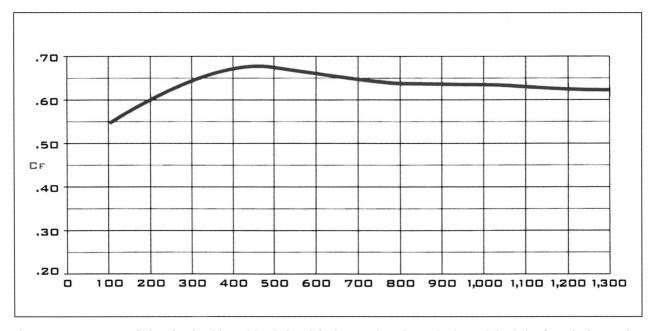

These are some very impressive brake pads. Wilwood designed these brake pads for the racetrack. You'll notice that they reach their highest friction level at around 450 degrees. You will never see these temperatures on a street driven Corvette. The really impressive thing, though, is how the coefficient of friction stays almost flat until 1,300 degrees.

Now we come to the advanced course in brake bias. You can change the brake bias by using different brake pads on the front and rear of the car. I'm going to use an example from Wilwood brakes since they have a pad numbering system that's easy to understand. The "A" pad is the most aggressive pad Wilwood makes. The "B" pad is a little less aggressive, and the "C" brake pad is the least aggressive of the race pads.

If you use an A pad in the rear and a C in the front, you're really making the rear brakes more aggressive, at least in relationship to the front. This is really a neat way to alter your brake balance without adding all the plumbing you normally need to install a line valve.

Almost all of the C4 Corvettes have anti-lock braking systems, or ABS. Only the 1984s and 1985s missed out on ABS. For this reason, few people want to put more rear brake into the hydraulic system by installing a proportioning valve. The use of different pads allows us to dial in the brake system. The only trouble is that it's going to take some seat time to find the correct combination.

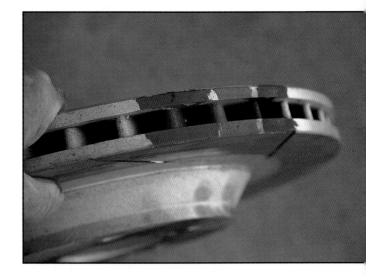

Temperature-sensitive paint is a wonderful thing. Most professional race shops use three different colors of paint on their brake rotors. Each of these colors is designed to change color at a different temperature. The changes in color give you an indication of the temperature your rotor is achieving out on the racetrack.

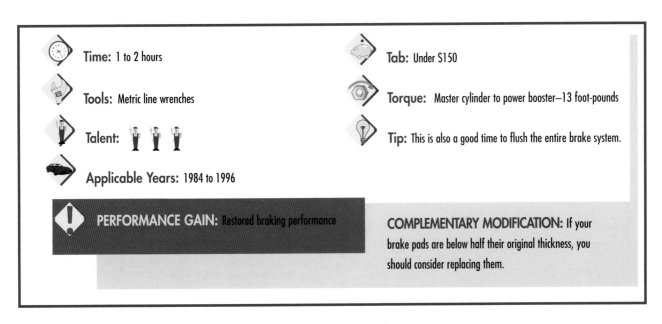

Brake Master Cylinder Replacement

Time: 1 to 2 hours

Tools: Metric line wrenches

Talent: ♟♟♟

Applicable Years: 1984 to 1996

PERFORMANCE GAIN: Restored braking performance

Tab: Under $150

Torque: Master cylinder to power booster—13 foot-pounds

Tip: This is also a good time to flush the entire brake system.

COMPLEMENTARY MODIFICATION: If your brake pads are below half their original thickness, you should consider replacing them.

BRAKES

Drive your Corvette long enough, and you'll eventually need to replace the brake master cylinder. There are a couple of ways to know when your master cylinder needs replacing. You might need to replace the master brake cylinder in your Corvette if:

• Your brake pedal slowly sinks to the floor while you wait for the light to turn green
• Your brakes work better after you pump the pedal a couple of times
• You have to open the hood to add brake fluid more than every few months
• You find brake fluid running down your brake booster

In my case, I was having to replenish my brake fluid supply every few weeks. Right away I knew that this was not a good sign. The other bad sign was that I was constantly finding peeling paint on my nicely enameled garage floor because the brake fluid was leaking onto it.

Two things tipped me off to the problem, and, upon closer inspection, I found that the underside of the master cylinder was covered in brake fluid. The interesting thing was that it was leaking out of the pressure differential switch. I'd never seen that before.

Master cylinders usually leak out of the rear seal. This means that your brake booster will be covered with brake fluid. The other failure happens when an internal seal breaks down, and your brake light goes on. Sometimes you can lose your rear brakes, in which case the rear rotors will get rusty. These maladies are all normal and easy to diagnose.

Master cylinders are easy to replace. It should only take you a half-hour to install a new unit. Most shops will charge you for an hour of labor, which is totally reasonable. They may also charge you additional time to bleed all four calipers, which is also a reasonable charge.

The master cylinder design changed during the production of the C4, but the basic things remained the same. After all, a master brake cylinder is a master brake cylinder. This particular unit is on a 1985 Corvette. If you have an ABS system, don't get overly concerned. The master cylinder is upstream of the ABS system and is easy to work on.

You can run into a few obstacles when replacing the master cylinder. First, you can have trouble when you try to break the old brake lines loose from the master cylinder. If you round the corners on these fittings, you're in a huge amount of hurt. You can simply start replacing lines halfway through the car.

I've installed possibly a hundred master cylinders in my lifetime, and the only line wrenches I trust for the job are Snap-On. Normally I'm a Craftsman type of guy, but when it comes to line wrenches, I go to the top of the line. These things really work. There are a lot of ways to save money, but skimping on line wrenches is not the best way to balance your budget.

Next make sure that all of your bleeder screws can be loosened. If you have a bleeder screw that won't loosen, or, worse yet, one that breaks off, be prepared to spend a lot of money on repairs. A frozen, or broken, bleeder screw means you're going to have to purchase a new caliper. I've heard of all the various ways of removing obstinate bleeder screws, and I don't like any of them. If you find yourself in this predicament, my advice is that you just go out and get a new caliper.

It takes two different line wrenches to break the lines loose from the master cylinder. You're going to need a 12-millimeter and a 14-millimeter flare-nut wrench. Regardless of the tool you use, remember that you want a wrench that won't spread apart as you turn the fitting. The cheap wrenches actually flex if the fitting is difficult to remove. Once you round the fitting, you're in serious trouble. You're better off to spend the money on a quality wrench than to spend money fabricating new brake lines.

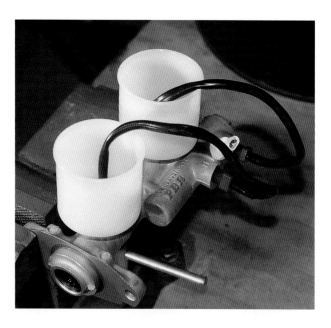

Now that you've gotten all the lines loose, we can turn our attention to bench bleeding the new master cylinder. Clamp one of the mounting ears in a vise and attach the bleeder kit. You can get a nice metric kit from Pep Boys or AutoZone for just a few dollars. The idea is to pump fluid through the master cylinder and remove any air from the internal passages in the master cylinder. I use a big Phillips screwdriver to pump the master cylinder piston. Once you have nice clear fluid with no air bubbles coming out of the little plastic hoses, you're ready to begin the great master cylinder swap.

Now that you have the new master cylinder in place, you want to bleed the final amount of air out of the unit. There's a trick here that your local Corvette shop probably never showed you. Get your buddy to sit in the car as you loosen one of the master cylinder line fittings so that a little fluid leaks out. Now have him push the brake pedal slowly to the floor. Now repeat this with the other brake line.

Any air in the master cylinder will be expelled before it gets to the brake lines that go to the corners of the car. Do this with both the front and rear brake lines about three times. Just remember to close the brake line before your friend lets the brake pedal return. If you do this correctly, you won't have to bleed the individual calipers.

PROJECT 42
Replacing an ABS Sensor

 Time: 1 hour

 Tools: 1/2-inch metric sockets drive

 Talent:

 Applicable Years: 1987 to 1996

 Tab: $25 to $50

 Torque: Sensor retaining bolt—89 inch-pounds

 Tip: You want to keep everything as clean as possible during the wheel sensor replacement.

 PERFORMANCE GAIN: Your anti-lock braking system, or ABS, will work properly.

COMPLEMENTARY MODIFICATION: This is really a stand-alone project, and you don't need to delve into the entire braking system.

The Corvette was endowed with an anti-lock braking system, or ABS, in 1986. This was due to the driving force of Dave McLellan who held his engineering team to the fire. He wanted an ABS braking system on the Corvette as quickly as possible. McLellan felt that in order for the Corvette to be considered technologically advanced it had to have an ABS braking system.

Anti-lock braking systems terrified service technicians at the time. We all thought there were going to be major, and extremely complex, problems with these electronic wonders. As it turned out, we were all wrong. ABS braking has been virtually foolproof. About the only time that something goes wrong is when a wheel sensor fails. That's the most common problem with the ABS systems.

If this happens to you, I suggest that you let a professional diagnose your ABS problem. Owning and operating the scan equipment needed to perform a complete diagnosis is simply not practical for the weekend warrior.

If you want to be part of the process without having to purchase you own scan tool, you can try to get a good Corvette shop to diagnose the reason your ABS light is coming on. If the only problem is the wheel sensor, you can drive the car home and replace the appropriate wheel sensor yourself.

Before I describe the technique of replacing a speed sensor, I want to take a second to remind you that an ABS failure is not a brake system failure. All of the anti-lock braking systems are designed in such a way that when they fail, you still have a normal brake system. There is simply no need to panic that you're going to go flying through a red light on your way to work in the morning.

Very few of us even get to the point where we activate the ABS system during normal driving. I suggest that on a nice, wet Saturday morning, you find a totally deserted area of road, or a parking lot, and brake hard enough to activate the ABS. This will show you what the brake pedal does under heavy braking and give you an idea of how easy it is to control the car.

You should also learn how to keep your foot on the brake pedal under conditions that activate the ABS. Most

This toothed ring is a part of the wheel bearing. It's really rare for this part to break and need to be replaced. However, if it does break, you should start trying to figure out why it happened. The other reason to replace this unit is if the bearing itself should wear out.

BRAKES

107

of us grew up with the notion that when your brakes start to lock up, you should come off the brake pedal slightly to regain control. That's not necessarily true if you have ABS. With ABS, you can just keep standing on the brakes until the car comes to a complete stop. The ABS will do exactly what you used to do for yourself—back off of the brake pedal.

The Wheel Sensor

Replacing a defective wheel sensor couldn't be easier. First, you trace the sensor wires back to the connector and unplug the sensor from the harness. Now go back to the sensor and remove the two little bolts that hold the sensor in place. You also have to remove the little brackets and grommets that are used for routing the wiring. This sensor won't just pull out; it's been there for a while so you may have to help it out. The good part is that, since you've already determined it's defective, you don't have to worry about damaging it. On the other hand, you need to be very careful so you don't damage the aluminum knuckle. Pry bars and screwdrivers may help you get the sensor out of the hub, but they could also scratch the hub.

Once you have the sensor out, take some time and clean the area really well. Brake cleaner usually works best in this situation. The silicone is going to fight you a little bit. Just keep telling yourself that the cleaner you get this area, the greater are your chances for success. You really don't want to go back to the shop that did the diagnosis and admit that you couldn't properly install the sensor.

The Corvette engineering team spent a lot of time working with the sensor's coatings. The Corvette was one of the first cars to use aluminum suspension pieces held together with steel bolts. This is why things like the ball joints and the ABS sensors all have special coatings designed to ward off any possible corrosion problem.

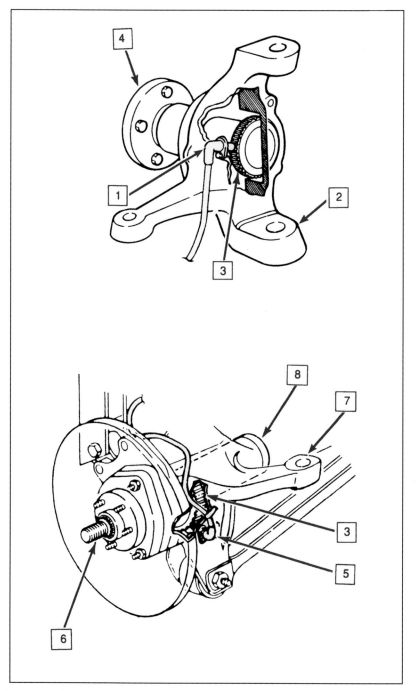

1 - Right Front Speed Sensor
2 - Front Steering Knuckle
3 - Toothed Ring
4 - Front Hub and Bearing Assembly
5 - Left Rear Wheel Speed Sensor
6 - Rear Driveshaft Spindle
7 - Suspension Knuckle
8 - Rear Wheel Shaft

Changing the Brake Bias Spring

Time: 2 hours

Tools: Sockets, screwdrivers, and an arbor press

Talent:

Applicable Years: 1984 to 1996

Tip: The most important thing you can do for your braking system is to keep good pads installed and change the brake fluid once a year.

 PERFORMANCE GAIN: The braking force will be more evenly distributed, and you'll shorten your braking distance.

COMPLEMENTARY MODIFICATION: Make sure the rotors and pads are in good condition. If your brake rotors have runout, or are too thin, this is a good time to change them. If you have less than half the friction material remaining on your brake pads, they should be changed as well.

All street cars, and especially those from General Motors, have braking systems that are set up with most of the braking force generated by the front brakes. There are some very good reasons for doing this, and most of them have to do with your safety.

Brake bias is the term used to describe the ratio between the amount of brake torque exerted on the front brakes compared with the rear. Brake bias is normally expressed as a percentage of brake torque at one end of the car to the total brake torque, as in "60 percent front."

If you should lock up the front brakes, you'll have a few problems with the steering, but nothing a reasonably skilled driver can't handle. If the rear wheels should lock up first, the rear of the car will usually swing around and try to meet the front of the car.

When the front tires lock before the rears, steering control is lost, and the car continues straight ahead. Understeer is a stable condition, and steering control can

be regained by simply reducing the pedal pressure. If, however, the rear tires lock first, the result is instantaneous oversteer, and the car will want to spin. This is more difficult to recover from, especially when entering a corner.

If all you do is drive on the street, you might not want to get involved in this project. If you lock up your rear brakes in the rain or snow, the rear end will spin around to meet the front of the car. That's not a good experience. On the other hand, if you drive in autocrosses or track events, this is a very worthwhile project.

The best way to get more braking force into the rear of your Corvette is to change the brake bias spring in the master cylinder. This spring determines the amount of hydraulic pressure that goes to the different ends of the car.

Brake people use a term called the "crack point" to describe the point at which the front and rear brake system pressures change from being the same front and rear to where (normally) the rear brake pressure increases in a smaller proportion to the front.

That means that, as you brake, the front and rear brake lines have the same pressure until you reach the crack point. At this point, the rear pressure increases in

I suggest that you start with three different colors of heat-sensitive paint. You can go out and do about five to ten laps. If your rotors have reached certain temperatures, their paint colors will have changed. This is really the most accurate way to check brake temperatures.

Changing the bias of the braking system will raise the temperature of your rear brakes. This is exactly what you want to happen. It means your rear brakes are working harder than they were before.

109

proportion with the front pressure according to the bias ratio of the valve you have. The crack point, a number such as C150, is normally stamped onto the proportioning, or bias, valve.

Adjustable Bias Valves

There are several aftermarket adjustable bias valves, including ones from Tilton, AP Racing, Wilwood, and PBR. In these designs, turning a knob or moving a lever will change your brake bias. The problem is that they do it by limiting the line pressure to the rear brakes.

The adjustable bias valve is really a dedicated race car part, and it's something you should stay away from if you use your Corvette on the street. The only cars on which you might even consider such a part are the 1984 and 1985 models.

Checking Your Bias

With all of different configurations available for the C4 Corvette, there's a very simple way to check your bias. You merely need to measure the temperature of your brake rotors after a half-dozen laps. If your braking is balanced, you should have approximately the same temperatures at both ends of the car.

The best way to do this is to check your brake rotor temperatures with heat-sensitive paint. Brake rotors cool down so fast that it's hard to get a good reading in the pits. While an infrared gun, or pyrometer, can provide you with an estimate of the temperature, it's incapable of offering anything more than an approximation.

Braking Affects Your Handling

You have to keep in mind that your Corvette is a total system. If you change the braking forces, you're going to change the handling of the car. The normal Corvette braking system actually contributes to the understeer found in the car.

If you change the bias to get more rear braking force, you're going to add a little oversteer to the Corvette. Remember, as you come into a corner with a significant amount of rear brake, the rear is going to be using up a lot of the traction circle in just braking. Simply put, a tire only has a given amount of traction that it can provide. If you use more traction in braking, you're going to have less available for turning. When you start the turn, you won't have a great deal of traction available for turning. As a result, the rear is more likely to break away from you. This is really brake-induced oversteer. Make sure that you adjust to this condition, or you'll have a very exciting day.

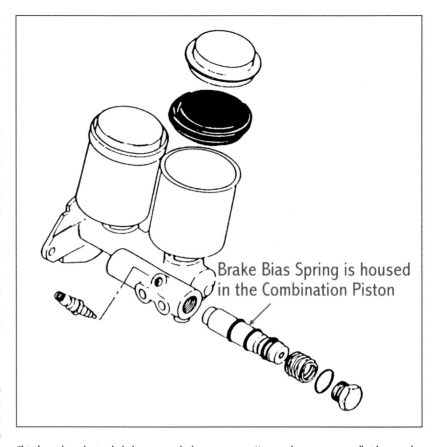

Brake Bias Spring is housed in the Combination Piston

This shows the order in which the master cylinder comes apart. You may have to use a small pick to get the piston assembly out of the bore. You can do all of this with the master cylinder in place. As difficult as it may seem, this process is actually faster than removing the master cylinder from the car.

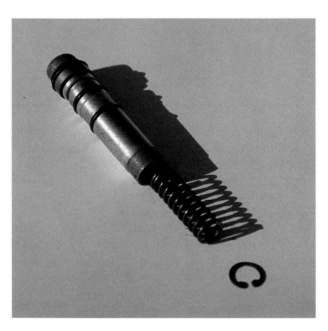

The hardest part of this whole job is compressing the new spring back into the piston. You have to compress the bias spring enough to allow installation of the circlip that holds everything together. The best way is to do this is by using a small arbor press. This will allow you to keep the spring compressed while you install the circlip that holds it in place.

Adjusting the Parking Brake

Time: 1 hour to 1 day

Tools: Screwdrivers and brake spring tool

Talent:

Applicable years: 1984 to 1996

Tab: $25 to $250

Tip: You should use your parking brake on a regular basis. This is especially true if you have a 1988 to 1996 model.

PERFORMANCE GAIN: The parking brake is an important part of the braking system. For the other brakes to work properly, It should be at peak efficiency.

COMPLEMENTARY MODIFICATION: This is a good time to replace the rear brake pads.

U se your parking brake every time you drive your Corvette. Never using your parking brake can lead to a host of little problems such as frozen cables and rusted parts that will never work properly. In later model C4 Corvettes, not using your parking brake will even lead to excess wear on the front brake pads. This is because the rear brakes will go out of adjustment. Remember, you really can't wear out your parking brake by using it, but you can cause a lot of problems by not using it.

It's even a good idea to use your parking brake before you place the transmission into park. You should shift out of park before you release the parking brake. This prevents driveline motion that could possibly strain the parking pawl in the transmission. This little technique will also help slow wear in the differential gears and universal joints. It may seem like a minor thing, but it really does help.

The C4 Corvette used two types of parking brakes. In 1967, when the Corvette went to a four-wheel disc brake system, Chevrolet created a small drum brake in the center of the brake disc. This miniature drum brake system func-

tions as a parking brake. The best way to describe this is to simply call it "a brake in the hat." You even adjust this parking brake the same way as you used to adjust the old drum brake Corvettes.

A new parking brake system was introduced in 1988 that used the rear brake pads as the parking brake. A system was designed in which a pull on the parking brake handle forced the caliper piston out and pushed the brake pads against the rear brake rotor.

1984 to 1987: Chevrolet simply continued to use the miniature drum brake inside the center of the rear disk brake rotor. When you would pull on the parking brake handle, you were actuating the small brake shoes.

Adjusting the parking brake is relatively easy. First, you should back off the cables at the equalizer bar. This ensures that everything is free to move. Then tighten the brake rotor into place using three lug nuts, making sure that the adjustment hole lines up with the hole in the hub.

Rotate the rotor until you locate the adjuster sprocket and turn it counterclockwise until the rotor can't rotate.

When you remove the rear brake rotor from the 1984 to 1987 Corvette, you'll find the parking brake mechanism. This is really a drum brake, complete with the adjuster mechanism. You might even use this as an opportunity to adjust the brake so the parking brake lever won't have to be moved quite so far. You adjust it the same way you adjust any drum brake. Use the adjuster tool while you rotate the disc. When the disc locks up, back the adjuster off three or four clicks. If you find that it's really out of adjustment, you'll have to adjust the cables using the equalizer bar.

111

This might take as many as twenty clicks on the adjuster. When the rotor is locked in position, back off the adjuster screw about eight to ten clicks. The brake disc should rotate freely now. If you have any drag, back off about two more clicks.

Now pull the parking brake lever up about two clicks. At this point, both of the drums should move freely. If you've adjusted both of the drums properly, you can go to the equalizer bar rod and take the slack out of the cable. Keep checking the rear rotors for drag when you do this. If you get any drag, you'll need to back off the equalizer nut. The idea here is to get both rear brake shoes to apply at the same time. Getting this to happen involves some back-and-forth adjustment.

The final goal is to have the parking brake assembly fully engage the rear wheels with about five clicks on the lever. If you ever have to adjust the parking brake again, simply start with the adjusters. Resist the temptation to tighten the cable at the equalizer bar. You should only need to do that for a major adjustment. The only time these brake shoes will get any real wear is if you try to drive the car with the parking brake engaged. If you keep everything properly adjusted that shouldn't even be possible.

The cable shouldn't stretch any substantial amount during its normal lifespan. The only real reason to replace a cable is it if it's frozen or rusted in place. This seldom happens in the 1984 to 1996 Corvette.

1988 to 1996: In 1988, the Corvette got the same type of rear brake caliper found on most of the other GM cars with four-wheel disc brakes. It's absolutely imperative that you use the parking brake every day with these Corvettes.

Most brake calipers are self-adjusting. One of the wonderful things about disc brakes is that the old brake adjustment procedures became a thing of the past. This changed slightly with the incorporation of the parking brake into the rear brake caliper. The interesting aspect of this system is that you can adjust the rear brake caliper by simply *using* the parking brake. Sit in the car and pull the parking brake about sixty times. Just make sure that you haven't got your foot on the brake pedal when you do this.

If this doesn't take care of things, you're going to have to remove the levers from the calipers and use an Allen wrench to move the caliper pistons into position. This is not a fun job. If you haven't done this before, you really should find a good Corvette shop that knows how to perform the work and can do it for you. Maybe once you actually have to pay someone to make the rear brakes function, you'll start using the parking brake every day.

The biggest problem with this system is that if you don't use the parking brake every day, you actually wear out the front brakes. If your Corvette's rear brakes aren't working, you're going to be putting all the braking into the front brakes. If you have to replace the pads several times before you replace the rear, you could have a problem with the rear calipers, *not* the front calipers.

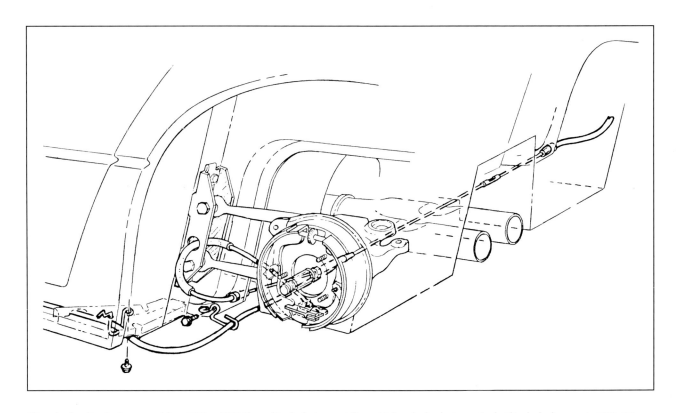

This style of parking brake was used from 1984 to 1987. The parking brake is essentially a mini drum brake that's contained within the brake rotor. In 1988, GM changed to a different style of rear caliper that incorporated the parking brake into the brake caliper.

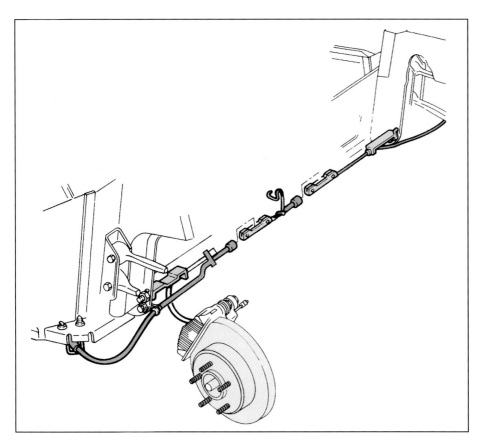

In 1988, when GM switched to a rear brake caliper that incorporated the parking brake, there was a slight change in the cable. The key thing here is to make sure all the cables are free to move in the way in which they were designed. Cars that have spent their entire lives in salt and snow usually require the most attention here. A nice Saturday morning project is to put the car up on jack stands and simply make sure everything is free to move. You can help loosen things up by using some anti-seize compound on the nuts and bolts.

Below: The rear calipers on the 1988 to 1996 Corvette are so expensive because they are very complex assemblies.

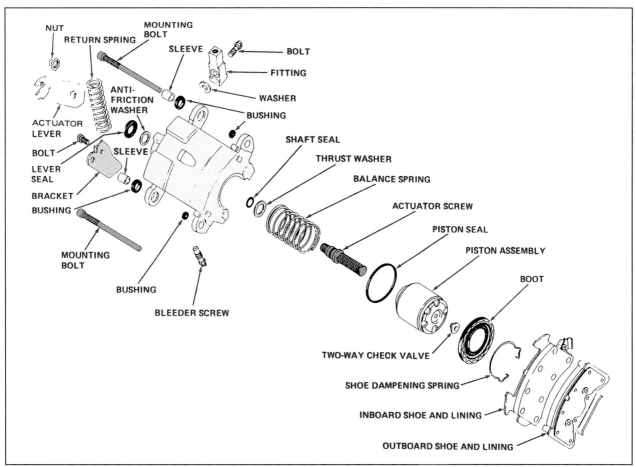

SUSPENSION

Parts courtesy Corvette Central

Replacing Rear Control Arm Bushings

 Time: 3 hours

 Tools: 1/2-inch drive metric sockets

 Talent:

 Applicable Years: 1984 to 1996

 Tab: $50

 Torque Numbers: Spindle control rod to control rod bracket—63 foot-pounds; Spindle control rod to hub carrier—140 foot-pounds

 Tip: Make sure that you use the grease that comes with the bushing kit to prevent any squeaking.

! PERFORMANCE GAIN: Improved stability in cornering, braking, and acceleration.

COMPLEMENTARY MODIFICATION: Replace other rubber suspension bushings with polyurethane as well.

I like low-frustration jobs. I also like the sort of tasks that allow me to take my Corvette apart on Saturday morning and have it back on the road by Saturday afternoon. Low-frustration jobs are even more satisfying if they improve the way my Corvette handles. Replacing the rear trailing arm bushings on your 1984 to 1996 Corvette is one of those jobs.

Four trailing arms, or spindle control rods, hold the rear axle in place. On the earlier Corvettes, a single trailing arm was used. From 1963 to 1982, an arm was attached to the frame and ran toward the rear of the car. This trailing

arm held the rear spindle in place. The C4 design is really just an improvement on that earlier effort.

An interesting aspect of this design is that a side view of the rear suspension would show that the best arrangement would be a long arm inclined to the front of the car, pointing above the center of gravity. This long arm would produce a force under acceleration that countered the body pitch caused by the center-of-gravity height. Obviously, an arm this long could never be used, so the same effect was produced by using two arms. With two arms, the virtual intersection point produces the same results as a single arm.

These four trailing arms take a tremendous amount of force every time you accelerate or brake. The purpose behind the four arms is to provide anti-dive and anti-squat control. This means that they come into play every time you accelerate or apply the brakes. Just consider how many times your Corvette has accelerated and then braked in the last 100,000 miles.

Stop and think about what happens as you place your foot on the brakes. As the trailing arm moves forward, it compresses the bushings on both ends of the trailing arm. When you accelerate, it does the very same thing except it goes in the opposite direction. This means that these trailing arm bushings get a tremendous amount of use.

The factory originals were designed to take care of the necessary forces, and, at the same time, transmit very little noise. The factory had a different set of priorities than you might have. As you accumulated the miles on your Corvette, the rubber bushings got a little softer with age, and deterioration set in. The anti-dive and anti-squat

You'll need a block of wood and a jack for this little trick. If you push just right on the rear arm of the hub, you can get everything aligned. The bolts should all just slide out. If you have to force something, do this by moving the jack up or down slightly.

115

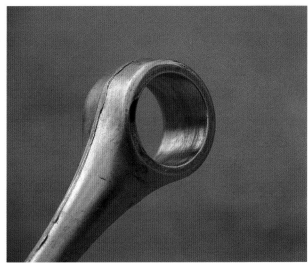

While the trailing arm is off the car, you can drill holes all around the bushing. If you drill enough holes, you'll be able to easily push the old factory bushing out of the arm. Just make sure you don't drill into the aluminum arm.

Once you get the old bushing out of the arm, make sure you clean the area of all the old adhesive and rubber. The new bushings simply won't work properly if you leave any of the old bushing in place.

SUSPENSION

quality in your Corvette is now different from what existed when it left the Bowling Green plant.

You've lost a little consistency in your suspension. Since the bushings softened, they now need to compress before any of the anti-dive and anti-squat geometry actually takes effect. If you replace the bushings, everything will take hold just a little bit sooner. Better yet, it will react the same way every time.

The good thing about simply replacing the rubber bushings with polyurethane equivalents is that you can take things apart without having a slew of parts all over your garage. If you want, you can do one side of the car each week. This isn't one of those jobs that requires taking your car out of service for weeks at a time.

Chevrolet doesn't sell trailing arm bushings separately. Your local Chevrolet dealer will only sell you the complete trailing arm.

There are also adjustable trailing arms on the market today. These adjustable trailing arms have Heim joints on either end of the rod, allowing you to either shorten or lengthen the rod. Since both of the rods are adjustable, you can lengthen the lower rod and shorten the upper rod. You're controlling anti-dive and anti-squat by changing the nature of the hypothetical triangle.

These Heim-jointed units are wonderful if you know what you're doing and can get enough seat time at the track to actually sort everything out. There are computer programs available to help you make the necessary changes, but you have to have a really good understanding of what's going on with your suspension to maximize their use. For most of us, the polyurethane replacement bushings work just fine.

This is the new polyurethane bushing. Before you install it, make sure you cover any contact points with the lubricant that's included in the bushing kit. You should use the lubricant on the metal insert and on the area where the two halves contact in the center of the bushing.

PROJECT 46
Lowering the Rear

 Time: 1 hour

 Tools: 1/2-inch drive metric sockets

 Talent:

 Applicable Years: 1984 to 1996

 Tab: $50

 Tip: Make the front of the car slightly lower than the rear. You want a very mild nose-down attitude on your C4 Corvette.

 PERFORMANCE GAIN: Handling will be improved, and the car just looks better when it's lower to the ground.

COMPLEMENTARY MODIFICATION: Lower the front of the car by replacing the spring bushings.

There are really only three ways to improve Corvette handling. The first way is to widen the track, or put the tires out farther from the center of the car. The second is to add larger sway bars to control body roll. The third way to improve handling is to lower the car's center of gravity. To do this, you'll need to get the whole car lower to the ground.

Lowering the rear is the least expensive and easiest of the three options. The C4 Corvette handles best with a slight nose-down attitude. I prefer to run about two degrees of rake, with the front being lower. If you do this

Polyurethane spring bushings really don't add anything to the performance of your Corvette, but they last longer than the stock parts. The important part of the lowering kit is the longer bolt. The original bolt uses a cotter pin to make sure the bolt doesn't back off the nut. All of the aftermarket parts use a Nylock nut for the same purpose.

backwards and have the rear lower than the front, you're going to have problems.

With the 1984 to 1996 Corvette, getting the correct ride height is absolutely critical. You have to get the ride height balanced all the way around. You can adjust this ride height from the rear spring height.

Not only is ride height absolutely critical to the C4 Corvette, it's also very difficult to get correct. Ride height issues used to drive the Bowling Green assembly plant crazy. That's the reason why ride height adjustment on the C5 Corvette is so easy to perform. After fighting with the C4 ride height for more than a decade, the engineering team wasn't about to make the same mistake with the new C5 Corvette.

The actual work to lower the C4 rear is very simple. The idea is to get the ends of the rear spring to ride lower in relationship to the chassis than they normally do. This means you're going to need longer bolts at the outer attachment points. The good part is that all you have to do is replace the two stock bolts with longer bolts. Every Corvette supplier in the world sells a kit that contains all the parts you'll need. The kits normally cost less than $40.

When you order the lowering kit, you should make sure you also get the polyurethane spring cushions. There's very little actual performance gain from using the polyurethane cushions, but since they hold up so much better, it would be foolish to use the bushings that were originally installed on your Corvette.

Once you have the new bolts and bushings in place, you need to take a few minutes to adjust the ride height. Find a handy place on the frame and mark it with a yellow paint stripe. Make sure that the left and right stripes are at the same point on the frame.

Now measure the distance from the ground to the bottom of the frame at the point where you've placed the yellow stripe. This distance should be as close as you can

SUSPENSION

117

The car is supported by jack stands placed under the frame. Clamp a small piece of wood on the spring—this will keep the jack from sliding. Then, as you raise the jack, the pressure will be removed from the nut and bolt on the end of the spring. This allows you to remove the stock bolt and spring cushions.

The ride height is adjusted by changing the distance between the head of the bolt and the nut on the lower end. You should drive the car a mile or so between adjustments so that everything settles. Make your measurements from a given point on the frame.

possibly get it. If one side is significantly different from the other side, move the nut on the spring bolt up or down until both sides of the frame are an equal distance from the ground.

Make sure that you do this with the car on a level piece of ground. Measuring the ride height with the car on an incline isn't going to do much good. Every time you make a change, make sure that you take the new measurement from the same place you took the old measurement. Four strips of tape on the garage floor work nicely to remind you where the car was located for the previous measurement.

Every time you change the position of either nut on one of the rear bolts you'll need to drive the car around the block to settle the suspension. Remember, an object at rest tends to stay at rest. You really need to get the car settled before you take any new measurements. That's why you placed the tape stripes on the floor. If you place the car in the same location each time you make an adjustment, you're going to get more accurate measurements.

When you run track events, you're generally all alone in the car. You might consider putting several hundred pounds of sandbags in the driver's seat while you adjust the ride height. You could also get a friend of similar weight to sit in the car as you check the ride height. This

allows you to get the ride height correct for the car as it's driven down the road.

The easiest way to check the rake on the car is to park it on a level surface and stand back about twenty-five feet. The car should have a slight nose-down attitude. You can get crazy and check this angle with a digital level if you wish. You're looking for a one- to two-degree angle from the front to the rear.

Not only should the ride height be equal from side to side, but the nose should also be slightly lower than the rear. I find this little protractor makes measurement very simple. If the nose of the C4 is higher than the rear, you'll never get optimum handling from the car.

Lowering the Front

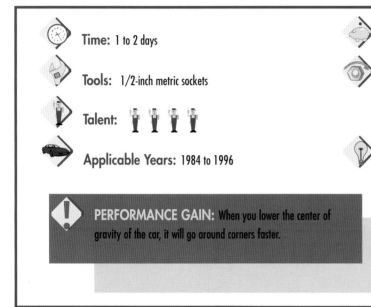

Time: 1 to 2 days

Tools: 1/2-inch metric sockets

Talent: 👤 👤 👤 👤

Applicable Years: 1984 to 1996

PERFORMANCE GAIN: When you lower the center of gravity of the car, it will go around corners faster.

Tab: $25 to $150

Torque: Make sure you check the factory manual — there are a lot of bolts and nuts in this project. You want everything tightened properly here.

Tip: Consider purchasing the tool designed to release the belt tensioner. This works very nicely and is cheap. Otherwise use a 1/2-inch breaker bar.

COMPLEMENTARY MODIFICATION: Make sure you lower the rear at the same time. That's a much easier task, thank goodness.

This is a project that you should carefully consider. There is a tremendous amount of effort involved and the gains are pretty minimal. The most you're going to drop the car is about one inch. That's a lot if you're a racer or you run a bunch of track events. If you're a cruiser or waxer, it's not much at all. No one will even be able to tell that you did anything.

There's another problem with this project. The C4 Corvette likes a slight nose-down attitude. That ride height attitude is really more important than how low the car is. If you drop the front, you're going to need to drop the rear as well. The problem is getting the rear down low enough to get that one- to two-degree front-to-rear rake on the car. The bolts that are sold by the Corvette mail-order guys to lower the rear aren't quite long enough to get that desired angle.

Now that I've explained why you should skip this project, let's talk about why you might consider doing it. If you're going to be rebuilding the front suspension of your C4 Corvette, you'll find it worthwhile to lower the front of the car.

• Here is the process to follow to execute this task:

• Unplug the wiring to the speed sensors. They're in the back of the wheel bearings. Just unplug the two-wire clip connector and move the speed sensor connectors out of the way so they won't get damaged.

• Remove the lower bolts from the front sway arm linkage to lower control arms on both sides of the car (15mm). You may need to wiggle the sway arm to get these bolts out of the sway arm linkage. Do both sides of the sway bar at this point.

• Remove the upper nut and washer from the shock absorbers.

• Place your jack in the same plane as the spring—meaning left to right and **not** front to back. Raise the control arm about two inches and remove the shocks from the lower control arms.

• Next you can remove the block that holds the spring to the frame. It's just in front of the motor mounts in the crossmember that the spring runs through.

• Now remove the cotter pin and castle nut (22-millimeter) from the lower ball joint. Break the lower ball joint loose with a ball joint separator. If you don't have one, purchase a ball joint separator. Don't, under any circumstances, bang on your control arm with a hammer.

• After the ball joint is loose, get the upper control arm and spindle out of the way. Get a 1x4-inch piece of wood that is about one yard long. Place it across the top of the fender well, front to back. Take some rope and tie the upper control arm/ hub assembly up out of the way. Get it as high as you can. Make sure you don't kink the brake line as you raise it up.

• Now slowly lower the control arm.

• The control arms should now be floating on the spring and should be pointing down at roughly a 45-degree angle. The crossbrace behind the passenger side rear lower control arm bolt has to be removed. There are two

119

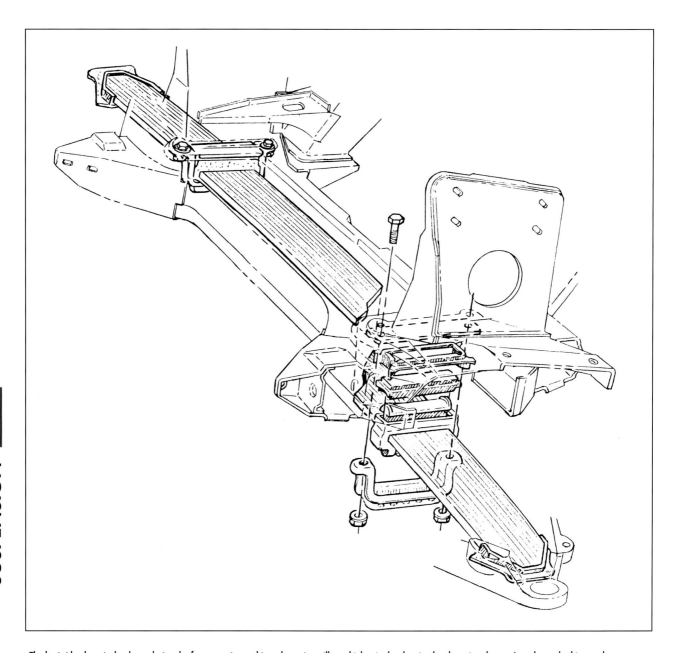

The basic idea here is that by replacing the factory spring cushions the spring will rest higher in the chassis, thus lowering the car. In order to do this, you have to remove the spring. Once you have the control arms apart, you can start to attack the two brackets shown in this drawing.

13-millimeter bolts on the side frames, two 15-millimeter bolts in the center crossmember frame, and one 18-millimeter bolt under the engine mount.

• Make sure the spring isn't under tension. You can do this by pushing down on one of the control arms. You should be able to move the control arm about 3/4-inch up and down if the spring tension has been removed.

• Remove the passenger side lower control arm from the car.

• Slide the spring out of the crossmember frame from the passenger side.

• The rubber bumpers need to be cut off the top of the transverse spring and replaced with the smaller urethane wedges included in the lowering kit. You can cut the rubber bumpers off from the top of the spring and glue the urethane wedges in their place.

• It may be difficult to get the new spring lined up left to right when putting the car back together. This is because of the uneven pressure exerted on the spring as it is worked back up into place one side at a time. While it's fairly easy to move with the control arms down, any tension at all on the spring will make it difficult, if not impossible, to move.

• Tighten the lower control arm bolts to 45 foot-pounds and start putting everything back together.

Finally, drive the car around the block to seat the bushings on the control arms. Then tighten the control arm bolts to 96 foot-pounds. This prevents the bushings from being put under a torsional load.

Changing the Spring?

As long as you're going to all this trouble to remove the front spring, you need to consider if you want to put the same front spring back into the car. Then there's the obvious question: "If not this spring, then which one?" Remember, there are only two good reasons for lowering the front of the C4. You either want your Corvette to look cooler, or you want to go faster.

Let's deal with the cosmetic issue first. If you're going to stay on the street and do cruise nights, you want a very comfortable car. That means you want the softest possible spring. The 1986 and 1987 Corvettes have some of the softer front springs of any of the C4 cars. If you have the Z51 suspension in your car, these springs would be the way to go.

If you're more interested in going faster, you need to consider the type of driving you will be doing. On the racetrack, you want the softest possible spring you can find. You should never control body roll with springs. That's why you have sway bars on your car. It's interesting that the road race or track event guys want the very same soft springs that the cruisers want.

The folks who drive Solo 2 cars still prefer the very stiff springs. They're still using the spring to control body roll. They're relying on the theory that the quick transitions of the Solo 2 course require the extra control. Some of these guys are pretty fast with stiff springs.

Like everything else, make sure you talk to a variety of people before you start exchanging springs. When it comes to running on a racetrack, always ask the fast guys what they have. The interesting thing is that the fast guys are generally more open about telling what they've tried in the past and sharing how they like their current setup.

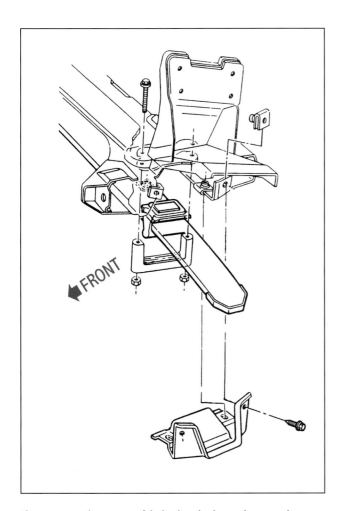

These are the new spring cushions you get in the mail-order lowering kit. You'll probably never spend so much time (or money on labor charges) to install such an inexpensive part.

This gives you a close-up view of the brackets that have to be removed. Nothing is very hard about this project. It's just that there is so much to remove — and so much to put back together.

PROJECT 48
Front Shock Replacement

 Time: 1 hour

 Tools: 17-millimeter 3/8-inch socket

 Talent:

 Applicable Years: 1984 to 1996

 Tab: $100 to $2,500

 Torque: Lower shock mounting bolt—19 foot-pounds

 Tip: Tighten the upper mounting bolt until the rubber pads begin to bulge, then stop. This final tightening should be done with the car on the ground.

 PERFORMANCE GAIN: When it comes to things that you can replace on your Corvette, shock absorbers may make the single biggest difference in the way your car runs.

COMPLEMENTARY MODIFICATION: You might want to consider polyurethane bushings for the front sway bar at the same time. It's a slightly more difficult job, but, as long as you have the car on jack stands and the wheels removed, it'll only take a few more hours.

This is an easy job and takes very little time. I would do both the front and rear shocks at the same time. You'll spend more time thinking about which brand of shock to purchase than it takes to replace them.

The front shocks are not as critical to ride control as the rear shocks are. Here I'm talking about the ride quality on the street, not on the track. There doesn't seem to be very much difference from one brand to the next when it comes to ride quality on the front shocks. The rear shocks make a noticeable difference in ride quality. Therefore, you might want to select a brand of shock based on what's best for the rear. I've had dozens of different shocks on my car, and the best all-around shocks came from TPIS in Minnesota. They aren't the best shock in any single category but they are certainly a great all-around shock. Plus, they're reasonably priced.

The best way to make your purchase is simply to buy what your friends and neighbors are using on their Corvettes. Unless you drive at the track, you'll see very little difference between the various brands. While you're shopping, you might also look for one with a lifetime guarantee. Almost everyone offers one these days.

The front is easier to work with than the rear. Place your jack stands under the frame of the car and let the front suspension hang free. Now start at the top of the shock absorber and remove the upper nut. Most shock absorbers have some sort of arrangement where you can hold the shaft while you loosen the mounting bolt. In the case of these Bilsteins, you'll need a very small wrench to hold the shaft in place while you release the nut. If you have Koni shocks, you'll need an Allen wrench to do the same thing. If all else fails, people have been know to use Vise-Grips to hold the shaft stationary while removing it.

SUSPENSION

122

The lower mount on the 1984 to 1987 Corvette consists of two bolts that screw into captive nuts. The easiest way to get to these nuts is to use a socket with a universal and a long extension. With the suspension in full droop mode, you can thread the shock bolt out toward the front of the car.

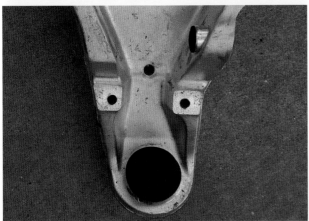

In 1988, the suspension was changed and a nut and bolt arrangement was used. Instead of being assembled with a number of parts, the later control arms are a one-piece design. The 1984 to 1987 control arms aren't interchangeable with the 1988 to 1996 control arms, but the shock replacement technique is the same.

You only want to tighten the nut until you get a slight bulge on the rubber cushions. There's no need to clamp down with excessive force. Once you lower the car back onto the ground, you should look at the cushions and see if they need any additional tightening. Remember, we're talking about a slight bulge here.

PROJECT 49
Rear Shock Replacement

SUSPENSION

 Time: 30 minutes

 Tools: Metric sockets and a 1/2-inch breaker bar

 Talent:

 Applicable Years: 1984 to 1996

 Tab: $250 to $1,000

 Torque: Lower shock mount—61 foot-pounds; Upper shock bolt (late)—19 foot-pounds

 Tip: Raise and lower the car to get the shock mounting holes aligned.

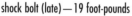

 PERFORMANCE GAIN: Even the inexpensive shocks will improve your handling.

COMPLEMENTARY MODIFICATION: Use polyurethane bushings in the lower shock mounts.

Jack up one side of the Corvette and place a jack stand under the rear hub assembly. The reason for this is that you're going to move the car up and down slightly as you install the shock. Gas shocks are almost impossible to compress by hand. It's a lot easier to move the car up and down than it is to compress the shock during installation.

This is the upper mount on the rear of the early C4 Corvette. You might need a small plastic hammer to drive the bolt out once the nut is removed on these early mounting systems.

This is one of those fun jobs that allows you to improve your Corvette and, at the same time, spend a pleasant day hanging out in the garage. Changing the rear shocks on the 1984 to 1996 Corvette doesn't take much time at all, but your wife doesn't know that. I've always liked using the KYB shocks for just about any car I've owned, and I use them on one of my Corvettes. I have a couple of sets of Bilsteins for my 1985 Corvette and love them as well. The only shocks I currently use at the track are Bilstein. That's mainly because Bilstein created a special set for track use. Plus, the company even sent me a dyno printout with the shocks.

There are two mounting arrangements used on the C4 Corvettes. The early cars, those made between 1984 and 1987, use a conventional bracket at the top for the shock. The mounting bolts run horizontally through a bracket and the top of the shock. They present no problem at all in installation. I usually take the top bolt out before I

remove the lower bolt, but removing them in either order works fine.

One thing you need to watch for on these early cars is that the nut doesn't loosen on this upper bolt. This is fairly common on the early cars. If you hear a clunking sound

The upper mount was changed in 1988 to this type of mount which used two bolts, but the process for changing the shock is the same.

coming from the rear of your car, take the rear wheel off and tighten the bolt. You might find yourself doing this once a year. On the other hand, every time you take a rear wheel off the car, tighten this upper shock mount as a routine item.

On the later cars, there are two bolts that have to be removed. Once these are removed, the bracket, which is part of the shock, drops down. This is also a very easy shock to work with.

One thing you should consider is using a polyurethane bushing on the lower shock mount. The C4 was designed to use a very solid shock mount. The factory went with a very stiff rubber compound. You can improve on this by using the bushings from Energy Suspension. It's simply a matter of pressing the bushing out and then installing the polyurethane in its place.

Rear shocks are much more critical to ride quality than the front shocks. I can put almost any brand of shock on the front of the car and it makes very little difference. It's a whole different matter with the rear of the car. I'll often leave the front track shocks on the car all season and never notice that I've done this. If I leave the rear track shocks in place, I can feel every pebble in the road. It seems that about 70 percent of the ride quality in the C4 is determined by the rear shocks. The fronts seem to make only a minimal difference.

Above: With the top bolt removed, you can remove the lower nut that holds the shock to the bottom of the hub assembly. The higher your Corvette is off the ground, the easier it is to remove this nut. A large 1/2-inch breaker bar with a socket on the end helps a great deal.

Mount the new shock on the lower stud and place the nut and washer in place. Then gently lower the car back on the jack stand so that the upper mounting hole is lined up with the holes in the bracket. With the later Corvettes, start the two upper mounting bolts, but leave them loose until you get the lower mount in place with the nut and washer.

You can purchase polyurethane bushings for the lower shock mount, and any local shop with a small press can install them. The advantage with these bushings is that they last longer than the standard rubber bushings. There's no actual gain in performance, but these bushings do help to maintain the rear shock performance as you roll up the miles.

SUSPENSION

PROJECT 50
Sway Bar Choices and Replacement

 Time: 1 to 2 hours

 Tools: 1/2-inch drive metric sockets

 Talent:

 Applicable Years: 1984 to 1996

PERFORMANCE GAIN: You will get less body roll when you go around a corner.

 Tab: $25 to $150

 Torque: End links for front sway bar — 35 foot-pounds

 Tip: Just install the biggest sway bars you can find, and your C4 Corvette will out-handle all the other Corvettes — including the C5.

COMPLEMENTARY MODIFICATION: Install polyurethane bushings in all the sway bar links.

SUSPENSION

There were two different styles of sway bars used on the C4. Most of the C4 Corvettes used solid bars in varying diameters. Beginning in 1986, the front bars on cars with the base suspension were converted to a tubular design. The interesting thing is that, while the street cars got tubular bars, all the high-performance Corvettes stayed with the solid bars.

I'm a big advocate of large sway bars. If you want your Corvette to really handle well, use the 30-millimeter sway bar up front and couple it with a 24- or 26-millimeter bar in the rear. This will solve all of the body roll problems you might have in a corner—especially if you switch to polyurethane bushings at the end links.

At the risk of being repetitive, I have to point out that you shouldn't be trying to control body roll with stiff springs. Springs simply hold the car off the ground. Sway bars are the way you control body roll in a turn. Sway bars don't detract from ride quality either—at least not very much. Big sway bars will allow you to improve the handling of your Corvette at almost no cost to the ride quality.

There are no aftermarket bars worth considering. Several companies have tried to make sway bars for the C4, but none has really been successful. The big factory bars are wonderful and are as much sway bar as you really need.

The only real alternative to the big factory bars is to have a race shop fabricate a set of bars for the front and rear of your Corvette.

The end of the sway bars remained the same through the production of the C4 Corvette. This is the end link for the rear sway bar. It's pretty easy to replace the original bushings with the polyurethane replacements and well worth the effort.

That option aside, your best plan would be to visit salvage yards that have C4 Corvettes. Look around at what they have available and start measuring. Take a set of calipers with you and actually measure the sway bar.

Place the sway bar on a flat surface. The bar should lie flat with both ends the same distance from the surface. A bent sway bar will cause endless handling problems. Since the end links on the C4 are fixed, there's no way to make adjustments. They're either flat or they aren't.

Before you part with any money, always place the sway bar on a flat piece of concrete to make sure the bar isn't bent. Installing a bent bar is a sure road to frustration. Take a few minutes and make sure there's nothing wrong with the salvage-yard special you've chosen.

If you already have a solid front sway bar on your car, you won't need any of the end links. The end links are the same for all the C4 Corvettes. There's a really strange link that was installed on the front in 1984, but even that bolts up just fine.

The key bushing problem is on the front sway bars. The two bushings that hold the sway bar to the chassis seem to collect water, and this sets up a rusting situation on the sway bar. The tolerances are so close here that the rust buildup causes binding in the bushings. Before you install the bar, make sure that these two areas are absolutely clean. Don't put a lot of paint on the areas that fit in the bushings. The last thing you need here is additional thickness.

Here's a list of the variety of stock sway bars that were offered by the factory.

Rear Sway Bar Choices (All Solid)
19-millimeter
20-millimeter
22-millimeter
24-millimeter
26-millimeter

Front Sway Bar Choices (Solid)
24-millimeter
30-millimeter

Front Sway Bar Choices (Tubular)
24-millimeter
26-millimeter

Remove these end links first by removing the upper bolts on both sides. Now grab the sway bar by the arm and see if you can move the bar through its rotation.

Moisture can build up in the rubber bushings that mount to the chassis, and the sway bar will develop a lot of unnecessary friction between the mounts and the bar. This is no big deal. It simply means you're going to do a little extra cleaning and sanding. The rear sway bar doesn't usually have this problem, but you should probably check it as well.

You simply need to put the largest available bar on the front. If you have a solid sway bar, use the 30-millimeter. If you have the tubular bar, find a 26-millimeter bar and install it. Just keep searching until you find the largest bar made by GM.

Now with the front choice settled, you can do exactly what the Corvette engineering team did with the high-performance packages. You're going to tune your suspension with the rear sway bar. The basic Corvette is your traditional understeering American car. That means if you're really aggressive going into a turn, the front tires will break away first.

Understeer, or push, is not a bad thing. At least you're going to see what you're about to hit. Oversteer means the rear wheels will break away before the fronts. Then the rear of your car will come around on you. With oversteer, you back into whatever you're going to hit.

If you only drive on the street, you think that most of this information isn't very important. If you drive on the track, you'll find that it gets to be real important. You want to dial the understeer out of the Corvette without going over the edge into oversteer. Actually, you want a car that will slide all four wheels at the same time.

If you're a track guy, try to locate a 26-millimeter rear sway bar. This won't be an easy bar to find. It was used on very few cars, and even fewer of them have ended up in the salvage yards. The Grand Sports, the ZR-1s, and the Corvette Challenge cars all used this bar. In addition, the 1990 R9G cars—all twenty-three of them made—used this rear sway bar. You can see that Corvette engineering felt that a 30-millimeter front and a 26-millimeter rear bar was the way to go for serious performance.

Most likely you're going to end up with a 24-millimeter rear sway bar. This is very common and can be found in any number of salvage yards. The performance difference between the two sizes is minimal.

I finally decided to do something about the rust build up on the sway bar and installed a grease fitting in the bracket. I drilled a hole in the polyurethane bushing so that grease can get between the sway bar and bushing. Now the sway bar can move freely in the bushings. If your front sway bar doesn't move freely in the two mounting brackets, it's like having an extra set of springs in the front of the car.

This is the end link for the front sway bar. If you've purchased polyurethane bushings for this application, take some time and measure the size of the bushing sleeve's inner diameter. The original mount uses a metric bolt in this position, but for some reason a few aftermarket companies have the bushing sleeve sized for a standard inch diameter. This means the original bolt is too small for the application. Everything will bolt up, but there will be almost 1/16 of an inch of play in the final link assembly. If this happens, all you have to do is go to the local hardware store and purchase the correct-diameter bolt. Then drill out the holes in the end link to accept this standard bolt size. It's not a huge job—just a source of aggravation. If you don't check this measurement carefully, you could end up with worse performance instead of improved cornering from the polyurethane bushings.

Installing Upper Control Arm Spacers

Time: 1 hour

Tools: Deep sockets with a 1/2-inch torque wrench

Talent:

Applicable Years: 1984 to 1987

Tab: $75

Torque: Upper control arm bolts — 37 foot-pounds

Tip: It's easier to put a deep socket on the upper control arm bolts if you jack the side of the car up slightly. Also, don't forget that you'll definitely need to have the car aligned after installing the spacers.

PERFORMANCE GAIN: These new spacers will allow for more front wheel caster, which, in turn, will give your Corvette more straight-line stability.

COMPLEMENTARY MODIFICATION: Have the alignment shop add about a half-degree of negative camber at all four corners.

One of the keys to improving your Corvette's performance is the handling. A great chassis will help you go faster than any amount of horsepower. The key to improving the handling is the alignment. There are some basic mechanical limitations for changing the alignment settings, especially on the early cars.

In 1984, the C4 Corvette used very little caster and not a whole lot of negative camber. This was due, in part, to the thinking about chassis settings in the very early eighties. And part of it was due to the nature of the tires on these early cars. As the C4 evolved over the years, the suspension alignments changed as well.

With today's modern tires, you can move the settings around to maximize how the Corvette uses these tires. Before we talk about making the changes, let's look at the setting. Caster is one of the most neglected settings. Basically, caster describes how far the center of the upper ball joint is forward of the lower ball joint. The setting, like most alignment settings, is expressed in degrees.

The more caster you have in your car, the straighter it will go down the road. There's a point of diminishing returns, however. As you increase the amount of caster, you're also increasing the amount of effort that it takes to steer the car. With manual steering, this was a problem. Now that almost all cars have power steering, it's really not a concern.

European cars have always used a huge amount of caster. This is one reason that vehicles like Mercedes, BMW, and Porsche have always felt a little different when going down the road. Back in the seventies, John Delran built an Impala sedan with a lot of caster, and driving it almost made you feel like you were driving a Mercedes.

Now let's look at camber, which is the way the wheels tilt. Negative camber means the top of the wheel tilts in, and positive camber means the top of the wheel tilts out. One of the secrets for performance driving is to increase the amount of negative camber.

Here are the upper control arm spacers that are used to set the initial caster settings. As the Corvette was developed over the years, the engineers kept adding more caster to the front alignment. Eventually they went to these thicker spacers as a way of getting the proper alignment. You'll notice my little, white paint stripe on both the spacer and the alignment shims. I always use paint stripes on every suspension component. That way I can tell at a glance if something has changed. It's also a good way to verify if the alignment shop actually aligned your car.

SUSPENSION

With the early cars, you're limited in how much camber and caster you can get into the front wheel alignment. The good part is that you can readily fix this by substituting some upper control arm spacers from a later C4.

Open the hood and look at the point where the upper control arm mounts. You'll notice some small aluminum spacers. When the assembly plant decided to add more caster and camber, it found that the easiest way to make the change was to simply increase the width of the spacers in the upper control arms.

You can make the same change by removing the narrow ones that came on your car and then replacing them with the ones designed for the later cars. I would start with the left side because it's easier.

Take a minute to loosen the upper control nuts. It's a lot easier to get them loose while the car is on the ground than when it's up in the air on a jack stand. Don't remove the bolts; just get them loose.

All you have to do now is jack the corner of the car up and remove one bolt at a time. Take the bolt out, replace the spacer, and then tighten the nut reasonably tight. If you do one bolt at a time, you shouldn't have any problem. If you remove both bolts at the same time, there's a good chance everything will fall away from the car. That's not a lot of fun.

Now that you've practiced on the left side of the car, you can go around to the other side. After you've loosened the two nuts, your next job here is going to be removing both the serpentine belt and the belt tensioner. You simply can't remove the front control arm bolt unless you remove the tensioner. Trust me – I've tried. The good part is that there's only one bolt holding the tensioner in place.

From this point on, everything is the same as it was on the left side. Remember, you don't want to totally remove the control arm. Just get the bolts moved far enough to the center of the car so you can install the new spacers.

For all of you who want to run Solo 2 type events, you can simply remove the spacers altogether. This works really well for Solo 2 since you get maximum negative camber, and the caster isn't a real concern because of the slow speeds. The best part is you can actually do this at the event, and then put the spacers back in place before you drive home.

Just remember to put the thin alignment shims back in the proper place. It helps if you paint the left side and the right side different colors. Most of the seasoned folks can do both sides in less than twenty minutes. Then they simply drive home with a nice street alignment.

It's a lot easier to tighten the upper control arm bolts if you raise the car a little with your jack. When the car is off the ground, the lower control arm droops just enough to let you use a 1/2-inch-deep socket on the nuts. You can also use a torque wrench with an extension. Whenever you use an extension with a torque wrench, use the shortest possible extension. Keep in mind that, if these bolts loosen up, you will have a dangerous car, and all of your alignment shims will fall out. You really don't want to have to pay for yet another wheel alignment.

PROJECT 52
Replacing Front Control Arm Bushings

 Time: 4 to 6 hours

 Tools: Metric wrenches

 Talent:

PERFORMANCE GAIN: Improved handling

 Applicable Years: 1984 to 1996

 Tab: $200 to $400

 Torque: Upper control arm bolt—37 foot-pounds; Lower control arm bolt—82 foot-pounds

COMPLEMENTARY MODIFICATION: This is a good time to think about lowering the front of the car and replacing the lower ball joints. As long as you have to remove the lower control arm from the car, it's not a bad idea to have the entire control arm rebuilt.

This is going to be a big deal. There's no easy way to replace your front control arm bushings. If you have to pay someone to execute the job, you're going to be in for an expensive modification. On the other hand, if you do the work yourself, you can hold the costs to a reasonable level.

The good part is that very few C4 Corvettes actually wear out the lower control arm bushings. The upper ones are starting to go bad as the cars age, but the lower bushings are generally in good shape. Unless you check them yourself, these lower bushings are seldom checked for wear.

The bad news for the restoration folks is that the original bushings simply aren't sold separately. If you have

worn-out lower control arm bushings, you'll need to purchase an entire control arm. Four brand-new control arms will cost more than a thousand dollars. Remember, no one ever said that C4 restoration would be cheap.

The good news is that you can do this project for a whole lot less money if you aren't worried about keeping everything original. You can save money by removing the control arms and replacing the bushings with polyurethane units.

It is very easy to determine if you need new bushings. If you see a gap in the upper control arm where the bushing used to be, you need new bushings. The irony here is that the lower ball joints are the first to wear out. That means you might end up rebuilding the lower control arms before you tackle the upper control arms. On my personal car, the upper control arm bushings went bad before the lower ball joint wore out. That may have been because I normally grease the ball joints every ninety days.

You can replace the upper arms at one time and then wait until later to do the lower control arms. If you decide to replace the lower control arm bushings, you need to make a couple of fairly serious decisions. The entire lower control arm will be removed from the car. If you go to this much trouble, you should probably consider replacing

There were only two different control arms used in the C4 Corvette, and they weren't made to be interchangeable. There was a change in the chassis design for the 1988 model year. A lot of the reason behind the change had to do with simplifying the production process. The revised lower control arms had fewer pieces attached. The control arm shown here fits the 1984 to 1987 Corvettes.

131

both the lower ball joints and the bushings in the lower control arm.

When you take on a project like this, it's difficult to know when to stop working. If you have the lower control arms off the car, it's not a big deal to install a lowering kit for the front suspension. That means you should install the lowering kit in the rear of the car as well. It's a pretty easy task, but you'll come back to the question, "When is enough, enough?"

Any number of companies can rebuild your control arms for you. Any machine shop can replace the ball joints. It's the bushing removal that they may not want to deal with—although it's not a terribly difficult job. To make things easier, you can order the control arm bushings from someone like Energy Suspension and then take the control arms, and all the new parts, to your local shop. You should be able to pick up the completed control arms the next day.

Generally, I suggest doing a total rebuild if your Corvette has more than 100,000 miles. If you're just installing polyurethane bushings as an improvement, make sure you check the condition of the ball joints before you take anything apart.

Offset Bushings

Offset bushings are for people who are into track events. With the stock bushing location, you're limited in the amount of negative camber you can get into the front suspension. Normally, the lower mounting bolt is centered in the control arm holes. Then you adjust the camber by using the shims at the upper control arm.

Offset bushings push the control arm farther to the outside of the car. This means that you have the negative camber already built into the system. With offset bushings, you use the normal shim adjustment, but you're starting at a point with a lot more negative camber. You really only need about -2 degrees with the C4 Corvette, but it's nice to have the larger range.

The offset lower polyurethane bushing moves the range of negative camber adjustment into a different area. The starting point for your camber adjustment with offset bushings is almost at -2 degrees. This means you can actually get about -4 degrees of negative camber into the front suspension. You many never need that much, but at least it will be available to you. On the other hand, -2 degrees of camber is too much for normal street driving. The amount of adjustment is the same regardless of which bushings you use – what's different is where the starting point is.

The key to this task is figuring out how much negative camber you actually need to go fast. The best way to determine this is to just keeping adding negative camber until the tire temperature readings equalize across the tread after driving the car on the limit. The C4 Corvette doesn't seem to need a lot of negative camber because its tires are so wide. You can get almost -2 degrees of camber with the stock setup, and that works fine for most applications.

I would only install the offset bushings on a car that gets a lot of track time. They're just not necessary, nor desirable, on the average street Corvette.

Drilling out the old bushings is still the best way to remove them. Do this very carefully since you don't want to remove any of the aluminum control am in the process. Once you have a few holes drilled in the bushing it should be easy to push out using two large sockets and a bench vise.

This control arm was used from 1988 to 1996. The sway bar connection was cast into the lower control arm. There are a lot of other differences between the two versions of control arms, but that's the one you can see most easily with the naked eye. Remember, the two versions are not interchangeable.

These control arms can take a tremendous beating. One way to approach this job is to pick up a set of control arms in a salvage yard and then send them out to be reconditioned with new ball joints and bushings. When they're returned, you can start the disassembly/assembly project.

SUSPENSION

PROJECT 53
Replacing the Rear Spring

 Time: 2 to 3 hours

 Tools: Metric wrenches

 Talent:

 Applicable Years: 1984 to 1996

 Tab: $150 to $200

 Torque: Rear spring anchor plate bolts—37 foot-pounds

 Tip: This job is a lot easier if you simply remove the spare tire carrier.

PERFORMANCE GAIN: Changing the rear spring will make a tremendous difference in the ride quality and cornering performance of the C4 Corvette.

COMPLEMENTARY MODIFICATION: This is a good time to install the longer spring bolts that are used to lower the rear of the car. Remember, you don't have to actually lower the car. You can also set the rear ride height at the stock level if you wish. Using the longer bolts just ensures that it can be easily lowered in the future.

There's really not much reason to replace the rear spring on the C4 Corvette. Over the years, a lot of folks have put stiffer springs into base suspension cars. However, we now realize this was really the wrong way to go.

The Corvette engineering team had a goal of 1.0g force in lateral acceleration. Team engineers accomplished this with really stiff springs. If you look at the chart here, you'll see that by 1985, the Z51 suspension was actually softer than the 1984 base suspension. The 1984 Corvettes are really brutal for driving around town. The 1985 springs have almost half the spring rates of the 1984 cars.

I've spent some time driving a 1986 Corvette with the Z51 package, and it's not a fun experience. My opinion is that you really don't need to replace the rear spring unless you're going to get rid of a Z51 spring set.

If you're going to swap the rear spring, you should also swap the front one. GM spent a lot of time working with these spring rates. While some of them may be a little stiff, they're balanced front to rear. You need to maintain a similar balance.

There are adjustable rear springs available on the market today. They are a great option, but you need to put in a lot of seat time to get them adjusted correctly. Basically I feel about this rear spring the same way I feel about most adjustable suspension items. They're great in theory but most of us never get enough seat time to be able to evaluate the variety of choices these parts offer.

A long time ago, I visited a Corvette Challenge race shop. There must have been several hundred springs all crowded on the shelf. I noticed that they all had the same factory numbers on them. In chalk, a different set of numbers had been written. This team would take a dozen different springs out to the track for testing. Do you have that sort of time?

It seems that the stock rear springs never break. A friend of mine at GM said that, back in the late eighties,

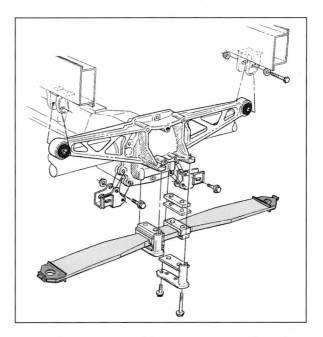

Removing the rear spring is one of the easiest projects you can do. It's almost as if they said, "Since we made the front spring so hard to remove, why don't we make the rear spring really easy for them to work with." You only have to remove six bolts, and you're done. Even better, this is a job that you can accomplish all by yourself.

they had a few problems but, in the end, they were traced to a specific wheel cleaner that folks were using. It seems that when the wheel cleaner got on the springs, it weakened them. Most broken springs seem to be caused by either the use of chemicals around the spring or by some sort of physical abuse.

Removing the rear spring couldn't be easier. The main thing to keep in mind is that everything goes a lot more smoothly if you simply drop the spare tire carrier out of the car. I actually dropped the carrier out of my car about a decade ago. Now I just carry a can of Fix-A-Flat and a cell phone.

Once you have the car on jack stands, you can remove the bolts on both ends of the spring. You might want to review Project #46 on lowering the rear of the C4. It goes into a little more detail on this procedure.

With both ends of the spring in full droop mode, you can simply release the four bolts that hold the center of the spring to the car. When you remove the center section, be careful to keep track of all the shims that are part of the assembly.

The rubber cushions are still available, and it might not be a bad idea to replace them. Most of the existing shims are in pretty good shape, though. Replacing them isn't a necessity—it's just one of those nice little touches you can add as long as you're taking things apart.

When you get the spring back in place, measure from the center of the spring mount to the end of the spring. You obviously want both ends to be equal in length. The arrangement has enough tolerance built in so this isn't critical, but it's still important.

Once you get the long mounting bolts attached at each end, take the car for a ride. You need to settle the rear suspension down before you take any measurements. When you come back from your drive, make sure you park the car in a level spot before you take your measurement.

Above left: These are the longer bolts that are used to lower the rear of the car. You'll notice that this car is fully dropped. The one thing I will never understand, however, is why every single mail-order company sells these bolts in standard thread when every bolt on the C4 Corvette is metric. Wouldn't it have been just as easy to use the same diameter bolts that came stock on the car? I'm sure they make metric bolts in that length.

Above right: When you remove these four bolts to drop the spring, make sure you remember where all the shims go. There's a very elaborate procedure for changing them and figuring out a new configuration. I just haven't found it necessary. It's a lot easier to simply keep track of them as you remove them.

Rear Spring Rates

Model Year	Suspension RPO	Rear Spring Rate (N/mm)
1984	FE1	72.0
	Z51	87.5
1985	FE1	39.9
	Z51	57.2
1986	FE1	39.9
	Z51	57.2
	FE1 (conv)	39.9
1987	FE1	57.2
	Z51	39.9
	Z52	39.9
	FE1 (conv)	39.9
	Z52 (conv)	39.9
1988	FE1	57.2
	Z51	39.9
	Z52	39.9
	FE1 (conv)	39.9
	Z52 (conv)	39.9
1989	FE1	39.9
	FX3	39.9
	Z51	57.2
	FE1 (conv)	39.9
	FX3 (conv)	57.2
	Chal.	57.2
1990	FE1	39.9
	FX3	39.9
	Z51	57.2
	FE1 (conv)	39.9
	FX3 (conv)	39.9
	ZR1	39.9
	R9G	57.2
1991	FE1	39.9
	FX3	39.9
	Z07	57.2
	FE1 (conv)	39.9
	FX3 (conv)	39.9
	ZR1	39.9
1992	FE1	39.9
	FX3	39.9
	Z07	57.2
	FE1 (conv)	39.9
	FX3 (conv)	39.9
	ZR1 39.9	33.0
1993	FE1	39.9
	FX3	39.9
	Z07	57.2
	FE1 (conv)	39.9
	FX3 (conv)	39.9
	ZR1	33.0
1994	FE1	39.9
	FX3	39.9
	ZR1	57.2
	FE1 (conv)	39.9
	FX3 (conv)	39.9
	Z07	33.0
1995	FE1 (early)	39.9
	FE1 (late)	26.0
	FX3	26.0
	Z07	572
	FE1 (conv)	39.9
	FX3 (conv)	26.0
	ZR1 39.9	33.0
1996	FE1	26.0
	FE1GS	26.0
	F45	26.0
	Z45GS	26.0
	Z51	33.0
	Z51GS	33.0
	FE1 (conv)	39.9
	F45	39.9

Ball Joint Replacement

 Time: 2 to 3 hours

 Tools: Ball joint press

 Talent:

 Applicable Years: 1984 to 1996

 Tab: $150 to $200

 Torque: Lower ball joint nut—33 foot-pounds (Never exceed 63 foot-pounds to align the cotter pin.)

 Tip: Renting or buying a ball joint press makes this job a lot easier.

 PERFORMANCE GAIN: Handling will be improved by adding precision to the turns.

COMPLEMENTARY MODIFICATION: This is also a good time to replace your brake pads since you're going to have the calipers removed anyway.

The ball joint is a very clever little device. It's designed so that the control arm can move up and down as you drive over bumps. At the same time, it allows the steering knuckle to pivot as you steer the car. The ball joint works a lot better than the old kingpins found on the pre-1963 Corvettes.

There are two ball joints on each side of your Corvette. The lower ones are called tension-loaded joints. The weight of your Corvette is really pushing down on the lower control arm, which is why the lower ball joints wear out first.

The spindle, or axle, of the Corvette is supported by the wheel and tire. As you drive down the road, your Corvette is actually attempting to tear this lower ball joint connection apart. The ball stud inside the housing is in constant contact with the internal bearing surface. This is just another reason why the lower ball joints will wear out first.

The ball joint on the upper control arm works in the opposite way. The control arm is above the spindle, and the weight of your Corvette is forcing the control arm down. This force actually pushes the bearing *into* the ball joint stud, or just the opposite of the lower ball joint. Some people refer to this upper ball joint as the follower ball joint. Its only real purpose is to provide a second pivot point for the suspension. This explains why the upper ball joints last a whole lot longer than the lower ball joints.

Place a jack stand under the lower control arm. This jack stand should be placed as far toward the outside of the car as possible. Next, move the top of the tire in and out. Because of possible wheel bearing play, you should have a helper look to see where any play is coming from. You can even take turns to ensure that you both see the same thing.

Checking for Wear

Wear occurs in two ways in the ball joint. Either one will allow excess movement in the suspension. With the Corvette, we're mainly interested in radial movement. Radial movement is side-to-side movement. The factory manuals don't even get into excess vertical play, or axial movement—that's how little axial wear takes place.

There's a very specific procedure for checking 1984 to 1996 Corvette ball joints. Actually, there are two ways to do this, and I'll explain both. We'll also get into how to change

your own ball joints. With the right tools, this isn't a bad job to do in your home garage.

The fastest way to check the condition of your front lower ball joints is to simply look at the position of the grease fitting. This lower ball joint is designed so that, as wear takes place, the grease fitting recedes farther into the body of the ball joint. A quick visual inspection of this grease fitting will tell you a lot about the condition of the ball joint.

Another way of determining if the ball joint is worn is to place a jack, or jack stand, under the lower control arm, raising the car just high enough that the front wheel is off the ground. The jack, or jack stand, should be as far to the outside of the control arm as is possible. In this position, the only weight on the lower ball joint is the weight of the wheel, brake caliper, rotor, and a few other minor parts. This is called unloading the ball joint.

The correct way to measure ball joint wear is to place a dial indicator on the lower edge of the wheel and get a reading on the amount of wobble. The specifications from Chevrolet say you shouldn't have any more than 0.125 inch of play at the edge of the wheel rim.

Remember that bearing play can act the same as a worn ball joint. Your ball joints can be in perfect shape, and you'll get a lot of wheel play at the edge of the rim from a worn-out wheel bearing. Luckily, the front wheel bearings are usually in pretty good shape. Nevertheless, check everything very carefully. Make certain you know what's allowing the movement.

This isn't a terribly difficult job if you have the correct tools. Of course, I might add that you should have the correct experience as well. Ball joints are easy for a professional technician to work with, but can cause great frustration for the novice. Under no circumstances should you resort to a hammer on this project.

I know that most of you enjoy working on your Corvette and absolutely feel inadequate if you can't do the job yourself. So I've come up with a procedure that will allow you to be part of the process.

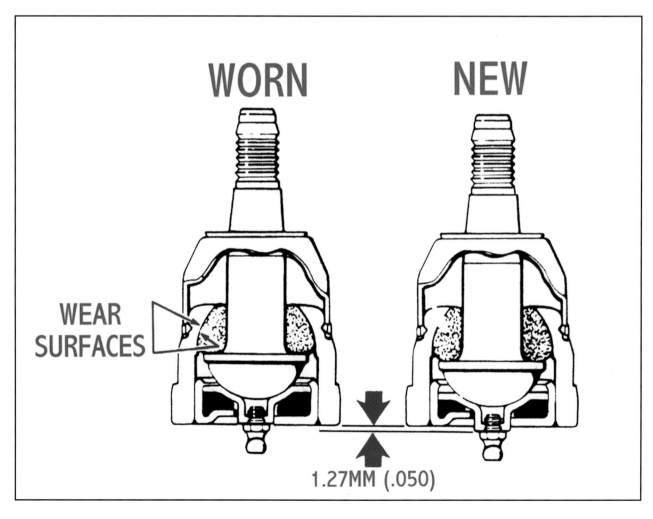

The alternative way to check your lower ball joints is to just look at the grease fitting. This is an almost foolproof process. As the ball joint wears, metal is removed from the wear surfaces highlighted in the drawing. This means the lower socket is moved higher in the housing. The grease fitting recedes into the housing as well. The specifications only allow for .050 inch of wear. That might be a little hard to see, but usually the recession is enough that you can easily see what's going on. One side usually goes bad before the other, so you can compare them from side to side. Another option is to stop at the local parts house and look at a brand-new ball joint.

The only good way to install the new ball joint is with a ball joint press. The presses are expensive so you should ask to borrow one from somewhere like your local AutoZone. Once you get started installing the new ball joint, the trick is to make sure everything is perfectly aligned. If you find you need to apply a lot of force, simply stop and check on the alignment of the ball joint as it proceeds into the control arm.

To begin, remove the tie rod from the control arm and then remove the lower control arm from the front spindle. This means you get to purchase some really neat pullers from your local NAPA store.

Remove the two bolts that hold the lower control arm to the chassis and remove the whole lower control arm. Now take these control arms, marked with a big L and R in bright yellow paint, to your local shop. Have an employee there use the shop press to install the new ball joints.

This is also a good time to ask a shop technician to install the polyurethane bushings you purchased several months ago. Go back to the shop in a couple of days to retrieve your parts.

Now everything should go together smoothly. You got to play with your car, spend money, and skip the really frustrating part of the job. See, working on Corvettes can be fun!

Use the ball joint press to remove the unit from the control arm. Under no circumstances should you hammer on the control arm. Remember, this is an aluminum control arm, and you don't want to damage it. Obviously I've removed the entire control arm from the car. This is something you could easily do, too. Then, instead of borrowing a ball joint press, just take the control arm to your local automotive machine shop.

The upper ball joint uses a riveted arrangement. I can't remember the last time I saw a replacement upper ball joint on a C4 Corvette. I'm sure they've been replaced, but they seldom wear out. There are a few possible reasons for their long lives. For one, they're easy to grease, so they're likely to get adequate lube. And secondly, they bear no load whatsoever.

Front Tie Rod Replacement

 Time: 30 minutes

 Tools: Metric sockets and metric combination wrenches, tie rod separator

 Talent:

 Applicable Years: 1984 to 1996

 Tab: $100

 Tip: You will need to have the car aligned when you finish installing new tie rod ends. You will only need the front toe checked and set, but most alignment shops will want to do a complete four-wheel alignment.

 PERFORMANCE GAIN: The car should go down the road with less need for steering correction. Tire wear should be significantly better as well.

COMPLEMENTARY MODIFICATION: Make sure you check all the front suspension components for wear at the same time. Since the price of a good alignment may run close to $200, it only makes sense to make sure that everything is in good shape before you have the car aligned.

One person should place his or her hands on the front wheel using a nine and three o'clock position. Then the other person should observe the tie rod end while the tire is moved in and out. If the tie rod is worn, you'll notice a lot of play.

Considering the variety of suspension design and innovation found on the C4 Corvette, the front tie rods are almost prehistoric. They're basically the very same item found on the original 1953 Corvette. The tie rod end is not only used to connect the steering rack to the wheels, it's also used to set the toe on the front wheels. Toe is a measurement that indicates whether or not the front tires are parallel to each other. Toe-out is when your front tires are pointing away from each other, and toe-in is when the fronts of the tires are pointing toward each other.

The tie rods are the connection between the steering rack and the front tires. When you turn the steering wheel,

you move the gears in the steering rack. This means the rack moves to the left and right. This movement is transferred to the front spindles, or axles, through the tie rod. Since the front spindle has to move left and right, as well as up and down, we need a ball socket type of connection to allow for all this movement.

A very basic fact of life is that ball sockets eventually wear out. Luckily, with the C4 Corvette, they take a long time to do that. If you grease the outer tie rods on a regular basis, they'll last until your odometer reaches at least 100,000 miles and maybe even 150,000 miles.

The other bonus is that when the outer tie rods finally do wear out, they're easy to change. They're also easy to check for wear. This is one more time you're going to need a helper to move the wheel back and forth as you check for movement.

Keep in mind that there is also an inner tie rod end where the tie rod enters the steering rack. These seldom wear, but you need to check for wear at that point as well. If there is play at the wheel, and you don't see any significant play at the outer tie rod, look carefully at the inner tie rod.

You'll notice that the inner tie rod moves, but nothing happens with the steering. This ball socket is a little more

SUSPENSION

difficult to diagnose since the rubber dust boot covers it. However, if it's worn out, you'll be able to see some excessive play. Remember, you shouldn't have any play in your wheel as it's moved back and forth. There should be a very direct connection between all the steering parts. Any play is an indication of a worn part. The trick is determining which part is worn.

The inner tie rod end is only about half the price of the outer unit, so you may want to consider replacing it at the same time. The downside is that it's twice as difficult to access. If several of the four tie rods are worn, you need to consider replacing the entire steering rack.

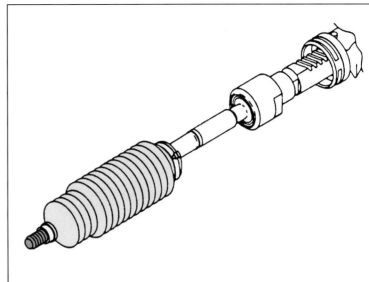

This traditional pickle fork is used to remove tie rods from the spindle. It's a pretty efficient tool that has been around forever. The problem is that it's a brutal instrument. The pickle fork usually tears up the rubber boot on the tie rod end, making replacement a certainty. The other problem is when it's used on the C4 Corvette, it also tears up the aluminum spindle. Using a steel tool like this on soft aluminum is not a good idea.

The correct tool is much more expensive, but how much do you prize your Corvette? You can purchase the tools you need from your local Sears or NAPA store.

Don't forget that each tie rod has two ball sockets that need checking, or four in total. While the inner tie rod socket doesn't seem to wear as rapidly as the outer one, it still wears and can cause the same sorts of problems as a worn outer tie rod end.

You should also examine the area around the boot carefully for oil leaks. This rubber boot is really a dust cover. No power steering fluid should leak past the inner ball socket. If you suspect you have a problem, you can cut the metal band and pull the boot back. If it's full of power steering fluid, start shopping for a new steering rack. While it can be repaired, it's really more cost-effective to simply install a new long rack, complete with four new tie rods.

Replacement of the outer tie rod end is really simple if you follow the basic procedure. Start by loosening the jam nut that holds the tie rod end in place. Then, before you do anything else, count the number of exposed threads on the arm that comes out of your steering rack. The idea is to thread the brand-new tie rod onto this arm in exactly the same position.

After you write down the number of threads exposed, you can remove the tie rod from the front spindle. The special tool is much better to use for this purpose, but you can still use the old-fashioned pickle fork if you wish. Just be careful you don't tear up that nice cast aluminum spindle with the nasty steel pickle fork.

Now it's simply a matter of threading the new outer tie rod end onto the tie rod. Make sure you go back and check your notes about how far to screw it onto the tie rod. When you get it into the proper location, install the socket into the spindle and tighten the jam nut.

This procedure might, and I use the word "might" very tentatively, save you from having to have the car aligned. At the very least it will allow you to drive the car a few days until you can get back to the alignment shop.

SUSPENSION

Rear Tie Rod Replacement

 Time: 30 minutes

 Tools: Metric sockets and metric combination wrenches, tie rod separator

 Talent:

PERFORMANCE GAIN: Improved handling

 Applicable Years: 1984 to 1996

 Tab: $250

 Torque: Tie rod center section—54 foot-pounds; Axle tie rod nuts—37 foot-pounds

 Tip: You will need to have the rear aligned when you finish.

COMPLEMENTARY MODIFICATION: You should also replace the rear spindle rod bushing. You can either do it at the same time or very soon after you finish with the tie rods.

SUSPENSION

While the rear of the 1984 to 1996 Corvette is very similar to the earlier Corvettes, there were some important differences. One of the new items that emerged in 1984 was a tie rod arrangement that connects the rear wheels to the differential cover. This assembly is bolted solidly to the differential and then uses a ball socket arrangement where the connection is made to the rear hub assembly.

The tie rod is where you make the rear toe adjustment. This rod also controls the roll steer geometry and moves the steer stiffness center as far to the rear as possible. The reason all of this is important is that it minimizes steering deflection from tire-induced lateral forces. Remember, when the C4 was introduced, it had the largest tires in the industry.

These huge tires presented new challenges for keeping the suspension in order. To make things even worse, many of us insist on putting even larger tires and wheels on our 1984 to 1996 Corvettes. The amazing thing is that this rear tie rod arrangement seldom causes problems and has a tremendous lifespan.

Dave McLellan, former Corvette chief engineer, has discussed how the forces of these tires act on the suspension and create elastic steer effects. He points out that it's best to control these elastic movements and then put them to work. The chassis engineer is then able to introduce controlled understeer and oversteer effects due to the compliance of the suspension.

The stock arrangement is very stiff and presents no wear problems—unless you forget to lube the ball socket

on a regular basis. I've seldom seen a problem with this unit on a Corvette with less than 120,000 miles. This is a testimony to one of the toughest suspensions ever to come out of General Motors engineering.

You can check the ball socket for wear the same way that you would check any other ball joint. Jack up the rear of the car and have a friend move the rear wheel in and out. His hands should be at the three and nine positions. You

The best way to check for wear is to raise the rear of the car and have a friend move the rear wheel back and forth. He should have his hands at the three and nine o'clock positions when he does this.

Watch to see if you have excess movement at any of the four connections. This is the outer ball joint, and any movement should be obvious. Since you'll be looking at all four connections, you'll have a good basis for comparison — unless, of course, all four are worn out.

the earlier cars, you're going to have to purchase an entire assembly in order to replace a worn tie rod end. The entire assembly, including the two new tie rod ends, will be more than $200.

Don't confuse wheel bearing play with play in the tie rod ball socket. You may very well get play in the wheel that comes from the rear wheel bearings. These wheel bearings are legendary for going bad. You're looking for excessive play in the outer tie rod end. That's why it really takes two people to check for this in the home garage. One person can move the wheel, and the other can crawl under the car to look for play in the tie rod ends.

Once you've established that you have movement, you need to determine where that movement is taking place. Replacing parts is the easy task. The secret is in making the correct diagnosis.

If you're really intent on building a perfect track car, you might want to replace the factory parts with an aftermarket Heim jointed unit. These are available from Vette Brakes & Products. This modification is really for a track car, and it's something I can't recommend on a street Corvette. The wear and dirt issues are just too significant for street use.

The Heim joint arrangement used by Vette Brakes & Products gives you a much more positive arrangement than the ball socket. It's not that much better than a brand-new ball joint, but it's been a long time since your C4 was new. A lot of times, people use fancy aftermarket parts and extol their virtues when all they did was replace a totally worn-out part with a brand new one. A brand-new ball socket on the end of the tie rod is really just as good as a Heim joint. The downside is that Heim joints are very sensitive to dirt.

If you have to drive your Corvette in snow and ice, you'll have a serious problem with Heim joints. There is

might also want to have him move the wheel with his hands at six and twelve. You're looking for play at the ball socket. Any play here should be minimal.

Now, with your friend still moving the wheel back and forth, look at the inner, or center, location. This is a ball socket arrangement as well, and it can wear just like the outer ball socket. That means you have four different sockets that need checking.

If you have an early car, one with a male outer tie rod end, you're not going to be able to find parts. GM switched over to a different assembly with the start of the 1992 production run. This means that, if you have any wear in

This center section is also a wear item. This unit provides a solid place for the inner attachment of the tie rods. The bad news is that if you have wear on the early cars, none of the parts are available. The only solution is to purchase the entire assembly that was designed for a later car. This is an easy bolt-on, so it's not a great deal of hassle to install — it's just one more item that you didn't expect to have to charge to your credit card.

just no way that Heim joints are suitable for climates with winter weather.

The other problem with this Heim joint conversion is noise transmission. Remember, the one thing that makes a Heim joint very nice to use is that it connects everything tightly together. This tight connection is also great for transmitting noise all over the car. The very feature that makes it great for use on the track contributes to problems on the street.

What we have here is a very specialized part that works great in the application for which it was designed. Just don't push the envelope and try to ask it to do more than it was designed to do.

Above: This puller works a lot better than the standard "pickle fork" to remove the ball socket from the rear spindle, or rear upright. The best part is it doesn't damage the rubber boot. Once you've removed the socket from the rear upright, or hub, it's simply a matter of unscrewing the socket from the tie rod link. I usually add a dab of white paint on the rod so I'll know how far to screw the new ball socket onto the rod. You can also count the number of threads showing before you remove the old assembly. Either method will at least get the rear toe setting close enough to drive to your favorite alignment shop.

Below: Here's the aftermarket version of the tie rod designed for track use. This unit uses the same center mounting holes as the factory unit. It's just that it uses Heim joints for a connection rather than a ball socket arrangement.

PROJECT 57
Rear Spindle (Strut) Rods

 Time: 1 hour

 Tools: Metric sockets (3/8-inch and 1/2-inch drive) and metric combination wrenches

 Talent:

 Tab: $25 to $150

 Torque: Spindle rod to knuckle—107 foot-pounds; Spindle rod adjustment nut—186 foot-pounds

 Tip: You will need to have the rear (actually the whole car) aligned when you finish installing new bushings.

! PERFORMANCE GAIN: Polyurethane bushings will improve your handling with no loss of ride quality.

COMPLEMENTARY MODIFICATION: Replace the rear trailing arm bushings with polyurethane bushings as well.

Thirty-three years is a long time in the world of automotive engineering. Yet the Corvette used the same basic design for maintaining the camber on the rear of the Corvette from 1963 to 1996. The parts may have changed slightly over the years, but the design remained the same. A rod is used to connect the lower part of the outer axle housing to the rear differential housing. This rod, or, in the

The first step is to remove the standard aluminum strut rod from the car and put it on your workbench. Take a straightedge and make sure that the rod hasn't been bent. A surprising number of C4 Corvettes are showing up with bent camber rods. Tow-truck operators cause most of this damage. They use these camber rods as a place to tie your Corvette to the flatbed truck. These rods were never meant to be used this way. If you ever have to have your Corvette placed on a flatbed truck, make sure you check these rods as soon as possible after you get your car back. If you purchased your car used, check the rods at the first possible convenience.

C4, an aluminum beam, holds the tire in a specific location. This determines the camber of the rear tires.

On the inner end, an eccentric bolt can be rotated to push the lower edge of the tire in and out. Turning the eccentric will lengthen, or shorten, the effective length of the rod. Chevrolet calls the eccentric bolt a spindle rod adjustment nut, or the rear camber adjustment cam. Chevrolet calls the whole part a rear spindle rod, but most of us know it by the name of rear strut rod.

Let's just take a second to review what camber is. Camber is the amount of lean your tire has. If your tire is at a ninety-degree angle to the ground, it has zero degrees of camber. If the top of your tire leans in, we say it has negative camber. If the top of the tire leans toward the outside of the car, we call it positive camber.

The goal is to get as much rubber on the road as possible. This even applies to when you go around corners. In a driving situation, you want to have zero degrees of camber as often as possible—especially in a corner. You want to set the *static* camber at some setting other than zero degrees.

I'm not going to get into the best camber setting for the Corvette here. I will, however, point out that, whatever your camber setting is, you would like it to stay consistent. This means the connection on the ends of your rear strut rod should be as firm as possible. This is what's going to allow your Corvette to corner exactly the same way every time.

When your Corvette was new, the standard bushings worked just fine. Then wear and age took their toll. What was, at one time, a very firm connection has become sloppy. When you take a corner, the bushings are compressed. The problem is that this compression is never consistent with a worn-out rubber bushing.

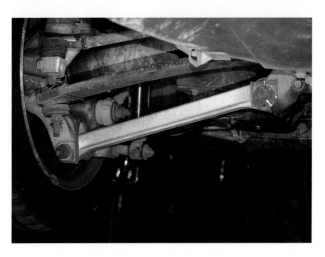

Above left: Think about how the various forces push on the ends of this rod. These control rods take tremendous forces. The good part is they hold up very well. Most Corvette owners seldom give them a thought. Replacing them is left to those owners who want top-quality performance. This particular replacement rod is from Vette Brakes & Products.

Above right: This eccentric bolt is used to set the camber on the rear tires. Alignment guys love this. The Corvette may be one of the easiest cars in the world for rear camber adjustment.

This digital camber gauge can be used for checking the amount of camber in your suspension. You simply set the gauge in position and look at the digital readout. I've used this for several years now and love it. I've even checked it out on one of the high-tech, $30,000 alignment machines a friend of mine has, and I'm happy to report that this thing is dead accurate to a tenth of a degree.

If you're working on the rear of your Corvette, you really have three options for replacement. The first option, and one that works just fine for most people, is to remove the strut rod and replace the rubber bushings with polyurethane bushings. This tightens up the suspension, and you still use the normal eccentric to adjust the camber. The whole job can be done on a Saturday morning. It does require that you get your Corvette aligned, though, since you did move everything around.

While you're back there, it's not a bad idea to replace the rear camber adjustment cams. Keep in mind that the 1963 to 1996 Corvette uses the same part for adjusting the camber. These take a lot of abuse from road dirt and salt. The cost of a new pair is minimal. Actually the most expensive thing about this whole job will be the new alignment.

The next option is to replace the entire strut rod assembly with adjustable strut rods. These strut rods have a left-hand thread on one end and a right-hand thread on the other end. When you turn the strut rod, you're lengthening and shortening the length of the rod. These rods give you a huge range of camber adjustment. If you run autocross or track events, you want these rods on your Corvette. If you have any reason to regularly change your rear camber, these adjustable camber rods are what you need.

Finally, there's a set of rear strut rods for the Corvette used only on the track. Instead of using a polyurethane bushing, they use spherical rod ends. These really aren't at all suitable for the street. First, spherical bearings transmit a tremendous amount of noise to the car. You may be fast, but you'll have one noisy Corvette with these rod ends.

You also have to remember that race cars are totally checked every hundred miles or so. Spherical rod ends don't like dirt. Racers clean them constantly. If you run them on the street in rain and snow, you're just asking for problems.

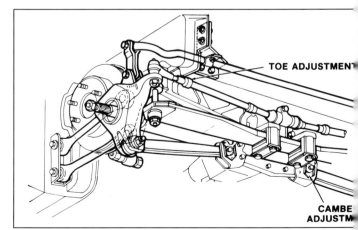

This drawing should clear up any problems you might have about what adjusts what at the rear of your Corvette.

FX3 Chip Replacement

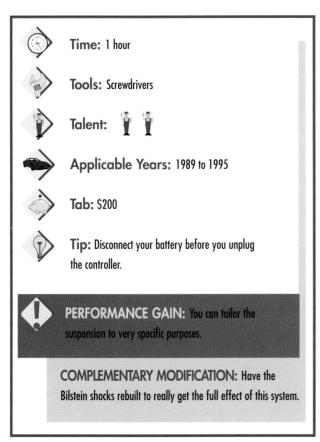

Time: 1 hour

Tools: Screwdrivers

Talent: 👤👤

Applicable Years: 1989 to 1995

Tab: $200

Tip: Disconnect your battery before you unplug the controller.

PERFORMANCE GAIN: You can tailor the suspension to very specific purposes.

COMPLEMENTARY MODIFICATION: Have the Bilstein shocks rebuilt to really get the full effect of this system.

Selective ride control, or FX3, was first offered in 1989. The idea behind the FX3 was that the shock valving would change as you drove the car. If you wanted to drive out to dinner on Saturday night, you would have a nice plush ride. If you wanted to carve the canyons near your house on Sunday morning, you would get an all-out competition ride.

That was the concept. What actually came out of the GM pipeline was so neutered that it really wasn't worth the effort. I can still remember wondering if the switch on the console was really connected to anything. There were days when I figured FX3 was nothing more than a $1,695 switch with no wires attached.

Now you can take this option and actually make it do something. Everything that's necessary for a wonderful ride-control system is in place. We can thank the people at Chevrolet for getting the unit in place, even if they did very little with the actual system.

With very few changes, you can turn the FX3 option into a wonderful thing. Let's look at the system and then look at how we can actually get this thing to work as we

drive down the road. I'm going to start backwards with the system and look at the shock absorbers first.

The shock absorber has a series of internal valves that control the rate that it dampens the suspension. You can take the shock absorber apart and change the internal valves to give different rates of compression and rebound. A nice solution, but not the most convenient.

Let's put a little electric motor on the top of the shock absorber shaft allowing the shaft to turn inside the shock absorber. This changes the oil flow through the bypass orifices, or valves, inside the shock. By doing this, we've just created an infinitely adjustable shock absorber. Well, not literally infinite, but one with six different positions, which is a lot better than the one setting with which the basic Corvette arrived.

Now, how do you control all this variation? Once again it's a fairly simple deal. By 1989 the Corvette computer system was collecting a tremendous amount of data. The vehicle speed was being monitored and stored in the computer and could be used as one of the parameters in the FX3 system. If you're just going down to the 7-Eleven, the speed was slow enough that you didn't need much control from the shock absorbers. If you were cruising down the interstate, a different shock setting might be needed.

This is the inside of the controller. The chip can simply be unplugged and replaced with a different one. Be careful that you don't bend the prongs on the chip when you're installing the new one. It's also not a bad idea to disconnect the battery when you do this.

SUSPENSION

145

The engineers took the vehicle speed data and sent it to a controller device that analyzed the information. Then, after analysis, the controller would tell the little motor on top of the shock absorber how far to turn the control rod. None of this was space-age technology. Rather, it was simply using a lot of computer data that was already floating around in the Corvette and putting it to use in a new application.

Now let's look at the specifics of the system as it was introduced in 1989. The decision was made to create three different maps. This way, rather than having the computers control everything, the driver could make a decision regarding when he wanted certain levels of shock absorber control to activate.

One of the little-understood features was that this switch on the console did nothing to actually control the compression and rebound of the shock absorber. Rather, it was simply a way to let the driver determine *when* things would happen. A driver could control three different settings. They were called touring, sport, and performance.

This system is not *totally* variable. Within each of the three settings, there are a finite number of adjustments. Let's say you've selected the touring mode. As you drive down the road, the controller will select one of six shock absorber settings.

Let's Go for a Ride

When you turn the key on your ignition, the FX3 computer runs a diagnostic check and lets you know that everything is functioning correctly. This means it not only checks the electrical circuits, but it also rotates the shock absorber shafts through their full 160 degrees of motion. Once this is complete, the rods are placed in the 60 degrees setting.

Once you begin to accelerate, the speed sensor starts to send a signal to the controller. Once you're going at least five miles per hour, everything is reset to whichever setting you have on the selective ride switch.

Let's suppose that you have the switch set to the TOUR position. This one is interesting because absolutely nothing will happen until you get to fifty miles per hour. At that point, a message is sent to the little electric motors on top of the shocks to move the shaft 20 degrees. As you move up to 75 miles per hour, the shaft will be moved again. In total, there are six different settings for the shock absorber valving. Take a look at the chart for the stock FX3, and you'll see that the final changes don't take place until 125 and 150 miles per hour. That's one reason why the FX3 suspension left you with the feeling that nothing was happening when you pressed the button. Nothing was happening.

If you move the switch to PERF, the controller starts with a firmer setting. The PERF setting is actually stiffer below 20 miles per hour than the TOUR setting is at 150 miles per hour. The interesting thing is that when you examine the chart, you'll notice that all the settings change at the same speeds. The changes take place at 25, 50, 75, 100, 125, and 150 miles per hour, regardless of whether you've selected TOUR, SPORT, or PERF.

Now that you understand how the system works, you can understand why it never really feels like it's working.

This chart shows what is really happening as you drive down the road with an FX3 Corvette. It also shows why you really can't feel much difference in the various settings. You can't feel much happening because not much is actually happening. The stiffer settings really don't operate until you're going over a hundred miles per hour. The stock system has all the right components, but the edges were really taken off the system. Compare this chart with what's available from Bilstein.

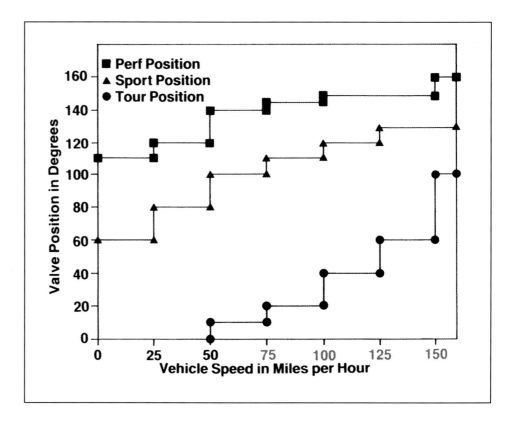

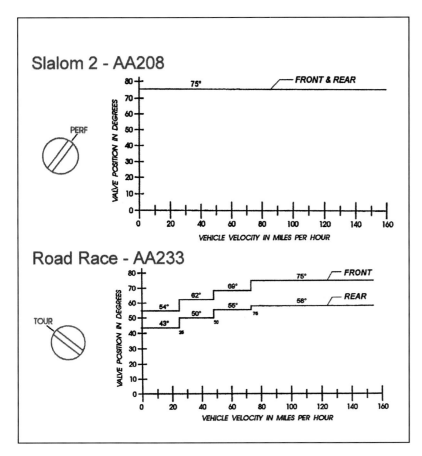

Slalom 2 - AA208

Road Race - AA233

These charts show just two of the many different chips that are available from Bilstein. This chip sets the shocks to full stiff at both the front and rear in the PERF setting. This is for Solo 2 events.

The Road Race chip keeps the rear shocks a little softer than the front shocks. The interesting thing with this chip is that the settings are all the same whether you select TOUR, SPORT, or PERF.

The only way to make a good chip replacement choice is to call Bilstein and talk with them about what you're trying to accomplish. They can then make a recommendation. They can also recommend what type of valving you want in the shock absorbers.

Chevrolet took the edge off all the settings. This is a wonderful system for street driving, but it never really comes into its own on the track. That's because the people at Chevrolet never intended for you to use it on the track. In fact, when they took the Corvette to the track, they used a very different map for the system. The good part is you can do the same thing.

Let's Change Things

When it comes to the FX3, things can be changed. First, you can change the controller. This changes the speed at which the shock is shifted to a new setting. Remember, this won't change the stock absorber setting one iota. All that changing the controller will do is to make the switch to a different valve setting at, say, fifty miles per hour rather than at 125.

If you want to change the way the shock absorbers act, you're going to have to actually change the valving inside

the Bilstein shock absorber. Remember, the shock absorber moves up and down, and the internal valving in the shock absorber sets the degree of resistance. If you don't change this internal valving, nothing will really change in the actual ride and control of the Corvette.

You want to start this process, though, by changing the controller first. This way you can get a feel for what one change does. You may decide that for the street all you need is to simply have the stiffer positions activate a little sooner. If you feel that you need more, move on to the shocks.

There's really no free lunch, but the FX3 may be the closest you can get to a really good, cheap buffet. If you manipulate the controller and the shock valving, you can get a well handling Corvette without too much loss of ride comfort.

Keep in mind that there's one very serious reservation with this FX3 arrangement: the valving is changed as a function of vehicle speed, not shock absorber shaft speed. Generally a shock absorber is calibrated so that the degree of resistance is a function of shaft speed. It's only logical that a shock absorber is most needed when going over a series of bumps. When traveling down a smooth road, particularly if you are not going around corners or accelerating or decelerating, there is very little need for damping.

Installing a new computer, or controller, will not change how the shock works. The actual functioning of the shock is strictly mechanical. That's why you truly won't get the most out of your FX3 system unless you change both the shocks and the controller. You really need to call Bilstein and talk to the people there. They'll talk to you about how you drive your Corvette and make the appropriate suggestions for changes.

In general, the FX3 suspension option is a really nice thing once you get it to work. The fact that you can customize the system to the type of driving you do makes it a worthwhile item. If you already have the system on your 1988 to 1995 Corvette, it's well worth talking to the people at Bilstein about making the necessary changes to the shock absorbers and controller.

You can make all of the necessary changes and still have a Corvette that appears to be dead stock. Eventually these C4 Corvettes will be NCRS eligible. A lot of owners are already concerned about maintaining a totally stock Corvette. With the FX3, you can change how your Corvette drives and handles while still maintaining the originality of the car.

Restoring FX3 Shock Actuators

Time: 1 hour

Tools: Screwdrivers, socket set

Talent:

Applicable Years: 1989 to 1995

Tab: $50 to $100

Torque: Front lower shock bolts—19 foot-pounds; Rear lower shock bolts—61 foot-pounds

Tip: When you remove the actuator wiring harness, tape it to the frame so it doesn't get lost.

PERFORMANCE GAIN: Restores the operation of your suspension to original condition.

COMPLEMENTARY MODIFICATION: Have the Bilstein shocks rebuilt and revalved to different specifications.

SUSPENSION

The FX3 suspension really has two components. We talked about the controller in the previous chapter. Now, let's look at the shocks themselves. We all know that the shock absorbers have a series of internal valves that control how the suspension dampens. Normally you have to keep taking the shocks off and installing different shocks when you go to a track event. Remember that different rates of rebound and compression give you very different handling characteristics. Also, keep in mind that what's good for the track isn't the best arrangement for the street.

Street driving is always a compromise between comfort and performance. You want to back off on the rebound for the street. In other words, the setting that works best on the track will make your Corvette miserable for the street. This is why the FX3 is really a great idea.

If you want to change the way the shock absorbers act, you're going to have to actually change the valving inside the Bilstein shock absorber. Remember, the shock absorber moves up and down, and the internal valving in the shock absorber sets the degree of resistance. If you don't change this internal valving, nothing will really change in the actual ride and control of the Corvette.

The true goal of your shock absorber is to keep the tires planted firmly to the ground at all times. This means that you're using the shocks to push the tire back to the pavement any time it's inclined to move up into the air. Most race cars are designed using this same thinking.

When you drive down the road and hit a bump, the shock absorber shaft is pushed into the body of the shock. This is shock compression. The oil in the shock simply can't be forced back fast enough, and resistance is created. If you vary the size of the orifices in the inside of the shock, you can change the amount of resistance, or compression.

The reverse happens when the car arrives at the top of the bump. The shock absorber is still compressing, and the wheel will come off the pavement unless you take control of the situation. The very instant you no longer need compression, you need to push the shock piston back into place so that the tire can remain on the pavement. This is the rebound phase.

The real secret to modifying the shocks is to make an accurate judgment about how you drive – and how you want your Corvette to feel. If all you do is drive on the

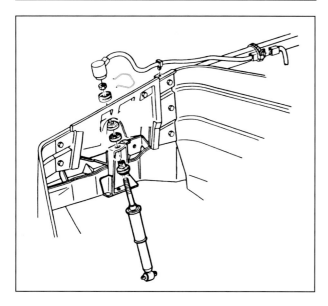

The front shocks are very easy to change. The best part is that you can easily reach the clips that hold the controller to the top of the shock. In addition, the wiring is really easy to work with. It doesn't hurt, though, to make a drawing of the direction that the pigtail is pointing before you remove things.

street, it might be best to leave the whole thing alone. The FX3 was really designed as a street system, and, if that's all you do, leave it alone.

Wear Problems

There are only a few wear problems with this system. One of the more common is that the inner seal on the shocks will deteriorate. Keep in mind that the piston rod assembly is actually two shafts, one inside the other. This is manufactured as a single unit. The outer shaft doubles as both the piston rod and the outer section of a sleeve valve that controls the flow of oil. The inner shaft is the other part of the valve. As the inner shaft rotates, the bypass valve opening varies. The top of this inner shaft is splined and engages the little electric actuators which, in turn, are operated by the SRC controller. To vary the bypass valve opening, this actuator turns the inner shaft. The larger the bypass valve opening, the softer the shock valving. The smaller the opening, the more aggressive the shock valving. This is where the wear usually takes place. When the seal between these two shafts fails, the shock will begin to leak oil. If you look at your shock absorber with the actuator attached, the leakage looks as if it's coming from underneath the actuator. When the inner seal fails, the oil is forced up through the space between the two shafts and out the top of the shock through the small gap between the splined end of the inner shaft and the outer shaft. Any oil leakage out the top of the shock or, if the actuator is in place, from under the actuator, means you have piston rod inner shaft seal failure. It's time to send your shocks to Bilstein for rebuilding.

This failure is affected by how much valve movement has taken place during the life of the shock. Every time an FX3 car is started, the actuators index themselves by moving through their full travel then returning to the valve adjustment called for by the selector switch setting and vehicle speed. The more often the inner shaft is moved, the more likely there will be a problem with leakage.

The front shocks can be inspected for leakage while they're in place. If leakage has existed for some time, shock oil will be present inside the actuator retaining bracket at the very top of the shock. The rear shocks really need to be removed to check for leakage. Any oil leakage from the top of the shock will be obvious once the shock is removed.

If you have FX3 shocks that are leaking oil out of the top, they can be repaired. Bilstein has the parts in stock, and the charge for repair is minimal compared to the price of new shocks. In fact, any Bilstein shocks can be repaired for a lot less money than it's going to cost you for new ones. They may not look as pretty as new ones, but your credit card statement will look a lot better at the end of the month.

There's one common problem that only seems to happen in certain parts of the country. Inside the actuator, there's a little plastic or nylon gear. This can become brittle, and the teeth can shatter or strip. However, these problems only seem to affect those Corvettes that reside where there are severe temperature extremes.

These gears seldom go bad on cars in Florida or California, but the ones that reside in Minnesota or Michigan have more than their share of problems. The type of material the gear is made out of appears to have a problem with temperatures that vary greatly during the course of the year. There's no scientific proof of this, but the anecdotal evidence is very compelling.

In general, the FX3 suspension option is a really nice thing once you get it to work. The fact that you can customize the system to the type of driving you do makes it a worthwhile item. If you already have the system on your 1988 to 1996 Corvette, it's well worth talking to the people at Bilstein about making the necessary changes to the shock absorbers and controller.

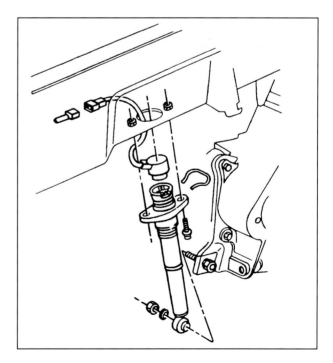

This is the rear shock setup, which is where most of the problems arise. First, be very careful that you don't lose the actuator wiring into the rear frame member. Secondly, getting the clip back on the controller is not the easiest task. Do it carefully and make sure you've got it right.

This retainer goes on the top of the shock. You'll need to remove this if you're going to remove the front shocks from the car

Wheel and Tire Selection

 Tools: Torque wrench for tightening the lug nuts

 Talent:

 Applicable Years: 1984 to 1996

 Tab: Usually well over $1,000 for tires and wheels— maybe over $2,000.

 Torque Numbers: Lug nuts—100 foot-pounds

 Tip: Make sure that you find someone who can mount the tires on your new wheels without damaging them during the mounting process. Don't trust just anyone with your new wheels.

 PERFORMANCE GAIN: Larger tires will improve the cornering ability of your Corvette, but you probably won't notice it on the street.

COMPLEMENTARY MODIFICATION: You should have your Corvette aligned after you've installed a new set of tires and wheels.

SUSPENSION

The 1984 to 1996 Corvette is all about wheels and tires. These things are what got everyone's attention, and they're still what draws a crowd. The choices are pretty great, and you can get some really huge tires under the car.

This Corvette was actually designed around the tires. The ultimate goal was to get as much tire under the car as possible. Contrast this with the C5 Corvette that followed. The C5 tires were constrained by aerodynamic numbers and the use of run-flat technology. It took almost five years to figure out how to get real rubber under that chassis.

As the prototype Corvettes were being developed, they were hitting speeds of 142 miles per hour. The fact they were doing it with only 205 horsepower was pretty impressive. This meant that the Corvette would have to have "Z" rated tires as standard equipment, something very few

other companies had done. The Goodyear tires were modeled after the Pirelli 225/50R16 tires that were found on the Porsche 928.

Now, twenty years later, these original tires and wheels don't seem all that large. That's why a lot of C4 owners are on a quest to put even larger tires and wheels on their Corvettes.

The C4 is also the Corvette that will put you over your credit card limit when it comes time to buy new rubber. There are really three questions involved here. First, what size tires and wheels actually came on your Corvette? Next, what's the best tire/wheel combination for your Corvette? Finally, what's the biggest tire that I can fit under your fenders?

The first C4 Corvettes had 16-inch wheels. The main reason for this was that they were the biggest tires the Corvette group could find. In 1984, 255/50VR16 was a monster tire. These large tires were originally going to be an option, and a 215/65R15 tire was going to be standard. The group quickly dropped the optional tire idea, and the big tire/wheel became standard on the 1984 Corvette.

When it came to the width of these 16-inch wheels, there were two choices. The base 1984 Corvette got 16x8.5-inch wheels all around, and the Z51 cars got 9.5-inch wide tires in the rear. In the 1985 model year, the Z51 suspension option got 16x9.5-inch wheels all the way around. This arrangement continued through the 1987 model year.

This raises the question: Can you gain anything by putting stock 9.5-inch wheels on your early C4? The

This is a 17-inch wheel on a 1985 Corvette. Complete Custom Wheels in Daytona Beach, Florida, produced this wheel. The company can produce wheels in virtually any size you need. Complete Custom Wheels also has a reputation for getting larger wheels and tires under the C4 Corvette than anyone else in the industry.

Here is a stock 16-inch wheel on an early C4. These wheels were clear coated at the factory, and most of them are getting a little faded by now. The only solution is to have the wheels polished and refinished. That will cost you almost as much as a new set of wheels.

answer is yes, but it's probably not worth the effort. There's a real performance gain from having the wider wheels at all four positions—Chevrolet proved that on the test track. On the other hand, the difference is only noticeable at the extreme end of performance driving—a place where you will probably never go. The difference between an 8.5-inch wheel and a 9.5-inch wheel will be so far out there that you'll only notice it on a racetrack or at a very fast Solo 2 course. With a street Corvette, you'll never notice the difference between 8.5-inch wheels and 9.5-inch wheels.

The best place to find these 9.5-inch-wide stock wheels is at a swap meet or a junkyard that specializes in Corvettes. The price on the 16-inch wheel is very reasonable since most people are jumping to the 17-inch wheels. Just make sure that you purchase a decent wheel. There's no reason to purchase junk and hope that you can fix it up at home. The last thing you need is a bent or out-of-round wheel.

With the early cars, I wouldn't even bother with any wheel changes unless I was prepared to go to the 17-inch wheels. If you're going to spend money, you want to be able to feel a real difference, not to mention the fact that you want people to see the difference.

The 1988 suspension change was a big one. The wheels for the 1988 to 1996 have very different offsets from the earlier Corvettes. The 1988 8.5-inch wheels have a 50-millimeter offset as opposed to the previous 32-millimeter offset. The 9.5-inch wheels went to a 56-millimeter offset as opposed to the earlier 38-millimeter offset. You can't swap wheels from the 1988 model year to the earlier cars without using spacers.

The new 17-inch wheel sported a 275/40ZR17 Goodyear tire. This is also the most common tire size in the entire C4 range. It's also a tire produced by almost every tire company in the world.

By the beginning of the 1989 model year, the 16-inch wheels were totally gone, and the standard Corvette wheel was 17x9.5 inches. The Z51 wheel and tire combination became standard. This situation continued right through the 1992 model year. The design would change, but the wheel dimensions would stay the same.

When we get to the 1993 Corvette, things get a little confusing. Chevrolet decided to make a change to improve the steering. They reduced the base front wheels to 8.5 inches in width, and the front tire size was reduced to 255/45ZR17. The rear wheels were kept at the 9.5-inch width, but they enlarged the rear tire size to 285/40ZR17.

The ZR-1

The ZR-1 got some monster rubber. This Corvette introduced the 315/35ZR17 tires. The important thing to remember here is that the rear fenders on the ZR-1 are bigger than those on the standard Corvette. This means the really big tires can be placed up in the fender much easier than on a normal C4.

There's very little need to use bigger tires on the ZR-1. The ZR-1 may be one of those rare cars that really can't benefit much from larger tires and wheels. Some people are putting 18-inch wheels on the ZR-1, but the impact is mainly visual. There's not much performance gain from that swap.

What's the Best Combination?

The average C4 owner is best served with a 17x9.5-inch rim and a 275/45ZR17 tire on all four corners. This is as much tire as you really need for a street Corvette. When you step up to the 315/40ZR17 rear tires, you're either buying appearance or you spend a lot of the time on the racetrack. This 315/40ZR17 tire will fit up in the wheel wells on the early C4s with no modification if you buy the correct set of wheels. On the other hand, you really don't need this big of a rear tire on the rear of the C4.

This is an example of one of the less expensive wheels on the market. These wheels are generally not forged and tend to be weaker than the factory wheels. If you find any used ones at swap meets, check them for roundness on the inside edge. The inner side of these wheels has a tendency to become egg shaped, or elliptical.

If you decide you truly like the big rear rubber, pay attention to the type of wheel you're going to use. These 315/40ZR17 tires are mounted on 11-inch wheels, and you have to watch the offset carefully since different manufacturers use different offsets to put this much rubber into the early wheel wells. I have a set of Complete Custom Wheels that fit nicely into the fender wells. The problem is that, by stuffing this much wheel and tire in the rear fenders, the tires sometimes hit the plastic inner wheel wells.

I also have a set of 11-inch American Racing wheels that cause no problem with the inner wheel well, but they stick out of the fender just a tad too much. This isn't a problem really—it's just visually jarring.

The next step up in the C4 wheel/tire quest will be putting 335/40ZR17 tires on the rear. This is done with a 12-inch wheel. This combination requires using the export or Grand Sport wheel flares. There is no way that you can stuff a 335-millimeter-wide tire into the early Corvettes without having something hang out. Complete Custom Wheels has a wheel designed for this combination.

This wheel has had a long and hard life. When a wheel is this badly scuffed, it's going to take a major refinish effort to save it. Be very wary of buying a wheel in this condition at a swap meet. The refinish cost will be greater than how much you would've paid for a really nice wheel

These wheels can be restored to look better than when they left the Bowling Green assembly plant. There are a couple of shops around the country that can do miracles with old wheels. Don't forget NCRS judging has already started. Save those original wheels, folks.

1984 to 1987 Wheel Offsets

1984 - 1987
8.5-inch wheel   32-millimeter
9.5-inch wheel   38-millimeter

1988- 1996
8.5-inch wheel   50-millimeter
9.5-inch wheel   56-millimeter

This is a handy chart for looking at the most commonly used tires on the 1984 to 1996 Corvette. These numbers will vary slightly from one manufacturer to the other. A 275/40-17 is not always 275 millimeters wide. There seems to be about a five-percent variation. It's best to check with the tire store on the exact dimensions. They have all this data readily available.

Tire Size	Side Wall Height	Tire Diameter	Tire Revs per Mile
255/50-16	128 mm	661 mm	799
275/40-17	110 mm	652 mm	811
285/40-17	114 mm	660 mm	797
285/40-17	100 mm	631 mm	801
295/40-17	118 mm	668 mm	767
315/35-17	110 mm	652 mm	808

STEERING SYSTEM

Parts courtesy Corvette Central

PROJECT 61

Replacing the Steering Rack

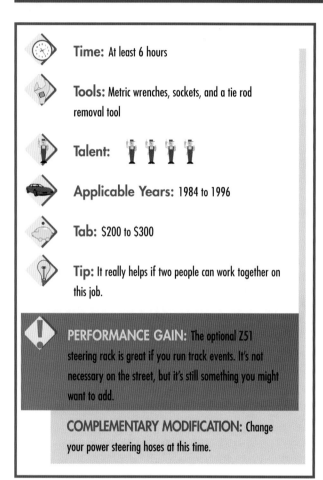

Time: At least 6 hours

Tools: Metric wrenches, sockets, and a tie rod removal tool

Talent: 👤 👤 👤

Applicable Years: 1984 to 1996

Tab: $200 to $300

Tip: It really helps if two people can work together on this job.

PERFORMANCE GAIN: The optional Z51 steering rack is great if you run track events. It's not necessary on the street, but it's still something you might want to add.

COMPLEMENTARY MODIFICATION: Change your power steering hoses at this time.

STEERING SYSTEM

The 1984 model was the first Corvette to use rack-and-pinion steering. This transition caused a variety of problems, although most of them have been taken care of by now. It wasn't just the Corvette that had problems with the steering rack. Steering rack problems during the middle 1980s troubled the entire GM product line. If it takes your power steering a couple of seconds to get going, you have a problem. This is the first sign of a steering rack going bad.

This symptom, best known as "morning sickness," is the result of an internal seal wearing inside the steering rack. In many cases, the Teflon seal was simply too hard and actually created wear on the aluminum parts, resulting in internal leakage. Once this wear has happened, it takes longer for the internal pressures to build up. Eventually the wear will get so bad that you might even lose your power steering as you drive down the road.

The only cure is to replace your steering rack with a new or remanufactured assembly. Several "miracle cures"

are offered on the market, but none of them have proven to be effective. Eventually the steering rack will have to be replaced.

When it comes to steering rack replacement, you have an interesting choice. The Z51 option included a steering rack with a different gear ratio, resulting in quicker steering. I see no reason why you wouldn't want this in your car. I've had the Z51 rack in my 1985 for almost a decade and love it. Several people have driven my car at the track and were surprised by how quickly it turned into a corner. One Porsche owner couldn't believe how quickly my Z51 responded and admitted he wouldn't be able to handle it. Maybe that's why he was driving a Porsche.

A second choice is to decide whether or not you want the "long" rack or the "short" rack. A "long" replacement includes both the right and left tie rod ends. The "short" version doesn't include the tie rod ends and is obviously cheaper. At this point you might as well replace the tie rod ends along with the steering rack. Remember, these are old cars, and everything on them is worn.

The first step when starting this task is to clean everything in the area. I generally use wheel cleaner and a strong hose to get all the oil and grease off the parts. You can also use a product like Gunk. Cleaning everything before you start removing the steering rack will make it a lot easier to see all the nuts and bolts that need removing.

Jack up the front end and place your jack stands on the frame just in front of the doors. Then place wheel chocks behind the rear tires and remove the two front tires.

The starting point is on the top of the engine compartment. You're going to be removing a lot of stuff here. Remove the air intake hose and the MAF sensor. You can leave the air filter box in place. Removing the cooling fan will give you better access to things.

Next you need to go under the car and remove the sway bar. The brackets holding it on the frame have 15-millimeter bolts, and a socket with extension works just fine to remove them. The end link bushing bolts are also 15 millimeter. You'll need a socket and wrench to hold the back side. Remove both frame mounts and two end links, then slide the sway bar out one side.

Next are the tie rod ends. There's a cotter pin holding the castle nut in place. Remove it. Then use an 18-millimeter socket on the nuts. You should then use the special tool that's designed to remove the tie rod ends from the spindle. The alternative is to use the traditional pickle fork for this job. If you use a pickle fork, you'll surely rip at least one of the rubber boots. If you've ordered a long rack

154

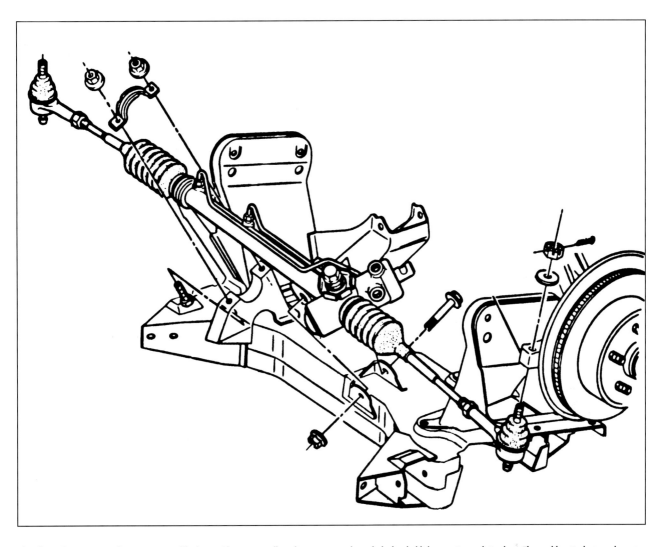

This shows the steering rack in a very simplified view. There are really only two nuts and one bolt that hold the steering rack in place. The problem is that you have to remove dozens of things to get to these three items.

assembly, this is no big deal since you've going to replace the tire rod ends anyway.

With the tie rod ends loose, you can start working on the rack mounts. The passenger side has two bolts and nuts, and the driver's side has one long bolt and nut. For the passenger side, you'll need a 13-millimeter socket/wrench, not to mention small fingers. From the wheel well area, you'll need to put the box end of a 13-millimeter wrench inside to hold the bolt while you come in from the top with a 13-millimeter socket and a bunch of extensions. This is one of those jobs where it helps to have two people working together.

With the mounts loose, you can remove the intermediate shaft. This is the part of the steering column that connects the rack to the upper steering column. There's a 12-millimeter bolt on each end on 1984 and 1985 cars.

Once the intermediate shaft is removed, you can move on to the fluid lines. Before loosening the lines, it's a good idea to get a turkey baster from the grocery store and use it to remove all the power steering fluid from the reservoir. This will minimize any possible mess when you unhook the lines at the rack. You'll need an 18-millimeter flare nut wrench and patience to remove the two power steering lines that feed into the rack.

Now that you have everything off, you have to work the rack out the driver's side. Once again, it helps to have a second person on this job.

The only tricky part of installing the new rack is threading the power steering lines into the rack. It's very easy to get these lines cross-threaded. If you do that, you've just destroyed your brand-new rack. There's really no way to cover this up should you attempt to take the rack back to the parts store for a warranty return. They've heard all the stories before. Just be careful.

The option here is to install a power steering fluid filter. Some people argue that you'll never get all of the Teflon and little metal particles out of the hydraulic system.

They say that as soon as you start the car, you're heading for your second rack failure.

The final step is bleeding the power steering system. Use a good synthetic fluid to fill the system. Then start the car and turn the wheel slowly to the left and right. Have your helper fill the reservoir as the level drops. When the bubbles stop, you're done. Replace the top and take the car for a 10- or 15-mile drive. When you get back home, check everything carefully for leaks.

The final step is to call your favorite alignment shop and have it align the car. You really only need the toe checked, but alignment shops can't make money just setting toe. You're probably going to get the full four-wheel alignment, which will probably cost you more than the steering rack.

One final caution. Some shops simply set the toe and charge you for a full alignment. Put yellow paint on all the bolts that relate to the alignment. If your car comes back without any changes in the settings, you need to change alignment shops.

Polyurethane bushings are a nice addition if you're replacing the steering rack. These bushings stabilize the rack just a little bit more than the stock bushings. They certainly do a better job than a set of worn-out original bushings.

Power Steering Hose Leaks & Replacement

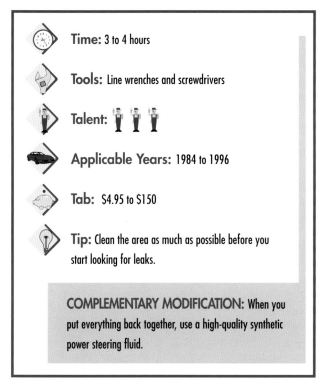

Time: 3 to 4 hours

Tools: Line wrenches and screwdrivers

Talent: ▮ ▮ ▮

Applicable Years: 1984 to 1996

Tab: $4.95 to $150

Tip: Clean the area as much as possible before you start looking for leaks.

COMPLEMENTARY MODIFICATION: When you put everything back together, use a high-quality synthetic power steering fluid.

Power steering leaks are all too common the C4 Corvettes. The worst part is leaks often happen right where they're most difficult to repair. On the other hand, hoses seldom just blow out. Instead, they develop a leak at the point where they're crimped to an end fitting. The only way they develop a hole is if they rub up against something in the engine compartment.

The first indication of a leak is a low fluid reservoir. If you find yourself filling the power steering fluid reservoir, you have a leak. Hopefully it's a power steering hose. I say that because the only other place for a leak to occur is the steering rack. As bad as it may be to replace a power steering hose, replacing the steering rack is worse.

The first step in this process is to clean everything as well as you can. If your car has had a hard life, using chemicals like Gunk may be necessary. If the car has just a light coating of dust, a good wheel cleaner is more than adequate for cleaning. Once everything is clean and dry you can set up for the white paper test.

Simply spread a large sheet of white paper under the area that you suspect is leaking. Leave it for a day or so and then go back and check to see what color the leaks are. Green fluid indicates antifreeze and a cooling system problem, while reddish spots signal a leaking transmission. Engine oil leaks are generally dark brown and power

steering leaks have an amber color. Power steering fluid will look a lot like automatic transmission fluid.

The fluid color generally identifies the leaking component. Most engine, transmission, and power steering leaks occur because of deterioration of the seals within the systems. As vehicles age, the seals often shrink and harden, permitting fluids to slowly leak. This often happens when Corvettes don't get driven often enough. Remember, the single most destructive thing you can do to your Corvette is let it sit idle in the garage.

Let's assume that you've determined where the leak is originating. If it's on the low pressure side, you simply need to purchase some new hose and some new clamps. That should take care of everything nicely. If it's on the high pressure side or the hose with the crimped ends, you have two possible sources for leaking. The first, and the most common, is the area right where the crimping meets the hose. This means you get to purchase a new hose.

If you need a new hose, I suggest that you order one from your local Chevrolet dealer right away. High-pressure hoses are no fun if they don't fit properly. The aftermarket retailers try to cut down on the amount of inventory they must carry, so if a hose is fairly close, they'll use one part to cover two applications. I've had too much experience with parts that almost fit. Try the dealer first and only go to the aftermarket if the part is no longer available.

Let's assume that you find that the fluid is leaking out of the O-rings at the point where the fittings screw into the rack or the pump. This is a situation where the stop-leak additives might work—at least for a while. These chemicals will cause the little rubber seals to swell beyond their normal size and can stop a lot of leaks.

Leaks can also happen right at the power steering pump. There are seals in the pump that can deteriorate just like the O-rings. A rebuild kit is available from most parts stores and is listed as Gates PN 35076. There's nothing hard about using this kit. It just takes a lot of time and care. It also requires that everything be spotlessly clean when you install the new seals.

If you have a problem with power steering leaks, I suggest that you ignore it until you have time to do a complete job. Just getting to the pump and hoses requires so much effort that it would be foolish to just go in and repair one component. The other thing to remember is that all these parts were installed at the same time at the Bowling Green assembly plant. That means everything is of the same age. If one seal has failed, it's a pretty good sign that the others are soon to fail as well.

Most leaks occur at the end of the hoses. It's rare for a hose to leak in the middle unless it's been abraded. If you think you have a leak, clean all the surrounding areas and then try to determine where the leak is coming from. After your car has put on 100,000 miles, be especially suspicious of the area where the hose joins the crimped steel end.

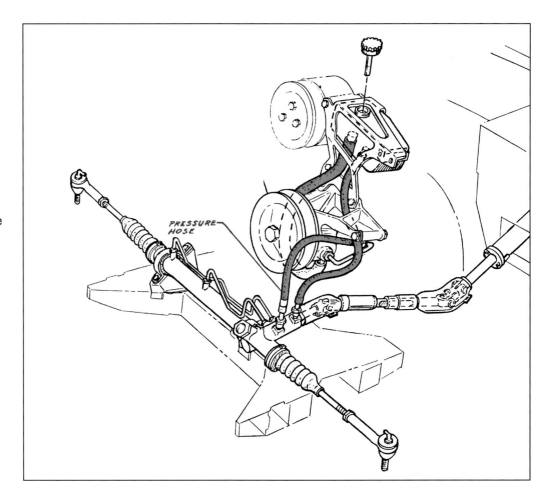

PRESSURE HOSE

Steering Rack Leaks

There's one more type of power steering leak that most people aren't even aware exists. The inner seal on the steering rack can leak. This was fairly common on the early C4 Corvettes. The problem was caused by wear in the spool-valve housing. The hard Teflon rings on the spool valve wore grooves into the relatively soft aluminum housing, allowing pressure to leak past the rings. The cure was to replace the rack with one that had a sleeved housing or a cast-iron housing.

In 1988, GM began switching to racks that had cast-iron housings. This cured the morning sickness problem,

which, over time, has reduced the demand for rack replacement. Nonetheless, you should check for this type of leak.

The easiest way to do this is to simply reach under the car and feel the rubber boot on each end of the steering rack. If you can feel fluid sloshing around inside the boot, start checking on prices for a new steering rack. If you're not sure what you're feeling, you can always remove the clamp and pull the boot back. Any steering rack that is leaking fluid past the rack or pinion shaft seals into the dust boot should be replaced.

When this seal begins to leak, it can force fluid out of the steering rack housing onto the rack or into the dust boot. The best way to cure this type of leak is to simply purchase a new steering rack.

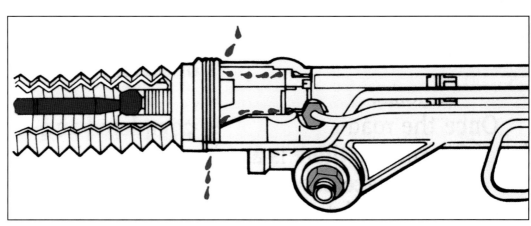

Power Steering Fluid Flush

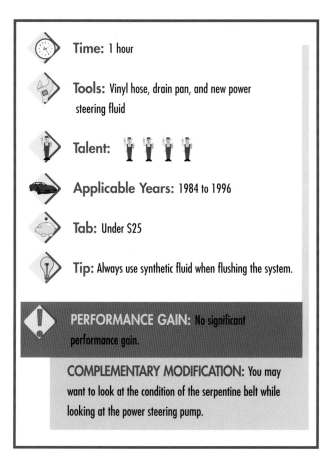

Time: 1 hour

Tools: Vinyl hose, drain pan, and new power steering fluid

Talent: ⚒⚒⚒⚒

Applicable Years: 1984 to 1996

Tab: Under $25

Tip: Always use synthetic fluid when flushing the system.

PERFORMANCE GAIN: No significant performance gain.

COMPLEMENTARY MODIFICATION: You may want to look at the condition of the serpentine belt while looking at the power steering pump.

Since the steering racks on the early C4 Corvettes are problematic, you really need to take all the possible precautions to ensure that they have a long and productive life. Most steering rack problems are caused by contaminants in the fluid. The other problem is the heat that breaks down the power steering fluid.

Most of the steering racks in the early cars have already been replaced. Hopefully, when the job was completed, all the old fluid was replaced. Since you have no way of knowing if this was done or not, it's best to add a fluid change to your list of things that need to be done.

Most of us don't think much about flushing the power steering fluid. As a general rule, you should flush the system every 30,000 miles. Flushing really doesn't take that long, and it's easy to do.

If you have any doubts about whether or not to do this, you can try the old paper towel test. Get a paper towel from the kitchen and put a spot of fresh power steering fluid on one side and a spot of your Corvette's power steering fluid on the other side. Then compare the two

spots to see how dirty your fluid really is. You should also sniff it to see if it's burned.

If you decide that you have some really nasty fluid in your Corvette, you can get started with flushing the old fluid out of the system. First drain the power steering pump reservoir. I like to use turkey basters from the supermarket. They're cheap and easy to find. Just suck as much of the power steering fluid out of the system as you can. Then inspect the pump lines or hoses to make sure they are not blocked, deteriorating internally, or leaking.

If the hoses are fine, you can disconnect the return line from the pump and place it in a container. Fill the pump reservoir with new synthetic power steering fluid that meets GM specifications. You can then disable the ignition and crank the engine. Don't turn the engine over for more than fifteen seconds or you could burn out the starter. Starters don't like to run continuously for much more than fifteen or twenty seconds. The last thing you need to do is burn out a starter attempting to change your power steering fluid.

Another technique for flushing the system is to remove the serpentine belt and then turn the power steering pump by hand. You should keep adding fluid to the reservoir until the fluid coming out of the return hose is clear. Then reconnect the return hose to the pump and fill the reservoir with some more new fluid.

Once the reservoir is full, you can start the engine and turn the steering from side to side in an effort to purge any air from the power steering system. Don't turn the wheel all the way and hit the steering stops during this process. Just go back and forth a few times while a friend checks the reservoir for bubbles. The level should be kept full when doing this. Keep turning the wheel until the air bubbles stop.

Add a Filter

A lot of people advocate using a filter in the power steering system. This is nothing more than a small oil filter installed in the system. It looks a lot like a small fuel filter and works the same way. Since these Corvette steering racks are very sensitive to dirt, it's not a bad idea to use a filter. If you've had problems with your steering rack, it's a very good idea to have a filter installed.

This filter is hose clamped into the low-pressure return line to the pump. First, drain the power steering fluid and then cut the rubber hose line within an inch or two of the inlet nipple. Hose clamp the aftermarket filter to the free ends of the hose. The filter's tiny screens remove abrasive particles that can cause pump failure.

STEERING SYSTEM

Just in case you're confused, there's an easy way to tell the low-pressure line from the high-pressure line. The high-pressure line takes fluid from the pump to the steering rack and uses a crimped-on steel sleeve. The low-pressure, or return, line is simply clamped to the return nipple with a hose clamp.

Power Steering Fluid Cooler

The power steering fluid in the C4 gets very hot. It gets so hot that Chevrolet even added a fluid cooler in 1987 for the cars equipped with the Z51 suspension option. The idea was that the Z51 cars were going to be driven more aggressively and would suffer the most from a breakdown of the power steering fluid.

Although you can do anything with enough time and money, retrofitting a power steering fluid cooler is really not something the beginning mechanic should consider. The job is just a little too involved for most people. At one time, GM offered a service kit—P/N 10080769—for installing a power steering cooler on a 1984 to 1986 Corvette. This was a pretty complete kit with everything necessary for adding a cooler to the early C4 Corvette.

This kit was intended for Corvettes used in racing where the power steering fluid temperatures got very hot. I'm not sure if they're available anymore, but it's worth having your dealer check out the part number for you. These kits used to be available from General Motors SPO and included the cooler, all the mounting/plumbing components required, and installation instructions.

This kit is really for the advanced class. If all you do is drive on the street, you really won't need this. On the other hand, if you do a lot of track events, it's worth trying to locate the kit.

Everyone should be using a synthetic power steering fluid, however. The cost is minimal, and it not only reduces wear in your steering rack, but it also protects your power steering system from heat-related damage.

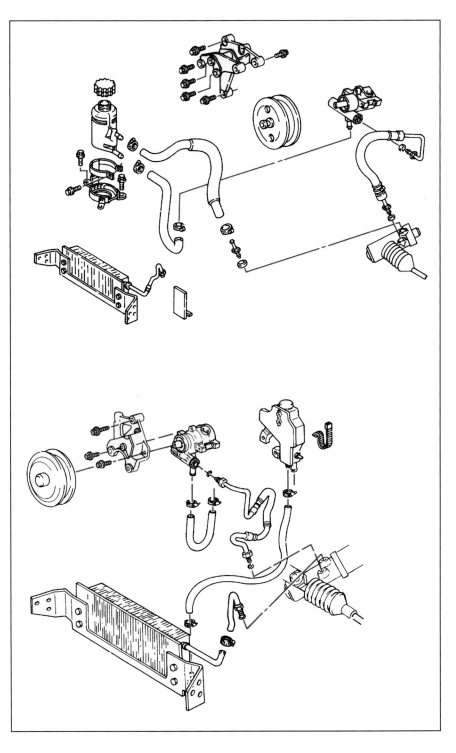

The Z51 power steering cooler changed over time. The upper picture is of the earlier system. It uses a round reservoir placed in the area between the front of the engine and the radiator. The reservoir was changed for the 1988 models but is really the same arrangement. The big difference is the hose configuration.

SECTION NINE
INTERIOR

Parts courtesy Corvette Central

Leather Care

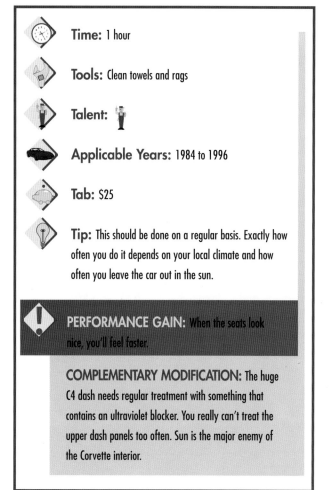

Time: 1 hour

Tools: Clean towels and rags

Talent: 👤

Applicable Years: 1984 to 1996

Tab: $25

Tip: This should be done on a regular basis. Exactly how often you do it depends on your local climate and how often you leave the car out in the sun.

PERFORMANCE GAIN: When the seats look nice, you'll feel faster.

COMPLEMENTARY MODIFICATION: The huge C4 dash needs regular treatment with something that contains an ultraviolet blocker. You really can't treat the upper dash panels too often. Sun is the major enemy of the Corvette interior.

INTERIOR

Leather is a natural product and has microscopic holes that allow moisture to pass through very tiny pores. These pores also absorb human perspiration. When the water evaporates, the salts remain to absorb the essential oils in the leather. This accumulation of salts and other grunge should be cleaned from the leather about twice a year. The loss of oils within the leather is really the first step in the leather's process of hardening, cracking, and shrinking.

You can clean your leather seats with a mild soap and water or, better yet, with a specifically designed leather cleaner. Of all the products I've tried, I still like Lexol pH Cleaner. It's both pH balanced and gentle. Any of the cleaners on the market, though, will rehydrate the leftover salts and grime and wash them from the leather fibers.

Make sure that you only use leather products on leather; don't use vinyl cleaners on your leather seats. These

vinyl cleaners tend to be much harsher and can actually damage your leather.

Any cleaner should be rinsed thoroughly from the leather. I've tried spraying it off with a hose. Unfortunately, this just seemed to fill the car with soapy water. I went back to using a damp cloth towel, repeatedly wiping down the leather. Once the leather is clean, a conditioner should be added to restore the lost oils.

You need to think of leather as a sponge. When the leather is new, the sponge is full of oil, and it's soft and pliable. Body salts, UV, heat, and other factors drive the oil from the sponge, allowing the leather to shrink and become brittle. A quality leather conditioner will help maintain the oil in the leather.

There are several conditioners on the market. My favorite is Lexol Leather Conditioner. I've tried other products over the years, but I always go back to the Lexol. It seems to be the product that is most easily absorbed into the leather fibers and tends to leave a relatively less greasy finish than any of the other products I have tried. It still leaves an oily surface, though, and you'll need to buff it before you sit in your seats.

Another good product is Connolly Hide Food. This is the product that Rolls Royce owners are known to use. It's made from rendered animal parts and will turn rancid in about two years. This, and the distinctive cow smell it possesses, removes it from the top of my list. Nevertheless, it's really a great product. Can several generations of Rolls Royce owners be totally wrong?

One Grand Leather Conditioner is a petroleum-based conditioner that seems to work great on Corvette leather. Again, don't use a vinyl product as a conditioner on your leather and avoid any products that contain raw silicone oils. Silicone oil dissolves the leather's natural oils and makes the leather sticky.

Silicone oil also has a very high electrostatic attraction and will invite practically every dust particle within five miles to set up camp in your interior. There's nothing worse than having a fully detailed interior and then having it covered in dust several hours later.

The application process is the same for all of the products you might use. Simply apply the conditioner to a soft cloth and work it into the leather. Then allow it to sit for a few hours, or a day, so the product can be absorbed into the leather. After a sufficient amount of time, you can buff off the excess material.

You can condition the leather as often as you wish. As a rule, however, condition your leather three to four times a year. The leather will tell you if you apply too much or

The first step is to clean the leather with a good-quality cleaner. Follow up with a leather conditioner. These conditioners contain oils that will keep your leather soft.

apply it too often. The leather fibers just won't absorb the excess. If you apply the conditioner and it immediately soaks into the interior, you should consider treating it a little more often. On the other hand, if it doesn't seem to sink into the leather very quickly, you can go a little longer between treatments.

If your leather has hardened or needs some intensive softening, there's a product called Surflex Leather Softener. This product is made from natural and synthetic oils that restore the natural softness to neglected leather. Clean the leather and then apply a liberal coat of the product. Then cover the treated area with plastic. Allow the Surflex to penetrate the leather for at least 72 hours.

Wipe off the excess. If it needs an additional application, repeat the above. For really bad areas, cover with plastic and allow to sit for a few days. Once the leather is sufficiently softened, allow to cure for another 24 hours and buff off any excess.

The real secret to leather care is that it needs to be done on a regular basis. Once the leather in the seats has hardened, you have a major task on your hands. The good part is that the seat leather in the C4 Corvette is very high quality and very tough. When it comes to seats, we really have far better seats than the folks who purchased C5s do. Take care of these seats, and they'll last forever.

Replacing the Dash Panels

 Time: 2 to 3 hours

 Tools: An electric drill and a very small Phillips screwdriver

 Talent:

 Applicable Years: 1984 to 1989

 Tab: $150 to $200

 Tip: Be careful not to crack the original plastic dash components. Most of these panels are now available, however, should you mess up and make a mistake. It's only money and time.

COMPLEMENTARY MODIFICATION: This is a good time to consider a complete interior detailing. The new dash panels are going to make everything else look a little scruffy.

D ash panel replacement, or conversion, is much more common on the early cars, those from 1984 to 1989. The aftermarket has fewer flat surfaces to work with after the dash redesign of 1990. Most of the carbon fiber and wood pieces that are available on the aftermarket are for the early cars.

A carbon fiber dash is really nothing more than the old wood panels that have been sold for the Corvette during the last several decades. These wood panels can be found on a lot of the late -1970s cars, but not many folks have gone for the wood look on the C4 Corvette.

Carbon fiber, or in most cases faux carbon fiber, gives the interior of the early C4s a nice high-tech look. It's also a very simple modification. One downside, however, is that it requires drilling holes into your original plastic dash panels. This means that if you ever want to put the car back to NCRS standards, you'll have to buy a lot of dash plastic. This won't turn off most people, but the restoration crowd will get very nervous about buying a car with these dash panels. They'll either pass entirely or try to lowball the price.

The only other downside of this project is that if you have to take the dash apart for repairs, you'll be removing two sets of panels. Each time you remove the screws, they strip out the threads a little. This is not a big deal, but something you should be aware of. If you remove the panels often enough, you'll have to figure out a way to fill the holes so that the screws will still hold the panels in place.

You shouldn't even consider a panel kit where everything just sticks on with an adhesive. The adhesive panels are really easy to install, but they're almost impossible to remove. Sooner or later this will become a problem.

If you have to remove an adhesive panel, and sooner or later you will, the only way to remove it is with a very sharp and flexible putty knife. This means you'll probably end up ruining the stick-on panel and the original panel as well. It's best to find the type of panels that screw into the original dash.

The one constant that you can surely count on is that the digital dash will eventually burn out in your early C4 Corvette. This means things will have to come apart. It's a lot better to plan for it right from the beginning than to go through a crisis later on.

If you decide to remove the breadloaf from the passenger side, plan on a major task. This unit can be unbolted, but you should assume you'll be spending a great deal of time doing it. The little nuts on the back side are

These panels are all mounted with very small screws. This requires drilling into your original dash panel. You need to consider if you really want to do this since there's no returning to original without purchasing all new stock panels.

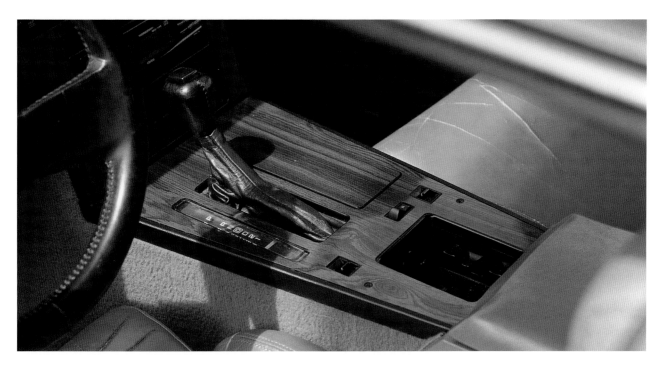

This center console panel shows that wood can be just as nice as carbon fiber. You need to be concerned about how this panel is mounted since the console may have to be removed at some time.

almost impossible to reach. This relatively simple— and boring—task will consume many hours of your weekend. You might just want to wait for your heater core to rust out and then do the whole thing as one job.

Another option is to simply break the breadloaf out of the dash. This is the easiest option, if not the most attractive. Actually it's just a psychological thing since, when you're all done, no one will ever know that you simply took a crowbar to your dash. It's just that we're not used to working on our Corvettes that way.

The center console kit usually includes a panel that covers the area where the seat adjuster switches are located. The panel that covers the ashtray/cup holder is secured to the original panel with adhesive. This means you won't be returning your interior to stock anytime in the very near future.

Steering Wheel Replacement

Time: 1 hour

Tools: Steering wheel puller and sockets

Talent: 🔧🔧

Applicable Years: 1984 to 1989

Tab: $300 to $600

Tip: Use a steering wheel puller, which you can find at any parts store.

PERFORMANCE GAIN: A larger diameter steering wheel just feels a lot better and will actually help you steer more effectively. Moreover, it looks a lot better than a steering wheel that has its leather falling off.

COMPLEMENTARY MODIFICATION: If your turn-signal return is broken, this is a good time to repair it.

INTERIOR

If you own your C4 Corvette long enough, you're going to replace the steering wheel. That's especially true with the early cars. The early cars came with a small-diameter leather wheel that was replaced with a thicker wheel in 1986. That wheel stayed in production until 1990 when the design was changed to make an air bag possible. The entire dash was also changed in 1990. That design lasted until the end of production in 1996.

The steering wheels in 1984 and 1985 Corvettes all seem to simply fall apart from normal use. The combination of the sun and the oils from the driver's hands cause the leather to rip and tear. This leather also twists around the wheel. The good part is it's really easy to install a new steering wheel. The bad part is it's not going to be cheap to do it.

The best choice is to purchase one of the upgraded wheels from any number of sources in the Corvette parts industry. The thick wheels just feel so much better as you drive down the road. It only costs about $30 more than re-

placing the old earlier thin-rim wheel. The only reason to ever install the original wheel back in the 1984 and 1985 Corvettes is if you intend to have the car NCRS judged.

Aftermarket steering wheels are a real problem because of the spoke designs. Almost any aftermarket wheel will bolt onto the steering column. The problem is that you won't be able to see your gauges once you've installed the aftermarket wheel.

When you get into the 1990 and newer models, you really don't want to start swapping steering wheels around because of the air bag. Air bags are very dangerous and can cause some serious damage if you're not very careful. Every professional mechanic I know has accidentally set an airbag off in a car. What do you think the chances are that a weekend warrior can change the steering wheel and get off incident-free?

One little trick for those of you who run Solo or track events. Coat your steering wheel with Lexol the day before the event. Lexol leather treatment leaves a sticky coating until it's buffed down. This sticky finish is just great in the middle of a tight turn. After the event you can simply buff the wheel with a towel, and you'll be all set to drive home.

Changing the Wheel

The first thing you need to do is purchase a steering wheel puller. The best place to do that is at your local NAPA store. NAPA stocks a reasonably priced professional one. The ones you get from AutoZone and Pep Boys are all produced as cheaply as possible offshore—usually in China—and they slip and bend easily.

You'll probably only use this puller twice in your life, but it's such aggravation working with poorly made tools that you should spend a few extra dollars to get a decent puller. Remember that being a tool addict is not a bad thing.

The first thing to do is disconnect the battery. The reason for this is you don't want to disturb your neighbors with the horn blowing. You'll lose your radio presets and the time on your clock, but it's still better than explaining why your horn kept going off.

The horn button is held in place with three little plastic prongs. A small screwdriver works best for pushing the prongs in to remove the cap. Be careful not to break one of these prongs off. Obviously, the cap won't stay on with only two prongs attached. You really don't want to have to purchase a new horn button because you tried to force things.

The horn button is held in place with three little plastic tabs. You can get a small screwdriver into the area and push the tabs back to remove the horn button. Be careful—if you break these tabs, you'll be looking around for a new horn button.

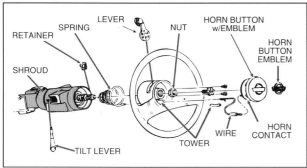

RETAINER   SPRING   LEVER   NUT   HORN BUTTON w/EMBLEM   HORN BUTTON EMBLEM

SHROUD

TILT LEVER   TOWER   WIRE   HORN CONTACT

All of this can be taken off with conventional tools. When you go into the shroud, you'll need a good-quality steering wheel tool sold by someone like NAPA. You'll need to compress the spring in order to remove the retainers. Just explain to the person at the counter what you need, and you'll not only have the tool, but their sympathies as well.

Once you get the horn button off, you can begin the descent into the bowels of the steering column. You'll see here that I've removed the telescoping mechanism. The next item to address will be the fancy circlip, followed by the nut that holds the wheel on. This whole job should take around 30 minutes, and, if it takes more than an hour, something's wrong.

Carpet Installation

 Time: 6 hours to 2 days

 Tools: Screwdrivers, carpet cement

 Talent:

 Applicable Years: 1984 to 1996

 Tab: $500 to $700

 Tip: You might want to do one section at a time.

COMPLEMENTARY MODIFICATION: This is a good time to replace any broken plastic parts in the interior. You may want to wait to place your order, however, since you may break some additional parts while installing the carpeting.

The first step to replacing the carpet is to decide how much carpeting you're going to replace. The 1984 to 1996 carpeting really consists of three different sections. You have the driver's side area, the passenger area, and the rear cargo area. If you really feel energetic and have a decent balance on your credit card, you can do all three sections at the same time. A more realistic approach is to simply do one area as the spirit moves you. If you're a typical person, you probably tend to lose interest about halfway through a project. Keep in mind that taking everything apart is easy. Putting things back together is where the frustration exists. However, you already knew that, didn't you?

A lot of people purchase the entire carpet set at one time because they want everything to match perfectly. Carpeting today is dyed in huge quantities, and the quality control is far better than it used to be. A few months, or even a year, between purchases won't make a great deal of difference in the carpet color. However, as we all know,

these projects tend to drag on far longer than we ever intended. This means it could be years between carpet purchases. And this means you could end up with carpet in different shades of the same color. More likely, though, the problem will come from having the first part of the project start to fade as you get around to finishing things up.

You should purchase carpet that matches the original perfectly. Corvettes that have been repainted will always lose some value, but if you install a different type, or even color, of carpeting in your Corvette, be prepared to take a serious financial hit upon resale. The $200 you save by purchasing something that is almost correct, instead of something that is perfect, won't be a wise decision.

The two carpet areas that take the greatest abuse are located in the rear area and on the driver's side. The rear area really fades quickly. If you want to see how much your carpet has faded, simply pull up the edge of the center section and look at the carpet that's been hidden from the sunlight. The good news is that the rear area is also the easiest section to work on.

The first job is to remove the front seats. This task takes a lot less time if you take off the roof—unless, of course, you own a convertible where you can simply lower the top for seat removal. Look at the chapter on swapping the seats around to remind yourself how to remove the four bolts that hold each of the seats in place. Also, be careful with all the electrical connections that have to be undone.

With the seats out of the way, you can progress to the most difficult part of the project—removing the sill covers without breaking them. The early sill covers come out easily in two pieces. The only problem is that's the wrong way

The later doorsills are a lot easier to work with than the early ones. The 1984 to 1987 cars have one huge piece of plastic that's almost impossible to remove. I suspect the assembly plant had the same sort of problems because in 1988 it went to a two-piece unit that lasted until the end of the C4.

You can always tell when a car has been repainted. This car was originally a black car. The body shop left the little adhesive pads for the sill plate in place during the painting process. This picture shows where you can expect to find the adhesive pads. Run your hair dryer in these areas to soften up the adhesive. Then carefully remove the huge plastic sill.

The center console is a difficult area. Make sure the carpeting tucks under the panels with no wrinkles.

When you remove the under padding, it might not be a bad idea to install some sort of sound deadener on flat panels in the rear. I used some cork that I found at Home Depot to do this. You can find better material at a local stereo store but plan on spending over $100 for it. You can also install a heat barrier kit in the front area of the car. The kit uses a ceramic cloth that's only 1/8-inch thick. Considering how hot the C4 Corvette gets, this may be a wise investment.

to do it. If you break one, the replacements are over $100 for the early cars. This is a task for two people working slowly and carefully.

The technique is to remove all the screws and then slowly move the sill cover around. They're really glued firmly down onto the doorsill. Chevrolet used some black putty between the plastic cover and the sill to prevent squeaks. There are three different areas under the sill where this putty was applied.

Over the years, the putty has hardened and will fight all reasonable attempts to remove the sill. One good technique is to use a heat gun to warm the sill cover so the putty will soften. While this makes the removal a little easier, it's still not the greatest job in the world. Just take your time here, and the cover will eventually pull off the doorsill.

Removing the carpeting from the floor is pretty simple. The only other area of difficulty is where the carpeting tucks up under the center console. It helps if you remove the screws that hold the center console plate in place. You'll have to do this to get the new carpeting tucked up into place so you may as well do it to remove the old carpeting now.

Don't try to remove backing that goes over the transmission. Although it's easy to remove, it is a nightmare to replace. The factory laid this insulation down over the tunnel and then placed everything over the top of the backing. If you try to replace this backing, you're going to have to remove all of the center console, not to mention the panels that go up the center of the dash on the early cars.

Be very careful with all the backing material since it isn't readily available. Before you start your project, check to see if this situation has changed.

PROJECT 68
Seat Swapping

 Time: Several hours

 Talent:

 Applicable Years: 1984 to 1996

 Tab: Under $20

 Tip: Be careful when you unplug the electrical connectors. Most of them have not aged well and have become very brittle.

 PERFORMANCE GAIN: You can put off restoring your seats for a few more years if you even out the wear patterns.

Most of the time, you're the only person in your Corvette. As a result, the driver's seat gets a whole lot more wear than the passenger seat. This means that the driver's seat is going to get nasty and worn-looking long before the passenger seat does.

When things get so bad that you're considering reupholstering, you'll have to make a decision as to whether or not to reupholster both seats – one of which is perfectly good. If you swap the seat cushions around, you can put off the inevitable for a while.

If you keep your Corvette long enough, when the inevitable finally happens, you'll have two seats that are both worn out. That way you can justify buying the reproduction seat covers for two seats.

The C4 Corvette has these nice little plastic covers over the front of the seat rails. They not only hide the seat rail, but they also hide the bolt you're going to have to remove as well. Take a very small screwdriver and simply pop the little round plug out. The whole cover can then be removed so you can loosen the seat bolts for removal.

This is a little lever arrangement that holds the lower seat cushion in place. You'll notice here that the seat is upside down. This really isn't necessary if all you want to do is just swap the lower cushions around. Once you've done this a couple of times, you'll be able to do it with the seat in place.

Above left: You'll notice the four little brackets on the seat shell. The seat back has four little rope loops that hook into these brackets. These little ropes are molded into the foam. Removal of the seat back is easy. You simply bend the seat cushion over far enough so you can see the loops. Using a long screwdriver, unhook the rope loops.

The part that's tricky is making sure that everything goes back together. You have to get the loops over the bracket. I've decided it either takes a special tool or a lot of experience, neither of which I have. I took the seat to my local upholstery guy, and he did it in about five minutes.

Above right: There is no reason for a Corvette seat to end up looking like this. If this seat back had been swapped around with the passenger seat, this left-side bolster would have been on the inside of the car and gotten virtually no wear. It could have easily gone another twenty thousand or more miles.

INTERIOR

170

Roll Bar Installation

Time: 6 to 8 hours

Tools: Welding equipment and cutting tools

Talent:

Applicable Years: 1984 to 1996

Tab: $500 to $1,000

Tip: Make sure you locate a skilled welder who's willing to work on cars before you even order the roll bar.

PERFORMANCE GAIN: Handling will be improved due to the added chassis stiffness.

COMPLEMENTARY MODIFICATION: This may be the time to consider replacement of the rear carpeting since it will all have to be removed for the roll bar installation.

Installing a roll bar is a big step. It's not all that difficult to do, but there's really no going back once you install one. Most modifications can be turned around, and your Corvette can be made original again. However, once you cut holes in the rear of the interior floor, it's pretty difficult to cover them up. Still, new carpeting does wonders.

While there are people who install bars for appearance, most use their Corvettes for track events. Even then, installing a roll bar is something you don't need to do until you've run track events for a couple of years. A roll bar, or, as the manufacturers call it, a chassis stiffener bar, is going to make some improvements. It will not make you fast. The way to be fast is to drive better. That's something none of us like to admit. We're all looking for that magic part.

A roll bar simply ties the frame together. This means that you'll pick up more precision in the rear suspension. And it means that when you enter and exit a corner, your car will be a lot more predictable. Less chassis flex means cornering will be the same every time you drive through a corner.

The ultimate solution to chassis flex is to install a full roll cage. This will tie everything together. The only problem is that you should never drive a car with a full cage on the street—it's just way too dangerous. At the track, you're strapped in with at least a five-point harness. Then your head is encased in a helmet. At the same time, the bar's all covered in energy absorbing foam. If anything bad happens, you're in pretty decent shape.

INTERIOR

This is a chassis stiffener, or roll bar, I acquired from Doug Rippie. I figured that Doug Rippie would have the best bar since he was very involved in the Corvette Challenge series and built any number of C4 race cars. I've installed a number of roll bars over the years, and this was one of the very few that actually fit.

171

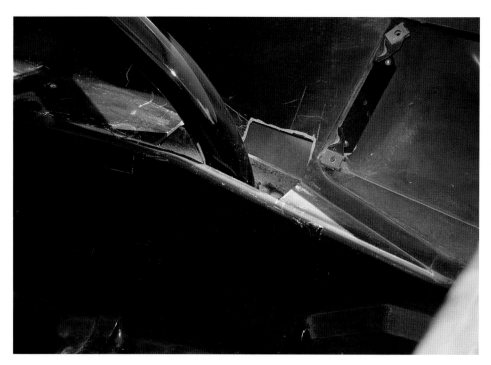

You're going to cut a couple more holes in the plastic for the rear legs. These cuts have to be large enough so the welder can work on the edges with reasonable ease. You're going to cover these holes with some aluminum plates before you're done so they don't have to look all that pretty. They just have to be fairly large.

Now let's pretend you're doing your morning commute. You have your lap belt on and maybe even your shoulder straps. You surely don't have a helmet on, and you would never wear your belts as tight as you do at the track. If you have any kind of accident, your head is going to impact the cage. When your skull meets steel tube, it's obvious who's going to win. You can easily end up with severe brain damage from this encounter.

The fad of running a full roll cage on the street needs to stop. It's a very dangerous practice. Simply having a roll bar isn't as dangerous since the head restraint in the seat should keep you from hitting any tubes in the bar. Make sure you check this, however. You may need to purchase some of the special high-density foam sold by the race shops just for this purpose.

This is also when you have to decide on what finish you want on the bar. If you want a classy look for the street, I suggest you take the bar to your local upholstery shop and have it covered in a nice soft black leather. Make certain that the upholstery can be removed for cleaning. Some people use Velcro for attachment and that works nicely. The leather covering really gives your car a high-end look and minimizes the boy racer look.

Another choice is to take the bar over to your local body shop and have urethane paint applied. The employees won't be happy to see you, and the total bill may be larger than what Rippie charged you for the bar in the first place, but the finished bar sure will look wonderful.

While your bar is being covered or painted, you can start to remove all the carpeting and sound deadener in the rear of the car. This includes the carpeting behind the seats. Everything comes out—including every last strip of plastic trim and all of the sound deadener under the carpet. Anything that can start a fire should be out of the car.

It's a lot easier to work on the car with every bit of fabric and plastic out of the car, and your welder is going to require this. Any welder you find willing to work on this bar will be very demanding about this situation. You might as well get started on the removal process right away.

You'll need to remove the front seats just for a trial fitting of the roll bar. It's a lot easier to get the bar in the car with the seats and roof panel removed. Remember, each seat is only held in with four bolts. Check out the chapter on seats again for a refresher course in seat removal. The good part is that only one seat has to go back in for the drive to the welder.

With the seats and all the rear carpeting removed, you can place the bar in the car. Mark out the areas of fiberglass that have to be cut away for the two front mounts. Chalk, or a yellow grease pencil, works nicely for this task.

Start with the front uprights. It's easy to see where these front uprights belong on the little ledge. You don't want to cut any of the metal ledge away, but you will need to remove some of the plastic. Once you get the bar situated, you can see how it has to move to the rear of the car. That will require some cutting.

With the cuts made in the area just behind the ledge, you can place the bar back in the car. You should be able to easily see where the cuts will have to be made for the rear legs. When you mark the area for cutting away the floor for these two rear mounts, make the cuts about two inches to the rear of where the mounts sit at this time. After you remove the roll bar, you can cut the fiberglass with a small circular carbide cutting saw. Then fit the bar back into the car. Check to see that you have enough room so that

There is some lack of rear vision, but that's why your Corvette has mirrors on the doors. You'll also notice how close the bar fits to the roof halo. That's a good thing. This helps a lot with any vision problems to the rear.

the sides can be welded. Make sure you take your carbide cutting tool with you to the welder in case he wants more plastic removed.

A bolt-in roll bar is really not a good option. Remember, the idea is to stiffen the chassis. A bolt-in roll bar really won't give you the stiffness you want. You've already cut four holes in the floor of your car, why quibble now?

Don't forget to disconnect the battery before the welding. There's a good chance that you could destroy the electrical system if you leave the battery connected while the welding takes place.

You should be able to weld at least three sides of each of the four legs. It seems that the fourth side is not all that easy to reach. A good secure weld on three of the sides should work just fine, however.

Now that you have the bar welded, you can put everything back together. When you drove home from the welding shop, you probably noticed a considerable increase in the noise level. It's almost impossible to get the noise level back to pre–roll bar levels, but you can come close. The first thing to do is to make up some plates to cover the holes you cut in the floor. I use aluminum plates that are about 1/16th of an inch, or something around .060 inch in thickness. Cut them with about an inch of overlap to the original body. You're going to create eight of these plates

since you need to cover the hole both to the front and the rear of the roll bar. Take your time shaping them around the roll bar braces. The better the fit, the less noise you're going to have.

Once you have the plates fitted, but before you rivet them in place, you can begin filling the hole with foam insulation to keep the noise level down. If your Corvette is a track-only car, you can skip this step.

Wrap the roll bar with something like Saran Wrap before you spray the foam in the cavity. You don't want the foam to stick to the roll bar. The floor panel in the rear area will move in relation to the bar, and there has to be some way for this movement to take place.

With everything taped up, you can spray the foam insulation in the cavity and watch the magic of chemistry take place. Once the insulation has hardened, you can smooth it off to the same level as the floor. Then put your aluminum plates in place with some sealant around the edges to further seal the area tightly. Add a few well-placed rivets, and you're done.

You should probably use new carpet underlay for the rear area making the necessary cuts around the four legs of the roll bar. Then put the carpeting in place and make the necessary cuts so the carpeting can lie flat. The final step is to take the carpeting to a carpet store to have the edges sewn. Now you have a truly professional-looking job.

PROJECT 70
Air Conditioning Maintenance

Time: 2 to 3 hours

Tools: You'll have to locate a shop with a refrigerant recovery machine.

Talent:

Applicable Years: 1984 to 1996

Tab: $150 to $200

Tip: Make sure the shop creates a vacuum in your air conditioning system to boil all the moisture out.

COMPLEMENTARY WORK: If you have to clean the condenser, you should clean the area behind the condenser. Remember, we're talking about enhanced airflow, and it would do little good to simply clean one side of the condenser. You want the air to flow through the condenser, not just bump up against it.

Air conditioning either works or doesn't work. When it comes right down to it, there just aren't many things that can go wrong with your air conditioning system. When something does go wrong, it's usually beyond the capabilities of the average weekend warrior.

In 1994 General Motors switched to R134 as an air conditioning refrigerant. There were a lot of dire warnings and several shouts of, "The sky is falling!" Now it can be seen that all of the talk was simply alarmist rhetoric.

If your Corvette is one of the 1984 to 1993 models, R12 refrigerant is going to be around for a long time. It's very expensive and will get even more expensive in the

future. On the other hand, I've never seen a retrofit to R134 that adequately cooled a C4. There's the simple fact R134 is 10 percent less efficient as a coolant than R12 is. You already know how hot your C4 can get in the summer. Do you really want a 10 percent drop in efficiency? There's so much glass in that back window that a system retrofitted to R134 just can't cope with the heat.

My suggestion is that if you have R12 in your car, keep using it, and just bite the bullet when it comes time to add, or replace, the refrigerant. As expensive as R12 may be, it will cost you more to convert the system with R134. And if you do, you will get less cooling. More money for less effectiveness doesn't sound like a very good deal.

At the very least, you may have to purchase a pound of R12 every couple of years. Even if your compressor destroys itself, you still shouldn't have to purchase any R12 since the shop working on the compressor will have to recover the R12, not lose it to the atmosphere. That means when the technicians complete their work on the system, they can simply put your old R12 back into your car.

One alarming trend in the service industry is the large numbers of what can best be called mystery refrigerant. As the price of R12, and even R134, increased, some very strange things started to come on the market. Even Butane is being packaged for use as a refrigerant. The EPA has approved some of these alternatives, but some of them have not been approved. GM has not authorized the use of anything other than R134 in its systems. This is a case of making sure you ask the service facility what it intends to place in your Corvette's air conditioning system.

If you have to open the air conditioning system for any reason, you'll need to replace the receiver/dryer. The receiver/dryer is nothing more than a storage tank for the liquid refrigerant that comes from the condenser. As the refrigerant flows through the condenser, it has to pass through a desiccant that absorbs the moisture in the system. If you insist on using the old dryer, your air conditioning system will perform very poorly.

174

This is the air conditioning compressor from an early C4. Getting one of these rebuilt will try your patience. Most places will want to sell you a factory-rebuilt unit. The problem is that it won't have the correct serial numbers should you have a desire for a matching-numbers car.

Most shops today use an analyzer to determine what type of refrigerant is currently in your air conditioning system. If you purchased your Corvette used, nothing should surprise you here. There are some strange things being found in air conditioning systems—I've even seen systems with propane in them. If you happen to have purchased a used Corvette with a unique refrigerant, be prepared for a sizable disposal charge. Some of these refrigerants have been declared hazardous by the EPA, and you will incur a hefty recovery/disposal charge because of that.

You need to learn all you can about air conditioning sealers. A lot of the discount outlets are selling these products. The sealers aren't new—they're just much more common than they used to be. They work the same way as any other seal sweller in that they contain chemicals that attack the rubber O-rings and cause them to expand. The interesting part is that they actually work as advertised. The problem with these is that when you take your Corvette to a shop, these sealants could easily clog the shop's refrigerant recovery machine. This could result in both you and your Corvette being banned from a very nice shop. If you use one of the sealants, please tell the shop what you have in the system.

The Compressor

The single most common problem, other than leaks, is compressor failure. The good part is that the Corvette air conditioning compressor is very rugged. The bad part is

that it will eventually go bad. Replacing the compressor is one job that's really beyond your own capabilities.

The compressor can fail, and the system still be full of R12 or R134. You should not vent this refrigerant into the atmosphere. That means you have to take your Corvette to an experienced air conditioning specialist with a recovery machine.

If you have a blown-up compressor, you have to deal with the possibility of the replacement meeting an early demise. Some people advocate flushing the entire system with a product such as Bright Solutions Terpene Flush. An equal number of people believe that it's all simply a waste of time and money. They argue that you're never going to get all the metal fragments out so just go ahead and replace the lines before you lose the new compressor.

One thing you might do if you've had an internal compressor failure is add a filter in the lines to ensure that metal shavings won't get into the new compressor. This is nothing more than a fine mesh screen. The idea is to trap any little particles before they destroy your new compressor.

The Restoration Question

If you want to keep your Corvette original, you're going to have to find someone locally that can rebuild your compressor. That's not going to be an easy task.

One alternative is to simply install a remanufactured compressor and keep the original on a shelf in the garage. A

This is the later compressor. These are no more, nor no less, reliable than the earlier ones. They can't be interchanged, though. Remember, if you have any intention of keeping your C4 totally original, you'll need to keep your original compressor.

lot of people do that with engines, so why not do the same with air conditioning compressors and alternators?

The problem is that both NCRS and Bloomington Gold are going to require a performance verification test of your air conditioning system for the highest award. This means that, at some point, you're going to have to have that old compressor repaired. In order to receive the top award, the air conditioning system will have to be operable. That means something resembling cold air has to come out of the vents.

Cleaning the Condenser Area

Earlier in the book, I discussed the process of cleaning out the area between your radiator and air conditioning compressor. Now you have one more reason to attack this project. If you remember, the problem is that dirt and paper get sucked up between the condenser and the radiator. Most people think of this as an engine cooling issue. It's also a big air conditioning issue.

Air has to flow though the condenser to cool the refrigerant. If the area behind the condenser is clogged, no air is going to get through the unit. This means the air conditioning will work, but it just won't be as effective as it could be.

It's critical to have proper airflow through the condenser. You already know that the area between the condenser and the radiator fills up with all sorts of road trash. You can improve the operation of the air conditioning system by cleaning the area between the condenser and the radiator. It helps if you actually remove the radiator to get the back of the condenser clean. Unfortunately removing the condenser involves evacuating the refrigerant. That's something you don't really want to do unless it's already leaked out.

You might want to locate a company in your local area that deals with commercial refrigeration. It will use some very effective chemical sprays for cleaning the tubes in commercial refrigeration units. These chemicals are equally effective at cleaning the condenser in your Corvette. You simply spray your condenser with the chemicals and let them soak in. Then rinse them with a hose. This generally makes a huge difference. All of this goes to prove that more refrigerant is not always the correct answer to effective cooling.

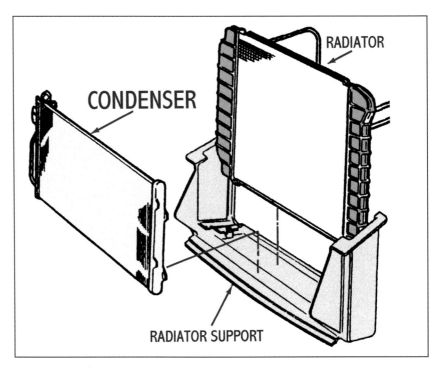

INTERIOR

176

Delco Bose Sound System Repair and Replacement

 Time: Several hours

 Tools: Screwdrivers

 Talent:

 Applicable Years: 1984 to 1996

 Tab: $150 to $1,000

 Tip: Make an early decision about whether you want to repair the Bose unit currently in your car or whether you would rather spend the money on a new system.

COMPLEMENTARY MODIFICATION: If you truly enjoy stereo in your car, and your system actually works, this might be a good time to investigate the use of sound-deadening materials. These can be placed under the carpet and upon any panel that might have a tendency to vibrate.

There are only two choices here. You can either fix what you have or put in a whole new stereo system. You can't upgrade the current system. The Delco Bose stereo system has always been more about hype than performance. I've never met a Corvette owner who thought this was a really great stereo system.

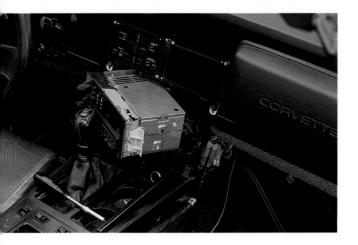

The Delco Bose is a unique system. It's different from any other stereo system. It relies on smaller speakers contained in their own boxes, each powered by a small amplifier rather than a larger speaker powered simply by the head unit. What was first heralded as being very innovative is now simply a pain in the rear. If anything goes wrong with the system, you're stuck with replacing the stock component. Forget putting those huge 12-inch bass speakers in the rear behind the seats.

In my opinion, if you're going to go to all the trouble of replacing the Delco Bose, you should get something that can play digital files. In fact, the ability to use digital files may be the single most important reason to simply rip out the whole Delco Bose system and replace it with some new technology.

The hardest part of working with the Delco Bose is diagnosing the system. You have five places where things can go wrong. The head unit that's installed in the center of your dash, or one of the four speaker units. The replacement of these items is really not much of a project. It's figuring out what's wrong that'll make you crazy.

Most Corvette mail-order companies sell remanufactured speaker/amplifier units, but they're not cheap. Each speaker, complete with the amplifier, is going to cost about $150. When you spend that sort of money, you want to be sure it really is the defective part.

The rear speakers are the easiest to replace since everything is right in view, and you only have to remove the speaker grille. The front units on the early cars require that you remove the door panels

Once you remove the front dash panel, you'll find four screws, or maybe small bolts, holding the head unit in the dash. Remove those and then unplug the unit from the color-coded plugs. Then do just what your Chevrolet dealer does. Drop the unit off at the nearest car audio store.

The best suggestion I can make is that the first time you have a problem with the Bose, you decide to replace it. I went through three Bose heads and about eight speakers before I simply ripped the whole system out. Track cars don't need stereos.

The only problem with installing a new system is that you'll have to snake some wires through the interior and under the carpeting. Luckily, that's not all that difficult.

On the cars with the early dash, you simply have to remove the center section. Then you'll find four little bolts that, when removed, allow you to simply slide the unit out of the dash. The good thing is the plugs are color coordinated.

INTERIOR

Another hard part of working with this system is the accessibility to the door speaker/amplifiers. The interior door skin has to be removed and a variety of things unplugged. This is no major effort, just an annoyance.

The other items that you should work on are the speaker enclosures. Chevrolet went to great efforts to design them properly. The only problem is that, at this point in time, they're over twenty years old. You should stop at your local audio store and ask for advice as to what you can do with these enclosures. A whole new level of technology has been created for these enclosures in the past few years.

There are a number of audio companies that specialize in repairing the Delco Bose systems. The problem is that most of them require that you remove the unit from your car and send it to them. This isn't a big deal unless you have a 1990 to 1993 Corvette. On these cars, the actual radio isn't what you see in your dash. The real radio is stuffed up under the dash on the passenger side of the car.

Here are examples of the processes to follow to remove a Delco Bose system:

1984 to 1989
• Remove the screws from the panel that go across the digital dash and the car stereo trim panel. There is a screw hidden behind the edge of the digital dash trim panel.

You see this unit in your dash. It's the control assembly. The real radio, or receiver, is hidden deep in your car on the 1990 to 1996 Corvettes. Any number of people have removed this control assembly and taken it to the radio shop for repair, only to be sent back home to retrieve the other part of the radio. A—Instrument Panel Carrier Locator, 1—Radio Control Assembly Retainer, 2—Radio Control Assembly, 3—Radio Control Assembly Screw, 4—Instrument Panel Carrier Assembly, 5—Instrument Panel Wiring Harness Connector

• Move the gear shifter to the lowest position.
• Pull the right edge of the bezel forward, unhook the left side, and remove.
• There are only four bolts holding the radio into the dash.

1990 to 1996
• Remove the two screws located in air conditioning vents and pull the vents from dash.
• Now open the center console and lift the corners of carpet.
• Remove the rubber inserts in the cup holders.
• Remove the three screws you find there.
• Set the parking brake and shift to drive.
• Remove the center armrest door.
• Lift the center console up and back.
• Remove the three screws from the car stereo trim bezel.
• Remove the stereo trim bezel by pulling it forward and releasing the three clips.
• Remove the two screws that secure the side panels. This will give you a little room to play when executing the next few steps.
• Gently push the right side of the dash trim out.
• Remove the four screws securing the car stereo to dash. Be aware that the left bottom side screw is difficult to move.
• Remove the stereo from the dash, reaching around to remove the two connectors.

The Amplifier Box—1990 to 1993.
• Remove the three screws securing the bottom dash panel.
• Open the fuse panel and remove the three screws that secure the panel.
• Remove the one screw exposed from removing the panel.
• Pull back the corner of the carpet that is attached by Velcro to the bottom dash panel.
• Drop the bottom dash panel, disconnecting the courtesy light connector.

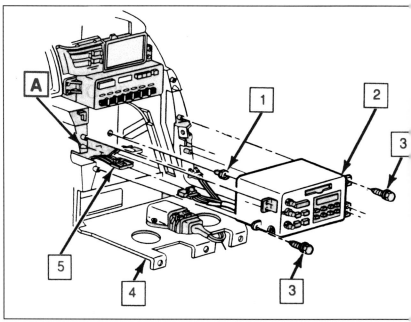

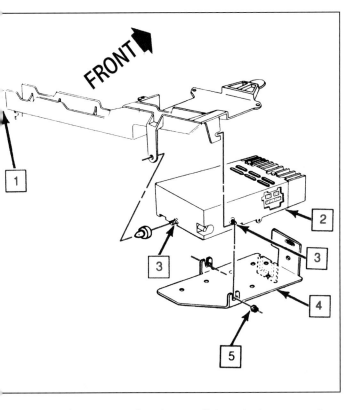

Here is the receiver unit. This is the part stuffed up under the passenger-side lower dash panel.
1 — Multi-Use Relay Bracket, 2 — Radio Receiver, 3 — Radio Receiver Stud, 4 — Instrument Panel Wiring Harness Bracket, 5 — Radio Receiver Nut

- Remove the two 10-millimeter nuts, one from each side of CDM box. One is buried—just keep looking until you find it.
- Look up at CDM box from under dash; there are four connectors clipped to the plastic covering CDM box.
- Remove two connectors from the CDM box on the side toward the center of the car. Release the trigger and remove.
- The CDM box has a guide pin hidden up behind the dash. This pin helps to secure unit to the dash. Since the two 10-millimeter nuts have been removed, there are two "L" shaped guides, one on each side that the screws are notched into. This part of the process is not much fun. The CDM box needs to be pushed toward the front of the car to release one of the clips and then back to release the second. When you release the second plastic panel below, the CDM can be dropped a little to give you some play.
- Remove the connectors and the antenna from side of the CDM.
- Now drop the CDM box down. Because it's wedged into the dash, it's going to require a little work to release.
- The side of the CDM box mounted toward the front of the car will come out first.

If you think this process is difficult, keep in mind that the actual removal is even worse.

The Amplifier Box—1994 to 1996
- Open the pocket behind the passenger seat.
- Remove the plastic insert.
- The CDM is located in the bottom of the well.
- Disconnect the antenna and connectors.

Front Speakers—1990 to 1994
- Remove the three screws from the panel.
- Pull the bottom edge of the panel away from the door jam, then pull down to unlock the upper edge of the panel.
- Remove two or three screws from the panel.
- Lift the panel from the rear to release it from under the front plastic panel. The entire panel needs to be worked out from around the emergency brake handle.
- Disconnect the Bose amplifier enclosure connector.
- Remove the two screws securing the leading edge of the Bose enclosure.
- Remove the two screws from the rear edge of the Bose enclosure.

Now we arrive at the speakers that resemble a big bulge in the carpet. The speaker covers are actually part of the doorsill covering. You have to remove the sill panel. Whatever you do, don't try to pry the covers off.

Interior Door Panel Removal

 Time: Several hours

 Tools: Screwdrivers

 Talent:

 Applicable Years: 1984 to 1996

 Tab: $10 to $400

 Tip: Don't get too carried away tightening the screws on the door panel. It's really easy to split the plastic panels.

COMPLEMENTARY MODIFICATION: Chevrolet added sound insulators in 1992. These are great updates for the earlier cars. The best part is that they cost less than $25.

I've had to take the interior door panels off so many times I would like to attach them with Velcro. There are several reasons you need to get into these door panels. For one, in the early cars, it's the only way to replace the Delco Bose amplifiers. Secondly, traditional power window problems are common with the earlier cars. Finally, almost every C4 is going to have to have the rubber window wiper strips replaced on the doors.

You'll also need to remove these panels if you need to replace the door handles or if you do any

work on the lock cylinders. Plus, if you have any rearview mirror problems, you need to have access as well. I trust you're getting the idea by this point. This all means that if you own a 1984 to 1987 Corvette, you're going to get really good at removing door panels.

If you own the 1988 to 1996 version of the C4, you won't need to get into the door panels except every few years, or maybe only once a decade. The big point is to be careful and don't break anything. Be especially careful that you don't split the vinyl on the panel. These door panels are around $400 each.

Taking the door apart should take you about a half hour. You can get started by disconnecting the negative terminal from the battery to protect the wiring. If you haven't noticed, I have this thing about working around electrical parts. It's so easy to disconnect the battery on the C4 Corvette that you should do it as an insurance policy. The only drawback is that you'll lose your radio station presets.

There are sheet metal screws located along the bottom edge of the door carpeting, in the door recess where you put your fingers to close the door, along with several hidden screws. One of the hidden screws is located behind the slide that locks the door. The door slide I'm referring to is under the inside door handle. Another screw is located inside the door and access is gained by removing the window switch. Disconnect the two wiring connectors from the switch and lay it aside. Using a small flashlight, locate the screw through the hole where the switch was removed. This screw is about 1-1/2 inch long and is the only one this

The door panels stayed the same from 1984 to the interior redesign in 1990. Still, the procedure for removing the door has remained essentially the same. One good thing about the Corvette is that things stay pretty much the same through a model run. GM is reluctant to spend a substantial amount of money on large changes. This is good for those of us who purchase the old cars.

INTERIOR

size in the door. There are also one or two screws behind the courtesy lamp bezel. The bezel is pried out from the top. Carefully remove the bezel so you don't break it or the two lamps mounted inside it. Make sure that you have something to place all the small parts in that you remove in this process. You'll end up with a pretty good collection.

Carefully remove the trim panel from the door. If it doesn't come off the doorframe easily, start checking to see if you've overlooked a mounting screw. This job is a lot easier if someone can hold the panel while you search around for things you forgot to remove or disconnect.

You might find something called a water deflector behind the trim. This is really nothing more then a sheet of dense foam rubber. Use care when removing it since it tears easily. It'll be necessary to remove the four to six plastic clips that run along the door, holding the wiring harness in place. Needle-nose pliers work nicely for prying the plastic clips out of the door. The water deflector is held onto the door with double-sided tape. The alternative to the double-sided tape is 3M weather-strip adhesive.

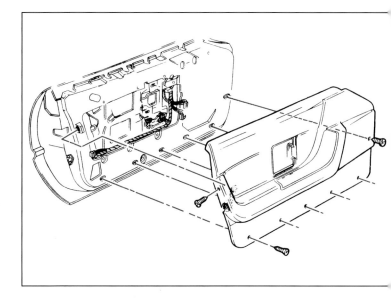

Most of the screws are down along the bottom edge of the panel. You have five of them, and they're generally hidden in the carpeting. Finding all the door panel screws is sort of like going on a scavenger hunt.

Be careful when you replace these screws. If you tighten them too much, you'll crack the plastic door skin. Stop when you're ahead here.

I thought these little metal inserts for the door handles were pretty silly. Then someone gave me a set, and I really like them. They give the door a solid feel when you pull it shut. They're sold as a way to keep your door panel from pulling apart. Since I've never seen a door panel that pulled apart you really don't need them. Still, they're just nice to have.

SECTION TEN
BODY

Parts courtesy Corvette Central

Rear Window Support Strut Replacement

 Time: 30 minutes to 2 hours

 Tools: Open-end metric wrenches

 Talent:

 Applicable Years: 1984 to 1996

 Tab: $35 per strut

 Tip: Get a board to act as a brace for the rear window while you replace a strut. You'll also need a helper for this task.

COMPLEMENTARY MODIFICATION: This may be a good time to repair the electrical grid that acts as a defroster. It's also a good time to think about replacing the weather-stripping around the rear window if you have any leaks.

The rear window struts are pretty sturdy units. Considering all the work that they do over the years, it's amazing that they hold up so well. They're also really easy to replace. It's probably a good idea to replace them in pairs since both are needed to hold the heavy glass window up.

The important point is to create a good brace that will hold the window in place as you replace the strut. The rear window is one very heavy item. It's also a very expensive item. The good part is that while you're replacing the struts, the window is still bolted in at the top of the halo, or Targa bar. You must also be careful with the struts themselves. Removing them improperly can cause them to release with a great deal of force. If you're in the way, the potential for injury is high. Refer to your GM service manual for the proper removal procedure.

The best way to approach this is to have a friend stop over to lend a helping hand. It's sort of like the process of bleeding brakes. The help is nice to have, even if it's not absolutely necessary. You really don't need to be reminded that this is one very large piece of glass. If anything goes wrong in this process, it's nice to have someone around to help with the glass.

Before you get started with the removal of the struts, make sure you have everything laid out on the garage floor. It's no fun having the window up in the air while you search for the correct tool.

Don't forget to disconnect the defroster wires from the struts before you unbolt anything. These have a little tab that you have to pull back and then they simply slide apart.

Adjustments

I've seen cases where the rear hatch glass has actually shifted over the years. You might want to look at how the glass aligns with the body panels on the rear of the car. If it's out of alignment, you'll notice it. If you can't see a problem, just leave well enough alone. Don't create problems where none exist.

If you see a problem, start by loosening the bolts that attach the glass to the roof assembly. Then make sure that the assist rods that go the glass are loose. You can move the glass by adjusting the rotating bracket assembly. This is a case where you need someone to help you. One person can help move the glass around and the other can lie in the back area to tighten the bolts. Don't forget that you have all the weather-stripping to push against. Take your time and make sure the glass is properly aligned with the body panels.

BODY

183

Even with the rear hatch glass braced, I wouldn't attempt this job by myself. This rear glass is heavy and any problems could get very expensive very quickly.

This is actually an eccentric and can be use to adjust the position of the rear hatch glass on the body. There are rare cases where the glass has shifted on the body. This usually means that the bolts that hold the glass to the forward hinge are loose. The trick is to loosen the four bolts and then use the eccentrics to shift the glass into position. This is one of those very time-consuming and tedious jobs. Make sure you really need to do this before you get started.

PROJECT 74

Broken Hood Cables

 Time: 1 hour

 Tools: Vise grips, metric sockets

 Talent:

 Applicable Years: 1984 to 1996

 Tab: $75

 Tip: Don't use the special tool that's sold by the mail-order companies. If you can't grab the broken cable at the point where it enters the handle, just take the car to a shop that specializes in Corvettes.

COMPLEMENTARY MODIFICATION: You might want to consider replacing the springs that cause the hood to pop open when the cable releases the hood latches.

I had read about broken hood cable and even thought about it a few times. Then I quickly dismissed the idea as being a little silly. I was under the assumption that broken cables don't happen, and was convinced that the tool was just another gimmick for the aftermarket to make money.

Then one day I reached in to open the hood, and the latch moved entirely too easy. At that point, I understood what people had been trying to convince me of.

The best solution to this problem is to simply take the car to an experienced Corvette shop. The people there will have the hood open in about ten minutes. If it's a really tough one, it might take a half hour. Corvette shops have replaced enough cables that this type of repair ranks right up there with the traditional oil change.

I can't recommend the tool that everyone sells in the catalogs. There are two problems with the tool. First, you need some experience using it. This is not a simple operation. You have to move it around just right to get everything in place. Considering you may only have one broken cable in your lifetime, do you really need the tool? More importantly, how will you ever develop the experience required to make this tool work?

Now comes the bad news. If you move it the wrong way at a certain point, you're going to break the windshield. Now you'll not only need to open the hood, but you'll need to replace the windshield. This is why shops won't use the tool. When experienced Corvette shops don't use the tool and can't recommend using it, why do I need this item in my toolbox?

After you've decided that you can't get the hood open, spend a few minutes investigating things. A very common breaking point is right at the handle that's used for opening the hood. If you're lucky, the cable will have already broken, and you can grab the cable with a pair of pliers. Once you have the hood open, you can simply replace the cable with a new one.

The other alternative is to fabricate a long hook and reach up from underneath the car. You need to use the hook to release the latch with the broken cable. I've seen this done, but has never been able to do it myself. If you run into a similar problem, find an experienced Corvette shop, and its employees will have it done before you can finish your coffee.

The cable can be adjusted at this point. If you're having problems, try adjusting it just a little bit at a time. After a half-dozen tries, you'll get it correct. Don't attempt major adjustments.

BODY

185

Over the years, this spring loses its tension. The hood was designed so that when you open the release, the hood will pop up off the latches. Most likely this won't happen with your Corvette. If you want to restore the original functioning, you can replace this plate.

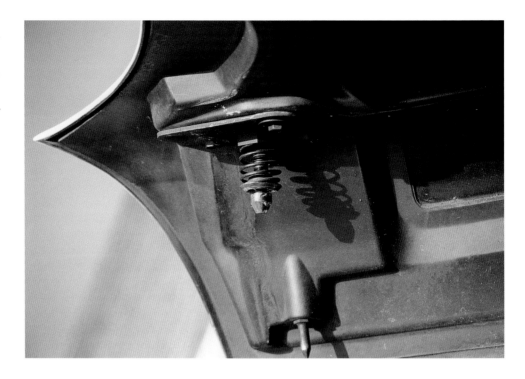

Keeping the area where the hood makes contact with the frame connector well greased is a good idea. White lithium grease works nicely on the contact areas. The grease will hold down the wear problems and any possible squeaking noise.

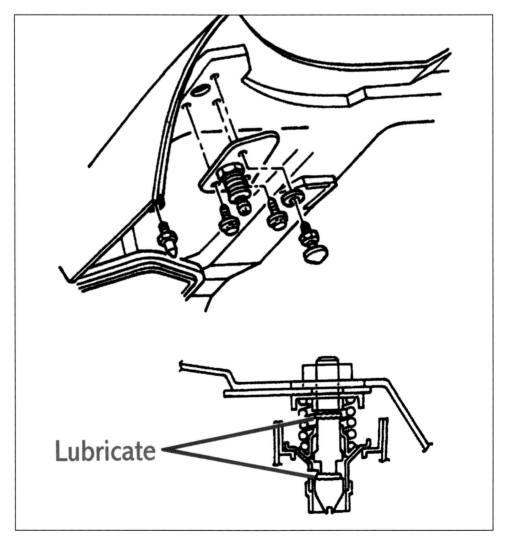

Lubricate

PROJECT 75
Side Window Wiper Strip Replacement

 Time: 2 to 3 hours

 Tools: Drill, rivets

 Talent:

 Applicable Years: 1984 to 1996

 Tab: $60 to $90

 Tip: If you have an early C4, you should use this project as an opportunity to install the door silencer, or insulator package, that was standard on the later cars. You can purchase a pair of these for around $50.

COMPLEMENTARY MODIFICATION: Actually, I would call this job itself complementary work. If you have to go into the door for any other work, you might as well replace the side wiper strip. It's a lot of work to go in just for this wiper strip, so try and combine it with another job. This is one project where you should combine several items.

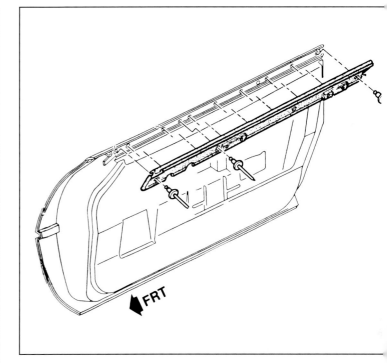

It looks so simple here. You just drill some holes and rivet the new window/door seal into place. Actually that's the easiest part of the job. Typical of everything else you do on the C4 Corvette, just getting to that point is the hard part. Take your time. Just don't drill holes in your doors when you drill out the old rivets.

If you keep your Corvette long enough, you'll get to do this job a couple of times. Whatever GM specified for the composition of these side window wiper strips was wrong. After a few years, the plastic hardens and starts to break away in big chunks. Not only does it start to look ugly, but the black starts to run down the side of the car.

This job has to rank right up there with replacing the front spoiler. If you keep your car long enough, it will become a part of routine maintenance. Every few years you'll get to do it again.

Replacing the wiper strips is actually the easy part. The hard part is getting to them. The door panel has to be stripped down. But you don't really have to remove the entire panel and set it aside. One little trick is to get a friend to work with you and hold the door panel while you drill the old door seal out. That way you don't have to unplug all the electrical connections.

Since I've covered the door panel in another project, I'm going to assume that you are at the point where you're ready to remove the old strip. The idea is to drill out the old rivets without drilling through your door. The trick here is to get some vacuum hose where the inside diameter is the same as your drill bit. I usually use a 1/4-inch drill bit since I only want to remove the head of the rivet, not make a new hole here.

Now slip the vacuum hose over the drill so only a little bit of the drill bit is exposed. You'll be able to drill out the rivet head, but the hose will prevent the drill from going any deeper. Nothing will ruin your day quicker than watching your drill bit come out the exterior side of your door.

Once you have all the old rivets drilled out, you can install the new wiper strip. Some of the kits include new rivets, and others do not. The genuine Chevrolet kit requires that you make a trip to the hardware store to purchase some new rivets. Get the aluminum ones since you really don't need rust in this location.

From this point on it's simply a matter of putting everything back together. Remember, don't get carried away tightening the screws that hold the door panel to the doorframe. It's really easy to split the plastic in an attempt to get everything tight.

One thing you can do is get some large plastic sheeting in a heavy thickness. Cut it to match the opening on the doorframe and then glue it in place using weather-strip adhesive. Stick it to the door before you install the door panel back in place. The other alternative is to use the factory insulator packet that was used on the later Corvettes.

Front Spoiler Replacement

 Time: 2 hours

 Tools: Sockets and screwdrivers

 Talent:

 Applicable Years: 1984 to 1996

 Tab: $100

 Tip: You don't have to replace the entire spoiler. Remember, it comes in three pieces. The way these spoilers get abused, you might want to consider doing one section each year. That way you won't be spending a lot money, and your car will always look decent.

 PERFORMANCE GAIN: Improved radiator flow may help the car run a little cooler on the highway. The spoilers don't have much effect on local driving.

COMPLEMENTARY MODIFICATION: If you have an overheating problem, it's probably because of a lot of dirt is trapped between the radiator and the air conditioning compressor. Broken spoilers usually won't cause your Corvette to overheat.

The front spoiler on the C4 Corvette will be the bane of your existence. If you keep a 1984 to 1996 Corvette long enough, you'll go through several of these spoilers. No matter how careful you might be, this spoiler is going to scrape the pavement at some time.

There's one basic fact that gets overlooked by most people: on the early cars, there were two different spoilers available. The base suspension cars got a shorter spoiler than the cars equipped with the Z51 suspension. The theory here was that the Corvettes with the Z51 suspensions wouldn't bounce as much going over bumps so the spoiler could be closer to the pavement.

The reality of the situation was that the Z51 spoilers just got torn up quicker. If I only drove my Corvette on the street, I would opt for the non-Z51 spoiler. If I were concerned about originality with my Z51-optioned car, I would go for the original spoiler. The third choice, and more people are doing this every year, is to keep a street spoiler and put the really nice correct one on the day before you go to a show.

This is really a two-person job. I have difficulty thinking about how I would do it by myself. One person has to use a 1/4-inch ratchet with a long extension and maybe

even a universal on the end. One person can use this socket from the top of the car while the second person is under the car keeping the nuts from turning. The center section is really easy. The side extensions test your collection of 1/4-inch extensions and swivel sockets.

With the old spoiler in the trash, you get to reverse the process. After a break, one person gets back on the ground and pushes the bolts up through the holes. The second person reaches around all of the stuff in the front corner and

By the time the average C4 gets over a decade old, the spoiler is usually a mess and is held together with an assortment of nuts and bolts, not to mention cable ties. Take a good look at the situation before you place your order. You may want to order the mounting kit that's available as well as the spoiler.

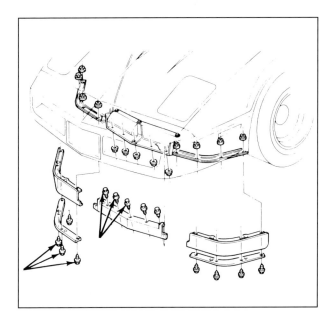

BODY

189

places the nut on the bolt. Continue this process for about an hour, and you'll be done.

The other thing to remember is to leave everything loose until you get it lined up properly. Carefully align the top edge of the spoiler with the body panel and then tighten each bolt as you go around. All that's left is to apply a coat of your favorite vinyl treatment to your shiny new spoiler.

This was one of my more foolish moves. This aftermarket spoiler has a place for attaching a brake cooling duct. I won't even elaborate on the fact that the opening is in the wrong place. What really amazed me was that there was no provision for attaching the cooling hose anyplace near the front brakes. Brake ducts are a great idea, but this particular one is the wrong answer. Save your money and stay with the original spoiler.

Everyone has tried to sell fiberglass spoilers for the front of the C4 Corvette. Even Chevrolet offered one in 1988. They just never caught on with the Corvette masses. The first reason is that they're generally pretty ugly and detract from the original C4 design. Secondly, if you hit the pavement with this spoiler, it's going to cost you a lot of money. Anyone who drives a C4 Corvette knows that no matter how careful you might be, you're going to rub the spoiler on the pavement.

BODY

PROJECT 77

Rear Spoilers

 Time: 6 hours

 Tools: Sockets, screwdrivers, and drills

 Talent:

 Applicable Years: All

 Tab: $500 to $1,000

 Tip: Make sure you talk to a Corvette owner who has actually installed the spoiler you're thinking about putting on your Corvette.

 PERFORMANCE GAIN: Probably no gain in performance and most of the spoilers may actually detract from top speed.

COMPLEMENTARY MODIFICATION: Rocker panel replacements are also very popular with people who like aftermarket spoilers.

Spoilers on the rear of the C4 Corvette are something you either like or you think are a complete waste of money. It's impossible to be neutral on the use of aftermarket spoilers.

The price you see in the catalog is only for the spoiler—very raw and usually very unfinished. A basic wing is going to cost from $200 to $500. That means you have a wing that arrives at your home in unfinished condition and fits reasonably well.

The next step is where the project starts getting a little more expensive. You're going to have to get the wing finished and installed on your car. A major step is simply finding a body shop that is skilled in working with fiberglass and is willing to take on the job.

Most body shops hate this type of work. The entire body shop industry is geared to turning out as much collision work as it profitably can. Working on fiberglass spoilers is the last thing professional mechanics want to do.

Not only will these body shops charge you a substantial amount of money, most will even complain about having to perform the work. They'll get over it once you hand them a check for their efforts, though.

The best way to select a spoiler is to attend cars shows and find one that looks right to you. None of them, except for the very rare factory spoiler, actually do any real good. The spoilers that you see in all the catalogs are simply cosmetic items. Make sure you pick one that you like.

The only spoiler that really adds downforce to the rear of your car is the original factory spoiler. That's also the most difficult one to locate. It was probably the least popular spoiler of all times. Chevrolet quickly discontinued it from production, and most of the fiberglass companies no longer manufacture it.

It's important to note that most of these spoilers will actually decrease the value of your Corvette. Over the years, the market has not treated Corvette body modifications kindly. If you spend a thousand dollars on the spoiler, you've taken at least five hundred dollars off the value of your car.

The biggest problem is that most of the spoilers require that you drill holes in the body of the car. That sort of thing is not going to make the next owner very happy.

This spoiler was beautifully done. Someone spent a great deal of time getting it to fit the body contours just right and then finished off the fiberglass to perfection. This is really a case study in how a spoiler should look. The only drawback is that it detracts from the value of the car.

BODY

191

Stock Corvettes traditionally bring the most money in the used car market. This is especially true when the cars get over thirty years old. Of course, if you want to shell out the money, the spoiler can be removed and the holes filled in. When it comes to aftermarket body parts, the expenses just never stop. You pay to put it on, and you pay to take it off.

The restoration crowd—yes, people are already restoring C4s—really gets upset about these body modifications. In addition, the average buyer thinks some sort of street racer maniac who most likely abused the car previously owned it. All this means that you really need to decide how much you truly want a spoiler.

This is the only spoiler that Chevrolet offered for the C4 Corvette. Rocker panels and a front spoiler were also available. It was designed for the IMSA racing program that required a factory body style. This type of spoiler was dealer installed or, more accurately, race shop installed. The dealers sold very few of them, and the part was dropped shortly after the close of the 1988 racing season.

Fixing Power Window Problems

 Time: 3 hours

 Tools: Screwdrivers and 3/8-inch drive metric sockets

 Talent:

 Applicable Years: 1984 to 1996

 Tab: $75 to $200

 Tip: If only the plastic ribbon is bad on the 1984 and 1985, you don't need to replace the whole mechanism.

COMPLEMENTARY MODIFICATION: Since you're going to have the inner door panel removed, you might consider adding the door insulators that were used on the 1992 to 1996 models. They do quiet the inside of the car a little, and they cost less than $25.

G M came up with a really wonderful idea. It was decided that the company could save a lot of money if it used a different type of mechanism for raising and lowering the side windows. The traditional power window mechanism used a lot of parts and was fairly expensive.

Instead of using a complicated scissors mechanism for the window operation, GM arrived at a process that used a nylon ribbon with teeth that ran through the power window motor. Actually this device was very similar to the nylon ribbon that's used to raise and lower the power antenna.

Getting the window up and down would be a little slower, but GM decided that people could easily live with that. Just think of how much money GM saved on this. The problem was that whatever money was saved in the production process was eaten up by the warranty costs.

This project is mainly for those of us who own the 1984 and 1985 C4 Corvette. This nylon ribbon idea didn't last very long. If you consider the lead time in Detroit for production changes, the nylon ribbon idea was dead before the first 1984s hit the showroom.

This project is about choices. If you own a 1984 or a 1985, you might want to try just replacing the nylon ribbon. If you own one of the later cars, you'll have a choice between simply replacing the motor or replacing the whole regulator. Here's a cost breakdown:

Power window ribbon	$18
Power window motor	$60 to $80
Regulator with motor	$200

While the costs vary tremendously, so does the work involved. The easiest and fastest way is to simply purchase the whole regulator assembly. You can save over $100 by just replacing the motor. The problem is you're going to spend several hours mounting the new motor. You have to make a decision about how much your time is worth.

This job begins with the removal of the inner door

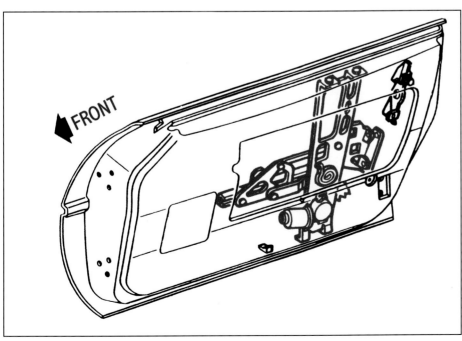

FRONT

This drawing illustrates how the power window mechanism fits inside the door.

BODY

panel. Once the inner panel is removed, you can see inside the door and view the motor and regulator mechanism. You can also test the motor using a battery charger, but you need to be careful when using this technique. A better technique is to have someone use the window switch to see if the motor is running. Now you can decide how many parts you need to order.

The first step after the inner door panel is off is to remove the metal accessory mounting plate. This is a large piece of sheet metal. It's almost the size of the door and various items are mounted on this panel. You have to reach behind the accessory mounting plate and disconnect the rods that activate the inside locking mechanism as well as the inside door handle.

These rods are held in place by a plastic or metal clip. Be careful you don't break the mounting clips. If you do, the rods can fall off after you reassemble the door. You should only have to disconnect one end of each rod in order to remove the accessory mounting plate. You'll have to twist the mounting plate inside the door to remove it. Once the mounting plate is out of the door, you have access to both the window and window regulator.

Removing the window regulator
• Mark the location of everything you remove from this point on. This helps when putting everything back together. A very sharp awl works nicely for scribing lines around the various components.

• Remove the window stabilizer pads.
• Remove the three nuts that hold the window to the regulator.
• Remove the four Torx screws from the cover of the motor.
• You can turn the motor armature with your fingers if it's necessary to lower the window. It takes a lot of turning to lower the window even a couple of inches.
• When the last nut that holds the window to the regulator is removed, carefully lower the glass into the door.
• Remove the mounting bolts that hold the window regulator in the door.
• Remove the entire regulator assembly from the door.

Removing the old motor from the regulator
• The window regulator contains a large, flat, coil spring that helps the motor to lower and raise the glass. Be careful when removing the motor from the regulator so that this spring doesn't go flying across the room.
• The motor is fastened to the regulator with three rivets.
• The rivets allow just enough clearance for the window regulator gear to move. You can use two 1/4 -20x1" stainless-steel nuts and bolts to mount the rebuilt motor. You may have to grind the head of one bolt to clear the operation of the regulator gear.
• Use Loctite on the threads of these bolts.
• After the regulator is installed, lubricate the window motor gear with grease. You can also grease the regulator after it's mounted to prevent getting the grease on the car's interior.

Emblem Replacement

Time: 15 minutes

Tools: deep metric sockets in 1/4-inch drive

Talent:

Applicable Years: 1984 to 1996

Tab: $25 to $200

Tip: Don't use a heat gun to remove the adhesive emblems. A hair dryer is less likely to cause damage.

I don't have a front emblem on my 1985. That's because I was so busy taking pictures for this book that I never replaced the nuts on the back side of the emblem. Then on one wonderful Sunday morning, as I came down the front straight at Sebring, something really ugly hit the windshield of my car. At first, I just assumed that it was a part that had fallen off one of the Porsches.

As I searched for the blind apex on turn one, it suddenly occurred to me that I had never bolted my hood emblem back to the hood. My own parts were hitting me. That's not a good thing. Coming down the backstretch, it crossed my mind that, with my luck, I would now proceed to run over my own part and destroy a tire. I never did hit the emblem. Of course, I never found it again either.

In the beginning, the C4 had what I consider real emblems. They had little prongs on the back, and they actually poked through the fiberglass. Other than my Sebring experience, my favorite emblem encounter was a gentleman who pulled up to a recent show with a beautiful 1989 red Corvette. After filling out the usual paperwork and moving his car to the designated area, he got out of the car and proceeded to carefully remove the emblems from both the front and rear of his car. He then reached back into the car and pulled out a box. There in this velvet-lined box were some of the most perfect gold emblems I've ever seen. Once the car was parked, he dusted the red paint very carefully and then systematically installed the new emblems. As the show finished, he went around the car and removed them and returned them to the box lined with velvet.

Corvette emblems are a big deal. Corvette Central has three pages of C4 emblems. Most of them are stock, just like the sort that came on your car when it left the dealership. And some of them are just ways of announcing what you own.

If you have some strange emblems on your car, or the dealer emblem is still attached, they're probably stuck on with some sort of adhesive. The two tools you need for removal are a hair dryer and a thin plastic putty knife. Don't use a metal knife on your paint. Get the emblem fairly warm and then use the plastic wedge to pry off the emblem. Do this slowly and carefully since you don't want to scratch the paint. The professionals use heat guns to do this, but you can do serious damage with those tools. Most of us should stick to hair dryers.

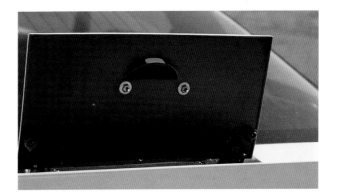

The front and rear emblems are held on with what we used to call speed nuts. You can get them at the local Home Depot store, and they work just fine. You really don't have to worry about whether they're metric or standard. Just take the emblem with you and try out the various sizes.

BODY

Roof Panel Replacement

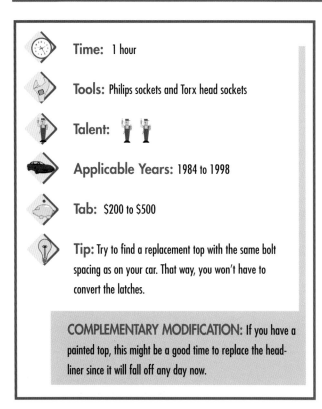

Time: 1 hour

Tools: Philips sockets and Torx head sockets

Talent: 👷 👷

Applicable Years: 1984 to 1998

Tab: $200 to $500

Tip: Try to find a replacement top with the same bolt spacing as on your car. That way, you won't have to convert the latches.

COMPLEMENTARY MODIFICATION: If you have a painted top, this might be a good time to replace the headliner since it will fall off any day now.

Roof panels are critical on the 1984 to 1996 Corvette. They actually hold the car together. When the design of the Corvette was changed from a T-top to a one-piece, the roof actually became a structural element of the car. This is why your car drives so much better with the roof attached. This is also why the C4 uses four big bolts to hold on the roof. Latches simply could not do the job here.

Unless your Corvette is a convertible, it came with a roof panel. A few C4 Corvettes even came with two roof panels. Starting in 1986, you could order your Corvette with the basic fiberglass hardtop, and then order a transparent one as an option. This option was listed as C2L, and it cost $895 in 1986. In 1996, it sold for $950. Considering that anywhere from 4,000 to 6,000 people selected this option every year, you can assume that about 50,000 more roofs were manufactured than cars. That's a lot of extra roofs floating around.

The transparent tops give the C4 interior a much more open feeling. The extra light that's allowed into the interior can make a tremendous difference in how the car feels on a sunny, but cool, day. Transparent tops generate a tremendous amount of heat, effectively warming up the interior. That's something to consider when you think about using a transparent top. Maybe that's why Chevrolet offered two tops—one for the summer and one for the winter.

The best place to purchase a top is really a salvage yard. Very few Corvettes ever go upside down. It seems most of the Corvettes you find in a salvage yard have had some sort of engine fire, which generally leaves the roof panels intact. Should you find a good one, you only need to have the roof painted to match your car. Of course, a new paint job may cost more than you paid for the salvage yard roof.

The good part about the transparent roofs is that you don't have to deal with the headliner. On the other hand, make sure you look carefully for small cracks in the roof before you fork over your money. These roofs have a way of developing very small spider-web cracks. You really can't see them from the outside of the car. They become obvious from inside the car, however. You should probably take some Windex and paper towels along with you as you go shopping just to be on the safe side.

You might also want to take your whole car with you. That way you can install the new roof on the car to make sure it fits. If the roof you want doesn't have the correct front mounting plates, make sure you get them while you're at the salvage yard. Ask the people there to include the hardware in the price of the roof.

The metal strip that fits along the edge of the roof seems to get damaged simply from normal use. It's always ending up with a series of dents or scratches along the edge. You can remove the old trim strip by tapping it with a wooden block. Carefully tap all the way around the roof, and the strip should simply pop off. Your Chevrolet dealer can order a new strip. To install it, I use a soft, rawhide hammer for installation, and I put a little weatherstrip cement into the groove of the metal strip to help it stay in place.

With so many roof panels on the market, I have to wonder why anyone would need an aftermarket panel. The only advantage is that you can get slightly different transparent shades.

Also, keep in mind that, although the roof panels may seem reasonably priced, the painting and detailing may well cost more than the roof. Make sure that you check out the total price on this project before you get too far along.

Are the roof panels stamped with a VIN number?
Yes, the factory did start numbering the see-through roofs because they were a high-theft item. Look on the left front corner of the frame. If it is an original factory top, it's last eight numbers should be the same as the vehicle identification number on your dash.

BODY

1984 - 1986 Early
1 Cone Pin Only
1 Bolt on Top

1986 late -1988
3 Holes

1989 - Up
3 Holes

The quickest way to identify a roof panel is by looking at the latch mechanism. The panel attaches at the windshield header, as shown in the photos.

You can remove the metal decorative strip by using block of wood and hammer. Simply tap around the roof, and the strip should slide off. The replacement procedure is the same as the removal procedure. The only hitch is that sometimes the strip doesn't like to fit and pop out at one edge. I typically use a little weathership cement to help the process along.

Weatherstrip Replacement

Time: 2 hours

Tools: Plastic scrapers, Phillips screwdrivers, 3M adhesive, and adhesive cleaner

Talent:

Applicable Years: 1984 to 1996

Tab: $100 to $1,000

Tip: Purchase a gallon of adhesive cleaner by 3M or an aerosol can of 3M Weatherstrip Release Agent. You'll need at least one of these before you're through. You may also consider getting your own hair dryer for use in the home garage since using one from the family bathroom usually causes some problems.

COMPLEMENTARY MODIFICATION: This is more than enough work for any project.

It sounds so simple. These strips are only rubber. How hard can it be to simply glue some new rubber strips on the car? Well, let me advise you, this job may be much more difficult than you envision.

Let's get one thing clear from the start. Weatherstripping at General Motors is a big deal. People have spent their entire careers at GM developing better weatherstrips. Now you're going to replicate all this work on a weekend with some new rubber parts and some glue. Yeah, right.

Not all weatherstripping is created equal. Weatherstripping is a miracle in rubber composition and complex forms. Before you buy any weatherstripping for your Corvette, ask around at the various shows to find out which companies people have used and how happy they've been with their new weatherstripping.

When it comes to weatherstripping supplies, you shouldn't order everything at one time. You may decide that this is a job you want to farm out to a professional once you've installed your first item. if so, you shouldn't

feel ashamed. Others have given up, and many more will do so in the future.

Removing the Old

The first step is to unwrap your brand new piece of weatherstrip and check it against what is already in your car. Here are some questions you should be asking:

Which way does the cross-section go?
Where is the seam?
Where is the original glue applied? Everywhere? Only in the corners?
Are there screws or fasteners?

Next, draw a picture or photograph the existing weatherstripping. Once you get the old weatherstripping off, it will be too late ask questions. Think of every possible question you might ever have and make sure you're prepared to label every single screw you remove.

Now start removing all of the old weatherstripping. This is easy if the weatherstrip utilizes small plastic pins and screws to hold it in place. Once you start finding weatherstrip that's been glued into place, things get more complicated.

Finding a loose end and pulling will result in some of the weatherstrip coming out and more being left behind, stuck in the channel. This is especially true of the weatherstrip that runs over the roof and down the rear edge of the side windows. The top weatherstrip, where the rear of the roof fits, is actually installed into a channel.

Just ripping out as much weatherstrip as possible and then going back to try to clean up the rest really isn't the best way to approach this task. The best way to remove glued-in weatherstrip is to use a hair dryer to heatup the channel as you are pulling. This should allow you to get the old weatherstrip out in one piece. Once again, be sure to pay attention to how the weatherstrip was installed while you are taking it out. If you run across any screws, put them in a plastic bag and label them.

Removing weatherstrip that has been glued in place requires the use of a combination of the hair dryer and an adhesive release agent. It's important to heat the old glue so it becomes pliable. Find a place where the weatherstrip is loose, then pull enough to raise the weatherstrip, but not tear it. Now start heating the channel to the left or right of the loose spot. As the channel warms, the glue should give way and the weatherstrip should easily separate from the car.

If your weatherstrip is stubborn, like mine always is, apply a release agent such as 3M No. 8971. Always carefully

BODY

follow the instructions and take the suggestions precautions listed on any product you use. One good thing is that, once you expose the screws in the weatherstrip retainer, you can easily remove the retainer from the car.

Now you can actually soak the retainer in a shallow tray of solvent. A plastic scraper works nicely in this case. Even sharpened tongue-depressors will do the job. Whatever you do, *do not* use a metal putty knife since that will dig into the metal channels. Keep telling yourself that the cleaner you can make these retainers, the less likely it is that you'll have leaks.

Install the New

If you've prepared everything correctly, the installation should be the easiest step. Use adhesive on any weatherstrip that is channel mounted or uses a combination of channel and fasteners. Refer back to your notes so you follow the same procedures that GM did in the Bowling Green assembly plant. The plant had tremendous problems with C4 water leaks so employees learned how and where to apply any adhesive. I've always used 3M weatherstrip adhesive— No. 8008. Follow the instructions on the package, and you shouldn't have any problems.

There's a new product available on the market that should be wonderful. 3M Weatherstrip and Sealing Attachment Tapes make the job of attaching weatherstrip easier. 3M says the bonds are far more effective than the old glue. The weatherstrip engineers like the tape system because it gives them the flexibility to place weatherstrip exactly where it's needed. Plus the tape provides a complete seal against noise, water, and dirt. This may replace our old standby, but it's too early to tell yet. At any rate, it's worth a try.

Now the fun really starts. Once your new weatherstrip is installed, you're most likely going to encounter some new problems. First you may have a problem closing the doors. Don't forget your old weatherstrip was pretty flat. Now you just put brand new, puffy, soft weatherstrip in place. Sometimes the new weatherstrip is thicker than the original factory product.

This means you're going to probably have to adjust both the doors and the windows. If you can, put this off for a while because there's a chance that the weatherstrip will flatten over the first few weeks.

Both the window and door adjustments are easy if you've done them dozens of times. Body shops are great at this sort of work. The only problem is they don't want to do just four adjustments. This is another occasion where you'll need to get the factory manual out and then go back and forth on the adjustments for several hours. If you did any of the side window weatherstrip, you'll need to take the inner door panel off to adjust the side windows. Remember, no one said this was an easy project.

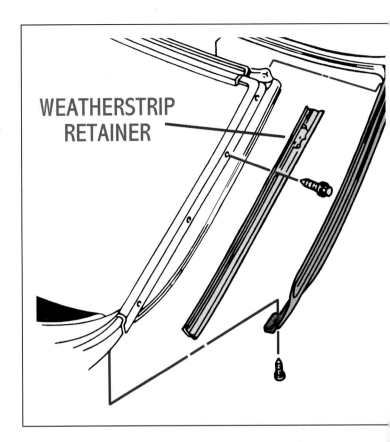

WEATHERSTRIP RETAINER

A great deal of the weatherstrip on the C4 Corvette uses aluminum retainers. These retainers are screwed to the body and then the weatherstrip is slid or poked into place. There's adhesive between the retainers and the weatherstripping that is almost impossible to remove. The worst part of this whole job is cleaning the retainers prior to installing the new weatherstripping.

Roof Panel Headliner

 Time: Several hours

 Tools: Large scrapers, sandpaper, and adhesive remover

 Talent:

 Applicable Years: 1984 to 1996

 Tab: $25 to $50

 Tip: Take your time and restore the whole interior of the roof panel in one sitting.

COMPLEMENTARY MODIFICATION: This job can really take on the nature of hardtop restoration. By the time the headliner starts to fall off, you may need a few other things replaced as well.

This job involves a little bit of fun and a lot of real boredom. If you have the clear hardtop, you can skip this step because you won't even know the C4 has this sort of problem. The trouble is usually caused by a decade of being in the hot sun. As a result, the original glue that holds the fabric to the roof's interior begins to deteriorate.

Every now and again you get this feeling like the car is closing in you—or at least the fabric on the roof is. You put up with it for a little while but eventually you decide you can't take it any more so you place the hardtop on the side lawn (so the paint won't get scratched) and start ripping the fabric out.

Once the fun is over you realize that eventually you're going to have to do something about all that old hardened glue that was put there over a decade ago by some highly paid union employee in Bowling Green.

Removing old glue is quite a challenge. There's a product designed by 3M that's made just for this type of situation. However, oftentimes, even that won't always do the trick. I'll share one way I decided to tackle this problem. One day, I fired up the compressor, got out my orbital sander, and put some 100-grit paper on it. The 100-grit paper made fast work of the glue. It was also a bit tough on the hardtop interior. Eventually I had to do something about all the sanded fiberglass on the interior of the car.

This is the inside of my roof panel after all the sanding took place, and I got a reasonably decent, smooth surface. You'll notice that one of my little rubber bits has fallen off. Corvette Central stocks all of these items. These little items keep your Corvette looking nice.

BODY

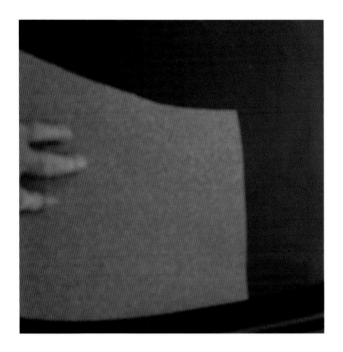

Here's the cork sheeting I found at Lowes. I thought about using the sound-deadening material that's available from the stereo stores, but that stuff is very heavy. The last thing I need is to add twenty pounds of weight at the highest part of the car. I was also concerned about how something that heavy would stay glued to the roof. When it came to cost, there was no comparison. Cheap cork trumps the stereo store stuff.

One of the problems with the C4 is the resonance that is set up from aftermarket exhaust systems. This is a particularly loud sound at certain rpm ranges. I never had any resonance until I bumped the compression ratio up in the engine. Then the noise became intolerable. I figured the bare roof panel wasn't helping the situation any.

That's when Lowes came to my rescue. The retailer sells cork sheeting in the roll. It actually fits the roof nicely. I made a pattern out of a piece of brown craft paper and then instantly had a pattern for the cork. The main thing you need to do is make the piece a little bit larger than the exposed roof area. That way you can insert the edges the way the factory did with the original fabric.

I used the spray can of 3M adhesive to seal the cork to the roof and all went well. The next trip was to the local fabric store for some black material to cover the cork. Once I found a lightweight fabric, I simply used my paper pattern again.

The trick here is to get enough adhesive on the cork so that the fabric will stay in place. The best tool for tucking the fabric into the edges is a large drywall putty knife. You may have to use a smaller knife to get the edges tucked in, but I'm sure you have a couple of those around the house already. When you're finished with this project, only an NCRS judge will be able to tell that it's not original.

The final touch is to glue some of the trim items back into place. If you're missing any of these little items, Corvette Central has them in stock. The factory used a double-edged tape that dries out the same way as the glue that held the original fabric in place.

You can now smooth the fabric out and get all the edges nicely tucked away. The other thing you should consider is adding the anti-squeak kit that was developed for the 1992 to 1996 Corvette. This kit can be used on any C4 hardtop and consists of some precut Velcro patches that fit right where most of the squeaks occur. At under $15, these kits are a nice item to add to your top.

Hood Prop Conversion

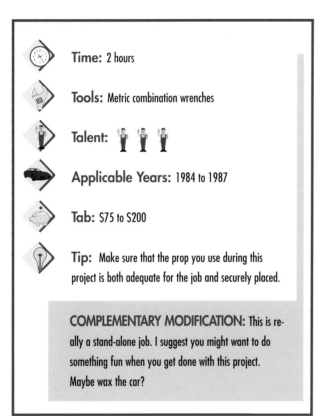

Time: 2 hours

Tools: Metric combination wrenches

Talent: ♟ ♟ ♟

Applicable Years: 1984 to 1987

Tab: $75 to $200

Tip: Make sure that the prop you use during this project is both adequate for the job and securely placed.

COMPLEMENTARY MODIFICATION: This is really a stand-alone job. I suggest you might want to do something fun when you get done with this project. Maybe wax the car?

The hood on the C4 is one very heavy piece of fiberglass. Checking the oil can almost be part of your daily workout. Obviously even the folks at Chevrolet agreed because, in 1988, they changed from the old-fashioned scissors-type of hood prop to a gas strut that actually helped the hood go up in the air. Just in case you folks with the post-1988 cars don't comprehend what I'm talking about, find one of the early cars and lift the hood, and you'll understand.

The least expensive way to approach this job is to simply purchase the one large strut that goes on the left side of the car. You can also purchase a kit that has two struts. The left side has the usual large strut rod, along with a smaller piston the fits on the right side.

The good part is that you can put this gas strut rod on all 1984 to 1987 Corvettes. This simple project takes less then two hours, and you don't have to modify anything. The gas strut makes a world of difference. The hood will open and close easier and be secure when it is fully opened.

The procedure I'm about to describe is for installing the large gas strut rod only.

- Use a safety rod to secure the hood while you are working. A four-foot piece of electrical conduit, or a 2"x2" piece of wood works nicely. There's going to be a point in the project where this safety rod will be the only thing holding the hood open so make an appropriate selection.
- Totally remove the old scissors-style prop rod. Save the bolts because you will use them later.
- Next remove the safety clips and washers on one of the old hood supports.
- Place the hood support lower shaft onto the lower mounting bracket and install a washer and the safety pin.
- Now gently rock the hood forward and attach the top end of the support to the upper mounting bracket. Make sure that your hood safety rod stays in place. Re-install the washer and safety clip. One side is finished. Repeat the procedure on the other hood support.
- At the front of the left inner fender, you'll see two 10-millimeter bolts. Remove the front one and loosen the rear one.Now slide the U-nut off the front hole in the inner fender. Save this U-nut because you'll be re-using it.
- Remove the 10-millimeter bolt that holds the vapor lines and bracket in place.
- Take the new prop rod-mounting bracket and place the U-nut that you removed from the inner fender onto the large hole in the end of the bracket.
- Mount the prop rod ball stud onto the bracket.
- Align the U-nut end of the mounting bracket with the first hole in the inner fender. Install the 10-millimeter bolt and snug it into place.
- Place the vapor line and clip over the front hole in the mounting bracket and install the bolt. Tighten it into place. Now go back and tighten the two bolts in the inner fender.
- Locate two threaded holes on the left side of the hood. This is where the upper mounting bracket will be installed.
- Install the upper bracket using the two 10-millimeter bolts you took off the old scissors prop rod mount. Align the mount with the ball stud pointing to the outside of the car. Now tighten the mount into place.
- Snap the new prop rod onto the ball stud mounts on each bracket. Make sure the strut rod end with the plastic boot attaches to the upper hood bracket.

Now it's all installed and ready to go. This prop rod also has a nice safety feature. The hood cannot be closed unless you pull the lower section of the prop rod in the direction of the arrow on the housing. This will allow the piston to slide into the housing allowing the hood to close safely.

BODY

202

This is the early-style hood support. It was cheap to make and easy to install. The only trouble was that the C4 hood was so heavy some people had trouble opening it.

This is the later-style hood prop. Not only is the hood easier to open, but it has a safety feature that won't allow the hood to close unless you move the piston housing in the direction of the arrow on the housing.

ELECTRICAL

Parts courtesy Corvette Central

Headlight Replacement

Time: 30 minutes

Tools: Philips screwdriver, No. 20 Torx socket, 7-millimeter socket

Talent: (1)

Applicable Years: 1984 to 1996

Tab: $25

Tip: Use halogen replacements.

PERFORMANCE GAIN: Halogen replacement headlights make a considerable difference at night.

COMPLEMENTARY MODIFICATION: Upgrade the driving lights with brighter bulbs.

The first time you go to change the headlights on your C4 Corvette, the process will absolutely baffle you. Fortunately, the job is really easy once you know the trick. The trick is that you have to change the light with the hood up and the headlight assembly halfway through its rotation. Once you do that, the whole operation will be much easier.

Open the hood and turn the ignition key to the "on" position. Then turn on the headlight switch. As the headlight gets about halfway through its rotation, turn the ignition key to the "off" position.

Now it's a matter of removing the two bolts that you can see on the rear side of the hood. These bolts can be removed with a 7-millimeter socket. Take note of where they're located since they also allow alignment of the housing. This housing should be centered in the opening when you reinstall the cover.

If you've rotated the headlight just right, you should be able to reach the two Torx screws with the headlight in the same position. It takes a No. 20 Torx driver to remove these two screws.

With the cover out of the way, you can simply rotate the headlight into full upright position and remove the metal retainer that holds the headlight in position. There are four screws here that must be removed. Please don't be tempted to mess with any of the two alignment screws.

Some new lighting systems are coming on the market with HID bulbs. The big problem is they cost over $500. A lot of folks say they have the latest greatest lighting system for your Corvette. The problem is that most of the things

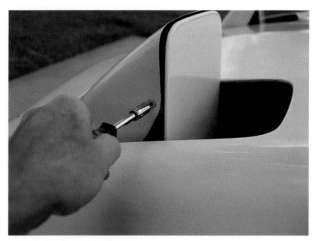

Above: You need to raise the hood and then turn on the lights. The trick is to stop the light assembly halfway through its travel. That allows you to reach the Torx screws that help hold the cover in place.

Left: These are the other two bolts that hold the cover in place. You can reach these from the back of the hood. You might want to scribe a mark around the cover edges. This will save you from having to figure out how to align the cover when you put it back in place.

205

they're selling take a degree in electrical engineering to figure out.

A sealed-beam unit is still the best and most reliable headlight system on the 1984 to 1996 Corvette. At one time, Hella offered a replacement lighting system that used replaceable halogen bulbs. This system was much brighter, but it wasn't very reliable in operation.

A halogen bulb is a delicate thing. Think about all the abrupt maneuvers that your headlights go through as they rotate up and down. The filaments in the halogen bulbs simply didn't hold up to all the banging around. Bosch eventually dropped the product.

A lot of Corvette owners prefer the basic halogen light, but they typically chose one with a plastic lens. They feel the plastic lenses are lighter, and they are convinced that this will ensure a longer life for the motors and the gears. This has never been proven, but it makes sense. Besides it won't cost you any extra money so maybe it's a worthwhile purchase.

When all is said and done, I usually end up purchasing the best halogen sealed-beams I can find at AutoZone or Pep Boys. The lights are plenty bright, and the price is very right. If you need the type of light that will melt the guy's license plate in front of you, it's time to consider an auxiliary lighting system. However, when it comes to this type of system, the choices are very limited and very expensive.

One additional thing you need to consider is that the headlights should be balanced from side to side. If you're improving one side with a brighter bulb, you should do the other as well – even though it might not be burned out yet. If you have a standard light in one side and a brand new bright halogen in the other side, the world is never going to look right. Spend the extra money and get two lights that have the same intensity.

Make sure you only remove the screws that hold the brackets in place. Don't remove the adjustment screws. Changing headlights shouldn't change the headlight alignment one bit.

Some Upgrades for Your Headlights

Upgrade	Benefits	Stock Light
H6054HO	High Output Halogen Upgrade: Up to 80 percent more light and more than two times the life of the standard H6054 halogen lamp	H6054
H6054XL	Longlife Halogen Upgrade: Up to six times longer life than a regular bulb.	H6054

Taillight/Back-up Bulb Replacement

Time: 30 minutes

Tools: You'll need a screwdriver to remove the license plate. You'll also need a screwdriver to remove the lens on the later cars.

Talent:

Applicable Years: 1984 to 1996

Tab: $4.95

Tip: If you have an early car, find someone with long, thin arms to help you.

COMPLEMENTARY MODIFICATION:

You might consider replacing the lens gasket on the later cars. At the very least, remove it and clean it before putting the lens back in place.

I simply don't know what they were thinking with the early C4s. Did they really believe that these taillight bulbs were going to last forever? Actually, these lights were done at the request of Chuck Jordan, who was, at that time, the head of GM styling. Remember, Chuck Jordan was also responsible for the design of the Chevrolet Caprice. That should give you some insight into the early C4 design.

There are two ways to get to these bulbs. A lot of people suggest removing the license plate and reaching in with your arm. That plan has never really worked all that well for me. I find that it's a lot easier to simply lie on the ground and reach up to twist the socket.

Below left: Round lights were the only option in 1984. The Corvette had possessed round lights since 1961, and no one was about to change them in 1983. This was one of those cases where upper management wouldn't budge, choosing to ignore the suggestions of the design team.

Below right: The design staff wanted to use these lights from the beginning. The micro-management style that was so common at GM during that time forced the design team into creating round lights. These rectangular lights were placed on the Corvette 1991 redesign. Not only do they look good, but you can actually change the bulbs.

The back-up lights are really simple to remove once you remove the license plate. Keep in mind that lenses of the backup lights can become very discolored. If you're really into having a pristine Corvette, you might want to install a whole new unit. This will do wonders for the look of your Corvette. A pair should cost less than $100. You can also install halogen bulbs in this location for less than $20. If you do a lot of backing up with your car, this might be a worthwhile purchase.

Just when things were going well, we got another light that required us to have to lie on the ground to change the bulb. These third brake light bulbs are still easier to change than the outer brake light bulbs.

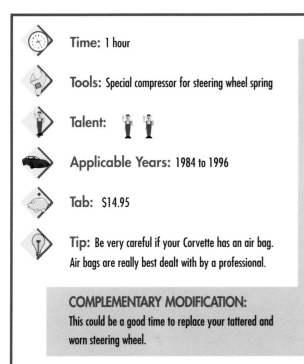

PROJECT 86
Turn Signal Repair

Time: 1 hour

Tools: Special compressor for steering wheel spring

Talent: 👷👷

Applicable Years: 1984 to 1996

Tab: $14.95

Tip: Be very careful if your Corvette has an air bag. Air bags are really best dealt with by a professional.

COMPLEMENTARY MODIFICATION:
This could be a good time to replace your tattered and worn steering wheel.

TROUBLESHOOTING:

Turn-signal Will Not Stay in Turn Position
> Broken or missing detent or canceling spring
> Faulty switch
> Steering shaft in the incorrect position

Turn-signal Will Not Cancel
> Loose switch mounting screws
> Switch out of adjustment
> Anchor bosses broken
> Broken canceling spring
> Canceling spring interference

Turn-signal Difficult to Operate
> Broken pressure pad or pivot assembly pin
> Jammed wires

Turn-signal Will Not Indicate Lane Change
> Dirt between the hazard support canceling leg and the yoke
> Turn-signal switch broken

Steering Wheel Loose
> Excessive clearance in support housing
> Upper bearing not seated in housing
> Upper bearing inner race seat broken
> Loose steering wheel retaining nut

Noise When Tilting Column
> Upper tilt bumpers worn
> Tilt spring rubbing in housing

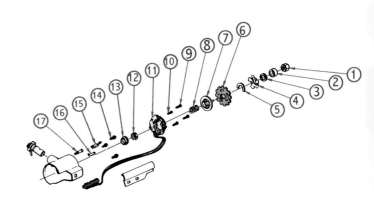

General Motors has been using the same little plastic parts for the turn-signal mechanism for years. And the parts have also been breaking for years. This is really only a project for those folks who own 1984 to 1989 Corvettes. In 1990 the air bag was added to the steering wheel. That modification puts this job beyond the abilities of the average weekend warrior.

One problem with the GM tilt steering wheel is that people use the steering wheel as a handle for getting in and out of the car. This is especially common on the Corvette. This steering wheel was designed as a way of steering the car—it's not a handle to make your life easier. If you continuously use the steering wheel as a handle, you're going to break things in the tilt mechanism. And the repairs won't be cheap.

There are a number of common problems with the turn-signals. What will most likely happen is that as you burrow down into the steering column, you'll start finding broken parts. The biggest problem you're going to have is locating these parts. This is especially true of the tilt mechanism parts. While it's fairly easy to get inside the column, don't plan on finishing this project over the weekend. It'll take several days just to locate some of the parts.

1 – Nut	10 – Screw
2 – Bumper	11 – Switch
3 – Spacer	12 – Seat
4 – Retainer	13 – Race
5 – Retainer	14 – Screw
6 – Lock	15 – Switch
7 – Cam	16 – Clip
8 – Spring	17 – Screw
9 – Screw	

Starter Replacement

 Time: 1 to 2 hours

 Tools: Metric socket set, a product like Brake Clean

 Talent:

 Tab: Under $150

 Tip: Gear reduction starters are great if you've installed headers.

 PERFORMANCE GAIN: Header installation is much easier with a gear reduction starter. The extra space provided by these small starters also allows more air to circulate around the starter, which theoretically should allow the starter to last longer.

COMPLEMENTARY MODIFICATION: Make sure that you check the condition of the battery and charging system when you replace the starter. The starter is only one part of the electrical system. You want to ensure that the entire system will be reliable.

This is the traditional Chevy starter. It's been around forever. It's big, heavy, and dead reliable. The best part is you can find a replacement at almost every corner auto parts store in the world.

The good news is that Corvette starters are really tough. After all, this type of starter has started millions of Chevy trucks over the years. The other good news is that replacing one is very easy. The only exception to this rule is the ZR-1, which involves removing the intake manifold to replace the starter. The L98 and LT1 Corvette starter is the basic Chevrolet starter that's been around for decades. These things are dead reliable. You shouldn't anticipate replacing more than one in the time you own your Corvette.

If your Corvette won't start, don't jump to the conclusion that the starter is defective. There's a good chance that the battery is dead or the alternator is defective. Either of these two problems is much more common than a failed starter. Before you run down to the local parts emporium for a new starter, make sure that the starter is really the problem. Most parts stores will not allow you to return a

starter once it's been installed. Almost all of the major parts stores have the capability to check the condition of your starter before you replace it. Simply remove the starter and take it down to the local store for a consultation.

New versus Remanufactured
It's hard to know whether to choose a new or a remanufactured starter. Most of the remanufactured starters are complete junk. Having said that, I also have to state that some companies, like NAPA, produce excellent units. The good part of dealing with NAPA and AutoZone is that they truly stand behind their warranties. Unfortunately, you really don't know what you're getting inside the starter. Professional technicians argue the merits of various electrical brands for hours. Most of this discussion is based on experiences they've had with different brands, not on a technical understanding of the components used in the various starters.

A local shop that specializes in automotive electronics is often the best place to find a rebuilt starter. Usually these local shops have been around for decades and have earned an outstanding reputation. It's simply a matter of asking around about where the best electrical shops are located.

The problem is that these shops usually require that you remove the starter from your car and bring it to them. They can usually turn it around within forty-eight hours,

This is the smaller lightweight replacement. There aren't too many reasons that you need these gear reduction starters, but they're definitely a neat little item. When you need a smaller starter, it's nice to have the option. Make sure you ask around about the various brands, though, because the reliability seems to vary tremendously. Remember, not all starters are created equal.

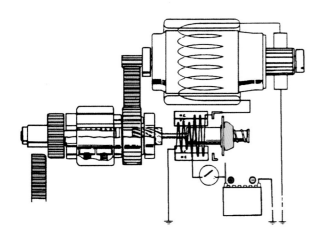

Here is the LT5 gear reduction starter. It's really all about basic physics. You can use the principles of gear ratios and force. Now you can use a small electric motor to turn another object with more force.

which is no big deal, but it's not as quick as running down to the local AutoZone.

One major reason for having your original starter rebuilt is that the Corvette community has an obsession with matching numbers. Starters all have numbers on the outside, and the NCRS has a record of what number should be on your starter.

Conventional Corvette Starters

The standard Corvette starter motor is the solenoid-operated, direct drive unit. Although there are construction differences between applications, the operating principles are the same for all these starter motors.

When the ignition switch is placed in the START position, the control circuit energizes the pull-in and hold-in windings of the solenoid. The solenoid plunger moves and pivots the shift lever, which, in turn, places the drive pinion gear into mesh with the engine flywheel.

When the solenoid plunger is moved all the way, the contact disc closes the circuit from the battery to the starter motor. Current then flows through the field coils and the armature. This develops the magnetic fields that cause the armature to rotate, thus turning the engine over.

Gear Reduction Starters

Over the last few decades, some manufacturers have started to use a gear reduction starter to provide increased torque. The ZR-1 Corvette even received a gear reduction starter. A conventional Chevrolet starter would never have fit below the intake manifold so Chevrolet went to the gear reduction style of starter.

Chrysler initially popularized these starters. The trouble with these early Mopar starters was the weight. Eventually, a number of Japanese vehicles began to appear with gear-reduction starters that were small and light. With

these developments, several aftermarket companies came up with new starter designs.

The gear reduction starter differs from most other designs in that the armature does not drive the pinion directly. These starter designs all rely on a gear reduction format. With a gear reduction of approximately 3.75 to 1, the actual starter motor can turn more freely and at significantly higher rpm.

Typically, a starter motor draws higher loads at low turning speeds. The gear reduction format solves that problem. Loads are decreased, the starter windings are not likely to become overheated, and less current is demanded from the battery. Some of these starters only require 250 amps to function—half that of a conventional starter draw. This leaves a considerable reserve for the ignition to supply spark to the powerplant.

In this gear reduction design, the armature drives a small gear that is in constant mesh with a larger gear. Depending on the application, the ratio between these two gears is between 2 to 1 and 3.5 to 1. The solenoid operation is similar to that of the solenoid-shifted direct drive starter in that the solenoid moves the plunger, which engages the starter drive.

These starters are one-third smaller than most original equipment starters, which means increased room for headers and oil pan, plus increased ground clearance. Most of these gear reduction starters provide 40 to 50 percent more cranking torque than stock and, at 10.6 pounds, are approximately 33 percent lighter. The motors are rated at 1.9 cranking horsepower with a 3.73 to 1 gear reduction.

There are even gear reduction starters for high-compression Chevrolet engines displacing over 500 ci. They provide a whopping 2.8 cranking horsepower. These are really great starters if you don't mind a non-Chevrolet part in your Corvette. Racers discovered the gear reduction starter several decades ago. Lotus introduced the gear reduction starter to the Corvette world when it designed the LT5 engine.

Now you have a choice of starters in your car. If your Corvette is purely stock, a high-quality rebuilt starter should work just fine. If you've installed headers or raised the compression on your Corvette, you might want to consider the gear reduction style of starter. At any rate, it's important to know that you have choices.

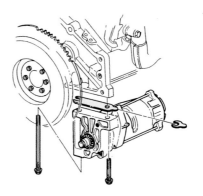

It's critical that the distance from the pinion gear to the flywheel be accurate. The general rule is that whatever shims you remove, you place back in with the new starter. The factory manual has a procedure for checking all this, but most people just check things by the way they sound. If the new starter sounds fine, just leave well enough alone.

Correcting Headlight Motor Problems

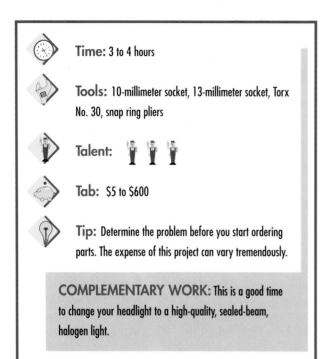

Time: 3 to 4 hours

Tools: 10-millimeter socket, 13-millimeter socket, Torx No. 30, snap ring pliers

Talent: ⚫⚫⚫

Tab: $5 to $600

Tip: Determine the problem before you start ordering parts. The expense of this project can vary tremendously.

COMPLEMENTARY WORK: This is a good time to change your headlight to a high-quality, sealed-beam, halogen light.

The good part is that the headlight motors are pretty reliable. The other good part is that they're fairly easy to work on. At least nothing is hidden, and the access is pretty good. The first hurdle is that you have to decide what is actually wrong with your headlights. You can have everything from a broken wheel to a burned out motor. That means you can spend anywhere from $5 to $600 on repairs and upgrades.

This is one time where the cheap way is most likely the best way. Try to determine what is wrong first and then order the necessary parts.

In 1988, GM revised the headlight system to make it a little more reliable. If you own a 1984 to 1987 Corvette, you can purchase a kit for the upgraded headlight system. I installed the kit in my 1985. While it's really nice, I'm not sure it's worth the money that it cost.

Here is a rundown of how to approach this job:
- Mark the position of the headlight assembly so you can put everything back in its correct alignment in the headlight opening when you finish. Use an awl, or sharp nail, to scratch along the headlight mounting brackets on the underside of the hood. Do this on all the mounting brackets.
- Disconnect the wiring harnesses. The motor and headlight have separate electrical harness plugs that must be

disconnected to remove the headlight assembly. Follow the wire from the motor and disconnect the gray connector.
- The headlight has a similar connector that is black.
- Use a 10-millimeter socket and remove four mounting bolts. Sometimes there's a small bracket on the right side of the left light (near the motor) that should be removed using the 13-millimeter socket. You should also remove the 10-millimeter bolt bracket.
- The headlight assembly can now be placed on a towel on your workbench.
- Use a Torx No. 30 bit to remove the two long bolts that hold the motor to the motor bracket.
- Look where the motor gear shaft passes through the headlight linkage, and you'll see a small retaining ring on the very end of the shaft. Remove this ring with the snap ring pliers.
- On the motor's gear shaft, you will see a small roll pin pressed into a collar and the shaft. Use a small punch to remove this pin from the collar and shaft.
- You can now remove the linkage from the shaft. There are some small shims and parts here, and these must be re-assembled in the correct sequence for the linkage to work.
- The motor should now be free from the headlight assembly, allowing you to remove the gear. You can do this by removing the three small hex head screws using a 1/4-inch socket or nut driver. Be careful not to snap off the heads.
- Rotate the worm gear adjuster one or two turns to relieve any pressure on the spur gear. Count the number of turns and write it down.
- Now loosen the two motor housing screws.
- Take your pliers and remove the yellowish gear that is about 3 inches in diameter. Be careful here that you don't damage the shaft. This gear is going to be tight, but eventually it will come off. Once again, you're going to find some small shims on this shaft. Don't lose them.
- You should now have a hollow gear with bad bushings inside or, in the most severe cases, a bunch of dust. Separate the two halves and dump out the dust and clean the gear.
- Place the three new delrin bushings in the triangular area of the bottom half and replace the top half.
- Clean all the dirt from the worm gear with an old toothbrush.
- Lightly grease the large gear and replace it back in the housing. This is going to be tight due to the way the teeth in the gear are cut. A light tap with a hammer will

ELECTRICAL

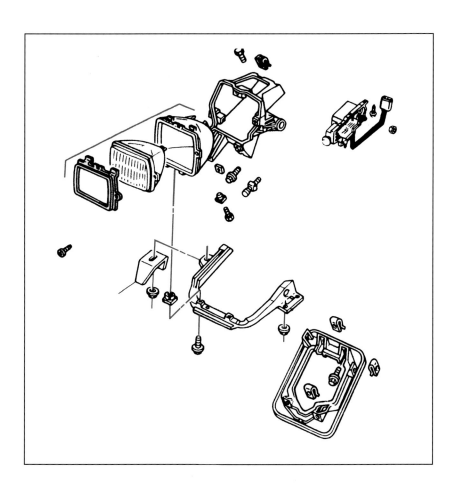

Part of the difficulty of this job is remembering where everything goes. This drawing should help.

put it in place. Replace the gear cover and reattach using the 1/4-inch screws. Do not over-tighten them.

• Tighten the motor casing screws and put the worm adjustment screw to its original position.

• Install the headlight motor back into the headlight assembly with the shaft protruding into the collar and linkage.

• Now insert the two motor mounting bolts into the motor bracket and tighten loosely.

• Slide the collar and linkage back onto the shaft.

• Align the hole in the collar with the hole in the shaft and press the roll pin back in with a hammer and punch.

• Tighten the two motor mount bolts.

• Reinstall the small snap ring onto the end of the shaft.

• Use the alignment marks you made in step one to place the assemblies back into the hood. If you don't do this,

hood/headlight damage could occur when you turn on the light switch.

• Reinstall the small bracket using the 13-millimeter and 10-millimeter bolts. Install and tighten the remaining four 10-millimeter bolts using the alignment marks as a guide.

• Before you test the headlights, make sure that the headlights are in the closed position. You can turn the motor by hand to rotate the headlight to its closed position.

• Now reconnect the electrical harnesses for the motor and headlights.

• Before you test the operation, it is a good idea to recheck the headlight linkage for correct assembly.

• Compare one headlight to the other to be sure they are the same. All that is left to do is to tidy up some of the wiring and turn on the lights to test them.

ELECTRICAL

Battery Replacement

Time: 1 to 2 hours

Tools: Metric socket set

Talent:

Applicable Years: 1984 to 1996

Tab: Under $150

Tip: Use only distilled water in the battery and check the level every couple of months.

COMPLEMENTARY MODIFICATION: Have the alternator checked at the same time you replace the battery. You should always make sure the dead battery wasn't caused by a problem with the charging system.

Once you figure out *how* to get the dead battery out of the car, this job is really simple. Just disregard any thoughts you might have about lifting the battery up and out. That simply won't work. Don't even think about removing the chassis brace that goes over the top of the battery. That won't help a bit. You have to get your metric wrenches out and remove the side vent panel on the body and then slide the battery out sideways. That's the only way to get it done. Taking the body of a car apart to replace the battery is a new experience for most of us, but it's the only way the battery is going to come out of your C4 Corvette.

Removing the side panel and getting the battery out isn't the hard part. The real trick is getting the body panel aligned properly once you have the new battery installed. Then you have to tighten everything up without cracking the fiberglass. Just be careful, and it should all go back together nicely. This is one job where it really pays to take your time.

The other problem is that someone has probably already replaced the battery before you. Just hope he or she used the proper bolts and put everything back together properly. Don't assume anything. You may find a couple of surprises along the way.

Three Things You Need to Know

There are three important things to look for in a battery. First, you should know about cold cranking amps, or CCA. Secondly, you should know the reserve capacity, or RC. Finally, you should get to know a thing called group size.

Cold Cranking Amps, or CCA, is the number of amps a battery can support for 30 seconds at a temperature of zero degrees Fahrenheit until the battery voltage drops to unusable levels. A 12-volt battery with a rating of 600 CCA means the battery will provide 600 amps for 30 seconds at a temperature of zero degrees before the voltage falls to 7.20 volts, or six cells.

Reserve capacity, or RC, is what will power your vehicle's electrical system if the alternator fails. It indicates the battery's "staying power"—how many minutes the battery can supply ample power without falling below the minimum voltage needed to run your vehicle. It's a very specific test, and it's widely understood.

The RC standard tells you how many minutes the battery can supply 25 amps of power at 80 degrees without falling below 10.5 volts. Notice that it's a very specific test carried out under standardized conditions.

If you go to your local discount auto parts store, you're going to see ratings called hot cranking amps, or HCA, and cranking amps, or CA. Ignore these items— they are tests that have no standards. When a battery can't meet the standardized tests for CCA and RC, companies come up with a test that has no real meaning. This allows them to put a big number on the side of the battery, hoping that you're sucker enough to purchase it.

Batteries are all given a standardized numbering system for their physical size. A battery's group size is really a standardized description of its length, width, height, and terminal configuration. The 1984 to 1996 Corvettes all use the same size of battery. It's called Group 75. Even though the ZR-1 got a more powerful battery, the physical size is the same as all the other C4 batteries.

Battery Load Test

Your local shop can test your Corvette's battery condition with what is called a load test. Don't let the shop's employees test a weak battery or the results will be meaningless. This traditional load test involves applying a specific load to the battery, then watching the battery's voltage to see if it stays above a certain level. The load created by the testing instrument is adjusted according to the battery's cold cranking amperage.

The load is applied to the battery for 15 seconds while the battery's voltage output is observed. If battery voltage

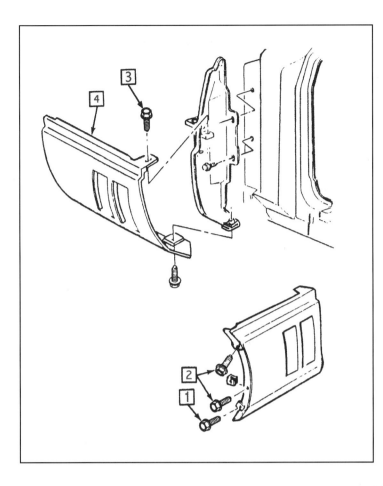

There's a certain sequence for removing this panel:
• Loosen the screw at the bottom of the front wheel well.
• Remove the two bolts just above that first screw.
• Now remove the bolt on the upper side near the rear of the panel. I usually remove the bolts at the lower edge last. Then I carefully pull the panel out from the body

Marine Batteries and Your Corvette

Marine batteries are designed to be almost completely discharged and then brought back up to a full charge. Some folks call them a deep cycle battery. There's really no reason to use one of these in your Corvette—unless you seldom drive your Corvette.

If you don't drive your car, the battery will slowly lose its charge. When you start the car, the alternator works at maximum capacity to put a charge back in the battery. Going from almost dead to a full charge is often called a deep cycle. This has a tremendous effect on the plates inside your battery. Automotive batteries need to be kept at or near full charge, otherwise the plates become sulfated and lose their capacity to accept and hold a charge.

remains above 9.6 volts, the battery is good and can be returned to service. If it drops below 9.6 volts, the battery will go dead on you some time in the very near future. Even if it's close to 9.6, it's not a bad idea to simply replace the battery. I like to replace anything determined to be below 10.2 just to be on the safe side.

Jump Starting Your Corvette

Jump starting a Corvette is not something you want to do. We've all done it, and, every time we do it, we put some very important electrical components at risk. In the old days, jump starting cars was a very common practice. Now, with all the very sophisticated computer components, there are a lot of problems associated with doing this.

Modern electrical components don't like voltage spikes. Make a simple mistake, and you've just fried the alternator and, quite possibly, the computer system. People still jump start cars all the time, but it's a real risk. Plus, a good percentage of the time it really doesn't work anyway.

When a modern battery is so run down that it can't crank your Corvette over, there's a good chance that jump starting won't do any good. You might as well simply replace the battery right there on the spot.

I've replaced batteries in parking lots to avoid jump starting them. While it isn't a great deal of fun, it sure beats jumping the car and then having to replace something like an alternator.

There is a bolt that goes through the battery hold down block. It's a good idea to put some grease on this bolt when you reinstall it into the battery tray. This bolt seems to get a lot of corrosion over time and usually needs replacement. Chevrolet doesn't list this bolt in the parts catalog, but any metric bolt will work. The best source for an original one is from a Corvette salvage yard.

Alternator Replacement/Upgrade

Time: 1 hour

Tools: 3/8-inch sockets and open-end wrenches

Talent:

Applicable Year: 1987 to 1996

Tab: $150 to $200

Tip: If your Corvette sits idle for several months, charge the battery before you start it. Most alternator problems come from the alternator overheating, which is caused by working too hard.

COMPLEMENTARY MODIFICATION: This may be a good time to replace the battery. I've always believed that the best way to make sure the car doesn't go dead again is to use a high-quality, rebuilt alternator and then install a new battery. Corvette batteries are cheap enough that you need to seriously consider purchasing a new one.

This is also a good time to carefully check the condition of your serpentine belt. Since you're going to have to remove the belt to replace the alternator, why not put a new serpentine belt on the car?

If you own a 1984 to 1986 Corvette, you can probably skip this chapter. The alternators only became a problem with the introduction of the new CIS alternators in 1987. These CIS alternators quickly acquired a bad reputation. The reality was that weak batteries, not a faulty alternator design, caused most failures.

Corvette alternators come in several varieties depending on which year C4 you have. In 1984, the alternator output amperage was 97 amps maximum load. In 1985, this was increased to 120 amps, and there were three different models of alternator with GM P/N 1049868 being the number for all of them. In 1986, the amperage was dropped back to 105 amps where it remained until the

conclusion of the C4. If you replace the alternator with a GM unit, you'll get the final version.

Alternators are designed to both maintain battery charge and meet the current demands of the vehicle's electrical system. They are not designed to recharge dead batteries. Installing a replacement alternator without testing and recharging the battery is asking for trouble. This is the most common mistake that's made when replacing an alternator. And it's the leading reason for alternator failures and warranty returns. A lot of us simply don't drive our cars often enough. This is especially true for people living in the snowbelt region. There Corvettes are put away for months at a time, and the batteries in them slowly drain down. Then on one nice spring day you'll get in the car and find it has enough power to crank over.

The problem is that even though the car started, the battery is so low that the alternator has to work overtime to run the car *and* charge up the battery. This sets up an alternator heat problem and the next thing you know the "check engine" light comes on, and your battery begins to go dead. What happened is that you just overworked your alternator and caused it to fail.

If you suspect an alternator problem, you have a couple of alternatives when it comes to fixing it. The first one, and usually the best one, is to find a quality rebuild shop in your local area. The best replacement alternators are still built by a local shop that has a lot of experience. I don't mean a general repair shop. Instead, I'm speaking of a high-quality electrical shop that specializes in electrical work. The staff there is usually able to add some heavy-duty parts and ensure that a better alternator goes back in your Corvette than what was installed originally.

The next alternative is to purchase a rebuilt alternator from a local parts house. The problem here is that almost all of the alternators are being rebuilt offshore today. Most of them are done in Mexico or China. The price of the unit is the major factor. When you contract to have several hundred thousand alternators rebuilt, every penny counts.

Most national parts houses offer a lifetime warranty, but that doesn't say much. If you have to replace two or three units on your Corvette, the thrill of the warranty soon fades.

Remember, just because the case and box say "AC Delco," don't assume that this means the parts are genuine. Alternators are being cloned every day. An exact replica of your Corvette alternator can be assembled without using a single GM part. Suppliers to the alternator rebuilding industry can provide any part desired for these alternators, including screws, insulators, brushes, bearings, voltage regulators, stators, rotors, rectifiers, diode trios, and small parts, too. They literally make a complete alternator out of aftermarket parts.

If you're having a local shop rebuild your alternator, you might want to inquire about the upgrades listed below. They can do all of these things, plus discuss if you really need the upgrades. The best part is that you keep your original case, which may be important for any future restoration project. Here are the parts that can be installed on your rebuilt alternator:

Improved rectifier for higher amperage output

Finned rear housing to remove heat from the rectifier and rear bearing area

10-millimeter-wide rear bearing; OEM uses only an 8-millimeter bearing

Metal internal rear fan

Copper heat transfer compound between the rectifier heat sink and housing for better heat transfer and electrical contact.

More than two-thirds of all alternators that are returned under warranty perform perfectly when tested to check their charging output. This means the original alternator was just fine and something else must have been causing the charging problem.

The most common installation problem is overloading the new alternator by asking it to start the car and charge a dead battery at the same time. The other big problem is that people jump to conclusions without doing the necessary tests. Many professional technicians feel too rushed to take the time to adequately test the battery and charging system. Accurate diagnosis is the key to fixing charging problems correctly the first time and to eliminating unnecessary warranty returns.

This large alternator was used on the 1984 and 1985 Corvettes. This one is totally reliable and causes very few problems. Nonetheless you might want to keep the battery charged if you're not driving the car for an extended period. Also, make sure that if you do replace the alternator, you fully charge the battery before you start the car.

This is the smaller, lightweight alternator used from 1987 to 1996.

Antenna Replacement

 Time: 2 hours

 Tools: 3/8-inch drive, short metric sockets, and combination wrenches

 Talent:

 Applicable Years: 1984 to 1996

 Tab: $150 to $200

 Tip: If your antenna motor is still operable, you might be able to use the AC Delco antenna mast kit, which is part No. 22535396.

COMPLEMENTARY MODIFICATION: You should consider installing the antenna booster ground plane kit if you have to do any work on your antenna. This was standard on the 1992 to 1996 Corvette.

The real secret to this repair is figuring out what is broken. Two things can go wrong with your Corvette's antenna. First the motor can be burned out. Secondly the nylon ribbon that makes the antenna go up and down is missing some teeth. This second item is most problematic. There are some rare times when the gear that drives the ribbon is broken. What happens is that the teeth break off and can no longer engage the ribbon. Before you start ordering parts, take a minute and check out all of these items.

If you can hear the antenna motor when the radio is turned on and off but nothing moves, the motor is probably fine. If you can get the antenna to go all the way up by turning the radio on and off several times, you should assume that the mast is probably just dirty and binding. Raise the antenna all the way up and clean it. You can even wax it.

Cleaning and waxing the antenna every time you wash or wax your car would be good preventive maintenance. Please don't use anything like WD 40 or a lubricant on the antenna. All of these lubricants attract dirt and will cause problems. Simply clean the antenna and use wax.

If the antenna only moves a short distance, or not at all, there are three things that could be causing this. First, the nylon cable attached to the antenna may have broken in two. Second, the teeth may be stripped from the cable. Or, last, the take-up gear in the motor may be stripped. The bad news is that fixing any of these problems requires removing the antenna motor.

Fix It

The directions that come with the repair kit and the authorized factory service manual indicate that you can repair the ribbon without removing the antenna motor. That's true, but it's easier if you simply remove the motor. Taking the motor out makes it a lot easier to get all of the old cable out. There's also a good chance you'll probably ruin the rubber grommet in the deck so plan on ordering one of these as well.

- Jack up the rear of the car high enough to comfortably lie on the ground and reach up into left rear quarter panel. Remember to use a jack stand under the car when you do this.
- Retract the antenna as far as possible, even if you have to push it down manually. If it can't be retracted and you are reasonably certain the cable is broken, simply cut the antenna off about three inches above the deck. This will help in getting the motor out.
- At the bottom of the antenna motor, you'll find two screws that hold the motor to the mounting bracket. One of these has a ground cable at the connection. Write yourself a note to remind yourself which side you removed it from.
- Now that you have the screws out, you can slide the bottom of the motor forward and off the bracket. Next pull the unit down out of the deck grommet.
- There's another ground wire connected at the top of the motor that you'll have to take off before you can remove the assembly.
- At this point, the unit will still have the radio antenna wire and power wires attached to it. These don't disconnect, but they're long enough so you can lower the assembly to the bottom of the fender lip.
- Hold the motor in a horizontal position with the antenna pointing toward the rear.
- At the very top of the motor housing (base of the antenna) is a plastic fitting. Look closely, and you'll see two square shoulders on the very top. These will unscrew from the remainder of the black plastic fitting.

If your antenna is stuck in the up position, try turning your radio on and off several times. If it finally decides to retract, you're having a good day. Bring the mast up and simply clean and wax it. If the motor runs and nothing happens, the ribbon is probably broken. Replacement is easier if you just cut the old antenna off a couple of inches above the body panel. You're going to replace it anyway during the repair, so why not get it out of the way right at the beginning?

- The motor housing is covered with a fitted rubber weather boot. You should be able to roll this up over the housing like a sock to expose the side of the gear case.
- Sometimes you'll find three self-tapping screws. Other times you'll find hot in jected plastic fasteners. These fasteners have to be drilled out for disassembly. The case can be reassembled with self-tapping screws.
- There is also one small nut at the center of the cover that must be removed.
- When you remove the cover, you'll find the take-up reel case. Be careful so you don't lose the two small washers that are between the cover and the reel case.
- When you remove the reel case, you'll probably find some of the white nylon gear strip that was originally connected to your antenna mast. Take a minute and inspect the nylon gear for damaged teeth.
- If you look at all this, you'll notice that the antenna cable feeds off the gear into the take-up reel case similar to an endless cassette tape. The factory used white grease inside the gear box. Clean out as much of this old grease as possible.
- Slide a lengthy piece of the gear strip down from the top just to make sure there aren't any small pieces still in the shaft.
- Apply a nominal amount of grease inside the take-up reel case and reassemble the unit. Replace the cover with some new self-tapping screws.
- Now roll the weather boot back down over the unit and temporarily connect the bottom ground wire back onto the bottom of the unit.
- Take the new antenna and extend it almost fully, leaving about a foot of the nylon cable dangling out the end.
- At this point, find someone to turn the radio on. The motor will cycle to fully extended and then stop. Insert the end of the new nylon cable into the top of the motor as far as it will go with the teeth facing down. This assumes the motor is lying in a horizontal position with the gear case facing toward the right side of the car. Now have your helper turn the radio off.
- Feed the cable into the shaft of the motor as it takes it up. The antenna most likely will not fully retract on this first cycle. Keep trying.
- Although it sounds complicated, this really isn't a bad project. Plan on a couple of hours. The big item here is to make the correct diagnosis. The repair kits are less than $30. The entire antenna assembly is close to $200.

- It's possible that your antenna may have been previously repaired. If this is the case, someone may have used the squeeze fittings just like the ones in your new kit. If so, you should be able to simply pull the old antenna mast out of the motor.
- You can remove the contact spring (actually a sleeve) off the old antenna by sliding it off the top end of the antenna. Clean the sleeve and be careful not to bend the metal fingers that touch the antenna mast when installed.

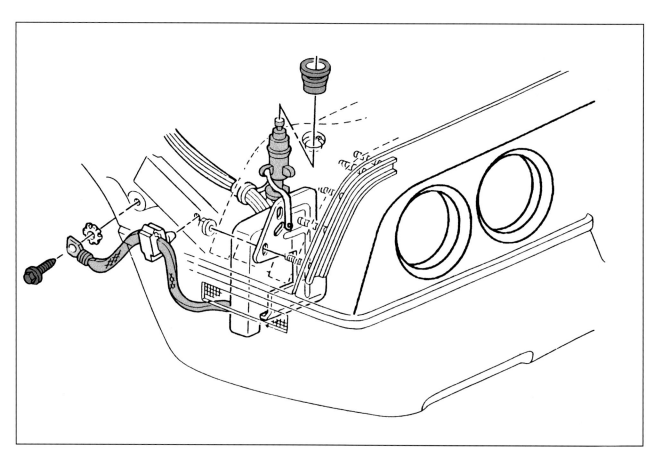

If the motor isn't running, I would take a few minutes to clean the ground connection. Bad ground connections are the source of many electrical problems in the Corvette. You might just get lucky on this one and not have to replace the antenna motor.

A Couple of Upgrades

In 1988 GM switched radio antenna suppliers. The new unit was superior to the old antenna. Logically, it's a good upgrade, but practically, how often do you really listen to FM radio in your Corvette? That may be the determining factor when deciding how much money you want to keep stuffing into the old Delco Bose stereo system.

If the motor in your 1984 to 1987 antenna is burned out, it might not be a bad idea to upgrade to the later motor. On the other hand, if the problem is just a broken ribbon, you can save a lot of money by not upgrading. Instead you can just replace the ribbon.

You should, however, consider adding the antenna booster ground plane kit. The kit creates a better ground connection and improves the clarity a little. Plus, it's easy to install and comes with nice directions.

Driving Light Upgrade

Time: 30 minutes

Tools: Fuse puller

Talent: 👤👤

Applicable Years: 1984 to 1996

Tab: $15

Tip: Make sure you don't put your fingers on the bulb surface.

PERFORMANCE GAIN: You'll gain a great deal of light for night driving.

COMPLEMENTARY MODIFICATION: Replace the headlights with halogen sealed beams.

Driving lights are great. The problem is that on the C4 they aren't real driving lights. You've probably already noticed that turning the driving lights on makes very little difference in lighting quality.

Before you get started, I need to point out that driving lights and fog lights are not the same thing. The 1984 to 1996 Corvette lights are driving lights in that the beam is narrow and goes a good distance down the road. Fog lights put out a very wide and diffuse pattern of light in front of the car. The difference between the two types of lighting has to do with the way the lens is designed. There's nothing you can do to these lights to change them to fog lights. Fog lights and driving lights oftentimes use the same bulbs, but remember, the execution is all in the lens.

A good fog lamp has almost no upward light and a very sharp cutoff. This means a well-placed fog light is mounted low to the ground, thus throwing light under the blanket of fog. It also means that you can use your fog lights to throw a wide beam of light directly in front of your car while you use the high beams in normal driving. In fog, you should turn your driving lights off. We all remember the old rule about using the low beams in fog and rain. The same goes with the Corvette driving lights.

The stock driving lights on a C4 are halogen bulbs rated at only 34 watts. This is less than the wattage of your low beam headlights, making the driving lights nothing more than a cosmetic, nonfunctional decoration. In Europe, driving lights are bright, high-wattage lights used on the open road or under special conditions. General Motors kept the wattage of these lights low, so you can have your driving lights on in city traffic, look cool, and not blind other traffic. However, it makes them pretty useless. However, I'm going to tell you how to fix that.

The stock bulbs in your driving lights are part number 880. This is a 34-watt bulb. This bulb is interchangeable with part number 885. This is a 50-watt bulb, or roughly one-and-a-half times as bright. The problem is that the 50-watt bulb will increase the amperage draw on the circuit. You have to make one more change so that the electrical system can handle this.

The driving lights are fused on the tail lamp circuit with a 10-amp fuse. Fuses are normally set to blow at about 10 percent above the rated load of the circuit, so a 10-amp fuse is normally installed in a circuit drawing about 8 amps maximum. The purpose of the fuse is to protect components, switches, and wiring in the circuit in the case of an overload condition.

The hardest part about this job is reaching in to unscrew the socket. You have to access the bulb from behind. It's a simple turn-and-pull type of plug. It's just difficult to reach it.

221

The fuse box is easy to reach, and everything is clearly marked. Be careful that you don't lose the little latch mechanism when you remove the access panel.

Switches and wiring are normally designed with a 2 to 1 safety factor to the level where the fuse will blow. In other words, a wiring circuit with a 10-amp fuse can normally reliably handle up to 20 amps without damage to components.

Remember, wattage is equal to volts times amps. In our 12-volt system, we can calculate that our stock 34-watt bulbs (two of them equal 68 watts) are drawing 5.6 amps. Changing over to the 50-watt bulbs (100 watts total), we will be drawing 8.3 amps. This is only 2.7 amps more than stock configuration, and still well below the 20-amp melt down level.

The stock wiring circuit is designed to operate within 10 percent of the stock fuse rating. This means about 8 amps is the normal load for a stock 10-amp fuse, so you'll blow the standard fuse by installing the 50-watt bulbs. However, by adding 2.7 amps to the stock 8-amp circuit, we're still within design limitations of the components— even if the fuse blows.

Actually, we'll be below a total circuit amperage of 11 amps —and the wiring circuit can handle up to 20. Simply remove the 10-amp fuse and put a 15-amp fuse in its place. This will provide adequate circuit protection and allow you to use 50-watt bulbs. It's that simple.

The change in the driving lights means that they will actually be brighter than the headlights and provide outstanding lighting under all conditions. It's just nice to be able to see better at night. Lots of light is a good thing.

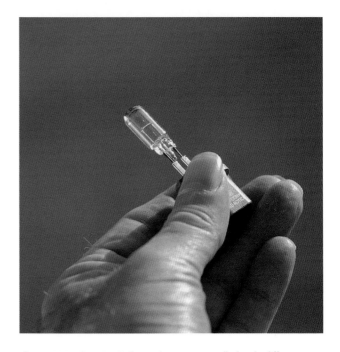

The No. 880 and No. 885 bulbs are the same externally, but the difference in output is considerable. When you install the new bulb, make sure that you don't touch the glass with your hand. The grease from your fingertips will contribute to an early failure.

NCRS Judging

 Time: This will totally consume your entire life if you want a Top Flight award.

 Tools: Lots of cleaning supplies and wax.

 Talent:

 Applicable Years: 1984 to 1996

 Tab: There's no limit to how much time and money you can spend on restoration.

 Tip: Buy the best C4 you can possibly find.

You might want to think of the National Corvette Restorers Society judging as a sport. It's a very expensive sport which can consume money faster than a bad 401K. Keep in mind that the NCRS began with the 1953 to 1962 Corvettes. These cars were very simple and consisted of primarily mechanical parts. The only electrical components in the cars were lights and an ignition system.

Now jump to 1984 and look under the hood of any C4 Corvette. Consider that the basic judging standard is that everything be exactly the way it was when this car left the Bowling Green assembly plant. That means every relay and electrical connector should be the same as it was twenty years earlier. If your C4 Corvette is the average used Corvette, getting your car to match these standards could be a major undertaking.

The best suggestion I can make is that if you're considering entering a C4 Corvette in NCRS judging, you must try to find the best original car you can possibly locate. The thought of taking a rough C4 and turning it into a Top Flight Corvette is really scary. There's just so much that has to be corrected. There are also a lot of C4 items that just

The ZR-1 will most likely be the favorite of the restoration crowd. Restoration guys love cars that are slightly rare. There has to be something unique about a car for it to get so much loving attention, not to mention money. The other point is that a lot of ZR-1s were put away upon introduction, which makes restoration only a matter of cleaning and detailing.

ELECTRICAL

aren't available anymore. Sure, you can buy all the relays, but will they have the correct serial numbers?

The C4 Corvette is going to be one of the most interesting NCRS judging programs for a variety of reasons. First, the C4 Corvettes are unique in that behind the cars is a tremendous amount of documentation. For instance, when the Bowling Green plant was having a problem with the air conditioning systems during the 1984 production, some workers ran down to the local hardware store for wiring and connectors. That's all documented in the manuals.

There is also a huge number of unmodified C4 Corvettes out there. The benchmark is pretty easy to ascertain. When we started restoring the early cars, it was pretty hard to find an original car. A tremendous amount of effort by people like Noland Adams helped us determine what was original.

With the 1984 to 1996 Corvette, we not only have all the documentation, but we have original cars. It doesn't get much better than that if you have to write a judging manual. It will take a couple of years to sort out the details, but the C4 will have the finest documentation of any of the Corvettes.

The most challenging part of C4 judging is the performance verification. Basically this means that everything must work on the dash displays. Right now it's still a question of *what* comes on, and *what time* does this display light up. I suspect this will always be the most difficult part of NCRS C4 judging.

The Strategy

I've already mentioned that you need to obtain the best possible original car you can find. This really shouldn't be that difficult. A lot of 1984 to 1996 Corvettes have been pampered beyond belief. There are a wide variety of cars out there with very low mileage and all the original parts still attached.

Purchase one of these cars and then purchase the judging manual. Study the judging manual the way you analyze the tax code. At this point, don't do anything to your car except put more wax and leather treatment on it. Keep it in your garage and keep it covered. Remember this Corvette is going to be your ticket to an NCRS Top Flight award.

You should then look for an NCRS regional meet being held reasonably close to your home. Take your C4 and have it judged. Remember, the judges are going to be learning as much as you are for the next decade. The goal here, however, is to find out how close your car is to being perfect.

The point deductions that you receive will turn into your plan for the coming year. NCRS judges will find something wrong—that's their job. The big question is what to do if you know something is original on your car, but the judges still deduct points because of it. This is the quandary of the NCRS.

The C4 may be the cheapest way to win a Top Flight award in the NCRS. It takes roughly $100,000 to restore a straight axle or a Sting Ray today. No one will confirm those numbers, but people who are in the restoration business will tell you that is approximately the amount it would cost to turn a good car into a Duntov award winner. If you purchase the right C4, you can create an award winner for less than $30,000. In show car circles, that's nothing.

The C4 Corvette is almost the perfect car for NCRS judging. You can literally buy a winner right out of someone's garage. Then all you have to do is maintain it. The Corvette life doesn't get much better than that.

The convertible is another favorite of the restoration crowd. These are a little more difficult, though, since there are usually a lot more items that will be judged. This might well be the reverse of the old straight axle Corvettes. Very few people will go for Top Flight with the early hardtop in place. There are just too many places to lose points. It's going to take a few years for people to develop a strategy for a Top Flight C4, but I'm sure it will happen.

Replacing the Digital Dash

Time: 3 hours

Tools: Metric wrenches and screwdriver

Talent: (4)

Applicable Years: 1984 to 1989

Tab: $200 to $500

Tip: I disconnect the battery to remove the dash display. I probably don't need to do this, but it makes me feel better.

COMPLEMENTARY MODIFICATION: If you have any broken panels in your dash, this might be a good time to replace them.

Replacing the digital dash isn't much fun. The display costs a lot of money, and there's a tendency to always feel as though you're doing the job incorrectly.

- Your first step is to remove the headlight switch knob. Use a small bladed screwdriver in position to release the knob retaining clip.
- Now loosen the radio panel. This helps you get to the dash pad retaining screws. You'll find, and remove, three screws under the cluster trim bezel and two screws under the radio trim bezel.
- The radio display cluster trim panel has four Phillips screws on the left edge and two screws on the right side.
- Tilt the steering column down and then unscrew the tilt lever.
- Now remove the four 7-millimeter screws that hold the digital display. There should be two screws near the steering column and two at the upper corners of the display.
- Sometimes it helps if you loosen the dash pad. Raising it up just a little helps you extract the display panel. Remove the dash pad screws and wedge the dash pad up ever so slightly. Now you can tilt the cluster forward and to the left to remove it.Once you have the digital display over the steering column, you can disconnect the dash harness. The best way is to remove the connectors by lifting the metal security clips with a small screwdriver.
- Next wedge the connectors off with a flat blade screwdriver. The cluster display should now be ready for complete removal.

The center panel has to be removed in order to remove not only the face plate on the driver's side, but the digital dash as well. It's really no big deal. Just remember to keep the screws with the panel.

The odometer will stay the same. On the early cars, the mileage was still recorded on a mechanical gauge. This also means that the mileage can be easily reset.

Notice that the wheel is fully lowered. Also note that the lever for the tilt mechanism has been removed. The tilt wheel lever simply unscrews. The next step will be to remove the four 7-millimeter screws that hold the display panel in place.

What Do Those Marks Mean?

At this point in time, a lot of digital dashes have been swapped around from car to car. There's a good chance that the one in your early C4 isn't the same one that was installed in the Bowling Green assembly plant. When you remove the cluster, you'll probably see some markings. It might be interesting to see if the cluster matches the driveline in your car.

LS	84 w/cruise
LT	83 exc. cruise
LAK	85 w/cruise
LAL	85 exc. cruise
LAW	86 w/cruise
LAX	86 exc. cruise
LBS	87-88 w/cruise
LBT	87-88 exc. cruise
LDL	89 w/cruise

REAR AXLE AND DRIVESHAFT

Parts courtesy Corvette Central

U-Joint Replacement

REAR AXLE AND DRIVESHAFT

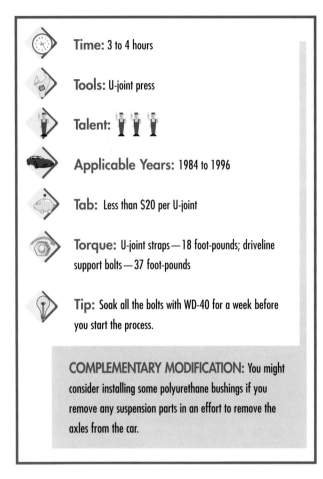

Time: 3 to 4 hours

Tools: U-joint press

Talent: ▮▮▮

Applicable Years: 1984 to 1996

Tab: Less than $20 per U-joint

Torque: U-joint straps—18 foot-pounds; driveline support bolts—37 foot-pounds

Tip: Soak all the bolts with WD-40 for a week before you start the process.

COMPLEMENTARY MODIFICATION: You might consider installing some polyurethane bushings if you remove any suspension parts in an effort to remove the axles from the car.

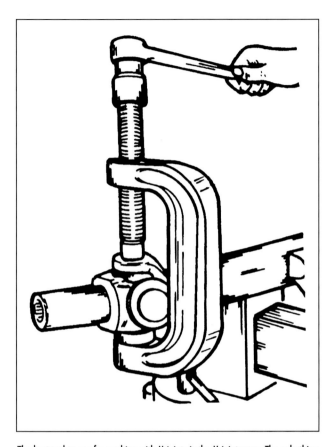

The best tool to use for working with U-joints is the U-joint press. The only thing you have to be careful of is that you don't bend anything. This press can exert a tremendous amount of force. If the U-joint doesn't appear to be moving nicely, stop and check things before you bend something.

You'll know when the universal joints, or U-joints, go bad on the C4 Corvette. Every time you accelerate, you'll get a clicking noise from the rear that sounds like the car has a serious problem. As soon as you back off the gas, everything will get quiet. What usually happens is the grease finally leaves the end of the universal joint, and the needle bearings start to break up The good part is that this usually doesn't happen until you have more than 100,000 miles on the car.

Replacing a U-joint isn't a very difficult task. The most difficult part is getting the axle shaft off the car and over to your workbench. It's almost impossible to thread the axle through the maze of parts that surround it. It's a whole lot easier to simply remove all of the clutter and then remove the axle. Remember that this axle is really a part of the suspension, so treat it accordingly.

A lot of people, maybe most people, replace U-joints with a bench vise. While that works, it's a whole lot easier to use the special tool that's designed for the purpose.

AutoZone, as well as some other discount chains, will loan you the tool if you purchase the U-joints from them.

The first step is to place a floor jack under this leaf spring on the side you're working on and raise the leaf spring up approximately three inches. This is the same thing you'd do if you were changing the bolt on the end of the leaf spring. You might want to look at the chapter on lowering the rear of the car again to refresh your memory on how to do that. Remember to use a jack stand under the frame rail.

Count the number of threads between the end of the spring bolt and the bottom of the nut. This will allow you to return the ride height to its setting without a lot of measuring. Just make sure you write this number down. Remember, it's always easier to take things apart than it is to get them back together. You can never predict how many days your Corvette will be resting on jack stands.

After you have the spring out of the way, the next task is to remove the tie rod, or outboard link, from the rear tie rod assembly. While you can separate the tie rod from the rear knuckle with a suspension fork, you usually end up ripping the rubber boot, which is not a good thing. It's far better to use a puller tool designed specifically for this purpose.

With the tie rod out of the way, you should attack the lower suspension link. Make sure you mark the camber eccentric bolt for realignment after reinstallation. It's tough to see, and you should paint a fine line on the bracket to the wheel of the camber bolt. When you reinstall this later, you'll only have to line the paint stripe up in order to maintain your car's alignment.

You can usually remove the camber bolt by gently hammering the rod down from its bracket with a rawhide mallet. Be careful not to lose the two washers, which will fall out with it on each side of the bushing. You can leave the end that's attached to the hub, or axle spindle, attached. You might want to loosen the bolt, however.

Now that you've got everything out of the way, you can simply rotate the axle so that the 5/16-inch universal strap bolts are accessible on the half shaft. It seems to work better if you start from the differential side. You can rotate this axle 180 degrees and remove the last two 5/16-inch strap bolts. You should have two

straps and four bolts at this point. Now remove the outboard straps.

At this point, it's nice to have a helper who can pull the lower edge of the wheel away from the car allowing you to remove the half shaft. You may have to use a pry bar in between the universal joints and mounting surface to help pry the half shaft out as they can be stuck in place. Just be careful since everything is soft aluminum.

At this point you really have a couple of choices. The first choice is to simply take the shaft with the old U-joints attached to a shop and have the people there handle the replacement for you. If you haven't done U-joints before, this isn't a bad idea. Keep in mind that the yoke which holds the U-joint is aluminum. That means if you screw up, you're going to be shopping for an axle shaft.

A second alternative is to locate the U-joint replacement tool that's designed for the job and do it in your home garage. This isn't a bad alternative either. These presses are readily available and make the job a simple process. You can usually borrow one from AutoZone or rent one from any variety of places. Most people simply call it a U-joint press.

A third alternative, and the least attractive, is to use your bench vise for the task. I've done this a few hundred times, and still don't like the process. Regardless, people have been doing this for years, and it works almost all of the time. Of course, when it doesn't work, you run the risk of bending the yoke, which means you'll be buying a new axle.

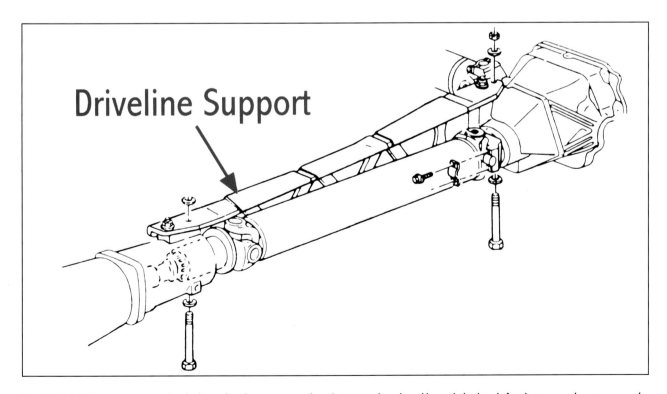

Driveline Support

The driveshaft U-joints come apart, and go back together, the same way as the axle U-joints. The only problem with the driveshaft is that you may have to remove the driveline support. I would loosen the bolts on the support and try to get the driveshaft out with the support in place. This way you might be able to avoid having to thread all the nuts back into place. That job alone can consume a considerable amount of time.

Remove the two snap rings from the half shaft end you're working on. Squeeze the two ends with a special pair of circlip pliers or needle-nose pliers. If the snap ring doesn't want to come out, try sliding a very small flathead screwdriver under the ring and pop it up and out of the groove.

Now start searching through your toolbox and find two sockets. One should be slightly smaller than the outer diameter of the U-joint (an 18-millimeter socket usually works here), and one should be slightly larger than the outer diameter of the U-joint (a 1.5-inch works nicely).

Now place the U-joint in the vice. It helps if you have a partner hold the other end while you arrange the sockets and the end of the shaft. The small socket should be on the outside of the vice lined up with the U-joint and the large socket on the inside of the vice lined up with the U-joint centered as much as possible. You're going to simply push the U-joint out of one side.

Once you've pressed the U-joint over as far as possible, remove the setup from the vice and pull off the cap from the large socket end with your hands.

At this point, you should be able to now pull the rest of the U-joint out of the half shaft easily. The caps may be difficult to remove, but a pair of pliers will usually be all the force that's necessary. Don't worry about scratching the cap since that's going to be thrown away.

Universal Joint Installation

If you've gotten this far, the rest is going to be easy. I always take a minute to clean up the area on the yoke of the shaft with 400-grit sandpaper. I don't want to remove any of the aluminum, but I just want to make sure there are no scratches that will hang up the new caps.

At this point, you should lubricate the inner side of the half shaft loops with some anti-seize compound. Then install the new U-joint into the yoke the same way you removed the old one, with one cap off. Install one of the snap rings on the loop of the half shaft on the outside of the vice.

Place the second cap on by hand and press it on as far as you can. Do this gently and make sure all is lined up squarely. Once you're convinced that everything is lined up, you can simply press the unit together the same way you took it apart.

Press the new U-joint in smoothly until you can feel it come up against the installed snap ring. The pressure will increase; this is how you can tell it's in the right position. Finally install the second snap ring.

This new U-joint may be a little tough to turn as pressing it in loads up everything to the side that had the large socket on it during installation. I usually take a large rawhide or plastic hammer and smack the new assembly.

You want to whack it toward the side where you put the cap on by hand. Just a slight tap should work. You should notice that the U-joint moves much more freely after doing this, as now the load will be distributed evenly throughout both sides.

Installation

Installation is the exact reverse of removal. There are just a couple of things to consider when reinstalling the assembly back into the car. First, remember to use some Loctite on the 5/16-inch strap bolts upon reinstallation. Next make sure the U-joints are on the inside of the little blocks that hold it in place side to side when it goes back in. They're not easy to see, but take a minute to make sure everything is right before you tighten it all down.

The axle shafts will necessitate working in some very close quarters. Take your time here. You may find that the job actually goes quicker if you get some parts out of the way. The first thing I got rid of on my car was the spare tire carrier. A can of Fix-a-Flat is a lot easier to carry around than a spare tire.

Rear Wheel Bearing Replacement

 Time: 2 to 4 hours (per side)

 Tools: You will absolutely need a No. 55 Torx socket. Make sure you get one before you attempt this project. Also, make sure that you get the long version, since the normal bit will not fit into the area.

 Talent:

 Tab: $150 to $300

 Torque: Spindle nut—164 foot-pounds; wheel hub mounting bolts—66 foot-pounds

 Tip: This might be a good time to replace the universal joints on the rear axles since you're going to have everything apart to do the rear wheel bearings.

The rear wheel bearings on the 1984 to 1996 work just fine if you don't put big tires on the rear and don't use the car at track events. That simply means that some of us are going to have to check the rear wheel bearings on a regular basis. Some people might even consider this to be routine maintenance.

The Corvette engineering team decided to give us what they called packaged bearings. We generally refer to them as a sealed bearing. The effect is the same. Once you get wear in the bearing, you simply throw the unit away and install a new one.

Check Your Bearings

The most important rule is that you check the bearings very carefully. Before you embark on this project, you need to determine whether or not you actually need rear wheel bearings.

These wheel bearings can be worn, and you'll never really notice. If the bearings are bad enough that you actually notice the wear while you're driving, you're way past the point of normal replacement. There's a very specific check for rear wheel bearing play.

Raise the rear corner of the car up enough to get the tire off the pavement and place a jack stand under the frame.

REAR AXLE AND DRIVESHAFT

The best way to quickly check the condition of a wheel bearing is to raise the corner of the car and wobble the wheel. You should have your hands on the top and bottom of the wheel during this check. There should be minimal play when you attempt to wobble the wheel. If you check all four wheels, you'll develop a good sense of how bad your wheel bearings really are. The front bearings seldom go bad, so they can usually be used as a good way to judge the condition of the rear bearings.

This shows the parts that have to be removed on the early cars, cars that use brake shoes for the parking brake. This job consists of removing parts and then putting them all back together. Unfortunately, there are a lot of parts. On these early cars, you're going to have to disconnect the parking brake cable. On the later cars, you can simply hang the caliper, complete with the parking brake cable, out of the way.

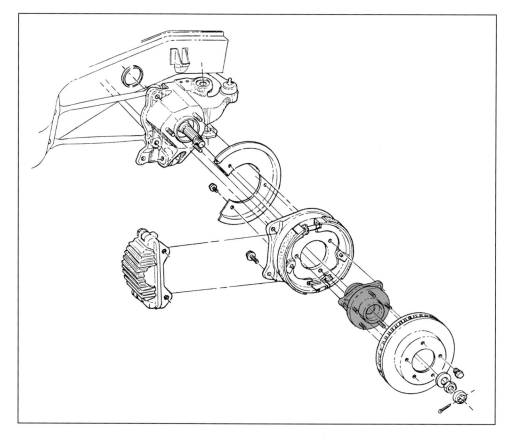

Below: This is the later car, which has the parking brake integrated into the brake caliper.

1 – Cotter Pin
2 – Wheel Nut Retaine
3 – Spindle Nut
4 – Spindle Washer
5 – Wheel Hub/Bearing
6 – Caliper Mounting Plate
7 – Wheel Spindle Washer

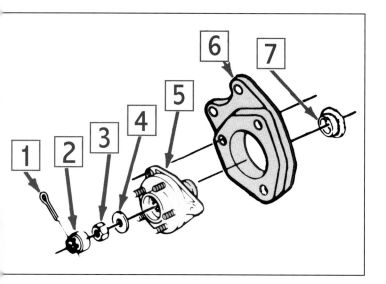

With your hands at 12 o' clock and 6 o' clock positions on the wheel, wobble the wheel up and down.

If you feel any significant amount of play, you either need to replace the wheel bearing or progress to a more precise way of checking for play.

Bearing Quality and Price
Rear wheel bearing prices are all over the map. AutoZone has Timken rear wheel bearings for $150 each. Most of the

Corvette specialty shops are a little more expensive. If you want an AC/Delco bearing, it's going to cost you almost twice as much as the others. The irony here is that there's very little difference in quality between the two products.

You want to avoid anything that comes in a white box. These "white-box" parts are built for one reason—to offer them at the lowest price possible. No one is currently offering a warranty on these wheel bearings, which should give you an indication of how long you might expect one to last. Unless you have really wide tires and wheels, you should expect quality bearings parts to last about 50,000 miles on your car.

Take It Apart
The part about this job that will get you frustrated is that there are three Torx bolts holding the bearing assembly to the spindle, and you can only reach them from the back side. The top bolt can give you a hard time because of the lack of room; the bottom two are easier to work with. You shouldn't have to remove the strut rod.

There are a couple of ways to approach this task. I prefer to do this disassembly on the car. Other people feel that the best way is to remove the whole corner of the car and do it on the workbench. If you do it on the workbench, you're going to remove the trailing arm links, the rear tie rod, and the rear camber strut rod. That just seems like a whole lot of stuff to remove. Granted, the actual bearing installation will go quickly if it's done on your workbench, but you're going to spend a lot of time removing and replacing all the additional parts.

Another way to approach this task is to simply remove the half shaft that runs between the hub and the differential. Just get it totally out of the way. Make sure you mark the ends with spots of yellow paint, or numbers, so you can remember how to get everything back together.

The hard part is removing the Torx bolts that hold the unit together. Make sure you use a really high quality Torx bit. The last thing you need on this job is to strip one the bolts.

Remove the rear wheel.
- Remove the ABS sensor (10 millimeter) from the housing. If you don't remove this now, you'll damage the sensor when you remove the bearing.
- Remove the caliper assembly and tie it out of the way. Make sure you unbolt the caliper bracket mounts, not the bolts that connect the caliper to the bracket.
- Remove the brake rotor.
- If you have a 1984 to 1987 model, you're going to need to disconnect the parking brake cable.
- Remove the cotter pin, nut (36 millimeter), and washer from center of each hub assembly.
- Mark the half shaft, or rear axle, so that you can replace it in exactly the same position that you removed it. Use something that won't come off, like yellow or white paint, not chalk.
- Remove the little straps that hold the universal joints to the half shaft.
- With the axle on the floor, locate the three bolts that secure the bearing to the housing (55 Torx bit). The bearing will fall off in your hand—maybe.
- Replace the old bearing and tighten the Torx bolts to 66 foot-pounds.

- Check the thin washers on the splined area of the half shaft. Make sure it fits up flush to the inside. If there's a gap, it's installed backwards. Put a little grease on both sides of it. It should fit directly up against the bearing.
- Install the half shafts with the retaining caps off.
- Place the caliper mounting bracket and the bearing on the rear spindle.
- Install the spindle washer and the nut. This nut has to be tightened to 164 foot-pounds. You can get it relatively tight while on the jack stands. Then do the final tightening with the car on the ground.
- Now replace the nut retainer and the cotter pin. Always use a brand-new cotter pin.
- Replace the brake rotor.
- Install the brake caliper.
- Install the ABS sensor.
- Install the wheel and lower your car to the floor.

Now that you have one side done, you're ready to attack the other one when the time seems right. There is no reason to do both sides if only one side is worn. Just keep in mind that if one side is worn, the other side is not going to last too much longer.

This is the correct and authorized procedure for checking rear wheel bearing play. The rotor is held in place with two lug nuts, and the dial indicator is placed on the center of the brake rotor. Wobble the rotor from the bottom and read the movement from the dial. The factory specification calls for no more than .005 inch of movement. I seriously doubt if many C4 Corvettes can meet that standard after 50,000 miles of driving. These rear wheel bearings are one of the weak points on the C4 chassis. It's especially bad when you install larger wheels and tires on the C4 Corvette.

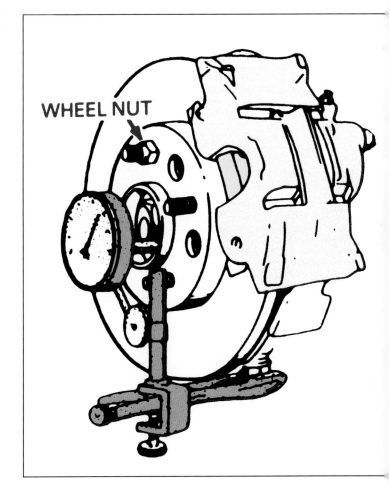

WHEEL NUT

Rear Differential Lube

 Time: 1 hour

 Tools: Drain plug kit and gear oil

 Talent:

 Applicable Years: 1984 to 1996

 Tab: $15 to $75

 Tip: Use synthetic gear oil.

 PERFORMANCE GAIN: There is a very marginal performance gain when you use a synthetic gear oil.

COMPLEMENTARY MODIFICATION: If you have to remove the differential cover, this would be a good time to replace the bushings in the differential cover/carrier.

Why would every Corvette built since 1963 lack a drain plug for the rear differential? I'm sure GM has a reason, but I certainly can't figure it out. No oil company will go on the record saying that their differential lubricant will last forever.

After putting about 120,000 miles on my car and competing in a dozen track events, I decided that it was time to change the rear axle lube. There are two ways to do this. The first way is to actually remove the rear cover on the differential. This is a pretty involved process.

In order to change the differential oil the GM way, you have to remove the rear cross-member and drop everything out of the way. Changing the differential oil involves removing not only the rear spring but the rear tie rods as well. Chevrolet obviously did not intend for you to change the oil in the differential.

Corvette Clinic in Sanford, Florida, developed a better way to do this. This process only entails drilling a hole in the lower part of the differential housing and tapping some threads for a small plug. Corvette Clinic sells a complete kit, which even includes a template that ensures you drill the hole in the proper location. This kit causes some apprehension when people first encounter it. There is a very serious concern that metal shavings will be floating around in the differential housing. This really isn't a factor since the metal shavings are all flushed out when the old oil starts draining.

DIFF DRAIN PLUG ←

Here is the drain plug from Corvette Clinic installed. Life is so much easier with this kit installed. Even though the differential gears in the C4 rarely go bad, it can't hurt to change this oil once a year.

Here is the fill plug on the side of the differential case. This is almost impossible to access while it's in the car. Once you remove the plug, you'll need a funnel with a long hose to fill the differential. We're talking about really cramped quarters in this area.

Checking and Adding

Checking your fluid level is fairly easy provided the last person who added oil didn't go crazy when he or she tightened the fill plug. The problem with the differential fill plug is that it's very close to the body (or floor) panel. This means you simply can't get a normal socket into the location. There's a good chance that when you look at your drain plug, you'll notice a series of teeth marks around the edge. These markings mean the vise grip technicians have been there.

It really takes a special tool to loosen the fill plug properly. Most shops don't have the necessary tool and resort to the standard vice grip technique. If you're going to a new shop, you need to ask how the employees intend to remove the fill plug. If they look at you like you're crazy, find another shop. An experienced shop will be familiar with this problem and explain to you that its employees have the proper tool.

You should ask the shop employees where they got the tool and then get one of your own. This way you can check the differential level at home. Once you get the fill plug out of the case, it's simply a matter of sticking your finger into the hole and checking the level.

The factory manual calls for the use of 75W90 gear oil in the rear gears. I would probably stick to this, but I suggest

This is the factory bushing in the differential carrier. I wouldn't go to all the trouble of removing this assembly just to install polyurethane bushings, but if I have to remove it for any reason, I would certainly spend an extra few minutes to install them.

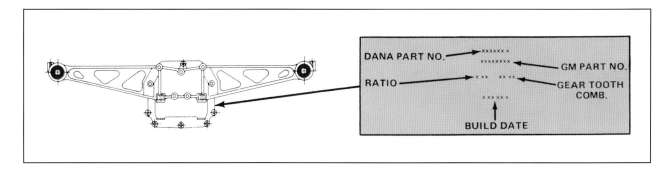

DANA PART NO. → XXXXXX X
XXXXXXXX ← GM PART NO.

RATIO → X XX   XX XX ← GEAR TOOTH COMB.

XX XXXX
↑
BUILD DATE

Your differential carrier has a wealth of information. You'll need to get up under the carrier with a light and some cleaner to see it all. The basic rule is that all the automatics received the smaller gears, and the standard transmissions got the big unit with the big gear. These Dana 44 units are bringing a premium price on the used market. On the other hand, you can hardly give the Dana 36 away.

that you use a synthetic gear oil. The advantage is that the synthetic oils can cope with extreme heat should they ever need to do that. Also make sure that the lubricant contains a Posi-Traction additive. If you can't find the correct oil, you can purchase the additive separately. The problem is that the only thing that smells worse than gear oil is a packet of Posi-Traction additive.

What Gears Are in My Corvette?

GM used two different limited slip rear axles in the C4. The automatic transmission cars had the Dana 36 with a 7.875-inch diameter ring gear, and the manual transmission cars had the Dana 44 with an 8.5-inch ring gear. The only exception to this was in 1984, which got the smaller Dana 36. Both units have held up remarkably well.

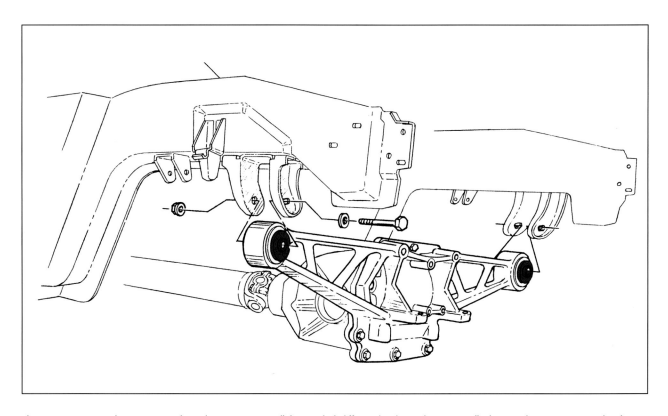

This rear suspension on the C4 is very similar to the 1963 Corvette. All the parts look different, but the two have essentially the same design. It's amazing that the basic design lasted for over thirty years. This also means that for over thirty years there was no way you could drain the differential oil without taking the whole rear suspension apart. Go figure that one out.

THE ZR-1

Parts courtesy Corvette Central

Changing the Oil in the ZR-1

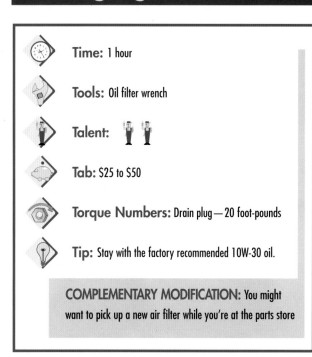

Time: 1 hour

Tools: Oil filter wrench

Talent: ∦ ∦

Tab: $25 to $50

Torque Numbers: Drain plug — 20 foot-pounds

Tip: Stay with the factory recommended 10W-30 oil.

COMPLEMENTARY MODIFICATION: You might want to pick up a new air filter while you're at the parts store

The first surprise is that the oil filter is upside down and sitting on top of the motor. The next surprise is that it sometimes takes almost a case of oil to fill the motor. The oil capacity is rather confusing. The best reference is the factory manual. Remember, too much oil can be almost as bad as not enough oil.

Without Filter Change	7.6 quarts
With Filter Change	8.6 quarts
With Oil Cooler Drain and New Filter	10.6 quarts
Complete System Drain (after engine rebuild)	11.6 quarts

A common concern among new ZR-1 owners is that, when they drain the oil, only about 8.5 quarts of oil comes out of the car. The oil is literally hiding out inside the motor. There are so many hiding places, in fact, that the manual suggests waiting two hours after shutting down the LT5 before checking the oil to get the most accurate reading.

Most owners come to accept that there will be no harm in the 3.2 quarts remaining in the system, since when mixed with the new fluid, it accounts for less than 30 percent of the oil in the system. The next time you change the oil, most of those three quarts will be drained. By the time you change the oil the third time, less than a half a quart of the original oil will be left in the system. You shouldn't get too alarmed about all the oil not draining out.

Oil and Filter Brands

You can decide for yourself which brand of oil to use. I've never heard of a name brand oil destroying a motor. I use Mobil 1 because it's readily available, and I've never heard of anyone having a problem with Mobil 1. A lot of people swear by Red Line and Motul. That's fine. I'll stick with what GM used.

When it comes to the oil filter, I'll do the same thing. The LT5 filter uses an anti-drain back valve. Anytime I run across a car that uses an anti-drain back valve in the filter, I stick with the original equipment filter. While there's no proof that the OEM filter is the best on the market, neither is there any real documented proof that any other filters are superior. I'll take the easy way out and use the GM filter.

Don't forget to use the GM drain plug gasket. That's one item that's well worth the money. Use a new drain plug gasket every time you change the oil.

The Dreaded Low Oil Light

It seems that some dealerships or quick lube shops aren't filling the LT5 engine with enough oil. This causes the "low oil" warning light to come on in the car. In order for the light to come on, a series of things has to happen. First, the oil temperature when the engine was last running must have been at least 195 degrees. Next, the oil temperature must have dropped at least 105 degrees from that temperature. Finally, the oil level sensor, located in the oil pan, must detect a low oil level before the car is started.

If you start your Corvette, and the "low oil" light doesn't come on, you shouldn't expect any problems during driving. The only way you'll be alerted to low oil levels will be because of high oil temps or low oil pressure. Since the LT5 has an oil cooler, excessive oil temperature is usually not a problem. The only exception might be if you run track events and have the LT5 engine running at high speeds for over a half hour or more. Even then this really is generally not a problem.

The electronic control module, or ECM, monitors the oil temperature and uses it for a few different functions. The first thing that changes with oil temperature is the actuation of the secondary throttle plates. These secondary throttle plates will only open when there is an oil temperature of between 68 degrees and 304 degrees. The 304-degree temperature actually corresponds to the maximum oil temperature the ECM will recognize so the max level is no big deal. Actually, you should shut the engine off long before you reach 304 degrees. In fact, if your oil temperature is above 284 degrees for longer than 30 minutes, you'll get an error code 62. Incidentally, an oil temperature of less than -36 de-

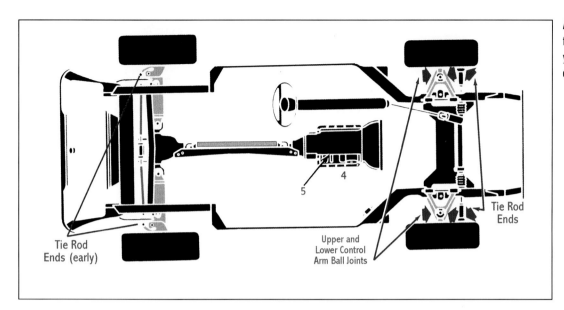

As you're changing the oil, make sure you grease the car as well.

Tie Rod Ends (early)

Tie Rod Ends

Upper and Lower Control Arm Ball Joints

grees for longer than 30 minutes results in error code 52 being set. That is most likely not going to happen.

In reality, a code 52 is an indication of something other than a temperature problem. The oil temperature sensor operates just like the inlet air temperature sensor since 5V is placed across the sensor, acting as a resistor. Higher temperatures produce lower resistance, which moves the 5V closer to ground. An open or shorted sensor, or a broken wire to the sensor, will result in a reading of -36. Then the ECM will set a code, which when you use the scan tool will be displayed as a code 52.

Three Things You Need to Know
The temperature of your oil actually controls three other functions on the LT5 engine. First, an oil temperature above 259 degrees will result in the air conditioning clutch being disabled. This reduces the load on the engine in an attempt to help bring the temperature down. High oil temperature also will trigger the cooling system fans to come on. An oil temperature of 228 degrees should result in a fan coming on.

The last function that uses oil temp is the oil life monitor. Oil temperature is one of the variables that is used in the calculation to determine when the "change oil" light is engaged.

Oil Pressure
The LT5 oil pump is rated for around 1.5 gallons per minute at idle and around 9 gallons per minute at 7,000 rpm. According to the manual, this should produce oil pressures, when hot, of at least 12psi at idle and over 40psi above 3,000 rpm. Unfortunately, the oil pressure sensors (yes there are two, both located on the oil filter housing, along with the oil temperature sensor) do not feed into either the CCM or ECM. This means that low oil pressure isn't used to turn the engine off. As a result, you have to detect the situation and turn the ignition key off as soon as possible.

One oil pressure sensor (the one with a light blue wire) drives the "check gauges" light, while the other oil pressure sensor (the one with a tan wire) drives the actual oil pressure gauge. When you notice an indication of ("low oil pressure" or "check gauges"), you have a right to be concerned. You don't need to get alarmed—just concerned.

There are really four possible causes for your dash display to light up. They are a faulty sensor, a low oil level, a critical oil system blockage, or a failed oil pump. Generally, if the culprit is one of the last three, the oil pressure will be abnormally low and the "check gauges" light will be on. If only one of those things is occurring, chances are a sensor has simply failed. Nevertheless, as soon as you see either dash light go on, the car should be stopped immediately. It's usually not a big deal, but why take a chance of destroying a motor?

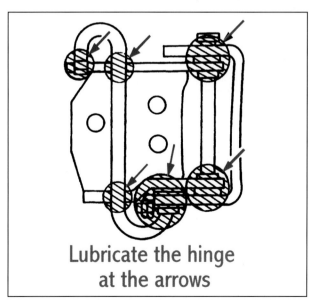

Lubricate the hinge at the arrows

This is one of the most forgotten items on the C4. The doors are big and very heavy. Spend thirty seconds and oil the hinges.

ZR-1 Air Filter

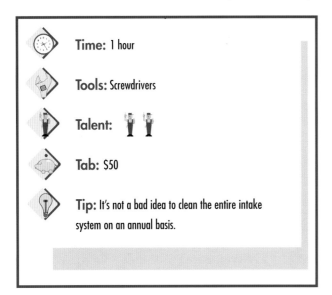

Time: 1 hour

Tools: Screwdrivers

Talent: 👤 👤

Tab: $50

Tip: It's not a bad idea to clean the entire intake system on an annual basis.

The intake system for the LT5 engine is very similar to that of the L98 and LT1 engines. From the air filter housing to the plenum, it's virtually the same as the other engines. The only difference is that when GM went back to a mass airflow system, the ZR-1 stayed with the speed density system. Considering that the car was failing in the marketplace, there was no money for any LT5 development. Remember, after its first couple of years, GM was just hoping the ZR-1 would go away.

Air Filters

Air filters are meant to keep the dirt out of our engines and create as little restriction as possible. The best all around air filter is the AC/Delco. K&N and some others have made millions selling high-performance filters that supposedly reduce restriction and, therefore, add horsepower. That may actually happen for some other cars, but it's not the case for the ZR-1.

Numerous people have tested stock air filter elements and K&N elements. No one found any difference between the two types, at least when they were both brand-new and clean. Unfortunately, though, the K&N element is an oiled design that must be cleaned and re-oiled periodically to maintain its efficiency. The oil seems to do a good job of trapping dust and other dirt, but it turns out that it actually does too good of a job. In other words, it's so efficient that it clogs up fairly quickly.

I've seen dyno tests where a stock AC/Delco air filter with 12,000 miles of use was compared to an empty filter housing. The dirty AC/Delco air filter produced only 2 horsepower less than an open passage. A K&N filter with 2,000 miles on it was tested, and the result was a 19 horsepower loss. Some of the other aftermarket foam type filters were even worse.

It seems that the K&N filter is really pretty good for the first few thousand miles. After that, it becomes severely restrictive. You can clean it every couple of thousand miles and hope for the best. Or you can use the AC/Delco filter and change it every ten thousand miles.

The good part about the LT5 engine is that it uses the old speed density system so at least the K&N air filter oil won't mess up the mass airflow sensor. Air filter oil deposits on the mass airflow sensor have been a problem with the K&N type of filter. It's most common on the AC/Delco MAF sensor since it doesn't have a burn-off cycle like the earlier Bosch system.

Air Filter Housings

The LT5 engine uses the same air filter housing as the other cars do, and it works just fine. If you feel the need to do something, you can cut the top of the lid off. You won't notice any appreciable power difference, but it will give you something to talk about at Corvette gatherings.

Flexible Air Ducts

Now we get to the real reason you need a good air filter with the LT5 engine. An increased pressure drop across the filter element will cause the air duct between the air filter housing and the throttle body to collapse. This problem of collapsing air ducts isn't as rare as you might first think. I saw one ZR-1 being tested with a foam-type air filter and watched the duct collapse almost completely as the rpm rose. Removal of the air filter element resulted in some very big gains—30 horsepower or more—for this owner.

Again, there are various aftermarket alternatives available to address this problem. Simply replacing the old, softened unit with a new GM duct will help a lot. The other thing you can do when you're cleaning the intake system is to totally remove the intake duct and spray it out with your air intake cleaner. You'll be amazed how much dirt comes out of this duct.

The aftermarket has come up with a variety of air filter housings that are supposed to offer all sorts of magical horsepower gains. People usually talk about how these housings are cold air induction systems. Think about this for a minute and go look at your stock Corvette. The air filter housing isn't even in the engine compartment. The stock air filter is drawing air from in front of the radiator. Your Corvette came equipped with a cold air induction

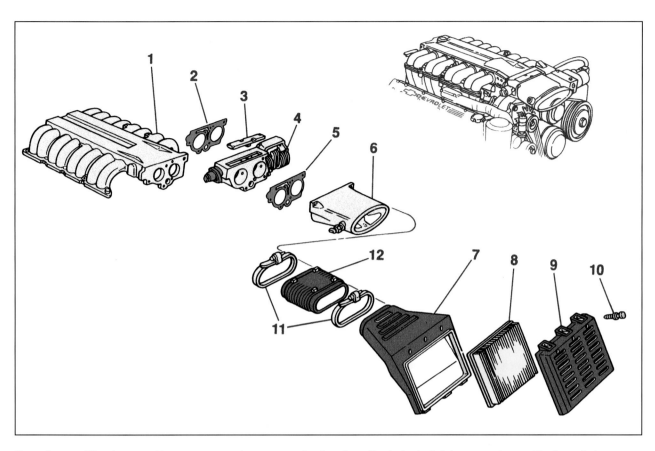

Here is the entire LT5 intake system. It's a very conventional system except that, from the air filter back, it's a little larger since there are 32 valves to feed.

1 – Plenum
2 – Gasket
3 – Cover
4 – Throttle Body
5 – Gasket
6 – Throttle Body Extension

7 – Air Intake Duct
8 – Air Filter
9 – Air Filter Cover
10 – Bolt for Air Filter Cover
11 – Clamp for Air Intake Intermediate Duct
12 – Air Intake Intermediate Duct

system. The idea of spending several hundred dollars for an intake system that draws air from the same location as the stock air filter doesn't strike me as a good use of my money.

A few years back, a company developed an intake system that drew air from the front license plate area. This was a frustrating item. It would never show any extra horsepower on the dyno because no air was being rammed through the front diffuser. The company readily admitted that it did nothing until you were moving at over 70 miles per hour. At that point there was no way to measure the horsepower gain. Thus it was a $1,000 air intake system that couldn't be properly evaluated. Most Corvette owners simply passed on the idea.

It's just hard to beat the stock Corvette air intake system. Many have tried, and many have failed. You should just ignore the hype, work on keeping the intake system clean, and buy a new AC/Delco filter once a year.

Throttle Body and Cleaning

Once you have the duct clean, you can spray the throttle body with the air intake cleaner. You shouldn't have to remove the throttle body since most ZR-1s have gotten very little use. On the other hand, make sure you spray both sides of the throttle plates with your air intake cleaner.

Doing this job correctly really means that you start cleaning at the air filter housing and don't stop until you reach the throttle plates. It just doesn't make much sense to only clean part of the intake passage. Even if you take everything off for cleaning, you'll still be spending less than an hour on this.

One item you should remove for cleaning is the throttle body extension. You'll need to unplug the sensor in order to do this. You'll also need a new gasket for the seal between the throttle body and the extension housing.

THE ZR-1

ZR-1 Cooling

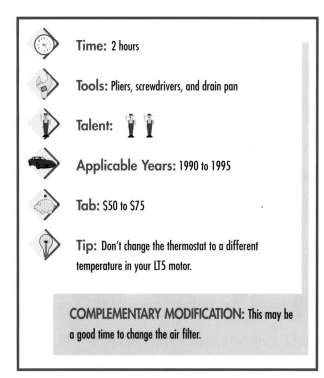

Time: 2 hours

Tools: Pliers, screwdrivers, and drain pan

Talent: ★★

Applicable Years: 1990 to 1995

Tab: $50 to $75

Tip: Don't change the thermostat to a different temperature in your LT5 motor.

COMPLEMENTARY MODIFICATION: This may be a good time to change the air filter.

Why shouldn't we be surprised that the ZR-1 has a history of cooling problems? All the other C4 Corvettes seem to have cooling problems, or, at the very least, they have owners that are greatly concerned about cooling problems. When I had questions about the LT5 engine, I went to Jim Van Dorn of Auto Masters in California. Van Dorn is the leading ZR-1 repair expert in the world, and he was very quick to point out that "the most common complaint made by the Corvette owner is overheating." He pointed out several concerns. "First," he said, "the Corvette ZR-1 has no front grille. Therefore, it relies heavily on the air deflectors underneath the front bumper to direct airflow through the radiator to dissipate heat. Damaged or missing deflectors will cause overheating. The bottom-breather design also works wonderfully as a vacuum cleaner for our roadways. However, the downside of this is

Here we have the air bleed hose junction block for the LT5 option. These units will be difficult to obtain in the future since so few were made. They can always be reproduced, but, because the demand will be so minimal, they'll be extremely high priced. This will always be a problem with the LT5 engines. During the next few decades, parts will become more difficult to locate.
1 – Air Bleed Hose Junction
2 – Air Bleed Hose

that the Corvette's radiator becomes highly susceptible to accumulating debris which will reduce airflow and, therefore, increase operating temperatures."

Van Dorn has always felt that the ZR-1's cooling system requires regular maintenance and feels that the system should be drained once a year. He pointed out that the best way to do this is by loosening the lower radiator hose. Van Dorn said that his facility, Corvette Masters, always uses distilled water because the aluminum alloys present in the LT5 and radiator actively promote the formation of scale within the system.

When it came to the inevitable discussion of thermostats for the LT5, he offered words of caution. "The LT5's thermostat has several functions. In addition to performing the duties of a thermostat, it also provides a bypass function for the radiator in the event the amount of coolant exceeds the capabilities of the radiator. Use of the incorrect thermostat can result in blown hoses and even blown radiators. The LT5 is equipped with a 195-degree thermostat but we have also had great results using the Stant 180 degrees." He was referring to part No. 14068.

Van Dorn also pointed out that the radiator is highly susceptible to restrictions and blockage, which are the main causes of any rise in operating temperatures. This airflow

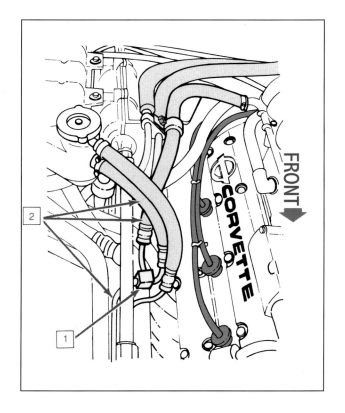

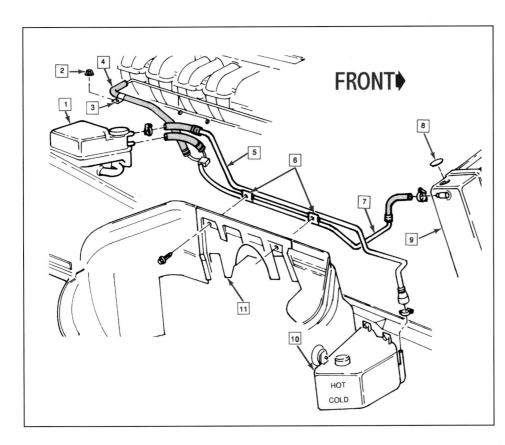

This is an illustration of the air bleed and recovery hoses on the LT5 engine.
1 - High Fill Reservoir
2 - Air Bleed Clip Retaining Nut
3 - Air Bleed Hose Clip
4 - Plenum Air Bleed Hose
5 - Coolant Recovery Hose
6 - Retaining Bracket
7 - Radiator Air Bleed Hose
8 - Radiator Air Bleed Access Plug
9 - Coolant Recovery Reservoir
10 - Center Wheelhouse Panel

FRONT▶

restriction occurs when particles are collected in the small space between the air conditioning condenser and the radiator. None of this is visible until the top radiator shroud is removed and the radiator is fully viewed from the top.

He pointed out that removing the radiator is not as involved as it may first appear, and he's found periodic removal and cleaning of the radiator to be very effective. "Also," he said, "be sure to inspect the air conditioning condenser due to the fact that it is installed in front of the radiator. It must not be obstructed or damaged by road debris."

Van Dorn said, "Keeping your LT5 cool and the cooling system serviced is crucial to the LT5's durability. Although there are some larger aluminum radiators available, the stock system should provide adequate cooling under most street operation if kept clean and unobstructed. The LT5 is susceptible to head gasket problems if allowed to overheat because of the close proximity of the lower part of the cylinder to the coolant passage. If your LT5 uses coolant and you see no external leakage, you may have a seeping head gasket and should have it checked immediately."

Drain, Flush, and Refill System:
• When the engine and radiator are cool, remove the pressure cap on the coolant fill reservoir located at the right rear of the engine compartment by slowly rotating cap counterclockwise to detent. Do not press down while rotating.
• Wait until any residual pressure (indicated by a hissing sound) is relieved from this reservoir.

• After all the hissing ceases, press down on the cap while continuing to rotate counterclockwise.
• Now open the radiator petcock to drain coolant.
• Close the petcock and add sufficient water to fill system.
• Run the engine for a few minutes and then drain and refill the system again. Continue to do this several times until the drained liquid is nearly colorless.
• This final time allow the system to drain completely and then close the radiator petcock tightly.
• Now remove the coolant recovery reservoir located at the right front of the engine compartment and clean it. Once you're happy that it's really clean, you can put it back in place.
• Add a 50-50 mixture of water and ethylene glycol antifreeze that meets GM specification 1825-M. Fill the reservoir to the base of the filler neck and add sufficient coolant to the recovery reservoir to raise the level to the full "COLD" mark on the dip stick. Now you can reinstall recovery reservoir cap.
• Run the engine, with pressure cap removed, until the normal operating temperature is reached and the upper radiator hose becomes hot.
• While the engine is still idling, add coolant until the level reaches the bottom of high fill reservoir filler neck.
• Do not use stop-leak pellets in the LT5 cooling system.
• Install the pressure cap, making sure the arrows line up with the overflow tube.
• Check the level in the recovery reservoir and add coolant until it reaches the full "HOT" mark on dip stick.

ZR-1 Thermostat Replacement

Time: 1 hour

Tools: Metric wrenches and screwdriver

Torque: Thermostat housing bolts—18 foot-pounds

Talent: 👤👤

Tab: Under $50

Tip: Use the stock Chevrolet thermostat.

COMPLEMENTARY MODIFICATION: This would be a good time to flush the entire cooling system.

The purpose of thermostats is to control the flow of the engine coolant. It helps provide fast engine warmup and regulates the coolant temperature by acting as a gate in the cooling system. The gate is either open or closed.

In the LT5 engine the function of the thermostat is a little different. The LT5 thermostat has a wax pellet which, when heated, exerts pressure against a diaphragm. This, in turn, forces the thermostat's valve to open. As the wax pellet cools down, the contraction allows a spring to exert pressure that closes the valve. This valve remains closed while the coolant is cold, stopping all circulation of coolant through the radiator.

This thermostat also combines a bypass function with temperature management. Under high rpm or cold operating conditions, the water pump can actually push more water through the system than the radiator can handle. When this happens, the coolant is bypassed to the engine. This system works all the time, letting a small amount of coolant bypass the radiator. The idea is that temperature regulation is enhanced.

Finding the Thermostat

The thermostat is behind the lower part of the radiator on the passenger side. The best way to get to this little guy is to jack the car up and remove the right front wheel. This job would be easy except there's a bracket attached to a frame cross-member that goes to the housing, so you also have to remove that first to get the thermostat out.

You can use a crowfoot wrench to get one of those bracket bolts out. Remember that the tapered side of the thermostat goes toward the radiator. To get the thermostat centered, insert the bolts into the housing. It helps to take the short piece of hose off the housing that goes to the radiator. Then, after you check for leaks, reattach the bracket to the frame.

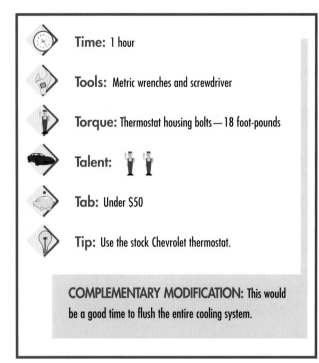
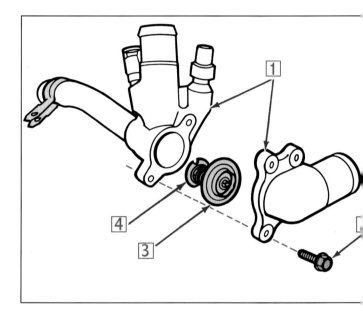

1 – Thermostat Housing, 2 – Bolt, 3 – Thermostat Seal, 4 – Thermostat

Which Thermostat?

There has been a lot of confusion as to which thermostat is really in the ZR-1. Some manuals say 180 degrees and others 195 degrees. The best answer is that your ZR-1 has a thermostat that starts to open at 180 degrees and is fully open at 195 degrees. This is really the best choice for normal use. In fact, it may be the best choice for any use.

VIN NUMBER DECODING

The Vehicle Identification Number, or VIN, decodes as follows for the C4 Corvette. The last five positions show the car's position in the build sequence for the model year.

```
1   G   1   YY   3   1   8   9   K   5        1 0 0 0 0 1
|   |   |   |    |   |   |   |   |   |        |—Plant Sequential Build Number
|   |   |   |    |   |   |   |   |   |—Factory Code (5 - Bowling Green, KY)
|   |   |   |    |   |   |   |   |—Model Year (See chart below)
|   |   |   |    |   |   |   |—Check Digit
|   |   |   |    |   |   |—Engine Code (8 = L83, L98, P = LT1, 5=LT4, J=LT5)
|   |   |   |    |   |—Seat Belt System (1 = Manual Belts)
|   |   |   |    |—Body Type (2 = Hatchback, 3 = Convertible)
|   |   |   |—Carline and Series (YY = Std Corvette, YZ = ZR1)
|   |   |—Division  (1 = Chevrolet)
|   |—Manufacturer  (G = General Motors)
|—Country of Origin  ( 1 = USA)
```

Designator	Model Year	Designator	Model Year
E	1984	M	1991
F	1985	N	1992
G	1986	P	1993
H	1987	R	1994
J	1988	S	1995
K	1989	T	1996
L	1990		

APPENDIX

This is a list of the significant changes that were made to the C4 Corvette. I haven't listed every running change since that would result in a document that's larger than this entire book. Neither have I attempted to duplicate the work of the NCRS by listing all the casting numbers and date codes.

The NCRS has now started judging the early C4 Corvettes, and you should get a copy of the judging manual. The best way is to simply log on to the NCRS web site at www.ncrs.org and place an order for the judging manual. That manual will list many more differences than I can possibly list here. If you're going to restore these Corvettes, you'll need information about the finish and serial numbers on the various parts.

This is merely a listing of what I call the major changes over the years from 1984 to 1996.

1984

• The 1984 Corvette was introduced in March 1983. Because it met all 1984 federal requirements, Chevrolet decided to skip the 1983 model designation. The result was a very long production run and the second highest model year volume in the Corvette's history. The 1983 Corvettes were built, given serial numbers, and tested by both Chevrolet and the media at the Riverside Raceway preview in December 1982.

• Design criteria specified that the 1984 Corvette have more ground clearance and more interior room, but less overall height. In order to achieve this, the engineers routed the exhaust system through the center tunnel.

• A 4+3, four-speed manual transmission, built by Doug Nash, had overdrive in the top three gears for improved fuel economy. This transmission wasn't available until later in the 1984 production year.

• All 1984 Corvettes were designed with one-piece, lift-off roof panels and rear hatch windows. At the time, the rear window glass was the largest compound glass ever installed in an American automobile. The front windshield was raked at a 64-degree angle.

• Brakes remained disc at all four wheels, but the components were all new and included aluminum calipers supplied by Girlock of Australia.

• Electronic instrumentation was standard and included digital readouts for engine monitoring and liquid crystal graphic displays for speed and engine revolutions. Analog instrumentation was not available.

• The 1984 Corvette was designed without fiberglass seams on exposed panels to eliminate factory finishing. The exterior seams were hidden under the rub strip extending around the entire body.

• The radiator was a new design using aluminum for the cooling fins and plastic for the reservoirs. The thermostatically controlled electric fan operated only when needed and only at under 35 miles per hour.

• Chevrolet built specially modified 1984 Corvettes for the export markets of Europe, the Middle East, Japan, and various Latin American countries. This required changes for license plate provisions and leaded fuel capability. It also involved electrical, glass, lighting, and mirror modifications.

• Single transverse composite leaf springs were used for both the front and rear.

1985

• Real fuel injection returned to the Corvette in 1985 for the first time in two decades. The 1985 tuned-port injection, built by Bosch, was standard equipment and featured a mass airflow sensor, or MAF. The system used aluminum intake runners, a cast plenum, and an air cleaner mounted forward of the radiator support. This new L98 engine delivered increased horsepower from 205 horsepower to 230 horsepower, and torque was increased from 290 foot-pounds to 330 foot-pounds. Fuel economy increased about 11 percent over the 1984 model.

• The overdrive selection switch for four-speed manual transmissions was moved during the 1985 model year from the console to the gearshift knob.

• The suspension rates were lowered in 1985. Springs for the base suspension were softer by 26 percent in front and 25 percent in the rear. The RPO Z51 springs were 16 percent softer in front and 25 percent softer in the rear.

- Larger-diameter stabilizer bars were included with Z51 equipped models. The front bar was 30 millimeters, and the rear was 24 millimeters.

- The Z51 package included 9.5-inch wheels at all four corners instead of just the rear as in 1984.

- The bore of the brake master cylinder was increased from 13/16 inch to 7/8 inch in 1985, and the vacuum booster was made of plastic, the first such application in an American car. This new plastic brake booster was 30 percent lighter and less subject to corrosion.

- Manual transmission cars came with a new, heavy-duty 8.5-inch ring differential. Rear axle gearing for manuals was 3.07:1 Standard gearing for automatic transmission was 2.73:1, but the 3.07:1 could be ordered as RPO 092.

- Wheel balance weights changed from the outside rim clip-on style to an inner-surface adhesive type. Chevrolet believed a better balance resulted because the adhesive weight was closer to the wheel's center.

- A full-length oil pan gasket reinforcement was added to the 1985 Corvette engine to improve the oil pan gasket seal.

- Electronic instrumentation continued much as the previous year, but displays were revised and improved with cleaner graphics, less color on the speedometer and tachometer, and larger digits for the center-cluster liquid crystal displays.

- A map strap was added to the driver-side sun visor.

- A heavy-duty cooling system was offered as RPO V08. This included a special radiator, an additional fan, an 18psi radiator cap, and the KC4 Modine oil cooler. It combined things that had previously been available under a series of single option codes.

1986

- The electronic air conditioning option, which had been announced as a late 1985, was finally introduced with the 1986 model year.

- The first Corvette convertible since 1975 was introduced in 1986. This was the pace car for the 1986 Indianapolis 500. All 1986 Corvette convertibles sold were designated as pace car replicas, and they all included decal packages for dealer or customer installation.

- An anti-lock braking system, or ABS, became standard with the 1986 Corvettes. An adaptation of Bosch's ABS, Corvette's ABS had rotational sensors at each wheel, which sent data to a computerized electronic control unit. Brake line pressure was automatically distributed for optimum braking without wheel lock and loss of steering control.

- The master brake cylinder was changed again. Earlier master cylinders had three brake lines exiting the master cylinder. There had been a separate line for each front wheel and one line serving both rear wheels. The new design had only two lines. One line served the front brakes, and the other line served the rear brakes. Both lines went directly to the ABS hydraulic modulator.

- Cracking around the head attachment, bosses required delaying the 1986's aluminum cylinder heads. The heads were ready in time for convertible production, and all 1986 convertibles as well as late production coupes had aluminum heads. Engines fitted with aluminum heads were rated at 235 horsepower, an increase of five horsepower.

- High center-mounted brake lights were added to 1986 Corvettes to conform to federal requirements. The coupe's light was mounted above the rear window; the convertible's was in a less-conspicuous rear fascia location.

- A new vehicle anti-theft system, or ATS, required a special ignition key with an embedded pellet. There were lock cylinder contacts that measured the pellet's electrical resistance (there were fifteen variations) before allowing the starter to engage.

- Caster was changed in 1986 from four degrees to six degrees to improve on-center road feel and to decrease highway wander.

- Fuel tank capacity was dropped to eighteen gallons to from the previous 20 gallons.

- Fifty "Malcolm Konner Commemorative Edition" 1986 Corvettes were built in a special arrangement honoring the New Jersey Chevrolet dealership's founder, Malcolm Konner. Each Corvette had special two-tone paint schemes—silver beige over black and coded "spec." Window stickers reflected 4OO1ZA as the RPO, and a $500 price tag for MALCOLM KONNER SP.EDIT.PAI. All were coupes, twenty with manual transmissions and thirty with automatics. All had graphite leather interiors.

- The angle of the 1986 digital instrument display was changed to improve daytime viewing by reducing glare.

- A new upshift indicator light for the manual and automatic transmission 1986 models was intended to improve fuel economy.

- Low coolant and ABS instrument displays were added.

- The wheel design was revised slightly for 1986, with the wheel center section having a natural finish instead of black as in 1984 and 1985.

1987

- Roller valve lifters were introduced in 1987. The reduced friction resulted in a power increase to 240 horsepower, up 5 horsepower from the 1986's aluminum-head engines.

- The center sections, as well as the radial slots, of 1987 wheels were painted argent silver. In the year prior, the wheel centers were not painted. The centers and radial slots for 1984 and 1985 were painted black.

- Convertibles, and some of the early coupes, had outside mirror air deflectors installed.

- Chevrolet planned a low tire pressure indicator option (UJ6), but the $325 option was placed on constraint during 1987 due to false signaling problems. Chevrolet records show that 46 units were sold before the option was pulled from production.

- A new RPO Z52 handling package combined elements of RPO Z51 with the softer suspension of the base models. RPO Z52 included the radiator boost fan, Bilstein base shock absorbers, engine oil cooler, heavy-duty radiator, l6x9.5-inch wheels, faster 13 to 1 steering ratio, larger front stabilizer bar (except early production), and the convertible-inspired structural improvements for coupes. The Z52 was available with coupes or convertibles, automatic or manual transmissions.

- The overdrive-engage light was moved from the center-dash area (1984-86) to a location within the 1987 tachometer display.

- The Callaway Twin-Turbo engine package introduced in 1987 was not a factory-installed option, but it could be ordered through participating Chevrolet dealers as RPO B2K. Fully assembled Corvettes were shipped from the Bowling Green Corvette plant to Callaway Engineering in Old Lyme, Connecticut, for engine modifications. The 1987 Callaway had ratings of 345 horsepower and 465 foot-pounds of torque, and reached a top speed of 177.9 miles per hour with .60 overdrive gearing. The first four 1987 Callaway Corvettes used replacement LFS (truck) short blocks, but subsequent cars had reworked production Corvette engines. All 1987 Callaway Corvettes had manual transmissions, and none was certified for sale in California. Of the 184 twin-turbos built in 1987, 121 were coupes, and 63 were convertibles.

- Electronic air conditioning control (C68) became an option for both coupes and convertibles in 1987. In 1986, it was only available in the coupes.

- New 1987 convenience options included an illuminated vanity mirror (D74) for the driver's visor and a passenger-side power seat base (AC 1). Twin remote heated mirrors became available for convertibles (DL8). The heated mirrors were included with the heated rear window in the defogger option (Z6A) for coupes.

1988

- Refinements for 1988 included carpeted doorsills, solution-dyed carpet, improved \"flow through" ventilation for coupes, and a lower, rearward relocation of the parking brake handle.

- Engine power remained at 240 horsepower for 1988 models, except for coupes with 3.07 to 1 and 2.59 to1 axle ratios, which were listed at 245 horsepower. This increase came from less restrictive mufflers. These mufflers created resonance problems in the convertibles and were not available.

- The rear suspension was revised to improve handling and stability. The rear trailing arm forward bushings were moved inboard, and the lateral arm inboard bushing mount was lowered. The outer tie rod attachment point was moved rearward and down, also.

- The upper shock absorber mount at the rear was relocated. The upper shock mount was relocated from the side of the body rail to the center of the rail.

- A 35th anniversary edition Corvette package was available for coupes only. It featured a two-tone exterior of white with black roof bow, white leather seats, and a white steering wheel. A console-mounted anniversary plaque and special emblems were also included. Sales totaled 2,050 units.

APPENDIX

248

- Chevrolet built 56 street legal Corvettes for the 1988 SCCA Corvette Challenge race series. The engines were stock but matched for power output and were built at the Flint engine plant. They were then sealed and shipped to Bowling Green for standard assembly. The cars weren't built in sequence because the Corvette plant built in color batches. Fifty of these cars were sent to Protofab in Wixom, Michigan, for installation of roll cages and other safety equipment.

- New six-slot 16x8.5-inch wheels were standard with P255/50ZR16 tires.

- The RPO Z51 and RPO Z52 content changed slightly for 1988. Both had newly styled 17x9.5-inch wheels with twelve cooling slots and 275/4OZR17 tires. Z51 had higher spring rates and the same power steering cooler as the year before, but in 1988 it also received larger front brake rotors and calipers. RPO Z51 was limited to manual transmission coupes. RPO Z52 was not restricted.

- All 1988 Corvettes had new dual-piston front brakes and parking brakes which activated the rear pads instead of activating small, separate parking drum brakes as in all previous Corvettes.

- Ratings for the 1988 RPO B2K Callaway Twin Turbo were 382 horsepower with 562 foot-pounds of torque.

- Automatic transmissions (actually reworked Turbo Hydra-Matic 400s) were available in the Callaway for $6,500. Either Z51 or Z52 suspensions could be specified. Later production with Z52 had Z5l's larger front brakes, mufflers, longer air dams, and steering coolers because RPO B2K triggered these through Special Equipment Option SEO Z50. Callaway, at its Old Lyme shop, reworked the engines in-house.

- The 1988 Corvette's also had an improved hood support rod.

- The air conditioning compressor was changed to a more efficient, higher capacity compressor manufactured by Nippondenso.

1989

- The new six-speed manual transmission (RPO ML9) was a no-cost option for 1989. It was designed jointly by ZF (Zahnradfabrik Friedrichshafen) and Chevrolet but built by ZF in Germany. A computer-aided gear selection (CAGS) feature bypassed second and third gears (and locked out fifth and sixth) for improved fuel economy in specific non-performance driving conditions.

- The Corvette Challenge race series ended at the end of 1989. Sixty Challenge cars were built with standard engines. Meanwhile, CPC Flint Engine built special, higher horsepower engines which were shipped to the Milford Proving Grounds for storage, then to Specialized Vehicles, Inc. (SVI), Troy, Michigan, where they were equalized for power output and sealed. Bowling Green sent thirty cars to Powell Development America, Wixom, Michigan, where the roll cages and safety equipment were installed, and the engines from SVI were switched with the original engines. At the end of the season, Chevrolet returned the original numbers-matching engines to each racer.

- RPO Z51 performance handling package option continued to be available only in coupes with manual transmissions.

- A new suspension option (FX3) permitted three variations of suspension control, regulated by a console switch. It could be ordered only with RPO Z51. However, all 1989 Corvettes with FX3 had Z52 springs and sway bars for a wider range of suspension control. The only exceptions were the sixty Corvettes built for the Corvette Challenge race series that had FX3 suspensions with Z51 springs and stabilizer bars.

- The standard six-slot, 16x8.5-inch wheel that was introduced in 1988 was discontinued for 1989. The twelve-slot, 17x9.5-inch style included with 1988 Z51 and Z52 options became the standard equipment wheel.

- On April 19, 1989, Chevrolet advised dealers that the ZR-1 would be a 1990 model, not a late-release 1989. The reason cited was :"insufficient availability of engines caused by additional development." A number of 1989 ZR-1 Corvettes were built for evaluation, testing, media preview, and photography, but not one was released for public sale.

- Seats were restyled, and the choices of cloth, optional leather, or optional sport leather continued. Chevrolet intentionally limited sales of the sport leather seats by making them only available to cars with the Z51 option during 1989. This was due to weight and fuel economy factors.

- The manual top mechanism was simplified for 1989 convertibles.

- A bolt-on hardtop was made optional for convertibles.

- The "pass key" system was introduced. This system used an electronically loaded pellet and a special ignition lock with a set of contacts.

1990

- The ZR-1 (RPO ZR1) finally arrived as a 1990 model with a 375 horsepower LT5 engine. It was designed with the same V-8 configuration and the same 4.4-inch bore spacing as the standard L98 Corvette engine. Otherwise, it was a totally new design with four overhead camshafts and 32 valves. LT5 engines were manufactured and assembled by Mercury Marine in Stillwater, Oklahoma, then shipped to the Corvette Bowling Green assembly plant for vehicle assembly.

- For a very limited time during 1990, dealers could order Corvettes destined for the new World Challenge race series. Merchandising code R9G triggered deviations from normal build, such as heavy-duty springs with FX3. Owners could buy race engines from Chevrolet or build their own, and all race modifications were the owner's responsibility. Twenty-three 1990 R9G Corvettes were built.

- The L98 engine no longer used a mass airflow sensor. A new speed density air control system, camshaft revision, and a compression ratio increase added 5 horsepower to base-engines, up from 240 horsepower to 245 horsepower (except coupes with 3.07:1 or 3.33:1 axle ratios which increased from 245 horsepower to 250 horsepower because of improved exhaust systems).

- The 1990 Corvettes had an improved ABS that used additional information from a lateral accelerometer.

- An engine oil life monitor calculated useful oil life based on engine temperatures and revolutions. An instrument panel display alerted the driver when an oil change was recommended.

- The RPO VO1 radiator and B4P boost fan were dropped in 1990. This package became unnecessary because of the more efficient, sloped-back radiator design that was introduced with the 1990 model year.

- Two premium 200-watt Delco-Bose stereo systems were available, the more expensive unit featuring a compact disc player. To discourage theft, the CD required an electronic security code input after battery disconnect.

- The instrument panel for 1990 was redesigned combining a digital speedometer with analog tachometer and secondary gauges. A supplemental inflatable restraint system, or SIR, with airbag was added to the driver side. A glove box was added to the passenger side.

- The "ABS active" light was removed from the driver information center.

- Seat designs were the same, except now the backs would latch in the forward position.

- Chevrolet service departments returned LT5 engines to Mercury Marine for certain repairs. Customers had the choice of a replacement engine or return of their original engine if repairable.

1991

- The 1991 Corvettes had restyled rear panels that were similar in appearance to the 1990 ZR-1. They had convex rear fascias with four rectangular tall lamps.

- The 1991 design featured a new front design with wrap-around parking/cornering fog lamps, new side panel louvers, and wider side moldings. These side moldings were now painted in body color.

- Despite similar appearance, the 1991 ZR-1 still received unique doors and rear body panels to accept the 11-inch-wide rear wheels. The center brake light for the 1991 ZR-1 continued to be roof-mounted. For all other Corvettes, the light was integrated into the new rear fascia.

- The base wheels were the same size as 1990. They were still 17x9.5-inchers, but they had a new design.

- Finned power steering coolers were made standard on all 1991 models.

- A new suspension option (RPO Z07) combined the previously available Z51 performance handling package with FX3 selective ride/handling. The new Z07 option used heavy-duty suspension parts so the ride could be adjusted from firm to very firm. This Z07 option was limited to coupes.

- The Callaway Twin-Turbo conversions ended with the 1991 model year. Callaway built the 500th twin-turbo on September 26, 1991, and subsequent builds were specially badged, for an extra $600, as "Callaway *500.*"

- A power wire for cellular phones or other 12V devices was added.

- A power delay feature was added to all models, which permitted the stereo system and power windows to operate after the ignition was switched to "off" or "lock." Power to the radio was only cut after the driver door was opened or after fifteen minutes, whichever occurred first.

- A sensor utilizing an oil pan float was added to all models. The words "low oil" appeared on the driver information center to signal a low oil condition.

- Mufflers were revised for 1991 with larger section sizes and different tuning of the exhaust note. The mufflers had lower back pressure for improved performance, but power ratings were not changed.

- The AM band for radios was expanded to receive more frequencies.

- The ZR-1 valet power access system continued but was revised to default to normal power on each ignition cycle. The "full power" light was relocated next to the valet key.

1992

- ZR-1 emblems were added above the side fender vents.

- Two rectangular exhaust outlets were used for both the ZR-1 and the base models.

- Instrument face-plates and buttons were changed to all black, replacing the gray-black. The digital speedometer was relocated above the fuel gauge, and the graphics were refined for better legibility.

- A new small block engine, the LT1, was introduced for 1992. This engine developed 300 horsepower at 5,000 rpm. Torque was 330 foot-pounds at 4,000 rpm, and the redline was 5,700 rpm, 700 higher than the L98. There was an automatic fuel cutoff at 5,800 rpm. Power increases were attributed to computer-controlled ignition timing, a new exhaust system with two catalytic converters and two oxygen sensors, higher compression ratio, new camshaft profile, revised cylinder heads, and a new multi-port fuel injection, or MFI, system. The 1992 LT1 outweighed the 1991's L98 base engine by 21 pounds, due partly to the replacement of stainless steel exhaust manifolds with cast-iron units.

- This new LT1 engine employed reverse flow cooling. Rather than route coolant from the pump through the block to the heads, the LT1 routed coolant to the heads first. This permitted higher bore temperatures and reduced ring friction. It also helped cool around the valve seats and spark plug bosses.

- Synthetic oil (Mobil 1) was used for all the LT1 engines. The engine oil cooler was deleted. This lowered production costs for the Corvette.

- Traction control was introduced as standard equipment on all 1992 Corvette models. Called acceleration slip regulation, or ASR, Corvette's system was created by Bosch and developed in cooperation with GM engineering. It was engaged automatically with the ignition, but it could be turned off by an instrument panel switch. Corvette's ASR used engine spark retard, throttle closedown, and brake intervention to limit wheelspin when accelerating. When the system was on and active, the driver could feel a slight accelerator pedal pushback.

- New Goodyear GS-C tires were introduced as standard equipment on all 1992 Corvettes and were exclusive to Corvettes during 1992. The GS-C tread design was directional and asymmetrical.

- Improvements in weather sealing were achieved with improved weatherstrip seals. Road noise reduction came from additional insulation in doors and improved insulation over the transmission tunnel.

- The stereo power delay feature was modified so that the passenger door also cut power in addition to the driver door. The fifteen-minute time delay feature was retained.

- The one-millionth Corvette, a 1992 white convertible, was built July 2, 1992.

1993

- Exterior appearance continued virtually unchanged for 1993, but a 40th Anniversary Package (RPO *Z25*) was optional with all models. The package included a Ruby Red metallic exterior, Ruby Red leather sport seats, power driver seat, special wheel center trim, and emblems.

- All leather seats in 1993 Corvettes had a "40th Anniversary" logo embroidered in the headrest area. The base cloth seats did not have any emblem.

- Horsepower for the base LT1 engine remained 300, but three changes made the engine quieter. First, the heat shield design changed from a single-piece stamping to a two-piece sandwich type that was self-damping. Secondly, new polyester valve covers with "isolated mounts replaced the magnesium covers. This was an effort at noise reduction, and no weight was saved in this change. In addition, the camshaft was changed ever so slightly. The camshaft redesign didn't change the horsepower, but it did increase the torque by ten foot-pounds at 3,600 rpm.

- The LT1 camshaft exhaust lobe profile was modified to reduce the exhaust valve closing velocity. In addition, a shortening of the inlet duration permitted more duration for the exhaust so there was no increase in overlap area. Emissions and idle quality weren't adversely affected. A side benefit of closing the inlet valve sooner was an increase in torque from 330 to 340 foot-pounds at 3,600 rpm.

- Horsepower increased for the optional ZR1's LT5 engine from 375 to 405 horsepower, a result of modifications to the cylinder heads and valve train. Other changes included four-bolt main bearings, a Mobil 1 synthetic oil requirement, platinum-tipped spark plugs, and an electrical, linear exhaust gas recirculation, or EGR, system for improved emission control.

- The 1993 Corvette featured a passive keyless entry, or PKE, system. Working by proximity, a battery-operated key-fob transmitter sent a unique code picked up by a receiver in the Corvette through one of the two antennas. In coupes, antennas were in the driver door and rear deck; in convertibles, antennas were in both doors. The transmitter required no specific action by the owner. Approaching the vehicle with the transmitter would unlock the doors, turn on the interior light, and disarm the theft-deterrent. Leaving an unlocked vehicle with the transmitter would lock the doors and arm the theft-deterrent. Transmitters for convertibles had a single button for programming and driver/passenger door unlocking; transmitters for coupes had an extra button for rear hatch release.

- Front wheels for base cars were decreased from 9.5x17 inches to 8.5x17 inches, and the front tire size from P275/40ZR17 to P255/425ZR17. Rear tire size was increased from P275140ZR17 to P285140ZR17. For RPO Z07, 9.5x17-inch wheels and P275140ZR17 tires were used front and rear.

- Although they had the same design as the previous model, the 1993 wheels had a different surface appearance due to a change in finish machining.

1994

- New nondirectional wheels were installed on the ZR-1 models.

- Power output of the base LT1 engine remained at 300 horsepower, but several refinements were added. A new sequential fuel injection system improved response, idle quality, drive ability, and emissions by firing injectors in sequence with the engine's firing order. A more powerful ignition system reduced engine start times, especially in cold temperatures.

- The standard four-speed automatic transmission was redesigned with electronic controls for improved shift quality and rpm shift-point consistency. In addition, a safety interlock was added which required depression of the brake pedal in order to shift from "park."

- Interior revisions included the addition of a passenger-side airbag and knee bolster (and removal of the instrument panel glove box), new seat and door trim panel designs, finer-weave carpet, "express down" driver's power window, and a redesigned two-spoke airbag steering wheel. New white instrument graphics turned to tangerine at night.

- The tire jack was relocated from the exterior spare tire well to a compartment behind the passenger seat.

- For 1994, all seats were leather. Base and optional "sport" styles were available. Both featured less restrictive bolsters to accommodate a wider range of occupant sizes and improved entry and exit. Controls for base seats with optional power assist were console-mounted with individual controls for driver and passenger. With sport seats, a single set of power assist controls for both seats was console-mounted. Also, individual motors adjusted the lumbar support for sport seats, and these controls were relocated from the seat to the console for 1994. Reclining mechanisms for all 1994 seats were manual.

- The rear window for convertibles was changed from plastic to glass and included an in-glass electric defogger.

- Spring rates for RPO FX3 were lowered to improve ride quality. For the same reason, recommended tire pressures were reduced from 35psi to 30psi (except ZR1).

- Air conditioning systems were revised to use R-134A refrigerant.

- Optional Goodyear Extended Mobility Tires (RPO WY5) had special bead construction to permit use with no air pressure. The low tire pressure warning system (RPO UJ6) was required because, if the tire was run deflated more than about fifty miles, damage could result.

- The mass airflow system returned to the Corvette.

1995

- The 1995 exterior was distinguished from 1994 by restyling of the front fender air vents.

- Corvette paced the Indianapolis 500 race in 1995. A replica, dark purple and white (convertible only) with special accents, sold 527 units.

- Optional sport seats had stronger "French" seam stitching.

- A readout for automatic transmission fluid temperature was added to the instrument display.

- Numerous Velcro straps to reduce rattles.

- A stronger radio mount to control CD skipping.

- A drip tube was designed into the A-pillar weatherstrip for improved water intrusion control.

- The base LT1 engine continued with the same 300 horsepower and 340 foot-pounds of torque ratings. Late in 1994 production, connecting rods were changed to a powdered-metal design to improve both strength and weight uniformity. Fuel injectors were revised to better cope with alcohol blend fuels and to reduce fuel dripping after engine shutdown. The engine cooling fan was modified for quieter operation.

- This was the ZR-1's last year. Mercury Marine in Stillwater, Oklahoma, completed all LTS engines in November 1993. Tooling, owned by GM, was removed from Marine's factory and all engines, specially sealed, were shipped to Corvette's Bowling Green assembly plant for storage until needed. Total 1995 ZR-1 production was predetermined at 448 units, the same as for 1993 and 1994. Total ZR-1 production for 1990 through 1995 was 6,939.

- Clutch controls in the four-speed automatic transmission were improved for smoother shifting, and its torque converter was both lighter and stronger.

- The automatic transmission fluid was changed to Dexron III, which GM said never required changing.

- The six-speed manual was redesigned by replacement of the reverse lockout with a high-detent design for easier operation.

- A larger brake package, previously only included with the Z07 and ZR-1 options, was made standard.

- All 1995 Corvettes had a new anti-lock/traction control system (ABS/ASR-5).

- The extended mobility, or run-flat, tires introduced as a 1994 option minimized the need for a spare tire. Therefore, 1995's RPO N84 created a delete spare option which reduced weight and included a credit of $100.

- Base suspension models had lower front and rear spring rates.

- Windshield wiper arms were redesigned with revised contact angles and higher contact force to reduce both chatter at all speeds and lift at high speeds.

1996

- A new version of the 350CID small block (RPO LT4) became optional with 1996 Corvettes. Rated at 330 horsepower, 30 horsepower more than the base LT1, the LT4 had higher compression (10.8:1 vs. 10.4:1), new aluminum head design, Crane roller rocker arms, and a revised camshaft profile. The LT4's redline increased to 6,300 rpm—5,700 rpm for LT1. LT4-equipped models had 8,000-rpm tachometers instead of the base 6,000 rpm. While the LT4 was available with all Corvette models, it could only be ordered with the manual transmission.

- LT1 engines were mated only to automatic transmissions that had improved friction materials for the intermediate clutch and front/rear bands, improved shift quality, and more durable torque converters.

- Grand Sport (RPO Z16) included the LT4 engine and distinctive Admiral Blue paint complete with a white center stripe. ZR-1 style five-spoke 17-inch wheels were used but painted black. Like the ZR-1, tires for Grand Sport coupes were P275/4OZR17 on the front and P315/35ZR17 on the rear. Grand Sport coupes had rear fender flares rather than the ZR-l's wider rear panels. Convertible Grand Sport tires were P255/45ZR17 on the front and P285/40ZR17 on the rear with no fender flares. Interior choices were limited to black or a red/black combination. Corvettes with the Grand Sport option had separate serial number sequences.

- Both the LT1 and LT4 engines had a new throttle body for 1996. Throttle bodies for LT4 engines had red "Grand Sport" lettering.

- The Collector Edition (RPO Z15) included Sebring Silver paint and special trim. ZR-1-style, 17-inch, five-spoke wheels were used, but they were painted silver with P255/45ZR17 front and P285/4OZR17 rear tires.

Black, red, or gray interiors were available, but soft top color choices were limited to black.

- RPO F45, selective real-time damping, was priced the same as 1995's FX3 Selective Ride option ($1,695), but it was substantially different. Using data from wheel travel sensors and the powertrain control module, a controller calculated the damping mode that would provide optimum control via special shock absorbers. It could alter each shock individually (unlike the earlier system which changed all shocks simultaneously) every 10 to 15 milliseconds or about every foot of roadway when traveling at 60 miles per hour.

- The performance handling package (RPO Z51) that was optional from 1984 through 1988 returned in 1996. It included Bilstein shock absorbers with stiffer springs and thicker stabilizer bars. If you ordered Z51 with an automatic transmission, a 3.07:1 axle was required. Tires were P275/40ZR17 on 17x9.5-inch aluminum wheels, except for the Z51 Grand Sports, which had P31 5/3SZR17 rear tires on 17x11-inch wheels. The Z51 option was limited to coupes.

- On-board diagnostics for 1996 were much more sophisticated and complex than in years past. This was the first year of the OBD II system and the number of diagnostic codes increased from 60 to 140.

THE RPO THING

Corvette owners talk a great deal about RPOs. RPO stands for regular production option. This was how General Motors codified the options installed at the assembly plant. Everything on your Corvette has a number. That's what makes the NCRS so much fun. It's also why restoration can be such a challenge.

The RPO list for a specific vehicle can be found on the inside of the console storage compartment lid in the form of a sticker, or it can often be found on a sticker attached to the gas tank. You can also purchase a "build sheet" from the National Corvette Museum by calling 1-800-53-VETTE.

When it came to the earlier Corvette models, the information was very incomplete. Records simply weren't available. In the case of the early cars, there isn't even a record of what color the car was painted.

Eventually the exterior color and the type of interior trim information was included on the trim tag installed on every car. But there still weren't any records about what options had originally been installed at the assembly plant. This led to a very productive industry where restoration shops could turn base cars into highly optioned and highly desirable Corvettes. This will never happen with the C4.

The C4 Corvette RPO list is lengthy, and each model year brought changes, additions, and deletions. Some of the basic RPO options that remained more or less constant throughout the life of the C4 generation Corvette were as follows:

RPO	Description
ACl	Passengers Six-Way Power Seat
AC3	Drivers Six-Way Power Seat
AS8	Restraint System Manual
CC3	Removable Roof (Transparent)
CF7	Removable Roof (Non-Transparent)
C2L	Removable Roof Package (Both Tops)
C49	Defogger, Rear Window, Electronic
C60	Manually Controlled Air Conditioning
C68	Electronically Controlled Air Conditioner
DL8	Heated Outside Mirrors
D74	Vanity Inside Visor
FE1	Suspension, Soft Ride
FE7	Suspension, Heavy Duty
FX3	Ride and Handling, Electronic
GH0	Rear Axle, 3.54 Ratio
GM1	Rear Axle, 2.59 Ratio
GU2	Rear Axle, 2.73 Ratio
GW4	Rear Axle, 3.31 Ratio
G44	Rear Axle, 3.07 Ratio
G92	Rear Axle, Performance Ratio
JL9	Brakes, Anti-Lock Front and Rear Disc
J55	Brakes, Heavy Duty
KC4	Cooler, Engine Oil
K09	Generator (Alternator), 120 Amp
K68	Generator (Alternator), 105 Amp
MD8	Transmission, Auto, Four-speed THM 700-R4
ML9	Transmission, Manual, Six-speed, ZF
NK4	Steering Wheel, Sport Leather
UJ6	Indicator, Low Tire Pressure Warning
UM6	Radio, AM/FM Stereo, Seek & Scan, Auto Rev cassette, Clock, ETR
UQ4	Speaker System, Bose
UU8	Radio, AM/FM Stereo, Cassette, Dolby, Clock, ETR
U19	Cluster, Kilometers & Miles
U52	Cluster, Electronic
V01	Radiator, Heavy Duty
Z51	Performance Handling
Z6A	Defogger, Rear Window and Outside Mirrors
24S	Roof, Removable Blue Transparent
K05	Heater, Engine Block
L83	EFI Engine, 5.7L V8 (1984 Only)
L98	TPI Engine, 5.7L V8
LT1	TPI Engine, 5.7L V8
LT4	TPI Engine, 5.7L V8
LT5	TPI Engine, 5.7L V8

APPENDIX

INDEX

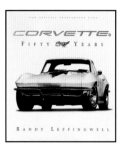

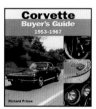
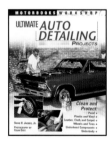